Fodor's

Turkey

"When it comes to information on regional history, what to see and do, and shopping, these guides are exhaustive."

—USAir Magazine

"Usable, sophisticated restaurant coverage, with an emphasis on good value."

—Andy Birsh, Gourmet Magazine columnist

"Valuable because of their comprehensiveness."

—Minneapolis Star-Tribune

"Fodor's always delivers high quality...thoughtfully presented...thorough."

—Houston Post

"An excellent choice for those who want everything under one cover."

—Washington Post

Fodor's Travel Publications, Inc.
New York • Toronto • London • Sydney • Auckland
http://www.fodors.com/

Fodor's Turkey

Editor: Daniel Mangin

Contributors: Steven K. Amsterdam, Robert Andrews, Glen Berger, Paula S. Bernstein, Robert Blake, David Brown, Audra Epstein, Gareth Jenkins, Laura M. Kidder, Bevin McLaughlin, Scott McNeely, Rebecca Morris, Heidi Sarna, Helayne Schiff, Mary Ellen Schultz, M. T. Schwartzman (Gold Guide editor) Dinah Spritzer, Aaron Sugarman, Meltem Türköz, Nancy van Itallie

Art Director: Fabrizio La Rocca

Associate Art Director: Guido Caroti

Photo Researcher: Jolie Novak

Cartographer: David Lindroth

Cover Photograph: Peter Guttman

Design: Between the Covers

Copyright

Third Edition

ISBN 0–679–03292–4

"The Art of the Kilim" is excerpted from *Living with Kilims,* by Alastair Hull and Nicholas Barnard, and is reprinted with permission of Thames & Hudson Ltd., London. Copyright © 1988 by Thames & Hudson Ltd., London.

Special Sales

Fodor's Travel Publications are available at special discounts for bulk purchases for sales promotions or premiums. Special editions, including personalized covers, excerpts of existing guides, and corporate imprints, can be created in large quantities for special needs. For more information, contact your local bookseller or write to Special Markets, Fodor's Travel Publications, Inc., 201 East 50th Street, New York, NY 10022. Inquiries from Canada should be directed to your local Canadian bookseller or sent to Random House of Canada, Ltd., Marketing Department, 1265 Aerowood Drive, Mississauga, Ontario L4W 1B9. Inquiries from the United Kingdom should be sent to Fodor's Travel Publications, 20 Vauxhall Bridge Road, London SW1V 2SA, England.

PRINTED IN THE UNITED STATES OF AMERICA

10 9 8 7 6 5 4 3 2 1

CONTENTS

ON THE ROAD WITH FODOR'S

WE'RE ALWAYS THRILLED to get letters from readers, especially one like this:

It took us an hour to decide what book to buy and we now know we picked the best one. Your book was wonderful, easy to follow, very accurate, and good on pointing out eating places, informal as well as formal. When we saw other people using your book, we would look at each other and smile.

Our editors and writers are deeply committed to making every Fodor's guide "the best one"—not only accurate but brimming with sound recommendations and solid ideas, right on the mark in describing restaurants and hotels, and full of fascinating facts that make you view your travels in a rich new light.

About Our Writers

Our success in achieving our goals—and in helping to make your trip the best of all possible vacations—is a credit to the hard work of our extraordinary writers.

Gareth Jenkins, who revised the Destination: Turkey, Istanbul, Southern Marmara Region, and Aegean Coast chapters, has a degree in Ancient Greek and Latin from Durham University, England. After graduating, Gareth worked as an archaeologist and writer in the United Kingdom before setting off to travel and teach English in the Mediterranean. He spent five years in Egypt, Greece, and Israel before moving to Istanbul, where he has lived since 1989. He works as a freelance journalist, writer, translator, and editor. He has published two books on Turkey and is researching a third on Turkish politics.

Freelance journalist **Paula S. Bernstein** updated the Mediterranean Coast, Ankara and Central Anatolia, and Black Sea Coast chapters. While spending her junior year of college in Tel Aviv, Paula went to Turkey for the Middle East equivalent of Spring Break and has since returned several times to visit and to purchase the kilims that decorate her Manhattan apartment. Paula's writings on film, travel, and the Internet have appeared in the *New York Times*, the *Village Voice*, *In Style*, and *Filmmaker*, and she was one of the first contributors to Fodor's World Wide Web site.

Scott McNeely, who revised the Far East chapter, is a former editor at Fodor's and the former executive editor of the Berkeley Guides. On his fourth trip to Turkey, Scott spent a few demanding but glorious weeks exploring the eastern portion of the country. The terrain wasn't so bad, but there was that 19-hour bus ride during which he was suffering from "sultan's revenge" yet found himself asked to "sing song, please, Mr. Tourist" for his entire vehicle. Scott is on a yearlong trek that will take him from Turkey to Syria, Jordan, Pakistan, China, Nepal, and India.

New This Year

This year we've reformatted our guides to make them easier to use. Each chapter of *Fodor's Turkey* begins with brand-new recommended itineraries to help you decide what to see in the time you have; a section called When to Tour points out the optimal time of day, day of the week, and season for your journey. You may also notice our fresh graphics, new in 1997. More readable and more helpful than ever? We think so—and we hope you do, too.

On the Web

Also check out Fodor's Web site (http://www.fodors.com/), where you'll find travel information on major destinations around the world and an ever-changing array of travel-savvy interactive features.

How to Use This Book

Organization

Up front is the **Gold Guide.** Its first section, **Important Contacts A to Z,** gives addresses and telephone numbers of organizations and companies that offer destination-related services and detailed information and publications. **Smart Travel Tips A to Z,** the Gold Guide's second section, gives specific information on how to accomplish what you need to in Turkey as well as tips on savvy traveling. Both sections are in alphabetical order by topic.

Chapters in *Fodor's Turkey* are arranged geographically, fanning out from Istanbul. The chapter on Istanbul begins with an Exploring section, which is subdivided by neighborhood; each subsection recommends a walking or driving tour and lists sights in alphabetical order. Each regional chapter is divided by geographical area; within each area, towns are covered in logical geographical order, and attractive stretches of road and minor points of interest between them are indicated by the designation En Route. Throughout, Off the Beaten Path sights appear after the places from which they are most easily accessible. And within town sections, all restaurants and lodgings are grouped together.

To help you decide what to visit in the time you have, all chapters begin with recommended itineraries; you can mix and match those from several chapters to create a complete vacation. The A to Z section that ends all chapters covers getting there, getting around, and helpful contacts and resources.

At the end of the book you'll find Portraits: a chronology of Turkey's history; an essay about the art of Turkish kilims (rugs); and suggestions for pretrip reading, both fiction and nonfiction, and movies on tape with Turkey as a backdrop.

Icons and Symbols

★   Our special recommendations
✕   Restaurant
🏠   Lodging establishment
✕🏠   Lodging establishment whose restaurant is among the best in town
☞   Sends you to another section of the guide for more information
⊠   Address
☎   Telephone number
FAX   Fax number
☺   Opening and closing times
💲   Admission prices (for adults, in U.S. dollars).

Numbers in white and black circles (⑳ and ❷⓿, for example) that appear on the maps, in the margins, and within the tours correspond to one another.

Dining and Lodging Price Categories

Prices in the restaurant chart below are per person and include an appetizer, main course, and dessert but not drinks and gratuities. A service charge of 10% to

15% is added to the bill; waiters expect another 10%. If a restaurant's menu has no prices listed, ask before you order—you'll avoid a surprise when the bill comes.

CATEGORY	MAJOR CITIES	OTHER AREAS
$$$$	over $40	over $30
$$$	$25–$40	$20–$30
$$	$12–$25	$10–$20
$	under $12	under $10

Prices in the lodging chart below are for two people in a double room, including VAT and service charge.

CATEGORY	MAJOR CITIES	OTHER AREAS
$$$$	over $200	over $150
$$$	$100–$200	$100–$150
$$	$60–$100	$50–$100
$	under $60	under $50

Hotel Facilities

We always list the facilities that are available—but we don't specify whether they cost extra: When pricing accommodations, always ask what's included. Rates at most *pansiyons* (guest houses) and many hotels include a light breakfast—often bread with feta cheese, tomatoes, cucumbers, and olives, plus coffee, tea, and juice. Assume that other meals are not included unless otherwise noted.

Restaurant Reservations and Dress Codes

Reservations are always a good idea; we note only when they're essential or when they are not accepted. Book as far ahead as you can, and reconfirm when you get to town. Unless otherwise noted, the restaurants listed are open daily for lunch and dinner. We mention dress only when men are required to wear a jacket or a jacket and tie. Look for an overview of local habits under Dining in Smart Travel Tips A to Z and in the Pleasures and Pastimes section that follows each chapter introduction.

Credit Cards

The following abbreviations are used: **AE,** American Express; **D,** Discover; **DC,** Diners Club; **MC,** MasterCard; and **V,** Visa.

Please Write to Us

You can use this book in the confidence that all prices and opening times are based on information supplied to us at press time; Fodor's cannot accept responsibility for any errors. Time inevitably brings changes, so always confirm information when it matters—especially if you're making a detour to visit a specific place. In addition, when making reservations be sure to mention if you have a disability or are traveling with children, if you prefer a private bath or a certain type of bed, or if you have specific dietary needs or any other concerns.

Were the restaurants we recommended as described? Did our hotel picks exceed your expectations? Did you find a museum we recommended a waste of time? If you have complaints, we'll look into them and revise our entries when the facts warrant it. If you've discovered a special place that we haven't included, we'll pass the information along to our correspondents and have them check it out. So send your feedback, positive and negative, to the *Turkey* editor at 201 East 50th Street, New York, New York 10022—and have a wonderful trip!

Karen Cure
Editorial Director

Western Turkey and the Greek Isles

Black Sea

T U R K E Y

THRACE

Makri

○ Istanbul

Sea of Marmara

Samothrace

Limnos

○ Çanakkale

■ **Assos**

Lesbos

○ Pergamum (Bergama)

Aegean Sea

N O R T H E R N   I S L A N D S

T U R K E Y

Chios

○ Izmir (Smyrna)

Andros

A E G E A N   I S L A N D S

Samos

Tinos

Ikaria

Mykonos

Delos

Patmos

Paros

Naxos

C Y C L A D E S

Leros

Kalimnos

○ Bodrum

○ Marmaris

Amorgos

Kos

○ Kos

■ **Knidos**

Ios

Astypalea

Nissyros

Symi

Santorini   *Anafi*

D O D E C A N E S E

Tilos

Chalki

○ Rhodes

○ Kaş

Rhodes

Sea of Crete

Karpathos

N

0   50 miles

0   75 km

C R E T E

Heraklion ○

Ay. ○
Nikoloos

Kassos

Ierapetra ○

Mediterranean Sea

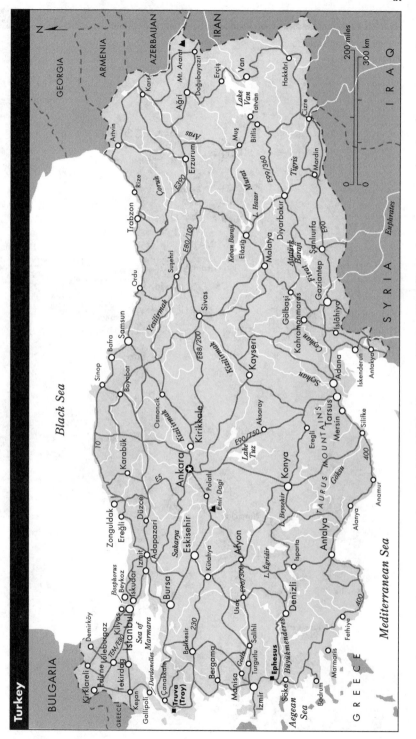

World Time Zones

Numbers below vertical bands relate each zone to Greenwich Mean Time (0 hrs.).
Local times frequently differ from these general indications,
as indicated by light-face numbers on map.

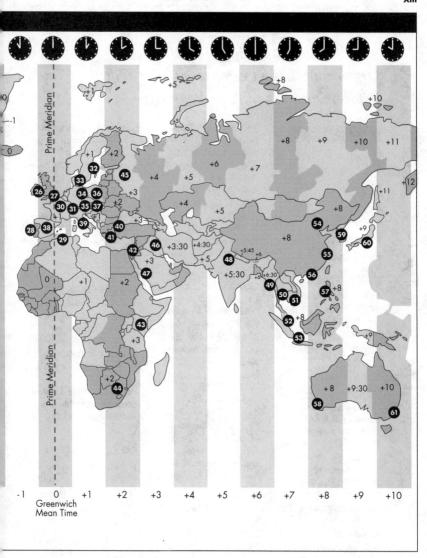

IMPORTANT CONTACTS A TO Z

An Alphabetical Listing of Publications, Organizations, and Companies That Will Help You Before, During, and After Your Trip

A

AIR TRAVEL

The major international gateway to Turkey is Istanbul's **Atatürk Airport** (☎ 212/663–6300).

FLYING TIME

Flying time is 11 hours from New York, 13 hours from Chicago, and 15 hours from Los Angeles. The flight from Toronto to Istanbul takes 11½ hours. Flying time from London is 4 hours.

CARRIERS

Carriers flying from the United States include **Air Canada** (☎ 800/776–3000), **Air France** (☎ 800/237–2747), **British Airways** (☎ 800/247–9297), **Delta** (☎ 800/241–4141), **Lufthansa** (☎ 800/645–3880), **Northwest/KLM** (☎ 800/447–4747), **Olympic Airlines** (☎ 800/223–1226), **Swissair** (☎ 800/221–4750), **TWA** (☎ 800/221–2000 or 800/892–4141), and **THY/Turkish Airlines** (☎ in the U.S., 212/986–5050 or 800/874–8875; in Istanbul, ☎ 212/663–6300 or, for reservations, 212/663–6363), the Turkish national airline.

If you are flying from Canada, contact **Air Canada** (☎ 800/776–3000), **British Airways** (☎ 800/247–9297), **Air France** (☎ 800/237–2747), **Alitalia**

(☎ 800/223–5730), **Finair** (☎ 800/950–5000), **KLM** (☎ 800/374–7747), **Lufthansa** (☎ 800/645–3880), **Olympic Air** (☎ 800/223–1226), **SAS** (☎ 800/221–2350), **Swissair** (☎ 800/221–4750), and **TWA** (☎ 800/221–2000 or 800/892–4141).

Carriers from the United Kingdom include **British Airways** (☎ 0181/897–4000 or 0345/222–111 outside London) and **Turkish Airlines** (⌧ 11–12 Hanover St., London W1R 9HF, ☎ 0171/499–9249 or 0171/499–4499), which fly to Istanbul. **Lufthansa** (☎ 0345/737–747) flies from London to Istanbul, Ankara, and İzmir, all via Frankfurt.

Turkey's main domestic carriers are **Istanbul Airlines** (☎ 212/509–2100) and **Turkish Airlines** (THY, ☎ 212/663–6300; 212/663–6363 for reservations). Turkish Airlines operates an extensive domestic network, with nine flights daily on weekdays between Istanbul and Ankara alone. In summer, many flights to coastal resorts are added. Try to arrive at the airport at least 45 minutes before takeoff because security checks can be time-consuming; checked luggage is put on trolleys and must be identified by boarding passengers before it is

put on the plane, and all unidentified luggage is left behind and checked for bombs or firearms.

COMPLAINTS

To register complaints about charter and scheduled airlines, contact the U.S. Department of Transportation's **Aviation Consumer Protection Division** (⌧ C-75, Washington, DC 20590, ☎ 202/366–2220). Complaints about lost baggage or ticketing problems and safety concerns may also be logged with the **Federal Aviation Administration (FAA) Consumer Hotline** (☎ 800/322–7873).

CONSOLIDATORS

For the names of reputable air-ticket consolidators, contact the **United States Air Consolidators Association** (⌧ 925 L St., Suite 220, Sacramento, CA 95814, ☎ 916/441–4166, FAX 916/441–3520).

PUBLICATIONS

For general information about charter carriers, ask for the Department of Transportation's free brochure **"Plane Talk: Public Charter Flights"** (⌧ Aviation Consumer Protection Division, C-75, Washington, DC 20590, ☎ 202/366–2220). The Department of Transportation also publishes a 58-page booklet, **"Fly Rights,"** available from the

Consumer Information Center (✉ Supt. of Documents, Dept. 136C, Pueblo, CO 81009; $1.75).

For other tips and hints, consult the Consumers Union's monthly **"Consumer Reports Travel Letter"** (✉ Box 53629, Boulder, CO 80322, ☎ 800/234–1970; $39 1st year).

B

BETTER BUSINESS BUREAU

For local contacts in the hometown of a tour operator you may be considering, consult the **Council of Better Business Bureaus** (✉ 4200 Wilson Blvd., Suite 800, Arlington, VA 22203, ☎ 703/276–0100, FAX 703/525–8277).

BOAT TRAVEL

Contact Turkish Maritime Lines for cruise and ferry information and reservations. Cruises are in great demand, so make your reservations well in advance, either through the head office (✉ Rıhtım Cad. 1, Karaköy, ☎ 212/249–9222) or through **Sunquest Holidays Ltd.** in London (✉ Alsine House, Alsine St., London W12 8AW, England, ☎ 0181/800–5455).

C

CAR RENTAL

The major car-rental companies represented in Turkey are **Avis** (☎ 800/331–1084; in Canada, 800/879–2847), **Budget** (☎ 800/527–0700; in the U.K., 0800/181181), **Hertz**

(☎ 800/654–3001; in Canada, 800/263–0600; in the U.K., 0345/555888), and **National InterRent** (sometimes known as Europcar InterRent outside North America; ☎ 800/227–3876; in the U.K., 0345/222–525). Rates in Istanbul begin at $42 a day and $264 a week for an economy car with unlimited mileage.

CHILDREN & TRAVEL

FLYING

Look into **"Flying with Baby"** (✉ Third Street Press, Box 261250, Littleton, CO 80163, ☎ 303/595–5959; $4.95 includes shipping), cowritten by a flight attendant. Every two years the February issue of **Family Travel Times** (☞ Know-How, *below*) details children's services on three dozen airlines.

KNOW-HOW

Family Travel Times, published quarterly by Travel with Your Children (✉ TWYCH, 40 5th Ave., New York, NY 10011, ☎ 212/477–5524; $40 per year), covers destinations, types of vacations, and modes of travel.

CUSTOMS

IN THE U.S.

The **U.S. Customs Service** (✉ Box 7407, Washington, DC 20044, ☎ 202/927–6724) can answer questions on duty-free limits and publishes a helpful brochure, "Know Before You Go." For information on registering foreign-made articles, call

202/927–0540 or write U.S. Customs Service, Resource Management, 1301 Constitution Ave. NW, Washington, DC 20229.

COMPLAINTS➤ Note the inspector's badge number and write to the commissioner's office (✉ 1301 Constitution Ave. NW, Washington, DC 20229).

CANADIANS

Contact **Revenue Canada** (✉ 2265 St. Laurent Blvd. S, Ottawa, Ontario K1G 4K3, ☎ 613/993–0534) for a copy of the free brochure **"I Declare/Je Déclare"** and for details on duty-free limits. For recorded information (within Canada only), call 800/461–9999.

U.K. CITIZENS

HM Customs and Excise (✉ Dorset House, Stamford St., London SE1 9NG, ☎ 0171/202–4227) can answer questions about U.K. customs regulations and publishes a free pamphlet, **"A Guide for Travellers,"** detailing standard procedures and import rules.

D

DISABILITIES & ACCESSIBILITY

ORGANIZATIONS

TRAVELERS WITH HEARING IMPAIRMENTS➤ The **American Academy of Otolaryngology** (✉ 1 Prince St., Alexandria, VA 22314, ☎ 703/836–4444, FAX 703/683–5100, TTY 703/519–1585) publishes a brochure, "Travel Tips for Hearing Impaired People."

TRAVELERS WITH MOBIL-
ITY PROBLEMS➤ Contact
**Mobility International
USA** (✉ Box 10767,
Eugene, OR 97440,
☎ and TTY 541/343–
1284, Ⅲ 541/343–
6812), the U.S. branch
of a Belgium-based
organization (☞ *below*)
with affiliates in 30
countries; the **Society for
the Advancement of
Travel for the Handi-
capped** (✉ 347 5th
Ave., Suite 610, New
York, NY 10016, ☎
212/447–7284, Ⅲ 212/
725–8253; membership
$45); and **Travelin' Talk**
(✉ Box 3534, Clarks-
ville, TN 37043, ☎ 615/
552–6670, Ⅲ 615/
552–1182) which
provides local contacts
worldwide for travelers
with disabilities.

TRAVELERS WITH VISION
IMPAIRMENTS➤ Contact
the **American Council of
the Blind** (✉ 1155 15th
St. NW, Suite 720,
Washington, DC
20005, ☎ 202/467–
5081, Ⅲ 202/467–
5085) for a list of
travelers' resources.

IN THE U.K.

Contact the **Royal
Association for Disabil-
ity and Rehabilitation**
(✉ RADAR, 12 City
Forum, 250 City Rd.,
London EC1V 8AF,
☎ 0171/250–3222) or
Mobility International
(✉ rue de Manchester
25, B-1080 Brussels,
Belgium, ☎ 00–322–
410–6297, ⅢⅩ 00–
322–410–6874), an
international travel-
information clearing-
house for people with
disabilities.

PUBLICATIONS

Several publications for
travelers with disabili-
ties are available from
the **Consumer Informa-**

tion Center** (✉ Box 100,
Pueblo, CO 81009, ☎
719/948–3334). Call or
write for its free catalog
of current titles. The
Society for the Ad-
vancement of Travel for
the Handicapped (☞
Organizations, *above*)
publishes the quarterly
magazine **"Access to
Travel"** ($13 for one-
year subscription).

The 500-page *Travelin'
Talk Directory* (✉ Box
3534, Clarksville, TN
37043, ☎ 615/552–
6670, ⅢⅩ 615/552–
1182; $35) lists people
and organizations who
help travelers with
disabilities. For travel
agents worldwide,
consult the *Directory of
Travel Agencies for the
Disabled* (✉ Twin Peaks
Press, Box 129, Van-
couver, WA 98666, ☎
360/694–2462 or 800/
637–2256, ⅢⅩ 360/
696–3210; $19.95 plus
$3 shipping).

TRAVEL AGENCIES
& TOUR
OPERATORS

The Americans with
Disabilities Act requires
that all travel firms
serve the needs of all
travelers, but some
agencies and operators
specialize in making
travel arrangements for
individuals and groups
with disabilities, among
them **Access Adventures**
(✉ 206 Chestnut Ridge
Rd., Rochester, NY
14624, ☎ 716/889–
9096).

TRAVELERS WITH MOBIL-
ITY PROBLEMS➤ Contact
Flying Wheels Travel
(✉ 143 W. Bridge St.,
Box 382, Owatonna,
MN 55060, ☎ 507/
451–5005 or 800/535–
6790), a travel agency
specializing in Euro-
pean cruises and tours;

Hinsdale Travel Service
(✉ 201 E. Ogden Ave.,
Suite 100, Hinsdale, IL
60521, ☎ 708/325–
1335), a travel agency
that benefits from the
advice of wheelchair
traveler Janice Perkins;
and **Wheelchair Jour-
neys** (✉ 16979 Red-
mond Way, Redmond,
WA 98052, ☎ 206/
885–2210 or 800/313–
4751), which can
handle arrangements
worldwide.

TRAVELERS WITH DEVEL-
OPMENTAL DISABILITIES➤
Contact the nonprofit
New Directions (✉ 5276
Hollister Ave., Suite
207, Santa Barbara,
CA 93111, ☎ 805/
967–2841).

TRAVEL GEAR

The **Magellan's** catalog
(☎ 800/962–4943,
ⅢⅩ 805/568–5406),
includes a section
devoted to products
designed for travelers
with disabilities.

AIRFARES

For the lowest airfares
to Turkey, call 800/
FLY–4–LESS ($10
research fee required for
international flights).

THY offers several
standard discounts on
flights within Turkey—
10% for passengers'
spouses and other
family members, 50%
for children 12 and
under, and 90% for
children under 2.

CLUBS

Contact **Moment's
Notice Discount Travel
Club** (✉ 7301 New
Utrecht Ave., Brooklyn,
NY 11204, ☎ 718/
234–6295; $25 per
year, single or family)

or **Worldwide Discount Travel Club** (✉ 1674 Meridian Ave., Miami Beach, FL 33139, ☎ 305/534–2082; $50 per year for family, $40 single).

AUTO CLUBS

The **Türkiye Turing Ve Otomobil Kurumu** (✉ TTÖK, or Touring and Automobile Club; Şişli Halâskar Gazi Cad. 364, Istanbul, ☎ 212/231–4631) has information about driving in Turkey and does repairs.

E

Ambulance: ☎ 112; **Emergency (police, etc.):** ☎ 155; **Tourism Police (Istanbul):** ☎ 212/527–4503.

G

ORGANIZATIONS

The **International Gay Travel Association** (✉ Box 4974, Key West, FL 33041, ☎ 800/448–8550, FAX 305/296–6633), a consortium of more than 1,000 travel companies, can supply names of gay-friendly travel agents, tour operators, and accommodations.

PUBLICATIONS

The 16-page monthly newsletter **"Out & About"** (✉ 8 W. 19th St., Suite 401, New York, NY 10011, ☎ 212/645–6922 or 800/929–2268, FAX 800/929–2215; $49 for 10 issues and quarterly calendar) covers gay-friendly resorts, hotels, cruise lines, and airlines.

TOUR OPERATORS

Cruises and resort vacations for gays are handled by **R.S.V.P. Travel Productions** (✉ 2800 University Ave. SE, Minneapolis, MN 55414, ☎ 612/379–4697 or 800/328–7787). For mixed gay and lesbian travel, contact **Hanns Ebensten Travel** (✉ 513 Fleming St., Key West, FL 33040, ☎ 305/294–8174), one of the nation's oldest operators in the gay market, and **Toto Tours** (✉ 1326 W. Albion Ave., Suite 3W, Chicago, IL 60626, ☎ 312/274–8686 or 800/565–1241, FAX 312/274–8695).

TRAVEL AGENCIES

Agencies serving lesbian and gay travelers include **Advance Travel** (✉ 10700 Northwest Fwy., Suite 160, Houston, TX 77092, ☎ 713/682–2002 or 800/292–0500), **Islanders/Kennedy Travel** (✉ 183 W. 10th St., New York, NY 10014, ☎ 212/242–3222 or 800/988–1181), and **Now Voyager** (✉ 4406 18th St., San Francisco, CA 94114, ☎ 415/626–1169 or 800/255–6951). **Skylink Women's Travel** (✉ 2460 W. 3rd St., Suite 215, Santa Rosa, CA 95401, ☎ 707/570–0105 or 800/225–5759) serves lesbian travelers.

H

FINDING A DOCTOR

For its members, the **International Association for Medical Assistance to Travellers** (✉ IAMAT, member-ship free; 417 Center St., Lewiston, NY 14092, ☎ 716/754–4883; 40 Regal Rd., Guelph, Ontario N1K 1B5, ☎ 519/836–0102; 1287 St. Clair Ave. W., Toronto, Ontario M6E 1B8, ☎ 416/652–0137; 57 Voirets, 1212 Grand-Lancy, Geneva, Switzerland, no phone) publishes a worldwide directory of English-speaking physicians meeting IAMAT standards.

MEDICAL ASSISTANCE COMPANIES

The following companies are concerned primarily with emergency medical assistance, although they may provide some insurance as part of their coverage.

Contact **International SOS Assistance** (✉ Box 11568, Philadelphia, PA 19116, ☎ 215/244–1500 or 800/523–8930; Box 466, Pl. Bonaventure, Montréal, Québec H5A 1C1, ☎ 514/874–7674 or 800/363–0263; 7 Old Lodge Pl., St. Margarets, Twickenham TW1 1RQ, England, ☎ 0181/744–0033), **Medex Assistance Corporation** (✉ Box 5375, Timonium, MD 21094, ☎ 410/453–6300 or 800/537–2029), **Near Travel Services** (✉ Box 1339, Calumet City, IL 60409, ☎ 708/868–6700 or 800/654–6700), or **Worldwide Assistance Services** (✉ 1133 15th St. NW, Suite 400, Washington, DC 20005, ☎ 202/331–1609 or 800/821–2828, FAX 202/828–5896).

WARNINGS

The hot line of the **National Centers for**

THE GOLD GUIDE / IMPORTANT CONTACTS

Disease Control (✉ CDC, National Center for Infectious Diseases, Division of Quarantine, Traveler's Health Section, 1600 Clifton Rd., M/S E-03, Atlanta, GA 30333, ☎ 404/332–4559, FAX 404/332–4565) provides information on health risks abroad and vaccination requirements and recommendations.

I
INSURANCE
IN THE U.S.

Travel insurance covering baggage, health, and trip cancellation or interruptions is available from **Access America** (✉ 6600 W. Broad St., Richmond, VA 23230, ☎ 804/285–3300 or 800/334–7525), **Carefree Travel Insurance** (✉ Box 9366, 100 Garden City Plaza, Garden City, NY 11530, ☎ 516/294–0220 or 800/323–3149), **Tele-Trip** (✉ Mutual of Omaha Plaza, Box 31716, Omaha, NE 68131, ☎ 800/228–9792), **Travel Guard International** (✉ 1145 Clark St., Stevens Point, WI 54481, ☎ 715/345–0505 or 800/826–1300), **Travel Insured International** (✉ Box 280568, East Hartford, CT 06128, ☎ 860/528–7663 or 800/243–3174), and **Wallach & Company** (✉ 107 W. Federal St., Box 480, Middleburg, VA 22117, ☎ 540/687–3166 or 800/237–6615).

IN CANADA

Contact **Mutual of Omaha** (✉ Travel Division, 500 University Ave., Toronto, Ontario M5G 1V8, ☎ 800/465–0267 [in Canada] or 416/598–4083).

IN THE U.K.

The **Association of British Insurers** (✉ 51 Gresham St., London EC2V 7HQ, ☎ 0171/600–3333) gives advice by phone and publishes the free pamphlet **"Holiday Insurance and Motoring Abroad,"** which sets out typical policy provisions and costs.

L
LODGING
APARTMENT & VILLA RENTAL

Villas International (✉ 605 Market St., Suite 510, San Francisco, CA 94105, ☎ 415/281–0910 or 800/221–2260, FAX 415/281–0919) is one source, particularly for homes along the Mediterranean Coast.

M
MONEY
ATMS

For specific foreign **Cirrus** locations, call 800/424–7787; for foreign **Plus** locations, consult the Plus directory at your local bank.

CURRENCY EXCHANGE

If your bank doesn't exchange currency, contact **Thomas Cook Currency Services** (☎ 800/287–7362 for locations). **Ruesch International** (☎ 800/424–2923 for locations) can also provide you with foreign banknotes before you leave home and publishes a number of useful brochures, including a "Foreign Currency Guide" and "Foreign Exchange Tips."

WIRING FUNDS

Funds can be wired via **MoneyGram℠** (for locations and information in the United States and Canada, ☎ 800/926–9400) or **Western Union** (for agent locations or to send money using MasterCard or Visa, ☎ 800/325–6000; in Canada, ☎ 800/321–2923; in the U.K., 0800/833833; or visit the Western Union office at the nearest major post office).

P
PASSPORTS & VISAS
U.S. CITIZENS

For fees, documentation requirements, and other information, call the State Department's **Office of Passport Services** (☎ 202/647–0518).

CANADIANS

For fees, documentation requirements, and other information, call the Ministry of Foreign Affairs and International Trade's **Passport Office** (☎ 819/994–3500 or 800/567–6868).

U.K. CITIZENS

For fees, documentation requirements, and to request an emergency passport, call the **London Passport Office** (☎ 0990/210410).

S
SAFETY

"Trouble-Free Travel," from the AAA, is a booklet of tips for protecting yourself and your belongings when away from home. Send a stamped, self-addressed, legal-size envelope to Trouble-Free Travel (✉ Mail Stop 75, 1000 AAA Dr., Heathrow, FL 32746).

EDUCATIONAL TRAVEL

The nonprofit **Elderhostel** (✉ 75 Federal St., 3rd Floor, Boston, MA 02110, ☎ 617/426–7788) offers inexpensive study programs for people 55 and older. Courses cover everything from marine science to Greek mythology and cowboy poetry. Costs for two- to three-week international trips—including room, board, and transportation from the United States—range from $1,800 to $4,500.

ORGANIZATIONS

Contact the **American Association of Retired Persons** (✉ AARP, 601 E St. NW, Washington, DC 20049, ☎ 202/434–2277; annual dues $8 per person or couple). Its Purchase Privilege Program secures discounts for members on lodging, car rentals, and sightseeing.

BOATING & SAILING

Yacht agencies are listed with the Turkish Culture and Information office in New York; in Turkey, Marmaris has a particularly helpful tourist office (☎ 252/412–1035) that can be called on for advice on chartering *gulets* (wooden boats with crew).

HOSTELING

In the United States, contact **Hosteling International–American Youth Hostels** (✉ 733 15th St. NW, Suite 840, Washington, DC 20005, ☎ 202/783–6161, FAX 202/783–6171); in Canada, **Hostelling International–Canada** (✉ 205 Catherine St., Suite 400, Ottawa, Ontario K2P 1C3, ☎ 613/237–7884); and in the United Kingdom, the **Youth Hostel Association of England and Wales** (✉ Trevelyan House, 8 St. Stephen's Hill, St. Albans, Hertfordshire AL1 2DY, ☎ 01727/855215 or 01727/845047). Membership (in the U.S., $25; in Canada, C$26.75; in the U.K., £9.30) gives you access to 5,000 hostels in 77 countries that charge $5–$40 per person per night, plus discounts on selected travel expenses.

Gençtur Tourism & Travel Agency (✉ Yerebatan Cad. 15, Sultanahmet, Istanbul, ☎ 212/520–5274, FAX 212/519–0864) and **7 TUR Tourism** (✉ Inönü Cad. 37/2, Gümüşsuyu, Istanbul, ☎ 212/252–5921) can tell Hostelling International members (☞ *below*) about youth discounts and accommodations. Student residences in Ankara, Bolu, Bursa, Çanakkale, İzmir, and Istanbul also serve as youth hostels.

T

The country code for Turkey is 90. For local access numbers abroad, contact **AT&T** USADirect

(☎ 800/874–4000), **MCI** Call USA (☎ 800/444–4444), or **Sprint** Express (☎ 800/793–1153).

Among the companies that sell tours and packages to Turkey, the following are nationally known, have a proven reputation, and offer plenty of options.

GROUP TOURS

SUPER-DELUXE➤ **Abercrombie & Kent** (✉ 1520 Kensington Rd., Oak Brook, IL 60521–2141, ☎ 708/954–2944 or 800/323–7308, FAX 708/954–3324) and **Travcoa** (✉ Box 2630, 2350 S.E. Bristol St., Newport Beach, CA 92660, ☎ 714/476–2800 or 800/992–2003, FAX 714/476–2538).

DELUXE➤ **Globus** (✉ 5301 S. Federal Circle, Littleton, CO 80123, ☎ 303/797–2800 or 800/221–0090, FAX 303/795–0962) and **Maupintour** (✉ Box 807, 1515 St. Andrews Dr., Lawrence, KS 66047, ☎ 913/843–1211 or 800/255–4266, FAX 913/843–8351).

FIRST-CLASS➤ **Collette Tours** (✉ 162 Middle St., Pawtucket, RI 02860, ☎ 401/728–3805 or 800/832–4656, FAX 401/728–1380), **General Tours** (✉ 53 Summer St., Keene, NH 03431, ☎ 603/357–5033 or 800/221–2216, FAX 603/357–4548), and **Trafalgar Tours** (✉ 11 E. 26th St., New York, NY 10010, ☎ 212/689–8977 or 800/854–0103, FAX 800/457–6644).

PACKAGES

Independent vacation packages that include

round-trip airfare and hotel accommodations are available from major airlines. Among U.S. carriers, contact **Delta Dream Vacations** (☎ 800/872–7786) or **TWA Getaway Vacations** (☎ 800/438–2929).

ADVENTURE➤ Contact **Adventure Center** (⊠ 1311 63rd St., #200, Emeryville, CA 94608, ☎ 510/654–1879 or 800/227–8747, FAX 510/654–4200) for an active tour of Turkey.

ARCHAEOLOGY➤ **Archeological Tours** (⊠ 271 Madison Ave., New York, NY 10016, ☎ 212/986–3054, FAX 212/370–1561) explores Turkey's rich history.

BALLOONING➤ **Buddy Bombard European Balloon Adventures** (⊠ 855 Donald Ross Rd., Juno Beach, FL 33408, ☎ 407/775–0039 or 800/862–8537, FAX 407/775–7008) operates balloon holidays in Istanbul and central Turkey's Cappadocia region, known for its unique geological formations.

BICYCLING➤ Bike tours available from **Backroads** (⊠ 1516 5th St., Berkeley, CA 94710-1740, ☎ 510/577–1555 or 800/462–2848, FAX 510/527–1444) begin in Bodrum and explore the Datça Peninsula; from there cyclists ferry to Greece.

HISTORY➤ History buffs should contact **Herodot Travel** (⊠ 775 E. Blithedale, Box 234, Mill Valley, CA 94941, ☎ FAX 415/381–4031).

JUDAISM➤ Jewish life in Turkey is the subject of a tour from the **American Jewish Congress**

(⊠ 15 E. 84th St., New York, NY 10028, ☎ 212/879–4588 or 800/221–4694).

LEARNING VACATIONS➤ For educational programs contact **Earthwatch** (⊠ Box 403, 680 Mt. Auburn St., Watertown, MA 02272, ☎ 617/926–8200 or 800/776–0188, FAX 617/926–8532), which recruits volunteers to serve in its EarthCorps as short-term assistants to scientists on research expeditions, and **Smithsonian Study Tours and Seminars** (⊠ 1100 Jefferson Dr. SW, Room 3045, MRC 702, Washington, DC 20560, ☎ 202/357–4700, FAX 202/633–9250).

NATURAL HISTORY➤ **Questers** (⊠ 381 Park Ave. S, New York, NY 10016, ☎ 212/251–0444 or 800/468–8668, FAX 212/251–0890) explores the wild side of Turkey in the company of expert guides.

SINGLES AND YOUNG ADULTS➤ Travelers 18–35 looking to join a group should try **Contiki Holidays** (⊠ 300 Plaza Alicante, #900, Garden Grove, CA 92640, ☎ 714/740–0808 or 800/266–8454, FAX 714/740–0818).

WALKING/HIKING➤ For walking and hiking tours in Turkey, contact **Adventure Center** (☞ Adventure, *above*), **Butterfield & Robinson** (⊠ 70 Bond St., Toronto, Ontario, Canada M5B 1X3, ☎ 416/864–1354 or 800/678–1147), **Mountain Travel-Sobek** (⊠ 6420 Fairmount Ave., El Cerrito, CA 94530, ☎ 510/527–8100 or 800/227–2384, FAX

510/525–7710) and **Wilderness Travel** (⊠ 801 Allston Way, . Berkeley, CA 94710, ☎ 510/548–0420 or 800/368–2794, FAX 510/548–0347).

YACHT CHARTERS➤ Try **Huntley Yacht Vacations** (⊠ 210 Preston Rd., Wernersville, PA 19565, ☎ 610/678–2628 or 800/322–9224, FAX 610/670–1767), **Lynn Jachney Charters** (⊠ Box 302, Marblehead, MA 01945, ☎ 617/639–0787 or 800/223–2050, FAX 617/639–0216), and **Ocean Voyages** (⊠ 1709 Bridgeway, Sausalito, CA 94965, ☎ 415/332–4681, FAX 415/332–7460).

IN THE U.K.

Companies that offer holiday packages include **First Choice** (⊠ First Choice House, Peel Cross House, Peel Cross Rd., Salford, Manchester M5 2AN, ☎ 0161/745–7000), **Inspirations** (⊠ Victoria House, Victoria Rd., Horley, Surrey RH6 7AD, ☎ 01293/822–244), and **Unijet** (⊠ Sandrocks, Rocky La., Haywards Heath, West Sussex RH16 4RH, ☎ 01444/451–515).

ORGANIZATIONS

The **National Tour Association** (⊠ NTA, 546 E. Main St., Lexington, KY 40508, ☎ 606/226–4444 or 800/755–8687) and the **United States Tour Operators Association** (⊠ USTOA, 211 E. 51st St., Suite 12B, New York, NY 10022, ☎ 212/750–7371) can provide lists of members and information on booking tours.

TRAIN TRAVEL

FROM THE U.K.

If you have the time—and money—consider the still glamorous **Venice Simplon-Orient Express** (⊠ Sea Containers House, 20 Upper Ground, London SE1 9PF, ☎ 0171/928–6000). The route runs from London to Paris, Zurich, St. Anton, Innsbruck, Verona, and Venice, where you transfer to a ferry for Istanbul; the trip takes more than 32 hours. Trains that are more mundane, passing through Venice or Munich, take some 40 hours: Don't expect a romantic journey.

TRAVEL GEAR

For travel apparel, appliances, personal-care items, and other travel necessities, get a free catalog from **Magellan's** (☎ 800/962–4943, FAX 805/568–5406), **Orvis Travel** (☎ 800/541–3541, FAX 540/343–7053), or **TravelSmith** (☎ 800/950–1600, FAX 415/455–0554).

ELECTRICAL CONVERTERS

Send a self-addressed, stamped envelope to the **Franzus Company** (⊠ Customer Service, Dept. B50, Murtha Industrial Park, Box 142, Beacon Falls, CT 06403, ☎ 860/723–6664) for a copy of the free brochure "Foreign Electricity Is No Deep, Dark Secret."

TRAVEL AGENCIES

For names of reputable agencies in your area, contact the **American Society of Travel Agents** (⊠ ASTA, 1101 King St., Suite 200, Alexandria, VA 22314, ☎ 703/739–2782), the **Association of Canadian Travel Agents** (⊠ Suite 201, 1729 Bank St., Ottawa, Ontario K1V 7Z5, ☎ 613/521–0474, FAX 613/521–0805) or the **Association of British Travel Agents** (⊠ 55-57 Newman St., London W1P 4AH, ☎ 0171/637–2444, FAX 0171/637–0713).

U

U.S.
GOVERNMENT
TRAVEL BRIEFINGS

The U.S. Department of State's American Citizens Services office (⊠ Room 4811, Washington, DC 20520; enclose SASE) issues **Consular Information Sheets** on all foreign countries. These cover issues such as crime, security, political climate, and health risks as well as listing embassy locations, entry requirements, currency regulations, and providing other useful information. For the latest information, stop in at any U.S. passport office, consulate, or embassy; call the interactive hot line (☎ 202/647–5225, FAX 202/647–3000); or, with your PC's modem, tap into the department's computer bulletin board (☎ 202/647–9225).

V

VISITOR
INFORMATION

Contact the **Turkish Tourist Office** (⊠ 821 UN Plaza, New York, NY 10017, ☎ 212/687–2194, FAX 212/599–7568; 1717 Massachusetts Ave. NW, Suite 306, Washington, DC 20036, ☎ 202/429–9844, FAX 202/429–5649. In Canada: ⊠ Turkish Tourist Office, Constitution Sq., 360 Albert St., Suite 801, Ottowa, Ontario K1R 7X7, ☎ 613/230–8654, FAX 613/230–3683. In the United Kingdom: ⊠ 170–173 Piccadilly, 1st Floor, London W1V 9DD, ☎ 0171/629–7771).

SMART TRAVEL TIPS A TO Z

Basic Information on Traveling in Turkey and Savvy Tips to Make Your Trip a Breeze

A

AIR TRAVEL

If time is an issue, **always look for nonstop flights.** If possible, **avoid connecting flights,** which stop at least once and can involve a change of plane.

CUTTING COSTS

MAJOR AIRLINES➢ The least-expensive airfares from the major airlines are priced for round-trip travel and are subject to restrictions and availability. Airlines generally allow you to change your return date for a $25 to $50 fee. If you don't use your ticket, you can apply the cost toward the purchase of a new ticket, again for a small charge.

FROM THE U.K.➢ To save money on flights, **look into an APEX or Super-PEX ticket.** APEX tickets must be booked in advance and have certain restrictions. Super-PEX tickets can be purchased right at the airport.

CONSOLIDATORS➢ Consolidators buy tickets for scheduled flights at reduced rates from the airlines, then sell them at prices below the lowest available from the airlines directly—usually without advance restrictions. Sometimes you can even get your money back if you need to return the ticket. Carefully read the fine print detailing penalties for changes and cancellations. If you doubt the reliability of a consolidator, **confirm your reservation with the airline.**

ALOFT

AIRLINE FOOD➢ If you hate airline food, **ask for special meals when booking.** These can be vegetarian, low-cholesterol, or kosher, for example; commonly prepared to order in smaller quantities than standard fare, they can be tastier.

JET LAG➢ To avoid this syndrome, which occurs when travel disrupts your body's natural cycles, move about the cabin to **stretch your legs and drink plenty of water or juice—not alcohol.**

SMOKING➢ **Contact your carrier regarding its smoking policy.** Some carriers have prohibited smoking throughout their system; others allow smoking only on certain routes or even certain departures of that route.

B

BOAT TRAVEL

In some regions, particularly the Black Sea and greater Istanbul area, ferries are the most efficient means of getting around. On the Aegean and Mediterranean coasts, the pace is slower and boats are mostly used for leisurely sightseeing. Turkish Maritime Lines operates both car-ferry and cruise ships from Istanbul; cruises last a day to a week, and ships are comfortable, rather like moderate-class Turkish hotels.

BUS TRAVEL

Buses are much faster than trains and provide excellent, inexpensive service virtually around the clock, between all cities and towns; they're fairly comfortable and sometimes are air-conditioned. All are run by private companies, each of which has its own fixed fares for different routes and, usually more significantly, standards of comfort. Most bus companies, such as Varan, Ulusoy, and Pamukkale, working between major cities and resort areas, can be counted on for fairly comfortable air-conditioned service with snacks. You could pay anywhere from $8 to $13 for Istanbul–Ankara, say, or $11 to $16 for Istanbul–İzmir. Outside the major cities, however, whether you end up on a new bus or on a rattling old one is simply a matter of luck. All fares include *su* (bottled water). Tickets are sold at stands in a town's *otogar* (central bus terminal); the usual procedure is to go to the bus station and shop around. All seats are reserved. When arranging, ask to sit on the shady side; even on air-conditioned buses, the sun can feel oppressive over the course of a long trip, especially given the clouds of tobacco fumes in the air—the no-smoking movement has yet to arrive in Turkey. For greater comfort on overnight trips, buy two seats and stretch out.

For very short trips, or getting around within a city, take minibuses or a *dolmuş* (shared taxi). Both are inexpensive and comfortable.

BUSINESS HOURS

Banks are open weekdays from 8:30 until noon or 12:30 PM, depending on the bank, and from 1:30 until 5. Museums are generally open Tuesday through Sunday from 9:30 until 5 or 5:30 and closed on Monday. Palaces are open the same hours but are closed Thursday. Shops and bazaars are usually open Monday through Saturday from 9:30 to 1 and from 2 to 7, and closed all day on Sunday. Smaller shops often close for lunch between 1 and 2, although all large stores and even most small shops in the major cities remain open throughout the day. However, in resort areas, shops may stay open until 9 PM and all day Sunday.

NATIONAL HOLIDAYS

January 1 (New Year's Day), February 9–11 (Şeker Bayramı, marking the end of Ramadan), April 18–21 (Kurban Bayramı, an important religious holiday, honoring Abraham's willingness to sacrifice his son to God), April 23 (National Independence Day), May 19 (Atatürk's

Commemoration Day, celebrating his birthday), August 30 (Zafer Bayramı, or Victory Day, commemorating Turkish victories over Greek forces in 1922, during Turkey's War of Independence), October 29 (Cumhuriyet Bayramı, or Republic Day, celebrating Atatürk's proclamation of the Turkish republic in 1923), November 10 (the anniversary of Atatürk's death, commemorated most notably by a nationwide moment of silence at 9:05 AM). Please bear in mind that Muslim religious holidays are based on the lunar calendar and will shift about 10 days backwards each year. The dates given here for the Şeker and Kurban holidays are for 1997.

C

CAMERAS, CAMCORDERS, & COMPUTERS

IN TRANSIT

Always **keep your film, tape, or disks out of the sun;** never put these on the dashboard of a car. Carry an extra supply of batteries, and **be prepared to turn on your camera, camcorder, or laptop computer for security personnel** to prove that it's real.

X-RAYS

Always **ask for hand inspection at security.** Such requests are virtually always honored at U.S. airports, and are usually accommodated abroad. Photographic film becomes clouded after successive exposure to airport X-ray machines. Videotape

and computer disks are not harmed by X-rays, but **keep your tapes and disks away from metal detectors.**

CUSTOMS

Before departing, **register your foreign-made camera or laptop with U.S. Customs.** If your equipment is U.S.-made, call the consulate of the country you'll be visiting to find out whether it should be registered with local customs upon arrival.

CAR RENTAL

CUTTING COSTS

Ask your agent to **look for fly-drive packages,** which save you money, and **ask if local taxes are included** in the rental or fly-drive price. These can be as high as 20% for some destinations. Don't forget to find out about required deposits, cancellation penalties, drop-off charges, and the cost of any required insurance coverage.

INSURANCE

You are generally responsible for any damage to or loss of a rental vehicle, as well as any property damage or personal injury that you cause. Before you rent, **see what coverage you already have** under the terms of your personal auto insurance policy and credit cards. If you do not have auto insurance or an umbrella insurance policy that covers damage to third parties, purchasing CDW or LDW is highly recommended.

LICENSE REQUIREMENTS

In Turkey your own driver's license is ac-

THE GOLD GUIDE / SMART TRAVEL TIPS

THE GOLD GUIDE / SMART TRAVEL TIPS

ceptable. An International Driver's Permit is a good idea (rental agents, but especially local police, are more familiar with the document); it's available from the American or Canadian automobile associations, or, in the United Kingdom, from the AA or RAC.

CHILDREN & TRAVEL

Turkey is not the easiest place to travel with young children. There are long distances to cope with, lots of hiking around rock-strewn ruins, and few child-oriented facilities. However, restaurants are generally casual and accommodating to families, and diapers and baby food are easy to find in most towns.

DRIVING

If you are renting a car, don't forget to **arrange for a car seat when you reserve.** Sometimes they're free.

FLYING

As a general rule, infants under two not occupying a seat fly at greatly reduced fares and occasionally for free. If your children are two or older **ask about special children's fares.** Age limits for these fares vary among carriers. Rules also vary regarding unaccompanied minors, so again, check with your airline.

BAGGAGE➤ In general, the adult baggage allowance applies to children paying half or more of the adult fare. If you are traveling with an infant, **ask about carry-on allowances** before departure. In general, for infants charged 10% of the adult fare you are allowed one carry-on bag and a collapsible stroller, which may have to be checked; you may be limited to less if the flight is full.

SAFETY SEATS➤ According to the FAA, it's a good idea to **use safety seats aloft** for children weighing less than 40 pounds. Airline policies vary. U.S. carriers allow FAA-approved models but usually require that you buy a ticket, even if your child would otherwise ride free, since the seats must be strapped into regular seats. However, some U.S. and foreign-flag airlines may require you to hold your baby during takeoff and landing—defeating the seat's purpose. Other foreign carriers may not allow infant seats at all, or may charge a child rather than an infant fare for their use.

FACILITIES➤ When making your reservation, **request children's meals or freestanding bassinets** if you need them; the latter are available only to those seated at the bulkhead, where there's enough legroom.

LODGING

In general you can't count on Turkish hotels to have cribs or cots, so be sure to request them in advance. Discounts on room rates are often available, however. Children of any age stay free in the same room with their parents at the Hiltons in Istanbul and Ankara; the Hilton in Mersin charges $20 for rollaways.

CUSTOMS & DUTIES

To speed your clearance through customs, **keep receipts for all your purchases abroad** and **be ready to show the inspector what you've bought.** If you feel that you've been incorrectly or unfairly charged a duty, you can **appeal assessments in dispute.** First ask to see a supervisor. If you are still unsatisfied, **write to the port director** at your point of entry, sending your customs receipt and any other appropriate documentation. The address will be listed on your receipt. If you still don't get satisfaction, you can take your case to customs headquarters in Washington, D.C.

IN TURKEY

Turkish customs officials rarely look through tourists' luggage on arrival. You are allowed to bring in 400 cigarettes, 50 cigars, 200 grams of tobacco, 1½ kilograms of instant coffee, 500 grams of tea, and 2½ liters of alcohol. Register all valuable personal items in your passport at your embassy on entry. Items in the duty-free shops in Turkish airports, for international arrivals, are usually less expensive here than in European airports or in flight.

IN THE U.S.

You may bring home $400 worth of foreign goods duty-free if you've been out of the country for at least 48 hours and haven't already used the $400 allowance, or any part of it, in the past 30 days.

Travelers 21 or older may bring back 1 liter of alcohol duty-free, provided the beverage laws of the state through which they reenter the United States allow it. In addition, regardless of their age, they are allowed 100 non-Cuban cigars and 200 cigarettes. Antiques, which the U.S. Customs Service defines as objects more than 100 years old, are duty-free. Original works of art done entirely by hand are also duty-free. These include, but are not limited to, paintings, drawings, and sculptures.

Duty-free, travelers may mail packages valued at up to $200 to themselves and up to $100 to others, with a limit of one parcel per addressee per day (and no alcohol or tobacco products or perfume valued at more than $5); on the outside, the package must be labeled as being either for personal use or an unsolicited gift, and a list of its contents and their retail value must be attached. Mailed items do not affect your duty-free allowance on your return.

IN CANADA

If you've been out of Canada for at least seven days, you may bring in C$500 worth of goods duty-free. If you've been away for fewer than seven days but for more than 48 hours, the duty-free allowance drops to C$200; if your trip lasts between 24 and 48 hours, the allowance is

C$50. You cannot pool allowances with family members. Goods claimed under the C$500 exemption may follow you by mail; those claimed under the lesser exemptions must accompany you.

Alcohol and tobacco products may be included in the seven-day and 48-hour exemptions but not in the 24-hour exemption. If you meet the age requirements of the province or territory through which you reenter Canada, you may bring in, duty-free, 1.14 liters (40 imperial ounces) of wine or liquor *or* 24 12-ounce cans or bottles of beer or ale. If you are 16 or older, you may bring in, duty-free, 200 cigarettes, 50 cigars or cigarillos, and 400 tobacco sticks or 400 grams of manufactured tobacco. Alcohol and tobacco must accompany you on your return.

An unlimited number of gifts with a value of up to C$60 each may be mailed to Canada duty-free. These do not affect your duty-free allowance on your return. Label the package "Unsolicited Gift—Value Under $60." Alcohol and tobacco are excluded.

IN THE U.K.

From countries outside the EU, including Turkey, you may import, duty-free, 200 cigarettes, 100 cigarillos, 50 cigars, or 250 grams of tobacco; 1 liter of spirits or 2 liters of fortified or sparkling wine or liqueurs; 2 liters of still table wine; 60 milliliters of per-

fume; 250 milliliters of toilet water; plus £136 worth of other goods, including gifts and souvenirs.

D

DINING

Lunch is generally served from noon to 3, dinner from 7 to 10. You can find restaurants or cafés open virtually any time of the day or night in cities; in villages, getting a meal at odd hours can be a problem. Breakfast starts early, typically by 7 AM.

Except for at restaurants classified as $$$$, where jacket and tie are usually appropriate, you can get by in jeans and sneakers, and men don't need a jacket.

PRECAUTIONS

Tap water is heavily chlorinated and supposedly safe to drink in cities and resorts. It's best to play it safe, however, and stick to *şişe suyu* (bottled still water), *maden suyu* (bottled, sparkling mineral water) or *maden sodası* (carbonated mineral water), which are better-tasting and inexpensive.

DISABILITIES & ACCESSIBILITY

In Turkey, many buses have special seats designated for passengers with disabilities, and some of those in larger cities "kneel" to make it easier for less-mobile travelers to board. University and city hospitals can be helpful to visitors with disabilities.

When discussing accessibility with an operator

or reservationist, ask hard questions. Are there any stairs, inside *or* out? Are there grab bars next to the toilet *and* in the shower/tub? How wide is the doorway to the room? To the bathroom? For the most extensive facilities, meeting the latest legal specifications, **opt for newer accommodations,** which more often have been designed with access in mind. Older properties or ships must usually be retrofitted and may offer more limited facilities as a result. Be sure to **discuss your needs before booking.**

DISCOUNTS & DEALS

When you **use your credit card to make travel purchases,** you may get free travel-accident insurance, collision damage insurance, or medical or legal assistance, depending on the card and bank that issued it.

SENIOR CITIZENS & STUDENTS

As a senior-citizen traveler, you may be eligible for special rates, but you should mention your senior-citizen status up front. Many state-run museums and sites are free to those 65 and older. If you're a student or under 26, you can also get discounts, especially if you have an official ID card.

DIAL FOR DOLLARS

To save money, **look into "1-800" discount reservations services,** which often have lower rates. These services use their buying power to get a better price on hotels, airline tickets, and sometimes even car rentals. When booking a room, always **call the hotel's local toll-free number** (if one is available) rather than the central reservations number—you'll often get a better price. Ask the reservationist about special packages or corporate rates, which are usually available even if you're not traveling on business.

JOIN A CLUB?

Discount clubs can be a legitimate source of savings, but you must use the participating hotels and visit the participating attractions in order to realize any benefits. Remember, too, that you have to pay a fee to join, so **determine if you'll save enough to warrant your membership fee.**

GET A GUARANTEE

When shopping for the best deal on hotels and car rentals, **look for guaranteed exchange rates,** which protect you against a falling dollar. With your rate locked in, you won't pay more even if the price goes up in the local currency.

DRIVING

The best way to see Turkey is by car, conditions notwithstanding; there are 25,000 mi of paved and generally well-maintained highways, but off the intercity highways, surfaces are often poor and potholes frequent. Archaeological and historic sites are indicated by yellow signposts.

BREAKDOWNS

A road rescue service is available on some highways; before you embark on a journey, ask your hotel how to contact it in case of an emergency. Turkish mechanics in the villages will usually manage to get you going again, at least until you reach a city, where you can have full repairs made. In urban areas, entire streets are given over to car-repair shops run by teams of experts—one specializes in radiators, another in electrical fittings, another in steering columns.

Prices are not high, but it's good to give a small tip to the person who has made your repairs. If you don't wait for the work to be done, take all car documents with you when you leave the shop.

GASOLINE

Mobil, Shell, British Petroleum, Total, Elf, and two Turkish oil companies, Petrol Ofisi and Türkpetrol, operate stations here. Those on the main highways stay open around the clock, others from 6 AM to 10 PM.

ROAD CONDITIONS

Signposts are few, lighting scarce, rural roads sometimes rough, and city traffic chaotic, and the country's accident rate is one of the highest in Europe.

In the countryside, watch out for drivers passing on a curve or on the top of a hill, and beware of peasant carts, unlit at night, and motorcycles weaving in and out of traffic while carrying entire families.

Urban streets and highways are jammed with vehicles operated by high-speed lunatics and drivers who constantly blast their horns. In Istanbul, it's safer and faster to drive on the modern highways. Avoid the many small one-way streets—you never know when someone is going to barrel down one of them in the wrong direction. Better yet, leave your car in a garage and use public transportation or take taxis. Parking is another problem in the cities and larger towns.

RULES OF THE ROAD

In general, Turkish driving conforms to Mediterranean customs, with driving on the right and passing on the left.

F
FERRIES

Turkish Maritime Lines' Black Sea ferry sails from June through September from the Karaköy dock in Istanbul to Samsun and Trabzon on Mondays. The 40-hour one-way Istanbul–Trabzon trip costs about $30 for a reclining seat, $38 to $94 for private cabins, plus $50 for cars. On board you'll encounter tourists and locals alike.

The Istanbul–İzmir car ferry down the Aegean Coast departs every Friday year-round. The 19-hour one-way trip costs from $38 for a Pullman seat to $122 for a cabin berth, plus $40 for a car.

G
GAY & LESBIAN TRAVEL

Gays and lesbians are still not accepted in Turkey, and the recent revival in conservative Islamic sentiment has made matters more difficult. Lesbians are virtually invisible. Gay men are more visible (a few well-known singers are generally acknowledged to be gay), and there are gay bars in the major cities. There have been attempts to start a gay movement and to organize conferences on gay rights and other such events, but these are invariably broken up by the police. Overt displays of affection between gay foreigners will undoubtedly attract, at best, stares, and, particularly in rural areas, are likely to generate considerable shock.

H
HEALTH

There are no serious health risks associated with travel to Turkey, although you should take precautions against malaria if you visit the far southeast. No vaccinations are required for entry. However, to avoid problems at customs, diabetics carrying needles and syringes should have a letter from their physician confirming their need for insulin injections. Travelers are advised to have vaccinations for hepatitis, cholera, and typhoid for trips to the southeast. Rabies can be a problem in Turkey, even occasionally in the large cities. If bitten or scratched by a dog or cat about which you have suspicions, go to the nearest pharmacy and ask for assistance.

For minor problems, pharmacists can be helpful, and medical services are widely available. Doctors and dentists abound in major cities and can be found in all but the smallest towns as well; many are women. There are also *hastane* (hospitals) and *klinik* (clinics). Road signs marked with an *H* point the way to the nearest hospital.

I
INSURANCE

Travel insurance can protect your monetary investment, replace your luggage and its contents, or provide for medical coverage should you fall ill during your trip. Most tour operators, travel agents, and insurance agents sell specialized health-and-accident, flight, trip-cancellation, and luggage insurance as well as comprehensive policies with some or all of these coverages. Comprehensive policies may also reimburse you for delays due to weather—an important consideration if you're traveling during the winter months. Some health-insurance policies do not cover preexisting conditions, but waivers may be available in specific cases. Coverage is sold by the companies listed in Important Contacts A to Z; these companies act as the policy's administrators. The actual insurance is

THE GOLD GUIDE / SMART TRAVEL TIPS

THE GOLD GUIDE / SMART TRAVEL TIPS

usually underwritten by a well-known name, such as The Travelers or Continental Insurance.

Before you make any purchase, **review your existing health and homeowner's policies** to find out whether they cover expenses incurred while traveling.

BAGGAGE

Airline liability for baggage is limited to $1,250 per person on domestic flights. On international flights, it amounts to $9.07 per pound or $20 per kilogram for checked baggage (roughly $640 per 70-pound bag) and $400 per passenger for unchecked baggage. Insurance for losses exceeding the terms of your airline ticket can be bought directly from the airline at check-in for about $10 per $1,000 of coverage; note that it excludes a rather extensive list of items, shown on your airline ticket.

COMPREHENSIVE

Comprehensive insurance policies include all the coverages described above plus some that may not be available in more specific policies. If you have purchased an expensive vacation, especially one that involves travel abroad, comprehensive insurance is a must; **look for policies that include trip delay insurance,** which will protect you in the event that weather problems cause you to miss your flight, tour, or cruise. A few insurers will also sell you a waiver for preexisting medical conditions. Some of the companies that offer both these

features are Access America, Carefree Travel, Travel Insured International, and Travel Guard International (☞ Important Contacts A to Z).

FLIGHT

You should **think twice before buying flight insurance.** A supplement to the airlines' coverage, it's expensive and basically unnecessary. Charging an airline ticket to a major credit card often automatically provides you with coverage that may also extend to travel by bus, train, and ship.

HEALTH

Medicare generally does not cover health care costs outside the United States; nor do many privately issued policies. If your own health insurance policy does not cover you outside the United States, **consider buying supplemental medical coverage.** It can reimburse you for $1,000–$150,000 worth of medical and/or dental expenses incurred as a result of an accident or illness during a trip. These policies also may include a personal-accident, or death-and-dismemberment, provision, which pays a lump sum ranging from $15,000 to $500,000 to your beneficiaries if you die or to you if you lose one or more limbs or your eyesight, and a medical-assistance provision, which may either reimburse you for the cost of referrals, evacuation, or repatriation and other services, or automatically enroll you as a member of a particular medical-

assistance company (☞ Health Issues *in* Important Contacts A to Z).

TRIP

Without insurance, you will lose all or most of your money if you cancel your trip regardless of the reason. Especially if your airline ticket, cruise, or package tour is nonrefundable and cannot be changed, it's essential that you **buy trip-cancellation-and-interruption insurance.** When considering how much coverage you need, look for a policy that will cover the cost of your trip plus the nondiscounted price of a one-way airline ticket should you need to return home early. Read the fine print carefully, especially sections that define "family member" and "preexisting medical conditions." Also **consider default or bankruptcy insurance,** which protects you against a supplier's failure to deliver. Be aware, however, that if you buy such a policy from a travel agency, tour operator, airline, or cruise line, it may not cover default by the firm in question.

U.K. TRAVELERS

You can buy an annual travel insurance policy valid for most vacations during the year in which it's purchased. If you are pregnant or have a preexisting medical condition make sure you're covered before buying such a policy.

L

LANGUAGE

In 1928, Atatürk launched sweeping

language reforms that, over a period of six weeks, replaced Arabic script with the Latin-based alphabet and eliminated many difficult and obscure Arabic and Persian words from the Turkish language. The result has been dramatic: The literacy rate today is 75%, compared with 9% before the reforms.

English and German are widely spoken in hotels, restaurants, and shops in cities and resorts. In villages and remote areas, you may have a hard time finding anyone who speaks anything but Turkish, though rudimentary communications are still usually possible. Try learning a few basic Turkish words; the Turks will love you for it.

LODGING

Accommodations range from the international luxury chain hotels in Istanbul, Ankara, and İzmir to charming inns occupying historic Ottoman mansions and caravansaries to comfortable, family-run *pansiyons* (guest houses) in the countryside. Plan ahead for the peak summer season, when resort hotels are often booked solid by tour companies.

Asking to see the room in advance is accepted practice. It will probably be much more basic than the well-decorated reception area. Check for noise, especially if the room faces a street or is anywhere near a nightclub or disco, and look for such amenities as window screens and mosquito coils—small,

flat disks that, when lighted, emit an unscented vapor that keeps biting insects away.

APARTMENT & VILLA RENTAL

Home-exchange directories list rentals—often second homes owned by prospective house swappers—and some services search for a house or apartment for you (even a castle if that's your fancy) and handle the paperwork. Some send an illustrated catalog; others send photographs only of specific properties, sometimes at a charge; up-front registration fees may apply.

HOTELS & MOTELS

Hotels are officially classified in Turkey as HL (luxury), H1 to H5 (first- to fifth-class); motels, M1 to M2 (first- to second-class); and P, *pansiyons* (guest houses). However, these classifications can be misleading because they're based on the quantity of facilities rather than the quality of the service and decor, and the lack of restaurant or lounge automatically relegates the establishment to the bottom of the ratings. In practice, a lower-grade hotel may actually be far more charming and comfortable than one with a higher rating.

The major Western chains are represented by Hilton, Sheraton, and the occasional Ramada and Hyatt. All tend to be in the higher price ranges.

The standard Turkish hotel room that you will

encounter endlessly throughout the country is clean, with bare walls, low wood-frame beds (usually singles or twins), and industrial carpeting or kilims on the floor. However, the less expensive properties will probably offer plumbing and furnishings that leave much to be desired. If you want a double bed as at home, go to a more expensive property, either Turkish or Western.

PANSIYONS

Outside the cities and resort areas, these small, family-run places will be your most common option. They range from charming, old homes decorated in antiques to tiny, utilitarian rooms done in Kmart modern. As a rule, they are inexpensive and scrupulously clean. Private baths are common, though they are rudimentary—stall showers, toilets with sensitive plumbing. A simple breakfast is typically included.

M
MAIL

Post offices are painted bright yellow and have PTT (Post, Telegraph, and Telephone) signs on the front. The central POs in larger cities are open Monday through Saturday from 8 AM to 9 PM, Sunday from 9 to 7. Smaller ones are open Monday through Saturday between 8:30 and 5.

Rates are frequently adjusted to keep pace with inflation, but the cost of sending a letter or postcard remains nominal. Shipping a 10-pound rug home via surface mail will cost about $25 and take from two to six months.

RECEIVING MAIL

If you're uncertain where you'll be staying, have mail sent to Poste Restante, Merkez Postanezi (central post office) in the town of your choice.

MEDICAL ASSISTANCE

No one plans to get sick while traveling, but it happens, so **consider signing up with a medical assistance company.** These outfits provide referrals, emergency evacuation or repatriation, 24-hour telephone hot lines for medical consultation, cash for emergencies, and other personal and legal assistance. They also dispatch medical personnel and arrange for the relay of medical records. Coverage varies by plan, so **read the fine print carefully.**

MONEY

The monetary unit is the Turkish lira (TL), which comes in bank notes of 10,000; 20,000; 50,000; 100,000; 500,000; and 1,000,000. Smaller denominations come in coins of 1,000; 2,500; 5,000; 10,000; and 25,000. In fall 1996, the exchange rate was TL 95,000 to the U.S. dollar, TL 70,000 to the Canadian dollar, and TL 152,000 to the pound sterling.

ATMS

ATMs can be found in even the smallest Turkish towns. Many accept international credit cards or bank cards (a strip of logos is usually displayed above the ATM). Almost all ATMs have a language key (*dil* in Turkish) to enable you to read the instructions in English.

CASH ADVANCES> Before leaving home, **make sure that your credit cards have been programmed for ATM use in Turkey.** Local bank cards often do not work overseas either; **ask your bank about a MasterCard/Cirrus or Visa debit card,** which works like a bank card but can be used at any ATM displaying a MasterCard/Cirrus or Visa logo.

TRANSACTION FEES> Although fees charged for ATM transactions may be higher abroad than at home, Cirrus and Plus exchange rates are excellent, because they are based on wholesale rates offered only by major banks.

COSTS

Turkey is the least expensive of the Mediterranean countries. Although inflation hovers between 70% and 100%, frequent devaluations of the lira keep prices fairly stable against foreign currencies (which is why prices in this guide are listed in U.S. dollars). Only in Istanbul do costs approach those in Europe, and then only at top establishments. In the countryside, room and board are not likely to come to much more than $50 per person per day.

Coffee can range from about 30¢ to $2.50 a cup, depending on whether it's the less expensive Turkish coffee or American-style coffee and whether it's served in a luxury hotel or a café; tea, 20¢–$2 a glass; local beer, $1–$3; soft drinks, $1–$3; lamb shish kebab, $1.50–$7; taxi, $1 for 1 mi (50% higher between midnight and 6 AM).

EXCHANGING CURRENCY

Because Turkey constantly devalues its currency, wait to change money until you arrive. And don't change all of your money; payment in American dollars can often lead to an extra discount on your purchase. If you are staying for more than a few days, do not change all your money as soon as you arrive, as the exchange rate changes every day. Shop around the exchange booths for the best rate and change enough only for the next few days.

A growing number of privately operated exchange booths offer significantly better rates than hotels or banks.

For the most favorable rates, **change money at banks.** You won't do as well at exchange booths in airports or rail and bus stations, in hotels, in restaurants, or in stores, although you may find their hours more convenient. To avoid lines at airport exchange booths, **get a small amount of the local currency before you leave home.**

TAXES

VAT> The value-added tax, here called *Katma Değer Vergisi,* or KDV, is 15%. Hotels typically combine it with a service charge of 10%

to 15%, and restaurants usually add a 15% service charge.

Value-added tax is nearly always included in quoted prices. Certain shops are authorized to refund the tax (ask). Within a month of leaving Turkey, mail the stamped invoice back to the dealer, and he will mail you a check—in theory if not always in practice.

TRAVELER'S CHECKS

Many places in Turkey, even in Istanbul, do not take traveler's checks. If you want to bring traveler's checks, you're better off with widely recognized brands such as American Express and Thomas Cook. Before leaving home, **contact your issuer for information on where to cash your checks** without a incurring a transaction fee. Record the numbers of all your checks and keep this listing in a separate place, crossing off the numbers of checks you have cashed.

WIRING MONEY

For a fee of 3%–10%, depending on the amount of the transaction, you can have money sent to you from home through Money-Gram^{SM} or Western Union (☞ Money Matters *in* Important Contacts A to Z). The transferred funds and the service fee can be charged to a Master-Card or Visa account.

MOSQUES

Turkey is comparatively lenient regarding the visiting of mosques—in many Muslim countries, non-Muslims are strictly forbidden to enter them at all. Most mosques in Turkey are open to the public during the day. Prayer sessions, called *namaz,* last 30 to 40 minutes and are observed five times daily. These times are based on the position of the sun, so they vary throughout the seasons but are generally around sunrise (between 5 and 7), at lunchtime (around noon or 1, when the sun is directly overhead), in the afternoon (around 3 or 4), at sunset (usually between 5 and 7), and at bedtime (at 9 or 10). During *namaz,* if quiet and still, non-Muslims are usually tolerated. Tourists should, however, avoid visiting mosques midday on Friday, when Muslims are required to congregate and worship.

For women, bare arms and legs are not acceptable inside a mosque. Men should avoid wearing shorts as well. Women should not enter a mosque without first covering their heads with a scarf, though some guardians will overlook it when a female tourist does not cover her head.

Before entering a mosque, shoes must be removed. There is usually an attendant, and shoes are generally safe. If you feel uncomfortable about leaving them you can always carry them in your backpack or handbag. It is considered offensive for a non-Muslim to sit down in a mosque (many tourists do sit down despite the signs requesting them not to).

A small donation is usually requested for the upkeep of the mosque. TL 50,000–100,000 (approximately 50¢ to $1 U.S.) is appropriate. Some mosques heavily visited by tourists may also have a "shoekeeper," who will ask for a tip. You should not feel obliged to give him any money.

P
PACKING FOR
TURKEY

Turkey is an informal country, so leave the fancy clothes at home. Men will find a jacket and tie appropriate for top restaurants in Istanbul, Ankara, and İzmir; for more modest establishments, a blazer will more than suffice. Women should avoid overly revealing outfits and short skirts. The general rule is: the smaller the town, the more casual and conservative the dress.

On the beaches along the Mediterranean, however, topless sunbathing is increasingly common—though it may well attract unwanted attention. Shorts are acceptable for hiking through ruins, but not for touring mosques. The importance of a sturdy, comfortable pair of shoes cannot be exaggerated. Istanbul's Topkapı Palace is incredibly vast, and the ruins at Ephesus and elsewhere are both vast and dusty.

Light cottons are best for summer, particularly

along the coast. If you're planning excursions into the interior or north of the country, you'll need sweaters in spring or fall, all-out cold-weather gear in winter. An umbrella is advisable on the Black Sea Coast.

Sunscreen and sunglasses will come in handy. Outside the bigger cities and resort areas, it's a good idea to carry some toilet paper. You'll need mosquito repellent for eating outside, from March through October; a flashlight for exploring in Cappadocia; and soap if you're staying in more moderately priced hotels.

Bring an extra pair of eyeglasses or contact lenses in your carry-on luggage, and if you have a health problem, **pack enough medication** to last the trip or have your doctor write you a prescription using the drug's generic name, because brand names vary from country to country (you'll then need a duplicate prescription from a local doctor). It's important that you **don't put prescription drugs or valuables in luggage to be checked,** for it could go astray. To avoid problems with customs officials, carry medications in the original packaging. Also, don't forget the addresses of offices that handle refunds of lost traveler's checks.

ELECTRICITY

To use your U.S.-purchased electric-powered equipment, **bring a converter and an adapter.** The electrical

current in Turkey is 220 volts, 50 cycles alternating current (AC); wall outlets take Continental-type plugs, with two or three round prongs.

If your appliances are dual-voltage, you'll need only an adapter. Hotels sometimes have 110-volt outlets for low-wattage appliances near the sink, marked FOR SHAVERS ONLY; don't use them for high-wattage appliances like blow-dryers. If your laptop computer is older, carry a converter; new laptops operate equally well on 110 and 220 volts, so you need only an adapter.

LUGGAGE

Airline baggage allowances depend on the airline, the route, and the class of your ticket; ask in advance. In general, on domestic flights and on international flights between the United States and foreign destinations, you are entitled to check two bags. A third piece may be brought on board, but it must fit easily under the seat in front of you or in the overhead compartment. In the United States, the FAA gives airlines broad latitude regarding carry-on allowances, and they tend to tailor them to different aircraft and operational conditions. Charges for excess, oversize, or overweight pieces vary.

If you are flying between two foreign destinations, note that baggage allowances may be determined not by piece but by weight—generally 88 pounds (40 kilograms) in first class,

66 pounds (30 kilograms) in business class, and 44 pounds (20 kilograms) in economy. If your flight between two cities abroad *connects* with your transatlantic or transpacific flight, the piece method still applies.

SAFEGUARDING YOUR LUGGAGE➤ Before leaving home, **itemize your bags' contents** and their worth, and label them with your name, address, and phone number. (If you use your home address, cover it so that potential thieves can't see it readily.) Inside each bag, **pack a copy of your itinerary.** At check-in, **make sure that each bag is correctly tagged** with the destination airport's three-letter code. If your bags arrive damaged—or fail to arrive at all—file a written report with the airline before leaving the airport.

PASSPORTS & VISAS

It is advisable that you **leave one photocopy of your passport's data page** with someone at home and keep another with you, separated from your passport, while traveling. If you lose your passport, promptly call the nearest embassy or consulate and the local police; having the data page information can speed replacement.

U.S. CITIZENS

All U.S. citizens, even infants, need a valid passport to enter Turkey for stays of up to 90 days. Application forms for both first-time and renewal passports are available at any of the 13 U.S. Passport Agency offices and at some post offices and courthouses. Passports are usually mailed within four weeks; allow five weeks or more in spring and summer.

U.S. citizens also need to purchase a visa, which can be done at the point of entry for $20.

CANADIANS

You need only a valid passport to enter Turkey for stays of up to 90 days. Passport application forms are available at 28 regional passport offices, as well as post offices and travel agencies. Whether for a first or a renewal passport, you must apply in person. Children under 16 may be included on a parent's passport but must have their own to travel alone. Passports are valid for five years and are usually mailed within two to three weeks of application.

U.K. CITIZENS

Citizens of the United Kingdom need a valid passport to enter Turkey for stays of up to 90 days. Applications for new and renewal passports are available from main post offices and at the passport offices in Belfast, Glasgow, Liverpool, London, Newport, and Peterborough. You may apply in person at all passport offices, or by mail to all except the London office. Children under 16 may travel on an accompanying parent's passport. All passports are valid for 10 years.

Allow a month for processing.

U.K. citizens also need to purchase a visa, which can be done at the point of entry for £10.

S

SAFETY

Violent crime against strangers is still very rare in Turkey. The streets of Turkey's major cities are considerably safer than their counterparts in the United States or Western Europe. Travelers should nevertheless take care of their valuables, as pickpockets, although not as common as in the U.S. or Europe, do operate in the major cities and tourist areas.

WOMEN TRAVELING ALONE

Turkey is a generally safe destination for women traveling alone, though in heavily touristed areas such as Istanbul, Antalya, and Marmaris, women who are unaccompanied by men are likely to be approached and sometimes followed. In rural towns, where visits from foreigners are less frequent, men are more respectful toward women on their own. To give Turkish men the benefit of the doubt, some are genuinely curious about women from other lands and really do want only to "practice their English." Still, be forewarned that the willingness to converse can easily be misconstrued as something more meaningful.

As for clothing, Turkey is not the place for

clothing that is short, tight, or bare. Longer skirts and shirts and blouses with a sleeve, however short, are what it takes here to look respectable. Though it may feel odd, covering your head with a scarf will make things easier on you. It also helps if you have the manager of the hotel where you are staying call ahead to the manager of your next hotel to announce your arrival. In their eyes, the call makes you no longer a female who is unaccounted for, and your next host will feel some responsibility to keep you out of harm's way.

As in any other country in the world, the best course is simply to walk on, if approached, and to avoid potentially troublesome situations, such as deserted neighborhoods at night. Note that in Turkey many hotels, restaurants, and other eating spots identify themselves as being for an *aile* (family) clientele, and many restaurants have special sections for women and children. Depending on how comfortable you are being alone, you may or may not like these areas, away from the action—and you may prefer to take your chances in the main room (though some establishments will resist seating you there).

SENIOR-CITIZEN DISCOUNTS

To qualify for age-related discounts, **mention your senior-citizen status up front** when booking hotel reservations, not when checking out, and before you're seated in restaurants, not when paying the bill. Note that discounts may be limited to certain menus, days, or hours. When renting a car, **ask about promotional car-rental discounts**—they can net even lower costs than your senior-citizen discount.

SHOPPING

Beware of antiques. When dealing with pieces purported to be more than 100 years old, chances are you will end up with an expensive fake, which is just as well since it's illegal to export the real thing without a government permit. If what you covet is less than 100 years old, snap it up. If your purchase looks old, it is advisable to have its date authenticated by a local museum to avoid problems when you leave the country.

BARGAINING

Outside the bazaars, prices are often fixed, though in resort areas many shopkeepers will bargain if you ask for a better price. But in bazaars, the operative word is "bargain." More social ritual than battle of wills, it can be great fun once you get the hang of it. As a rule of thumb, offer about 60% of the asking price and be prepared to go up to about 70% to 75%. It's both bad manners and bad business to grossly underbid or to start bargaining if you're not serious about buying.

STUDENTS ON THE ROAD

Travelers 26 and under can purchase an Inter-Rail pass, which allows unlimited second-class rail travel in Turkey and 19 other European countries.

T

TELEPHONES

Most pay phones are yellow, push-button models, although a few older, operator-controlled telephones are still in use. Directions in English and other languages are often posted in phone booths.

All public phones use *jetons* (tokens), available in 7¢ and 30¢ denominations; they can be purchased at post offices and street booths. More and more also accept debit-type telephone cards, available at post offices and hotels, in denominations of 30 ($2), 60 ($3.50), and 100 ($5) usage units; buy a 60 or 100 for long-distance calls within Turkey, a 30 for local usage.

To make a local call, deposit a 7¢ token, wait until the light at the top of the phone goes off, and then dial the number.

Telephone numbers in Turkey have seven-digit local numbers preceded by a three-digit city code. Intercity lines are reached by dialing 0 before the area code and number. In Istanbul, European and Asian Istanbul have been assigned separate area codes: The new code for European Istanbul (for numbers beginning with 2, 5, or 6) is 212, while that for Asian Istanbul (numbers beginning with 3 or 4) is 216.

LONG-DISTANCE

The long-distance services of AT&T, MCI, and Sprint make calling home relatively convenient, but in many hotels you may find it impossible to dial the access number. The hotel operator may also refuse to make the connection. Instead, the hotel will charge you a premium rate—as much as 400% more than a calling card—for calls placed from your hotel room. To avoid such price gouging, travel with more than one company's long-distance calling card—for example, a hotel may block Sprint but not MCI. If the hotel operator claims that you cannot use any phone card, ask to be connected to an international operator, who will help you to access your phone card. You can also dial the international operator yourself. If none of this works, try calling your phone company collect in the United States. If collect calls are also blocked, call from a pay phone in the hotel lobby. Before you go, **find out the local access codes** for your destinations.

To call long-distance within Turkey, dial 131 if you need operator assistance; otherwise dial 0, then dial the city code and number.

To call from a public phone, dial 00, then dial the country code, area or city code, and the number. Expect to pay $3–$5 per minute.

The country code for Turkey is 90.

OPERATORS & INFORMATION

For international operator services, dial 115. Intercity telephone operators seldom speak English, although international operators usually have some basic English. If you need international dialing codes and assistance, or phone books, you can also go to the nearest post office.

TIPPING

In restaurants, a 10% to 15% charge is added to the bill in all but inexpensive, fast-food spots. However, since this money does not necessarily find its way to your waiter, leave an additional 10% on the table. In top establishments, waiters expect tips of 10% to 15% in addition to the service charge. While it's acceptable to include the tip on your bill in restaurants that accept credit cards, a small tip in cash is much appreciated. Hotel porters expect about $2. Taxi drivers are becoming used to foreigners giving them something; round off the fare to the nearest 5,000 TL. At Turkish baths, the staff that attends you expects to share a tip of 30% to 35% of the bill. Don't worry about missing them—they'll be lined up expectantly on your departure.

TOUR OPERATORS

A package or tour to Turkey can make your vacation less expensive and more hassle-free. Firms that sell tours and packages reserve airline seats, hotel rooms, and rental cars in bulk and pass some of the savings on to you. In addition, the best operators have local representatives available to help you at your destination.

A GOOD DEAL?

Make sure you know exactly what is covered, and **beware of hidden costs.** Are taxes, tips, and service charges included? Transfers and baggage handling? Entertainment and excursions? These can add up.

Most packages and tours are rated deluxe, first-class superior, first class, tourist, or budget. The key difference is usually accommodations. Remember, tourist class in the United States might be a comfortable chain hotel, but in Turkey you might share a bath and do without hot water. If the package or tour you are considering is priced lower than in your wildest dreams, **be skeptical.** Also, **make sure your travel agent knows the accommodations** and other services. Ask about the hotel's location, room size, beds, and whether it has a pool, room service, or programs for children, if you care about these. Has your agent been there in person or sent others you can contact?

BUYER BEWARE

Each year a number of consumers are stranded or lose their money when operators—even very large ones with excellent reputations—go out of business. To avoid becoming one of them, take the time to **check out the operator**—find out how long the company has been in business and ask several agents about its reputation. Next, **don't book unless the firm has a consumer-protection program.** Members of the USTOA and the NTA are required to set aside funds for the sole purpose of covering your payments and travel arrangements in case of default. Nonmember operators may instead carry insurance; look for the details in the operator's brochure—and for the name of an underwriter with a solid reputation. Note: When it comes to tour operators, **don't trust escrow accounts.** Although there are laws governing those of charter-flight operators, no governmental body prevents tour operators from raiding the till.

Next, **contact your local Better Business Bureau and the attorney general's offices** in both your own state and the operator's; have any complaints been filed? Finally, **pay with a major credit card.** Then you can cancel payment, provided that you can document your complaint. Always **consider trip-cancellation insurance** (☞ Insurance, *above*).

BIG VS. SMALL➤ Operators that handle several hundred thousand travelers per year can use their purchasing power to give you a good price. Their high volume may also indicate financial stability. But some small companies provide more personalized service; because they tend to specialize, they may also be more knowledgeable about a given area.

USING AN AGENT

Travel agents are excellent resources. In fact, large operators accept bookings made only through travel agents. But it's good to **collect brochures from several agencies** because some agents' suggestions may be skewed by promotional relationships with tour and package firms that reward them for volume sales. If you have a special interest, **find an agent with expertise in that area**; ASTA can provide leads in the United States.

SINGLE TRAVELERS

Prices are usually quoted per person, based on two sharing a room. If traveling solo, you may be required to pay the full double-occupancy rate. Some operators eliminate this surcharge if you agree to be matched up with a roommate of the same sex, even if one is not found by departure time.

TRAIN TRAVEL

The term "express train" is a misnomer in Turkey. While they exist, serving several long-distance routes, they tend to be slow.

The overnight sleeper to Ankara (*Yataklı Ankara Ekpres*) is the most charming and convenient of the trains, with private compartments, attentive service, and a candlelit dining car. The *Fatih Ekspres* travels daily between Ankara and Istanbul and takes about 7½ hours. There are also train services to Pamukkale and Edirne.

AMENITIES

Dining cars on trains between major cities have waiter service and serve surprisingly good and inexpensive food. Overnight expresses have sleeping cars and bunk beds. Cost on the Istanbul–Ankara run is $35, including tips, for example; though advance reservations are a must, cancellations are frequent, so you can often get a space at the last minute.

FARES

They're lower for trains than for buses, and round-trips cost less than two one-way tickets. Student discounts are 10% (30% from December through April). Ticket windows in railroad stations are marked BILGISAYAR GIŞELERI. Post offices and authorized travel agencies also sell train tick-

ets. Book in advance, in person, for seats on the best trains and for sleeping quarters.

W
WHEN TO GO

Most tourists visit between April and the end of October. July and August are the busiest months (and the warmest). April through June, and September and October offer more temperate weather, smaller crowds, and somewhat lower hotel prices.

Istanbul tends to be hot in summer, cold in winter. The Mediterranean and Aegean coasts have mild winters and hot summers; you can swim along either coast from late April into October. The Black Sea Coast is mild and damp, with a rainfall of 90 inches per year. Central and eastern Anatolia can be extremely cold in winter, and its roads and mountain passes closed by snow; summers bring hot, dry weather, with cool evenings.

The following are the average daily maximum and minimum temperatures for major cities in Turkey.

Climate in Turkey

ANKARA

Jan.	40F	4C	May	74F	23C	Sept.	79F	26C
	25	– 4		49	9		52	11
Feb.	43F	6C	June	79F	26C	Oct.	70F	21C
	27	– 3		54	12		45	7
Mar.	52F	11C	July	86F	30C	Nov.	58F	14C
	31	– 1		59	15		38	3
Apr.	63F	17C	Aug.	88F	31C	Dec.	43F	6C
	40	4		59	15		29	– 2

ANTALYA

Jan.	59F	15C	May	79F	26C	Sept.	88F	31C
	43	6		61	16		67	19
Feb.	61F	16C	June	86F	30C	Oct.	81F	27C
	45	7		67	19		59	15
Mar.	65F	18C	July	94F	34C	Nov.	72F	22C
	47	8		74	23		52	11
Apr.	70F	21C	Aug.	92F	33C	Dec.	63F	17C
	52	11		72	22		47	8

ISTANBUL

Jan.	46F	8C	May	69F	21C	Sept.	76F	24C
	37	3		53	12		61	16
Feb.	47F	9C	June	77F	25C	Oct.	68F	20C
	36	2		60	16		55	13
Mar.	51F	11C	July	82F	28C	Nov.	59F	15C
	38	3		65	18		48	9
Apr.	60F	16C	Aug.	82F	28C	Dec.	51F	11C
	45	7		66	19		41	5

İZMIR

Jan.	49F	9C	May	74F	23C	Sept.	81F	27C
	36	2		54	12		58	14
Feb.	50F	10C	June	83F	28C	Oct.	72F	22C
	36	2		59	15		52	11
Mar.	56F	13C	July	88F	31C	Nov.	63F	17C
	38	3		63	17		47	8
Apr.	67F	19C	Aug.	88F	31C	Dec.	52F	11C
	45	7		63	17		40	4

TRABZON

Jan.	50F	10C	May	67F	19C	Sept.	74F	23C
	40	4		56	13		63	17
Feb.	50F	10C	June	74F	23C	Oct.	70F	21C
	40	4		63	17		58	14
Mar.	52F	11C	July	79F	26C	Nov.	61F	16C
	40	4		67	19		52	11
Apr.	58F	14C	Aug.	79F	26C	Dec.	54F	12C
	47	8		68	20		43	6

1 Destination: Turkey

LAND OF CONTRASTS

O WESTERN EYES, Turkey is exotic. Its domed mosques with minarets piercing the sky, its crowded bazaars gleaming with copper and gold and piled high with carpets, and its palaces and sultans' harems are the stuff of fable. The muezzin's call to prayer startles our ears five times a day, and the syllables uttered by native men and scarved women are like nothing we've heard before. This legendary strangeness both compels and confuses travelers. It also masks the reality that Turkey is a modern country, rapidly industrializing, constantly changing, growing too fast, and clamoring for recognition as a 20th-century European power.

Such strong contrasts are daily life for urban Turks, who maneuver between the ancient and modern as deftly as they cross the new Bosporus Bridge between Europe and Asia. Istanbul, they will tell you, is the world's only city that spans two continents, which makes it something of a metaphor for the nation whose largest city it is. The constant pull between East and West, between modern and traditional, creates an underlying tension that often erupts to confound Turkish society and politics. Although Turkey has been a secular democracy since 1923, Islam remains a strong force; 99% of the population is Muslim. Religious tradition prevails in rural areas, where women cling to head scarves and some are still veiled. In major Turkish cities, however, contrasting lifestyles are tolerated, and you find religious tokenism and devotion side by side.

Turkish matrons wearing baggy harem pants stride by chic young women in short skirts and boys with Western jeans. Schoolchildren of both sexes in neat blue uniforms run along a street carrying books and accost you with newly learned English. "Hello," they call shyly. "Welcome to Turkey!" they shout. In a fish restaurant along the Bosporus, male and female university students share a table and order mezes, the requisite Turkish hors d'oeuvres. They are drinking wine and the anise-flavored liqueur known as raki. On a rural bus, a woman in a flowered head scarf holds up her rosy-cheeked baby for you to admire. You mime back that he's a fine boy, and she beams a proud smile. Someday he'll wear his own school uniform—what will he think of his mother's old-fashioned clothes then? On a steep road to the Aegean, cars whiz past dignified old men leading donkeys; on sandy beaches below, tourists sunbathe in bikinis or go topless. You seek shade in a quiet Istanbul garden at noon to eat a sandwich and spot rows of men's black shoes outside a mosque. When the men finally exit in their stocking feet, all wear dark business suits and some carry briefcases. A Turk leaves his friend with the universal goodbye: "Allaha ısmarladık" (I put myself in the hands of God). "Güle, güle" (Go smiling), the friend replies.

Bridging the old and the new, East and West, has made the Turks a unique people. They occupy the sites of some of the oldest cities in history; their towns and villages have risen atop the strata of great warring civilizations. Therefore, Turks walk proudly, but always a bit guardedly. They are independent, extremely courteous, and industrious. They also have an inbred instinct for survival, and that instinct has shown them the opportunities to be had from the recent boom in tourism. In major cities, resorts, and villages near archaeological sites, everyone is an entrepreneur. Very few beg; everyone—from street urchins proffering shoe shines to old men hawking cold, peeled cucumbers by the Bosporus ferries—seems to have something to sell you.

Urban Turkey is bursting at its seams as the countryside pours into the cities in yet another replay of the Industrial Revolution. The population of Istanbul has soared from 700,000 inhabitants in 1923 to an estimated 12 million in 1996 and is still growing by half a million a year; that of İzmir, the Aegean port that's the nation's third-largest city, increased by nearly 40% a year in the 1980s. The immense effort of metropolitan areas to accommodate such staggering growth has resulted in crowding, overbuilding, and gridlock. Air pollution is a real urban plague, especially in winter, due to the sooty lignite coal still used for heating. Electricity is expensive and at times unreliable, as is water. In Istanbul, the water supply often goes off for short periods in summer to relieve droughts. Better hotels now have their own water depots in readiness for cutoffs. Such private solutions to Istanbul's water problem have historical antecedents in the underground cisterns of the old city. Among all of Istanbul's eerie wonders, the shadowy subterranean reservoir called Yerebatan Saray (Sunken Palace) is a prize: Where else in the world can you descend into a 6th-century waterworks with dramatic illumination and classical music?

While the country has struggled with rapid industrialization, it has also benefited from it. Growth and prosperity have spurred the preservation of landmarks, the restoration of fine historic districts, and the creation of handsome new parks. Turkey has virtually no Western-style drug problem and enforces stringent drug laws. (These laws apply to you; it's foolhardy to transgress them.)

If you come to his country, the Turk reasons, you must need a carpet. A sizable segment of the economy is based on this assumption, and there are thousands of rug sellers. Accept directions from a stranger and you may find yourself at a rug shop. Inside, everyone is charming and it's hard to escape. First you are invited to sit and have some tea. Before you can demur, a lad is sent off to fetch fragrant apple tea. Meanwhile, carpets are rapidly lifted off piles by other Turks and spread before you, one after the other. Everyone scans your expression, quick to catch the slightest glimmer of desire. The tea arrives, in small, hot glasses and smelling sweet, and is handed around to make you feel beholden. It works; you feel beholden. Carpets continue to unroll before your eyes, and it's impossible to resist the rich colors and lavish patterns, the sheer variety and beauty of them. Before you know it, you own a rug. But you must bargain: A well-managed negotiation raises everyone's esteem.

Many of the finest carpets can be found in mosques, where there are strictures against wearing shoes (most Turks even take their shoes off to enter private houses). To the unconverted, mosques, like churches,

require a little study, and Turkey presents unparalleled opportunities. Some Islamic countries won't let non-Muslims enter mosques.

TURKISH CUISINE provides another satisfying diversion. The country is a major food producer, and for Turks, meals are no occasion to rush. The alcoholic beverages of choice are raki and beer, though Turkey also produces an acceptable range of wines. The universal nonalcoholic drink is tea, served in tiny tulip-shaped glasses. Coffee is a more expensive and formal drink; traditionally, a cup of thick Turkish coffee ends a meal. Teahouses are where Turkish men (and sometimes women, if the teahouse is outside or has a terrace) sit with friends, sipping, talking—and, of course, smoking. Turks smoke cigarettes all the time and everywhere. In rural areas, teahouses are strictly male preserves, the center of village life. The picturesque bubbling *nargile* (water pipes) can still be seen in teahouses, but the more portable cigarette rules.

Should you get lost in Turkey, you will not lack for help. Men and boys are everywhere, offering to guide you or to sell you something. Inflation has been running 80%–90% per year since the early 1990s, and unemployment and underemployment have become widespread. More than half of Turkey's population of 60 million is under 20 years of age and readying to enter the crowded job market. Turkey's army siphons some of the excess; a 16-month military stint is compulsory for males.

But work remains scarce and shared in odd ways. In tiny Selçuk, near Ephesus, a local carpet dealer, cousin to the owner of our *pansiyon* (guest house), generously offered to have his nephew drive us to the archaeological site. "And my father will bring you back," he announced. The next morning, an eager teenager, trying out his English, dropped us at the site, and later, a courtly old man with an elaborate mustache rolled up in an old blue car: "Merhaba!" (Hello), he called to us. I don't know if any of these people were actually related, although rural kinship is flexible, but I expect that each got a cut of the very reasonable price we paid for a kilim. The trip was still a bargain—not only in money, but because we were sick of buses and the deal made us family, too. In Turkey, anyone who helps bring in a customer receives a cut, and it spreads the work around.

What about the future? Turkey has a challenging agenda. It is determined to prosper and claim its place among the modern states of Europe. Turkey applied for full membership in the European Union in 1987 but has been refused on a variety of grounds, including virulent objections from rival Greece (an EU member). Turks, who have suffered from bad press in the West ever since the Crusades, argue that the EU has focused on its problems while ignoring the country's huge potential, its wide resources, and its astonishing progress. Nonetheless, Turkey has taken steps to spur EU acceptance. In 1996 it entered a customs union with the EU, with both sides abolishing tariffs on the other's goods.

The liberalization of the economy in the early 1980s has unquestionably brought huge material and technological benefits to many Turks. Stores that a few years ago stocked only a handful of shoddily made local goods now carry the very latest products, many of them either imported or manufactured locally under license. Turkish yuppies have MBAs from universities in the United States and Europe, carry credit cards and mobile telephones, and surf the Internet. But opening up to the outside world has not been without its costs. While some have become spectacularly rich, others, particularly those in lower income groups, have seen their real living standards fall. Traditionally close family structures have been strained and often broken by the stress of migration to Turkey's sprawling cities.

"Turkey is a man running West on a train heading East," goes a Turkish saying. As one section of society has become increasingly integrated with the West, another is turning away from what it sees as the West's brash, amoral materialism and toward more traditional values and conservative Islam. Reconciling these divergent goals is just the latest challenge facing this fascinating nation, one that has negotiated and survived other philosophical, cultural, and political evolutions over the centuries.

—By Rebecca Morris

WHAT'S WHERE

The Aegean Coast
Along the turquoise Aegean Coast are long stretches of sandy beaches and pine-clad hills dotted with old port villages—Kuşadası, Bodrum (ancient Halicarnassus), Marmaris, Antalya—all reincarnated as modern resorts. Some of the finest reconstructed Greek and Roman cities in the world can be found here, including the 3,000-year-old ruins of Troy, made famous by the poet Homer; Pergamum on its windswept hilltop; and the magnificent temples, colonnaded streets, and theater at Ephesus.

Ankara and Central Anatolia
The civilizations that have passed through Central Anatolia have bequeathed a richly textured region. Many of the sites and sights in the region are utterly unique: churches carved into volcanic rock, underground cities once inhabited by thousands of people, and the whirling dance of the Mevlana dervishes. Then, of course, there is the political and cultural center of Ankara, which has attained Atatürk's ideal of a modern Turkish city.

The Black Sea Coast
The Black Sea Coast harbors some of Turkey's wildest and most primitive districts, undeveloped regions that are far—in both distance and character—from the modern tourist resorts along the country's south and west coasts. With their old wooden Ottoman houses, cobblestone alleys filled with chickens and donkeys, and spare-looking mosques, the tiny villages here, many of them unmarked on maps, feel barely touched by the 20th century.

The Far East
The far east of Turkey is a harsh but beautiful region, with lonesome plains, alpine forests, and imposing black mountains that attract a small but steady stream of hardy travelers who come to see the ruins of the remarkable Armenian kingdom of Ani; Mt. Ararat, where, according to Genesis, Noah's Ark came to rest after the Great Flood; the wild, desolate landscape around immense Lake Van; the mighty, black basalt fortress at Diyarbakır; and the awe-inspiring temple atop Mt. Nimrod.

Istanbul

Although the capital may have been moved to Ankara, Turkey's heart still beats in Istanbul. With its archaeological sites and the matchless beauty of the Bosporus, "The City," as it used to be known, is quite unlike any other place in Turkey if not the world—capable of fascinating, frustrating, enchanting, and bewitching, all in a single breath.

The Mediterranean Coast

Turkey's Mediterranean Coast stretches from the Aegean to the Syrian border. Most visitors head for its westernmost corner, to the resorts of Marmaris, Fethiye, and Antalya, an area crammed with archaeological ruins, peaceful coves, and sandy beaches. To the east of Antalya the land begins to rise into the rugged Taurus mountains that form the southern rim of the central Anatolian plateau. In many places the mountains run straight down to the sea in cliffs and headlands before opening out into the great plains of the Hatay and Antakya, sites of Roman ruins and some stunning mosaics.

PLEASURES AND PASTIMES

Architecture and Ruins

With more than 2,000 archaeological sites and historical monuments, spanning over 10,000 years, Turkey is a repository of much history, from the Stone Age settlements of Çatalhöyük, the ruins of once-thriving Greek cities on the Aegean and Mediterranean coasts, and the troglodyte warrens of Cappadocia, to the architectural splendors of the major cities, with their magnificent Byzantine churches and Ottoman mosques. Turkey began in the 1980s a concerted effort to preserve and protect its heritage. But the sheer quantity means that hundreds of sites lie unexcavated in overgrown fields.

Beaches

Turkey's best beaches lie along the Mediterranean coast. From Bodrum, as you head east, top choices include the shores of Sedir Island; İztuzu Beach near Dalyan, a sweeping strand around a lagoon; the Gemiler Island beaches; the placid, deep blue bay of Ölü Deniz; Patara, with its endless stretch of dazzling white sand; the private coves along the Kekova Sound; the strand among the Roman ruins at Phaselis; and Ulas Beach near Alanya. Beaches along the Aegean are pleasant enough, if not as grand. The most popular are, from south to north, Altınkum, Samsun Dağı National Park, Sarımsaklı near Ayvalık, and those along the Gulf of Edremit. Here the sand is still fine and white, but the beaches are shorter and more heavily used.

Boating and Sailing

Boating the Aegean or Mediterranean coasts opens up otherwise inaccessible sights and bypasses the bumps and bustle of travel by road. Bodrum and Marmaris are the home ports to an array of boats, from sleek, modern yachts, which can be chartered bare or with crew, to traditional wooden boats, called *gulets*, always chartered with crew.

Camping

As pansiyons are cheap and plentiful and official campgrounds few, Turks themselves seldom camp out. So the predominant clientele in the well-equipped campgrounds in the Kervansaray-Mocamp chain, located nationwide in some popular tourist areas, are Europeans, hippies, and international budget travelers. These properties have electricity, running water, and occasionally a pool; the operating season is from April or May through October. For specific camping information, contact the local tourist boards listed in the city and regional chapters.

Dining

Cuisine

Turkey is not just a geographic bridge between Europe, Asia, and the Middle East; it is a gastronomic one as well. Its cuisine reflects the long history of a people who emigrated from the borders of China to a land mass known as Asia Minor, and built an empire that encompassed Arabic, Asian, and European lands.

Turkish cuisine is healthful, full of vegetables, grains, fresh fish, and seemingly infinite varieties of lamb. Fish and meat are typically served grilled or roasted.

The core group of seasonings is unique: garlic, sage, oregano, cumin, mint, dill, lemon, and yogurt, always more yogurt. Turkish yogurt is among the tastiest in the world: Many travelers swear it helps keep their stomachs calm and stable while on the road.

This guide makes frequent references to "traditional Turkish cuisine." Here's what to expect.

MEZES➤ These appetizers are often brought to your table on a tray. Standard cold mezes include *patlıcan salatası* (roasted eggplant puree flavored with garlic and lemon), *haydari* (a thick yogurt dip made with garlic and dill), *dolma* (stuffed grape leaves, peppers, or mussels), *ezme* (a spicy paste of minced green pepper, onion, parsley, and tomato paste), *kızartma* (deep-fried eggplant, zucchini, or green pepper served with fresh yogurt), *cacık* (a garlicky cold yogurt "soup" with shredded cucumber, mint, or dill), *barbunya pilaki* (kidney beans, tomatoes, and onions cooked in olive oil), *imam bayıldı* (slow-roasted baby eggplant topped with olive oil–fried onions and tomatoes and seasoned with garlic). One taste of this last meze, and you'll understand how it got its name—"the imam fainted with delight." Inevitably there will be other dishes based on eggplant, called *patlıcan* by the Turks. Hot appetizers, usually called *ara sıcak,* include *börek* (a deep-fried or oven-baked pastry filled with cheese or meat), *kalamar* (deep-fried calamari served with a special sauce), and *midye tava* (deep-fried mussels). Individual restaurants have their own variations on these dishes.

KEBABS➤ Available almost any place you stop to eat, kebabs (*kebaps* in Turkish) come in many guises. Although the ingredient of choice for Turks is lamb, some kebabs are made with beef, chicken, or even heavier fish, usually grilled with vegetables on a skewer. *Adana kebaps* are spicy ground-lamb patties arranged on a layer of sautéed pita bread, topped with a zippy yogurt-and-garlic sauce. *Bursa kebaps* are sliced grilled lamb, smothered in tomato sauce, hot butter, and yogurt. *Şiş kebaps* are the traditional skewered cubes of lamb, usually interspersed with peppers and onions. *Köfte kebaps* are meatballs made from minced lamb mixed with rice, bulgur, or bread crumbs, then threaded onto skewers.

FISH AND MEAT➤ Fresh fish, often a main course, is commonly served grilled and drizzled with olive oil and lemon. You will find *alabalık* (trout), *barbunya* (red mullet), *kalkan* (turbot), *kefal* (gray mullet), *kılıç* (swordfish, sometimes served as a kebab), *levrek* (sea bass), *lüfer* (bluefish), and *palamut* (bonito). In the meat department, there is *manti,* a sort of Turkish ravioli made with garlicky yogurt with a touch of mint. Grilled quail is most common inland; it's often marinated in tomatoes, yogurt, olive oil, and cinnamon. *Karışık ızgara,* a mixed grill, usually combines tender chicken breast, beef, a lamb chop, and spicy lamb patties, all served with rice pilaf and vegetables. *Tandır kebap,* lamb cooked in a pit, is a typical Anatolian dish.

DESSERTS➤ You'll encounter several varieties of baklava (phyllo pastry with honey and chopped nuts) and *burma kadayıf* (shredded wheat in honey or syrup). Also popular are puddings, made of yogurt and eggs, or sweet rice, or milk and rice flour.

BREAKFAST➤ Usually taken in your hotel, breakfast typically consists of white goat cheese, sliced tomatoes, and olives, with a side order of fresh bread; the menu varies little, whether you stay in a simple pansiyon or an upscale hotel. Yogurt with honey and fresh fruit is generally available as well. If you don't see it, just ask.

Types of Restaurants

The simplest establishments, Turkey's fast-food joints, are the *kebapç* and the *pideci.* The former specializes in kebabs—marinated cubes of meat (generally lamb), usually grilled and cooked with vegetables on a skewer. The latter serves *pide,* a pizzalike snack made of flat bread topped with butter, cheese, egg, or ground lamb, and baked in a wood-fired oven. Often these eateries are little more than counters, where you belly up to the bar for instant gratification; on occasion they attain luncheonette status.

Lokantas are bistros, unpretentious neighborhood spots that make up the vast majority of Turkish restaurants. In smaller cities, there may well be three or four in a row, each with simple wooden chairs and tables, paper napkins, and maybe a touristboard poster on the wall. In towns, villages, and any city with a harbor, lokantas are often open-air, the better to take advantage of the waterfront and sky, or surrounded by flower-filled trellises. Often you serve yourself, cafeteria-style, from big display cases full of hot and cold dishes—a relief if you don't speak Turkish. If there is no menu, it is because the chef only serves what is fresh, and that changes from day to day.

In the more upscale *restoran,* you can expect tablecloths, menus, even a wine list, and dishes drawn from the richer, "palace" cuisine of Turkish royalty, often with Continental touches. Reservations, usually unnecessary elsewhere, are a good idea here. The best restorans are in Istanbul and Ankara, though others are scattered throughout the country.

Wine, Beer, and Spirits

Alcohol is readily available and widely consumed, despite Turkey's predominantly Muslim culture. Among the perfectly acceptable, inexpensive local wines, the best are Villa Doluca and Kavaklidere, available in *beyaz* (white) and *kırmızı* (red). The most popular local beer is Efes Pilsen, your basic American-type pilsner. The national drink is raki, a relative of the Greek ouzo, made from grapes and aniseed. Turks mix it with water or ice and sip it throughout their meal or serve it as an aperitif.

Hiking

Turkey has stunning national parks with sweeping vistas on high grassy plateaus: Uludağ, near Bursa; Kovada Gölü, near Isparta, off the E24 toward Konya; Güllük Dağ, at Termessos; and Yedigöller, "Seven Lakes," north of Bolu. Even more exceptional for hikers are Turkey's ancient cities. Ruins lie up and down the Aegean and Mediterranean coasts; some (Termessos, Pergamum) are atop cliffs, some (Patara, Phaselis) along beaches. At many smaller sites, you will find few—if any—other visitors. Yellow signs mark archaeological sites, both major and obscure.

Shopping

Exploring the bazaars, all brimming with copper and brassware, hand-painted ceramics, carved alabaster and onyx, fabrics, richly colored carpets, and (truth be told) tons of tourist junk, is the best part of shopping in Turkey. You won't roam the bazaars too long before someone offers you a free glass of *çay* (tea), whether you're a serious shopper or are just browsing.

Rugs

Persistent salesmen and affordable prices make it hard to leave Turkey without flat-woven kilims or other rugs. No matter what you've planned, sooner or later you'll end up in the cool of a carpet shop listening to a sales rap. Patterns and colors vary by region. The best prices and the best selection are in smaller villages. You may pay twice as much in Istanbul, particularly for older rugs, and you won't find the selection or the quality—shops here cater to the package-tour crowd. Salesmen will insist they can't lower the price, but they virtually always do.

Other Local Specialties

Made of a light, porous stone found only in Turkey, meerschaum pipes are prized for their cool smoke; look for a centered hole and even walls. You can also buy tiles and porcelain, though modern work doesn't compare with older craftsmanship. Some spices, saffron foremost among them, can be purchased for a fraction of their cost back home. Another good deal is jewelry, because you pay by weight and not for design—but watch out for tin and alloys masquerading as silver. Turkey is also known for its leather goods, but it's better to stick with merchandise off the rack and steer clear of made-to-order goods.

NEW AND NOTEWORTHY

In the general elections of December 1995, the pro-Islamic Welfare Party emerged as the largest Party in parliament, sending a shock wave through Turkey's traditionally secular establishment and toppling the government of Prime Minister Tansu Çiller, Turkey's first-ever female leader. But with only 22% of the vote, Welfare was unable to form a parliamentary majority. After six months of chaos as mainstream parties maneuvered to keep Welfare out of power, Necmettin Erbakan became Turkey's first militantly Islamic prime minister when Welfare formed a coalition government with Ms. Çiller's True Path Party.

Turkey moved closer to economic integration with the European Union in January 1996 when the two sides implemented a customs union, removing tariffs on each other's goods. But the agreement only affected the movement of goods. Turkish citizens still have to apply for visas to enter the EU and face severe restrictions on working there. Opposition from Greece continues to deny Turkey access to EU funds, and full Turkish membership in the EU remains a distant prospect.

In June 1996 Istanbul hosted the UN Habitat II City Summit on Human Settlement. Over 20,000 delegates from around the world met to discuss the problems of housing and living conditions in the last major UN summit of the 20th century.

By late 1996 there was still no sign of a letup in the bloody struggle between the Turkish military and the separatist Kurdish nationalists, the PKK, which has claimed more than 20,000 lives since 1983. Despite occasional incidents in Turkey's major cities, the fighting remains mostly concentrated in the underdeveloped, and predominantly Kurdish, southeast of the country. The PKK has occasionally attacked Western property in the southeast and has been known to seize tourists traveling in the region and hold them hostage in an attempt to gain publicity. Both the State Department of the United States and the British Embassy in Ankara advise their citizens not to visit the area, or if they do go there to remain within the major cities and either fly or travel by public transport on main roads (the latter during daylight hours only). For an up-to-date report on the situation, call the State Department hot line in Washington, DC, at 202/647–5225.

FODOR'S CHOICE

No two people will agree on what makes a perfect vacation, but it's fun and helpful to know what others think. We hope you'll have a chance to experience some of Fodor's Choices yourself while visiting Turkey.

Architecture and Ruins

Classical Sites

★**Aphrodisias, inland Aegean Coast.** The beauty of the city of Aphrodite, the goddess of love, is in its details—in statues, columns, and decorative friezes.

★**Preserved theater at Aspendos, Mediterranean Coast.** Built during the reign of Emperor Marcus Aurelius, the theater, whose design rivals that of the Colosseum in Rome, is striking for its broad curve of seats, perfectly proportioned porticoes, and rich decoration.

★**Ephesus, Aegean Coast.** One of the finest archaeological sites in the world is an entire city of ruined temples, houses, libraries, theaters, and colonnaded streets.

★**Mountaintop ruins at Pergamum, Aegean Coast.** The remains of one of the ancient world's leading architectural and artistic centers sprawl across a windswept mountain with superb views over the Selinos valley.

★**Priene, Aegean Coast.** The ruins of Priene, which include a temple, a well-preserved council chamber, a marketplace, and a home where Alexander the Great may have slept, lie atop a steep hill, overlooking the flat valley of the Büyük Menderes.

★**Mountain aerie at Termessos, Mediterranean Coast.** High in the mountains behind Antalya, the ruins at Termessos include a gymnasium and bath complex, a 5,000-seat theater, and a vast necropolis with nearly 1,000 tombs.

Ottoman Sites

★**Blue Mosque, Istanbul.** Officially known as Sultan Ahmet Cami, this mosque is renowned for its interior, which shimmers with blue İznik tiles.

★**Selimiye Cami, Edirne.** Süleymaniye Cami in Istanbul may attract more attention, but it was this perfectly proportioned mosque in the provincial town of Edirne that the great Ottoman architect Sinan considered his masterpiece.

★**Süleymaniye Cami, Istanbul.** The grandest and most famous creation of the Ottoman architect Sinan, this 16th-century mosque still dominates the Istanbul skyline.

★**Topkapı Saray, Istanbul.** The heart of Ottoman Istanbul for more than four centuries, this former imperial palace of the sultans looks out across the Golden Horn. It holds priceless jewels, porcelain, paintings, costumes, and holy relics.

★**Yeşil Cami, Bursa.** The beauty of this mosque in the old Ottoman capital of Bursa starts at its carved-marble entrance, which leads into a sea of blue and green İznik tiles, many with intricate floral designs.

Byzantine Sites

★**Hagia Sophia, Istanbul.** The greatest church in Christendom for more than a millennium—with a huge dome, massive pillars, and magnificent wall mosaics—the 1,500-year-old Hagia Sophia is one of the greatest buildings ever constructed.

★**Hagia Sophia, Trabzon.** This ruined church, which sits on a green hill overlooking the Black Sea, has some of the finest Byzantine frescoes and mosaics in existence.

★**Kariye Museum, Istanbul.** This museum on the outskirts of Istanbul occupies the former Church of the Holy Savior in Chora, which contains dazzling 14th-century mosaics and frescoes depicting biblical scenes.

★**Monastery of the Virgin, Sumela.** The monks who founded this 4th-century retreat carved their cells from sheer rock. The setting—a labyrinth of courtyards, corridors, and chapels—is incredible.

★**Yerebatan Saray, Istanbul.** This underground cistern is just part of the Byzantine underground network of waterways built to supply Istanbul. Its 336 marble columns lend it a haunting, almost cathedral-like beauty and provide a cool, serene refuge from the bustle of city streets.

Dining

★**Canlı Balık, Ayvalık.** Local boats sway a few feet away while diners enjoy the excellent food and romantic setting of this Aegean Coast fish restaurant. $$

★**Dört Mevsim, Istanbul.** Turkish and French cuisine are served at this fine restaurant at the southernmost end of İstiklal Caddesi. $$

★**Mest, Ankara.** The French-trained chef here prepares fine northern Italian cuisine in a two-story villa with an upstairs terrace. $$

★**Çakallar Aile Gazinosu, Amasya.** You need a car to reach this restaurant, but it's well worth the trip. While you eat your fish dish or meat kebab, you can watch the sunset and take in a panoramic view. $–$$

★**Kirkerdiven Restaurant, Antalya.** Once the barn of an Ottoman house, this restaurant serves high-quality meat and fish, as well as a large selection of mezes and salads. $–$$

★**Hacı Baba, Istanbul.** Just off Taksim Square, this large cheerful restaurant serves fine mezes and excellent lamb dishes; its shady terrace overlooks a Greek Orthodox church. $

Lodging

★**Çelik Palas, Bursa.** A 1930s design and a large pool fed by thermal springs are just two of the appealing features of the poshest hotel in Bursa. $$$$

★**Çırağan Palace, Istanbul.** A restored Ottoman palace on the edge of the Bosporus, the Çırağan is probably the most romantic hotel in Istanbul. $$$$

★**Talya, Antalya.** This luxurious eight-story resort curves around its own beach, which is accessible via an elevator that runs up and down the side of a cliff. Rooms are spacious, with big beds, private terraces, and a view of the sea from every window. $$$–$$$$

★**Ayasofia Pansiyons, Istanbul.** A preservationist group restored several 19th-century Ottoman houses and furnished them with carpets and kilims. The pansiyons' front rooms have superb views over Hagia Sophia. $$$

★**Kismet, Kuşadası.** This small hotel, run by a descendant of the last Ottoman sultan, feels almost like a private Mediterranean villa. $$$

★**Yeşil Ev, Istanbul.** A restored mansion on the edge of a small park in old Istanbul, the hotel has been decorated in old-fashioned Ottoman style with lace curtains, latticed shutters, brass beds, and carved wooden furniture. $$$

★**Assos Kervansaray, Assos.** The Kervansaray is well situated on the water's edge with superb views out cross the Aegean Sea. $$

★**Binlik Hotel, Dalyan.** Rooms at this family-run hotel are not luxurious, but it does offer more amenities than most hotels its size. Take the half-board option, as dinners here are satisfying. $$

★**Balıkçı Han, Kalkan.** This delightful pansiyon, the only hotel on the small street edging the waterfront, is in a converted 19th-century inn. Some rooms have old brass beds, a nice change from the usual wood platforms in similar hostelries. $

★**Herodot Pansiyon, Bodrum.** Rooms on the marina side of this popular pansiyon have fine views of Bodrum castle. $

★**Ottoman House, Göreme.** This cozy and very inexpensive hotel feels like a bed-and-breakfast. The rooms are simple but very clean. They're decorated with carpets from the owners' shop. $

Museums

★**Ankara Anadolu Medeniyetleri Müzesi, Ankara.** A 15th-century *bedestan* (covered bazaar) and *han* (inn) houses masterpieces from several eras. The heart of the museum is its collection of Hatti and Hittite arts and crafts.

★**Arkeoloji Müzesi, Istanbul.** This recently renovated museum exhibits Greek and Roman artifacts from throughout Turkey and has new displays on Troy and the history of Istanbul.

★**Hatay Müzesi, Antakya.** Experts consider the exceptional Roman mosaics here—which portray scenes from mythology and figures such as Dionysus, Orpheus, Oceanus, and Thetis—to be among the highest achievements of Roman art.

Special Experiences

★**Soaking in the Valide Baths, Termal.** The hot thermal water at the ornate spa is reputed to cure a number of ills. A bath followed by a walk in the beautiful gardens is hard to beat for relaxation.

★**A ferry trip up the Bosporous.** Boats leaving from Istanbul's Eminönü docks zigzag between Europe and Asia. Stops include old-fashioned villages with castles, waterside restaurants, and Ottoman houses.

★**A picnic on the grounds of Tokapı Palace.** Cap off a visit to Istanbul's number-one attraction with a bite to eat on the palace grounds. You'll feel like royalty.

★**Call to prayer at sunset.** One of the most moving experiences in Istanbul, listening to the chants of dozens of muezzins echoing throughout the city, doesn't cost a penny. Combine it with an early evening trip to the Galata Bridge, and watch the sun slip behind a spectacular skyline of mosques, palaces, and minarets.

★**Cruise in a traditional wood *gulet* along the Mediterranean Coast.** The best time to go is on the edge of summer, in May, September, and October, when the weather is cooler and the number of fellow travelers is low.

★**Swimming in a private cove, Kekova Sound.** Crusader castles and small churches form backdrops for coves and inlets with crystal-clear water.

FESTIVALS AND SEASONAL EVENTS

WINTER

DEC.➤ The **Festival of Saint Nicholas** in Demre celebrates the original Santa Claus, who was a bishop here in the 4th century. The **Rites of the Whirling Dervishes,** which take place during December in Konya, are a rare and extremely popular display by this mystic order.

JAN.➤ **Camel wrestling** takes place midmonth in Selçuk; there are beauty pageants for the camels, parties for their handlers, and a battle royal in the ancient theater at Ephesus.

SPRING

MAR. OR APR.➤ The **Mesir Festival in Manisa,** north of İzmir, celebrates *mesir macunu* (power gum), a healing paste made from 41 spices.

APR.➤ Early April sees one of Istanbul's most popular events, the **Istanbul International Film Festival,** when the city's silver screens come alive with a multinational array of images. In late April, the Istanbul suburb of Emirgan, full of gardens, stages a **Tulip Festival,** and

the flower beds in its park become a riot of color.

MAY➤ In Marmaris, the **Yacht Festival** attracts the international boating crowd, which gathers here before setting sail along the Aegean or Mediterranean. The **Ephesus Arts Festival,** held during the first full week of May, brings theater and music to the ancient city. At the end of May is the **Denizli-Pamukkale Festival,** notable for its setting amid calcified cliffs and natural hot springs.

SUMMER

JUNE➤ The **Rose Festival in Konya** brings together gardeners from throughout the region for a floral competition. **Wrestling tournaments** are held in mid-June in villages throughout the country; the most famous is in Edirne, where burly, olive-oil-coated men have been facing off annually for more than 600 years. Mid-June also brings the monthlong **Istanbul Arts Festival,** Turkey's premier cultural event. Toward the end of June, the castle at İzmir's resort town Çesme becomes the site for the **Çesme International Song Contest.**

JULY➤ **Folk Festivals** with ethnic dances, concerts, and crafts displays take

place in both Kuşadası and Bursa toward the end of the month.

AUG.➤ The **Assumption of the Virgin Mary** is celebrated on August 15 with a special mass at the House of the Virgin Mary near Ephesus. Also during August, a **Drama Festival in Troy** honors the work of Homer and culminates in the selection of a new Helen of Troy. From August 20 through September 10, the amusements and cultural and commercial displays of the **İzmir International Fair** fill the central Kültür Park.

AUTUMN

SEPT.➤ The **Cappadocian Wine Festival** in Ürgüp celebrates the grape harvest with midmonth tastings. Also in mid-September, special tours of archaeological sites are conducted as part of the **Hittite Festival,** centered in Corum; crafts shows and concerts accompany the event. For four days in the middle of September, the **International Song Contest in Antalya** brings open-air concerts to the area around the marina.

OCT.➤ For the first 10 days of the month, the Oscars of the Turkish film industry are presented at the **Antalya Film Festival.**

2 Istanbul

Day and night, Istanbul has a schizophrenic air. At dawn, when the muezzin's call to prayer rebounds from ancient minarets, a few hearty revelers make their way home from the nightclubs and bars while other residents kneel on their prayer rugs, facing Mecca. Women in jeans or elegant designer outfits pass others wearing long skirts and head coverings. Donkey-drawn carts vie with old Chevrolets and shiny BMWs for dominance of the noisy, narrow streets. And the seductive Oriental bazaar competes with Western boutiques: The props may be new, but the song of the shopkeeper and ritual haggling are as old as the city itself.

Revised and
updated by
Gareth Jenkins

THOUGH IT IS OFTEN REMARKED THAT TURKEY straddles Europe and Asia, it is really Istanbul that does the straddling: The vast bulk of the country resides comfortably on the Asian side. European Istanbul is separated from its Asian suburbs by the Bosporus, the narrow channel that connects the Black Sea, north of the city, to the Sea of Marmara, to the south. (From there it is only a short sail to that superhighway of the ancient world, the Aegean.) The European side of Istanbul is itself divided by a body of water, the Golden Horn, an 8-km-long (5-mi-long) inlet that separates Old Stamboul, also called Old Istanbul, from "the new town," known as Beyoğlu. The Byzantines once stretched an enormous chain across the mouth of the Golden Horn, in hopes of protecting their capital city from naval attack. The tactic worked for a time but ultimately failed, after the young Ottoman sultan Mehmet II (ruled 1451–81) had his ships dragged overland from the Bosporus and dropped in behind the chain.

To be sure, more than a mere accident of geography destined Istanbul for greatness. Much of the city's character and fame was created by the sheer force of will of four men. The town of Byzantium was already 1,000 years old when, in AD 326, Emperor Constantine the Great began to enlarge and rebuild it as the new capital of the Roman Empire. On May 11, 330, the city was officially renamed "New Rome," although it soon became better known as Constantinople, the city of Constantine. The new Byzantine empire in the East survived long after the Roman Empire had crumbled in the West. Under the Byzantine emperor Justinian (ruled 527–65), Constantine's capital flourished. Justinian ordered the construction of the magnificent Hagia Sophia in 532, on the site of a church originally built for Constantine. This awe-inspiring architectural wonder, which still dominates Istanbul's skyline, spawned untold imitators: Its form is copied by many mosques in the city and elsewhere in Turkey, most notably the Blue Mosque, which sits across Sultanahmet Square like a massive bookend. Under the Byzantines, Constantinople grew to become the largest metropolis the Western world had ever seen. Contemporaries often referred to it simply as The City.

The Ottoman sultan Mehmet II, known as Fatih (the Conqueror), is the man responsible for the fact that the Hagia Sophia clones are mosques and not churches. It was Mehmet who conquered the long-neglected, nearly ruined Constantinople in 1453, rebuilt it, and made it once again the capital of a great empire. In time it became known as Istanbul (from the Greek "eis tin polin," meaning "to the city"). In 1468 Mehmet II began building a palace on the picturesque hill at the tip of the city where the Golden Horn meets the Bosporus. Later sultans embellished and extended the building until it grew into the fabulous Topkapı Palace that can be seen today. But most of the finest Ottoman buildings in Istanbul date from the time of Süleyman the Magnificent (ruled 1520–1566), who led the Ottoman Empire to its highest achievements in art and architecture, literature and law. Süleyman commissioned the brilliant architect Sinan (1489–1587) to design buildings that are now recognized as some of the greatest examples of Islamic architecture in the world, including mosques such as the magnificent Süleymaniye, the intimate Sokollu Mehmet Paşa, and the exquisitely tiled Rüstem Paşa. The monuments built by these titans, or in their honor, dominate and define the city and lead the traveler into the arms of the past at every turn.

Istanbul has its modern side, too, with all the concomitant traffic jams, air pollution, overdevelopment, and brash concrete and glass hotels creeping up behind its historic old palaces. But the city is more than grime and noise. Paradoxically, its beauty in part lies in the seemingly random juxtaposition of the ancient and the contemporary. Some of the perks that come with modernity are luxury hotels, international casinos, designer clothing stores, and western-style department stores. After a long day of sightseeing, you might appreciate a night out at one of the city's trendy nightclubs or bars, or the opportunity to catch a new Hollywood movie.

Pleasures and Pastimes

Dining and Lodging

Istanbul has a range of restaurants—and prices to match. Most major hotels serve unchallenging international cuisine, so it's more rewarding to eat in Turkish restaurants. Beer, wine, and sometimes cocktails are widely available despite Muslim proscriptions against alcohol. Dress is casual unless otherwise noted. Virtually everything tourists want to see in Istanbul is in the older part of town, but the big modern hotels are mainly around Taksim Square in the new town and along the Bosporus, a 15- or 20-minute cab ride away. The Aksaray, Laleli, Sultanahmet, and Beyazıt areas have more modest hotels and family-run *pansiyons* (guest houses). The trade-off for the simpler quarters is convenience: Staying here makes it easy to return to your hotel at midday or to change before dinner. No matter where you stay, plan ahead: Istanbul has a chronic shortage of beds.

Marketplaces

Atatürk moved the political capital to Ankara, but Turkey's commercial heart still beats in Istanbul. The city is a hive of free enterprise. Wherever one looks, something is being traded: stocks or shares on Turkey's spanking new stock exchange; rugs; leather and jewelry in the 4,000 shops of the ancient Grand Bazaar; spices and dried fruit in the Egyptian Bazaar; fruit, vegetables, and clothing in the city's numerous open markets; and flowers, toolkits, soft drinks, and the many wares that children hawk as they weave through rush-hour traffic.

Museums

Until the early 1980s, Istanbul, with its crumbling ancient buildings, was its own best museum. Most of the artifacts of the city's past were locked away in storage areas or poorly displayed in dusty, ill-lit rooms. But in recent years Istanbul's museums have been transformed. Topkapı Palace, which for 400 years was the palace of the Ottoman sultans, contains a glittering array of jewels, ceramics, miniature paintings, and holy relics. The Archaeological Museum, which has recently been renovated and refurbished, houses one of the most important collections of classical artifacts anywhere in the world. The Museum of Turkish and Islamic Arts holds superb examples of artistry and craftsmanship. The mosaics in the former church at Kariye are believed by many to be the finest surviving Byzantine artworks.

EXPLORING ISTANBUL

How does one find one's bearings in such an unpredictable place? Head for the Galata Bridge, which spans the mouth of the Haliç (Golden Horn). Look to the north and you will see the new town, modern Beyoğlu, and Taksim Square. From the square, high-rise hotels and smart shops radiate out on all sides. Beyond Taksim lie the fashionable modern shopping districts of Şişli and Nişantaşı. The residential suburbs of

Arnavutköy, Bebek, Yeniköy, Tarabya, and Sarıyer line the European shore of the Bosporus. Look southeast, across the Bosporus, and you can see the Asian suburbs of Kadıköy and Üsküdar. To the south lies the old walled city of Stamboul and Sultanahmet (after the sultan who built the Blue Mosque), with Hagia Sophia and Topkapı Palace at its heart. Turn to look up the Golden Horn and you should be able to make out two more bridges, the Atatürk, favored by cab drivers hoping to avoid the Galata Bridge, and the Fatih, out at the city's northwestern edge.

Great Itineraries

Those who like their monuments in a pristine state will be sorely disappointed in this noisy and chaotic city. The Turks seem to take the mayhem in good spirits, though, and you should, too. The twisty, crowded, old city streets exude an infectious energy. See the sights, dodge the cars, eat heartily. Like strong Turkish coffee, Istanbul can be gritty, but its rich flavor is bracing.

IF YOU HAVE 2 DAYS

Your first stop should be **Topkapı Palace,** the heart of the Ottoman Empire for over 400 years. You could easily spend your whole two days here, but at least see the Treasure Room, the Harem, and the Porcelain Collection. After a late lunch at one of the many restaurants lining Divan Yolu in Alemdar, visit the **Blue Mosque** and the **Museum of Turkish and Islamic Arts** inside the **Ibrahim Paşa Palace,** and stroll by the Hippodrome. Spend the next day exploring **Hagia Sophia** and **Yerebatan Sarayı,** before heading to the 4,000 shops of the **Grand Bazaar.**

IF YOU HAVE 7 DAYS

Start with a visit to **Hagia Sophia** and **Yerebatan Sarayı,** catch lunch on Divan Yolu, pass by the **Hippodrome,** and then visit the **Blue Mosque,** and the **Museum of Turkish and Islamic Arts.** Spend day two at **Topkapı Palace** and stroll through nearby Gülhane Park before dinner. On the third day, take a day's cruise up the **Bosporus.** Visit the **Arkeoloji Müzesi** on the morning of your fourth day, and taxi to **Dolmabahçe Palace** in the afternoon. On day five, explore **Süleymaniye Cami,** taxi to the **Kariye Museum,** and then take another to the **Grand Bazaar.** On the sixth day take a cab to the **Rahmi Koç Industrial Museum,** then cab back to the **Galata Tower.** After surveying its panoramic views, either catch a cab or walk to **Tünel Square** and the **Divan Edebiyatı Müzesi** (where the dervishes whirl). From here, you can either take the trolley or walk along İstiklal Caddesi to **Taksim Square.** If you still have time, take a taxi to **Yıldız Park.** On the final day, take a side trip to the entrancing **Princes Islands.**

Old Stamboul

Old Stamboul isn't large, but it can be overwhelming, for it spans vast epochs of history and contains an incredible concentration of art and architecture. The best way to get around is on foot.

A Good Walk

Numbers in the text correspond to numbers in the margin and on the Istanbul and Bosporus exploring maps.

Start from **Topkapı Palace** ① and walk back past **Aya Irini,** a smaller-scale version of Hagia Sophia. The **Arkeoloji Müzesi** ② is just north of Aya Irini. A small square surrounding a fountain built by the Sultan Ahmet III lies just outside the Topkapı Palace gate. Take a right down Soğukçeşme Sokak, a beautiful cobbled street lined with restored wooden Ottoman houses. At the bottom of Soğukçeşme Sokak, just before the entrance

16

Istanbul

Halâskârgazi Cad.

Kurtuluş Cad.

Emlâk Cad.

TEŞVIKIYE

Nüzhetiye Cad.

Yıldız Parkı

BEŞIKTAŞ

26

Yenişehir dere Cad.

Küçük Çiflik Park

Spor Cad.

Barbaros Bul.

Muvezzi Cad.

Ciragan Cad.

YENIŞEHIR

Cumhuriyet Cad.

Askerocagi Cad.

Taşkışla Cad.

Kadirgalargecin

Sai Nedim Cad.

Seranceley

25

Beşiktaş Cad.

24

Inönü Stadium

Dalmabahçe Cad.

23

Beşiktaş Docks

Tarlabaşı Cad.

Mete Cad.

Istiklal Cad.

22 Taksim Meydani

KABATAŞ

Gümüşşuyu Cad.

Sıraselviler Cad.

Kabataş Seabus Port

Yeni Çarşı

21

i

BEYOĞLU

Postacılar S.

Defterdar Yokuşu

Meclisimebusan Cad.

20

Divan Edebiyatı Müzesi

Tünel Subway Line

9

18

Kemeraltı Cad.

Necatibey Cad.

Kemankeş Cad.

i

Karaköy Seabus Port

Bridge

Karaköy Ferry Terminal

17

Eminönü Docks

14

INÖNÜ

Kennedy Cad.

Sirkeci Station

Seraglio Point

CI

U

Ankara Cad.

Ihtilalahmen

e Cad.

Gülhane Park

2

1

ANAHMET

Alemdar Cad.

Aya Irini

4

3

Ayasafa Sq.

Yolu

i

8

7

5

6

Baths of Roxelana

Boğaziçi (Bosporus)

Şemşi Paşa Cad.

ÜSKÜDAR

Halk Cad.

Salacak

Ihsaniye Sok.

Tıbbiye Cad.

Çeşmei Kebir Cad.

SELIMIYE

Kavak İskelesi Cad.

Sea of Marmara

N

TO PRINCES ISLANDS

Haydarpaşa Station

TO KADIKÖY

to Gülhane park, take a left up Alemdar Caddesi to **Hagia Sophia** ③
and **Yerebatan Sarayı** ④. Cross to the far lefthand corner of the small
park between Hagia Sophia and the **Blue Mosque** ⑤ to Kabasakal Caddesi. Approximately 100 meters along Kabasakal Caddesi lies the **Mosaic Museum** ⑥, which is believed once to have been the imperial palace
of the Byzantine emperors. Backtracking around the southern face of
the Blue Mosque you can see the foundation of the **Hippodrome** ⑦, a
Byzantine stadium, stretching northeast for three blocks to Divan Yolu.
West of the Hippodrome is **Ibrahim Paşa Palace** ⑧; walk to the southwest down Mehmet Paşa Yokuşu to get to **Sokollu Mehmet Paşa Cami** ⑨.

TIMING
Allow approximately 45 minutes to an hour to walk this route, two
or more days to take in all its sights. Topkapı Palace and the Arkeoloji
Müzesi are open daily. The Blue Mosque is also open daily, but the
Carpet and Kilim Museums within it are closed Sunday and Monday.
Hagia Sophia and Ibrahim Paşa Palace are closed Monday, and the Mo-
saic and Kariye museums are closed Tuesday. It's best not to visit
mosques during midday prayers on Friday.

Sights to See

★ ❷ **Arkeoloji Müzesi** (Archaeological Museum). A fine collection of Greek
and Roman antiquities—including pieces from Ephesus and Troy,
along with a magnificent tomb believed by some to have belonged to
Alexander the Great—are among the highlights of this recently renovated museum. As most of the pieces have been removed from the archaeological sites of Turkey's ancient cities, touring the museum will
help you visualize later what belongs in the empty niches. Among the
museum's new sections is one for children, complete with a replica of
the Trojan Horse; a special exhibit on Istanbul through the ages; and
one on the different settlements at Troy. Because the children's wing
is primarily intended for Turkish schoolchildren, the captions there are
in Turkish, but the other two have labels in English. Outside the museum is a small garden planted with bits of statuary and tombstones.
In summer, a small café is open.

Admission to the Arkeoloji Müzesi is also good for entry to the nearby
Eski Şark Eserleri Müzesi (Museum of the Ancient Orient) and **Çinili
Köşkü** (Tiled Pavilion). The first museum is something of a disappointment, despite its Sumerian, Babylonian, and Hittite treasures. The place
needs a fresh coat of paint, the displays are unimaginative, and the de-
scriptions of what you see are terse at best. The Tiled Pavilion has ceramics from the early Seljuk and Ottoman empires and tiles from İznik,
which produced perhaps the finest ceramics in the world during the 17th
and 18th centuries. Covered in a bright profusion of colored tiles, the
building itself is part of the exhibit. ⊠ *Gülhane Park, adjacent to Topkapı Palace,* ☎ *212/520–7740.* ☜ *$2 (total) for the 3 museums.* ☉ *Ar-
chaeology Museum Tues.–Sun. 9:30–4:30; Tiled Pavilion Tues.–Sun.
9:30–noon; Museum of the Ancient Orient Tues.–Sun. 1–5.*

★ ❺ **Blue Mosque.** This massive structure, officially called Sultan Ahmet Camii
(Mosque of Sultan Ahmet), is studded with mini- and semidomes and
surrounded by six minarets. This number briefly linked it with the Elharam Mosque in Mecca, until Sultan Ahmet I (ruled 1603–17) was
forced to send his architect down to the Holy City to build a seventh
minaret and reestablish Elharam's eminence. Press through the throng
of touts and trinket sellers, and enter the mosque at the side entrance
that faces Hagia Sophia. You must remove your shoes and leave them
at the entrance. Immodest clothing is not allowed, but an attendant at
the door will lend you a robe if he feels you are not dressed appropriately. Women should cover their heads.

Only after you enter the Blue Mosque do you understand why this is called the Blue Mosque. Its interior is decorated by 20,000 shimmering blue İznik tiles, interspersed with 260 stained-glass windows; an airy arabesque pattern is painted on the ceiling. After the dark corners and stern, sour faces of the Byzantine mosaics in Hagia Sophia, this light-filled mosque is positively cheery. Architect Mehmet Aga, known as Sedefkar (Worker of Mother-of-Pearl), spent eight years getting the mosque just right, beginning in 1609. His goal, set by Sultan Ahmet, was to surpass Justinian's masterpiece—completed nearly 1,100 years earlier—and many believe he succeeded.

The **Hünkar Kasrı** (Carpet and Kilim Museums) (☎ 212/518–1330), two good places to prepare yourself for dueling with modern-day carpet dealers, are in the stone-vaulted cellars of the Blue Mosque and upstairs at the end of a stone ramp, where the sultans rested before and after their prayers. Here, rugs are treated as works of art and displayed in a suitably grand setting. ✉ *Blue Mosque: Sultanahmet Sq., no phone.* ▨ *Mosque free, Carpet and Kilim Museums $1.50.* ☉ *Mosque daily 9–5, access restricted during prayer times, particularly at midday on Friday; Carpet and Kilim Museums Tues.–Sat. 9–noon and 1–4.*

★ ❸ **Hagia Sophia.** The magnificent dome of Hagia Sophia (Church of the Holy Wisdom, Ayasofya in Turkish), the world's largest until St. Peter's Basilica was built in Rome 1,000 years later, was considered miraculous by the faithful. Though some were afraid to enter lest the whole thing come crashing down, others argued that the fact that it didn't was proof that God was on their side. Nothing like the dome's construction had ever been attempted before—new architectural rules had to be made up as the builders went along. Perhaps the greatest work of Byzantine architecture, the cathedral was Christendom's most important church for 900 years. It survived earthquakes, looting crusaders, and the city's conquest by Mehmet the Conqueror in 1453. The church was then converted into a mosque; its four minarets were added by succeeding sultans.

The Byzantine mosaics were not destroyed, but were plastered over in the 16th century at the behest of Süleyman the Magnificent, in accordance with the Islamic proscription against the portrayal of the human figure in a place of worship. In 1936 Atatürk made Hagia Sophia into a museum. Shortly thereafter American archaeologists rediscovered the mosaics, which were restored and are now on display. Above where the altar would have been is a giant portrait of a somber Virgin Mary with the infant Jesus, and alongside are severe-looking depictions of archangels Michael and Gabriel.

Ascend to the gallery above and you will find the best of the remaining mosaics, executed in the 13th century. There is a group with Emperor John Comnenus, the Empress Zoë and her husband (actually, her third husband; his face was added atop his predecessors'), and Jesus with Mary, and another of John the Baptist. According to legend, the marble and brass **Sacred Column** in the north aisle of the mosque "weeps water" that can work miracles. It's so popular that, over the centuries, believers have worn a hole through the column with their constant caresses. Today, visitors of many faiths stick their fingers in the hole and make a wish; nobody will mind if you do as well. In recent years there has been growing pressure for Hagia Sophia to be reopened for Muslim worship. Some radical elements often gather to pray at the museum at midday on Friday. As with mosques, it is best not to try to visit then. ✉ *Ayasofya Sq.,* ☎ *212/522–1750.* ▨ *$4.50.* ☉ *Tues.–Sun. 9:30–4:30.*

For a real treat, spend an hour in a Turkish bath. One of the best is **Ca-ğaloğlu Hamamı** (✉ Prof. Kazı Gürkan Cad. 34, Cağaloğlu, ☎ 212/522-2424), in a magnificent 18th-century building near Hagia Sophia. Florence Nightingale and Kaiser Wilhelm II have soaked here; the clientele today remains generally upscale (Turks of lesser means head for plainer, less costly baths). You get a cubicle to strip down in—and a towel to cover up with—and are then escorted into a steamy, marble-clad temple to cleanliness. Self-service baths cost just $10; an extra $5–$10 buys you that time-honored, punishing-yet-relaxing pummeling known as Turkish massage. The baths are open daily from 8–8 for women and until 10 PM for men.

🟊 **Hippodrome.** Once a Byzantine stadium with 100,000 seats, the Hippodrome was the center for public entertainment, including chariot races and circuses. Disputes between rival groups of supporters of chariot teams often degenerated into violence. Thirty-thousand people died here in what came to be known as the Nike riots of AD 531. The original shape of the Hippodrome is still clearly visible. The monuments that can be seen today on the grassy open space opposite the Blue Mosque—the Egyptian Obelisk (Dikilitaş) from the 15th century BC, the Column of Constantinos (Örme Sütün), and the Serpentine Column (Yılanlı Sütun) taken from the Temple of Apollo at Delphi in Greece—formed part of the central barrier around which the chariots raced. The Hippodrome was originally adorned with a life-size sculpture of four horses cast in bronze. That piece was taken by the Venetians and can now be seen at the entrance to the cathedral San Marco in Venice. You'll encounter thousands of peddlers selling postcards, nuts, and souvenirs in this area. ✉ *Atmeydanı, Sultanahmet.* 🎟 *Free.* 🕙 *Accessible at all hrs.*

★ 🟊 **Ibrahim Paşa Palace.** The grandiose residence of the son-in-law and grand vizier of Süleyman the Magnificent was built circa 1524. The striated stone mansion was outfitted by Süleyman to be the finest private residence in Istanbul, but Ibrahim Paşa didn't have long to enjoy it: He was executed when he became too powerful for the liking of Süleyman's power-crazed wife Roxelana. The palace now houses the **Türk Ve Islâm Eserleri Müzesi** (Museum of Turkish and Islamic Arts), which yields superb insight into the lifestyles of Turks of every level of society, from the 8th century to the present. ✉ *Atmeydanı 46, Sultanahmet,* ☎ *212/518–1385.* 🎟 *$2.* 🕙 *Tues.–Sun. 10–5.*

🟊 **Mosaic Museum.** Tucked away behind the Blue Mosque, the often-overlooked Mosaic Museum is actually the ruins of the Great Palace of Byzantium, the imperial residence of the Byzantine emperors when they ruled lands stretching from Iran to Italy. The mosaics that give the museum its name lay hidden beneath the earth for 1,000 years before being uncovered by archaeologists in 1935. Scenes of animals, flowers, and trees in many of the mosaics depict rural idylls far removed from the pomp and elaborate ritual of the imperial court. ✉ *Kabasakal Cad., Sultanahmet,* ☎ *212/518–1205.* 🎟 *$1.50.* 🕙 *Wed.–Mon. 9–5.*

🟊 **Sokollu Mehmet Paşa Cami** (Mosque of Mehmet Paşa). This small mosque, built in 1571, is generally regarded as one of the most beautifully realized projects of the master architect Sinan, who designed more than 350 other buildings and monuments under the direction of Süleyman the Magnificent. Rather than dazzle with size, the mosque integrates all its parts into a harmonious whole, from the courtyard and porticoes outside to the delicately carved *mimber* (pulpit) and well-preserved İznik tiles set off by pure white walls and stained-glass windows done in a floral motif inside. ✉ *Mehmet Paşa Cad., at Özbekler Sok.,*

Küçük Ayasofya, no phone. ✉ *Free.* ☉ *Daily sunrise–sunset, except during prayer times.*

★ ❶ **Topkapı Palace** (Topkapı Saray). Istanbul's number-one attraction sits on Seraglio Point, where the Bosporus meets the Golden Horn. The vast palace was the residence of sultans and their harems until 1868, when Sultan Abdül Mecit I (ruled 1839–61) moved to the European-style Dolmabahçe Palace farther up the Bosporus. Plan on spending several hours and go early, before the bus-tour crowds pour in; gates open at 9 AM. If you go by taxi, be sure to tell the driver you want the Topkapı Saray in Sultanahmet, or you could end up at the Topkapı bus terminal on the outskirts of town.

Sultan Mehmet II built the first palace during the 1450s, shortly after his conquest of Constantinople. Over the centuries, sultan after sultan added ever more elaborate architectural frills and fantasies, until the palace had acquired four courtyards and quarters for some 5,000 full-time residents, including concubines and eunuchs. The initial approach to the palace does little to evoke the many tales of intrigue, bloodshed, and drama attached to the structure. The first entrance or Imperial Gate, leads to the **Court of the Janissaries,** also known as the First Courtyard, an area the size of a football field that now serves as a parking lot. As you walk ahead to the ticket office, look to your left, where you will see the **Aya Irini** (Church of St. Irene, Hagia Eirene in Greek). This unadorned redbrick building, now used for concerts, dates back to the earliest days of Byzantium.

Formed in the 14th century as the sultan's corps of elite guards, the Janissaries were taken as young boys from non-Muslim families in Ottoman-controlled territories in the Balkans, taught Turkish, and instructed in Islam. Though theoretically the sultan's vassals, these professional soldiers quickly became a power in their own right, and more than once their protests—traditionally expressed by overturning their soup kettles—were followed by the murder of the reigning sultan. During the rule of Sultan Mahmut II (ruled 1808–39), the tables were finally turned and the Janissaries were massacred in what came to be known as the Auspicious Event.

Next to the ticket office is the **Bab-ı-Selam** (Gate of Salutation), built in 1524 by Süleyman the Magnificent, who was the only person allowed to pass through it on horseback; others had to dismount and enter on foot. Prisoners were kept in the towers on either side before their execution next to the nearby fountain. Once you pass this gate, you begin to get an idea of the grandeur of the palace.

The **Second Courtyard,** just slightly smaller than the first, is planted with rose gardens and ornamental trees, and filled with a series of ornate *köşks,* pavilions once used for both the business of state and more mundane matters, like feeding the hordes of servants. To the right are the palace's immense kitchens, which now display one of the world's best collections of Chinese porcelains including 10th-century T'ang, Yuan celadon, and Ming blue-and-white pieces dating from the 18th century, when the Chinese produced pieces to order for the palace. Straight ahead is the **Divan-ı-Humayun** (Assembly Room of the Council of State), once presided over by the grand vizier. When the mood struck him, the sultan would sit behind a latticed window, hidden by a curtain so no one would know when he was listening, although occasionally he would pull the curtain aside to comment.

One of the most popular sections of Topkapı is the **Harem,** a maze of 400 halls, terraces, rooms, wings, and apartments grouped around the sultan's private quarters to the west of the Second Courtyard. Only

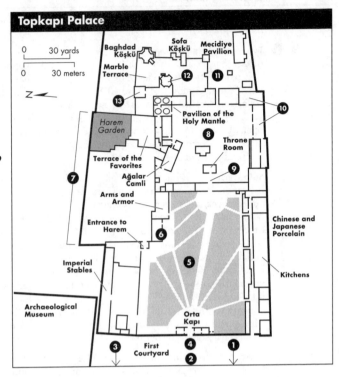

40 rooms, meticulously restored, are open to the public (and only on tours, which leave every half hour and cost $1.50). But they give you an idea of both the opulence and the regimentation of harem life. Only a few qualified for presentation to the sultan; even then, not all walked the Golden Way, by which the favorite of the night entered the sultan's private quarters. The first areas you see, which housed the palace eunuchs and about 200 lesser concubines, resemble a monastery; the tiny cubicles are as cramped and uncomfortable as the Harem's main rooms are large and opulent. Private apartments around a shared courtyard housed the chief wives (Islamic law permitted up to four); the Valide Sultan (Queen Mother), the absolute ruler of the Harem, had quite a bit of space as well as her own courtyard and marble bath. The sultan's private rooms are a riot of brocades, murals, colored marble, wildly ornate furniture, gold leaf, and fine carving. Fountains, also much in evidence, were not only decorative; they made it hard to eavesdrop on royal conversations. All told, it is a memorable, worthy backdrop to the rise and fall of princes and pretenders. You exit the Harem into the somewhat smaller **Third Courtyard.**

To see it to best advantage, make your way to its main gate, the **Bab-ı-Saadet** (Gate of Felicity), then exit and reenter. Shaded by regal old trees, the Third Courtyard is dotted by some of the most ornate of the palace's pavilions. Foreign ambassadors once groveled just past the gate in the **Arz Odası** (Audience Chamber), but access to the courtyard was highly restricted, in part because it housed the **Treasury,** four rooms filled with jewels, including two uncut emeralds, each weighing about 8 pounds, that once hung from the ceiling. Here, too, is the dazzling emerald dagger used in the movie *Topkapi* and the 84-carat Spoon-maker diamond that, according to legend, was found by a pauper and traded for three wooden spoons. Not surprisingly, this is one of the most popular sections of the palace, and it can get quite crowded. Also within this courtyard you can view a collection of thousands of Turkish and Persian miniatures, relics of the prophet Mohammed, and the rich costumes of the Imperial Wardrobe. Imperial fashion (male, of course) evolves slowly in the magnificent display of sultans' robes from the first to the last ruler. Some robes are bloodstained and torn from assassins' daggers, garments stiff with gold and silver thread, tooled leather, gold, silver, and jewels.

The **Fourth Courtyard,** the last, contains small, elegant summer houses, mosques, fountains, and reflecting pools, scattered amid the gardens. Here you will find the cruciform **Rivan Köşkü,** built by Murat IV in 1636 to commemorate a military victory. In another pavilion, the **İftariye** (Golden Cage), the closest relatives of the reigning sultan lived in strict confinement under what amounted to house arrest, ostensibly to help keep the peace, although it meant that heirs had no opportunity to prepare themselves for the formidable task of ruling a great empire. The custom began during the 1800s, superseding an older practice of murdering all possible rivals to the throne. Just off the open terrace with the wishing well is the lavishly tiled **Sünnet Odası** (Circumcision Room), where little princes would be taken for ritual circumcision during their ninth or 10th year. ⊠ *Topkapı Palace, Gülhane Park, near Sultanahmet Sq.,* ☎ *212/512–0480.* 🖃 *$3.50, plus $1.50 for harem tour.* ☉ *Wed.–Mon. 9:30–5.*

NEED A BREAK?	Just past the Topkapı Palace's Treasury, on the right side of the courtyard, are steps leading to the 19th-century Rococo-style Mecidiye Pavilion, also known as the Köşk of Sultan Abdül Mecit I (ruled 1839–61), for whom it was built. It now houses the **Konyalı Restaurant** (☎ 212/513–9696), which serves traditional Turkish dishes (albeit with a mass-produced flavor) and has magnificent views. On a terrace below is an outdoor café with an even better view. Go early to beat the tour-group crush. The restaurant and the café are open for lunch only.

★ ❹ **Yerebatan Sarayı** (Sunken Palace). Also known as the Basilica Cistern, Yerebatan Sarayı is the most impressive part of an underground network of waterways said to have been created at the behest of Emperor Constantine in the 4th century and expanded by Justinian in the 6th century (most of the present structure dates from the Justinian era). The cistern was always kept full as a precaution against long sieges. Today it is an atmospheric space, with 336 marble columns rising 26 feet to support Byzantine arches and domes. Piped-in classical music accompanies the sound of endlessly dripping water. ⊠ *Yerebatan Cad., at Divan Yolu,* ☎ *212/522–1259.* 🖃 *$1.* ☉ *Daily 9–5.*

OFF THE BEATEN PATH	**KARIYE MUSEUM** – Often passed over because of its inconvenient location at Istanbul's western edge, near the remnants of the city's Byzantine walls, this museum occupies what was once the Church of the Holy Savior in Chora, erected in the 5th century under the aegis of Justinian and rebuilt several times since. You come to see not the architecture but the dazzling 14th-century mosaics and frescoes depicting biblical scenes from Adam to the life of Christ; they are considered to be among the finest Byzantine works in the world. The historic Ottoman buildings around the museum have been restored as well, and there is a tea shop with light fare served on a garden terrace. Just west of the Chora are the Constantinian Walls, built by Emperor Theodosius II in AD 413. The massive walls, several stories high and 10 to 20 feet thick in spots, protected Constantinople from onslaught after onslaught of Huns, Bulgarians, Russians, Arabs, Goths, and Turks. The walls were breached only twice: by the crusaders in the 1200s and Mehmet the Conqueror in

1453. ⊠ *1 block north of Fevzipaşa Cad., by Edirne Gate in city's
outer walls,* ☎ *212/631-9241.* ☏ *$1.50.* ⊙ *Wed.–Mon. 9:30–4:30.*

Grand Bazaar to Eminönü

This tour makes its way through several markets, including two of Istanbul's largest, and also takes in two of the city's most beautiful
mosques.

A Good Walk

After a visit to the **Grand Bazaar** ⑩, exit through its front entrance on
Yeniçeriler Caddesi and head west to that street's junction with Çadırcı
Camii Caddesi. You'll see **Beyazıt Cami** ⑪ as you turn right into Çadırcı
Camii Caddesi, which runs into Fuatpaşa Caddesi. Follow Fuatpaşa
Caddesi along the eastern side of the grounds of **Istanbul University** ⑫.
Continue along Fuatpaşa Caddesi, keeping the grounds of the univer-
sity on your left, until the junction with Prof. Sıddık Sami Ona Cad-
desi and Ismetiye Caddesi. Turn left along Prof. Sıddık Sami Ona
Caddesi to **Süleymaniye Cami** ⑬. After visiting this mosque, retrace your
steps along Prof. Sıddık Sami Ona Caddesi, continue straight across
into Ismetiye Caddesi, and then turn left down Çarşı Caddesi. The narrow road leading downhill is a thriving market lined with barrows and
small shops selling mostly cheap clothing. Continue down the hill to
Hasırcılar Caddesi; you'll head into **Eminönü** ⑭. The **Rüstem Paşa
Cami** ⑮ is at the western edge of this neighborhood. After visiting this
mosque continue along Hasırcılar Caddesi to the **Egyptian Bazaar** ⑯.

TIMING
Not counting the streets of the Grand Bazaar, it takes about an hour
to complete this walk. Spending a brief amount of time in each of the
mosques and bazaars would take four to five hours, including a stop
for lunch. The Grand and Egyptian bazaars are closed Sunday. The
Beyazıt, Rüstem Paşa, and Süleymaniye mosques are open daily.

Sights to See

⑪ **Beyazıt Cami.** No, your eyes do not deceive you; this domed mosque,
too, was inspired by Hagia Sophia. It dates from 1504 and is the oldest of the Ottoman imperial mosques still standing in the city. ⊠
Beyazıt Meyd., Beyazıt, no phone. ☏ *Free.* ⊙ *Sunrise to sunset daily,
usually closed during prayer times.*

★ ⑯ **Egyptian Bazaar** (Mısır Çarşısı). Also known as the Spice Market, the
Egyptian Bazaar is much smaller than the Grand Bazaar but still lively
and colorful. It was built in the 17th century to generate rental income
to pay for the upkeep of the Yeni Cami (New Mosque) next door. Once
a vast pharmacy filled with burlap bags overflowing with herbs and
spices, the bazaar today is chockablock with bags full of fruit, nuts,
and royal jelly from the beehives of the Aegean, as well as white sacks
of spices. ⊠ *Hamidiye Cad., across from Galata Bridge, no phone.* ⊙
Mon.–Sat. 8–7.

NEED A
BREAK?
The **Pandelli,** up two flights of stairs over the arched gateway to the
Egyptian Bazaar, is a frenetic old-Istanbul restaurant serving typical Turk-
ish fare for lunch (noon–4 except Sunday) in a decor of incredible tiles.
The eggplant *börek* (pastry) and sea bass cooked in paper are good. ⊠
Mısır Çarşısı 1, Eminönü, ☎ *212/527-3909. No credit cards.*

---

⑭ **Eminönü.** The main transportation hub of Old Stamboul, Eminönü, is
at the southern end of the Galata Bridge. It has quays for the hydro-
foil sea buses, the more traditional Bosporus ferries (including those

for the day-long Bosporus cruises), and the Sirkeci train station and tramway terminal. The main coastal road around the peninsula of the old city also traverses Eminönü. Thousands of people and vehicles rush through the bustling area, and numerous street traders sell everything from candles to live animals.

★ ⑩ **Grand Bazaar** (Kapalı Çarşı). This early version of a shopping mall, also known as the Covered Bazaar, consists of a maze of 65 winding, covered streets crammed with 4,000 tiny shops, cafés, and restaurants. It's reputedly the largest number of different stores under one roof anywhere in the world. Originally built by Mehmet II (the Conqueror) in the 1450s, it was ravaged in modern times by two fires—one in 1954 that virtually destroyed it, and a smaller one in 1974. In both cases, the bazaar was quickly rebuilt in something resembling the original style, with arched passageways and brass-and-tile fountains at regular intervals.

In one sense, it's a shopper's paradise, filled with thousands of items—fabrics, clothing (including counterfeit brand names), brass candelabra, furniture, and jewelry. A sizable share of junk tailored for the tourist trade is sold as well. A separate section for antiques at the very center of the bazaar, called the Bedestan, is definitely worth checking out. Outside the western gate to the bazaar, through a doorway, is the Sahaflar Çarşısı, the Old Book Bazaar, where you can buy new editions and antique volumes in Turkish and other languages. The best way to explore the bazaar is to take a deep breath and plunge on in. And always remember: The best prices are those called out to you when the would-be seller thinks that you are about to slip away. ⊠ *Yeniçeriler Cad. and Fuatpaşa Cad.* 🎫 *Free.* ⊙ *Apr.–Oct., Mon.–Sat. 8:30– 7; Nov.–Mar., Mon.–Sat. 8:30–6:30.*

⑫ **Istanbul University.** The university's magnificent gateway faces Beyazıt Square. The campus, with its long greens and giant plane trees, originally served as the Ottoman War Ministry, which helps explain the grandiose, martial style of the portal and main buildings. In the garden stands the white marble 200-foot Beyazıt Tower, the tallest structure in Old Stamboul, built in 1823 by Mahmut II (ruled 1808–39) as a fire-watch station. ⊠ *Fuat Paşa Cad., Beyazıt.*

⑮ **Rüstem Paşa Cami** (Rüstem Paşa Mosque). This small and often overlooked mosque is another Sinan masterpiece. Tucked away in the backstreets to the north of the Egyptian Bazaar, it was built in the 1550s for Süleyman's grand vizier. Though unassuming from the outside, its interior is decorated with İznik tiles in an array of colors and patterns. ⊠ *Hasırcılar Cad., south of Sobacılar Cad., no phone.* ⊙ *Daily.*

⑬ **Süleymaniye Cami** (Mosque of Süleyman). The grandest and most famous creation of its designer, Sinan, houses his tomb and that of his patron, Süleyman the Magnificent. Its enormous dome is supported by four square columns and arches, and exterior walls buttress smaller domes on either side. The result is a soaring space and the impression that the dome is held up principally by divine cooperation. This is the city's largest mosque, but its decor is less ornate and more spiritual in tenor than that of other imperial mosques. Note the İznik tiles in the *mihrab* (prayer niche). ⊠ *Süleymaniye Cad., near Istanbul University's north gate, no phone.* ⊙ *Daily.*

Galata to Taksim

This tour explores the heart of the new town, where the first thing you will learn is that "new" is a relative term. Much of what you will see dates from the 19th century—except for the shops and imported American movies, which are strictly 20th century. Some may find the climb up Karaköy to Tünel Square tough going. But they can cheat by taking the tiny underground from Karaköy to Tünel Square. Only 90 seconds, it saves a stiff walk.

A Good Walk

Cross over the **Galata Bridge** ⑰, stopping to take in one of the world's great city views as you go. Continue due north up Karaköy Caddesi and then up some steps near the junction with **Voyvoda Caddesi** ⑱. Go straight up the appropriately named Yüksek Kaldırım Caddesi (Steep Rise Street), lined with shops selling electronics equipment. Halfway up the hill is **Galata Tower** ⑲. The views from the top (there is an elevator) will take away any of the breath you have left after your steep climb. From Galata Tower continue up the same road, which has now become Galip Dede Caddesi, to the **Divan Edebiyatı Müzesi,** and into **Tünel Square** ⑳, which is also the northern terminus of the mini-underground from Karaköy. From **Tünel Square** a trolley runs along İstiklal Caddesi through **Galatasaray Square** ㉑ to **Taksim Square** ㉒. But if your legs have made it this far, or if you took the underground before, it is more fun to travel on foot, stopping along the way to have a look at the Üç Horan Armenian Church, marvel at the many splendid old buildings that line the street (some now house Western consulates), or browse in the lively flower and fish markets.

TIMING

The time needed for the tour will depend as much on your stamina as how long you spend at the sights along the route. If you are reasonably fit and walk the whole way, allow three to four hours. The Galata Tower is open daily. The Divan Literature Museum is closed Monday.

Sights to See

Divan Edebiyatı Müzesi (Divan Literature Museum). Also called the Galata Mevlevihane, this museum contains costumes, instruments, and memorabilia used by the Sufi mystics known in the West as the whirling dervishes. There are dance performances and Sufi music at 3 PM on the last Sunday of each month. ⊠ *Galip Dede Cad. 15, southeast of Tünel Sq., off İstiklal Cad., Beyoğlu,* ☎ *212/245–4141.* ⊡ *$5.* ☼ *Tues.–Sun. 9:30–4:30.*

★ ⑰ **Galata Bridge.** The bridge that joins Istanbul's older, European districts to the new town yields one of the world's great city views. In Old Stamboul, behind you as you cross the bridge towards Karaköy, the landmarks include Topkapı Palace and the domes and minarets of Hagia Sophia and the Blue Mosque, and the Süleymaniye and Yeni mosques. Ferries chug out on the Bosporus, and the Galata Tower rises high on the Beyoğlu side of the Golden Horn, beyond Karaköy. The new drawbridge you will be standing on opened in 1993, when it replaced the old pontoon bridge that had been around since 1910, in the days when horse, ox, or mule-drawn carriages rattled across it for a fee. ⊠ *Sobacılar Cad. in Eminönü to Rıhtım Cad. in Karaköy.*

⑳ **Galatasaray Square.** This is the heart of the Beyoğlu district. The impressive building behind the massive iron gates is a high school, established in 1868 and for a time the most prestigious in the Ottoman Empire. Across İstiklal Caddesi, at No. 51, is the entrance to the **Çiçek Pasaji** (Flower Arcade), a lively warren of flower stalls, tiny restaurants, and bars. Street musicians often entertain here. Curmudgeons swear that the passage is a pale shadow of its former self—its original neo-Baroque home collapsed with a thundering crash one night in 1978 and its redone facade and interior feel too much like a reproduction—but you can still get a feel for its bohemian past. Behind the Flower Arcade is the **Balık Pazarı** (Fish Market), a bustling labyrinth of stands peddling fish, fruits, vegetables, and spices—with a couple of pastry shops thrown in—that makes for great street theater. The Fish Market is open Monday through Saturday during daylight. At the end of the Fish Market, at Meşrutiyet Caddesi, is the **Üç Horan Armenian Church** (⊠ İstiklal Cad. 288). With its crosses and haloed Christs, the church is an unexpected sight in Muslim Istanbul.

⑲ Galata Tower. The Genoese built the tower as part of their fortifications in 1349, when they controlled the northern shore of the Golden Horn. In this century, the rocket-shape tower served as a fire lookout until 1960. Today it houses a restaurant and nightclub (☞ Nightclubs *in* Nightlife and the Arts, *below*), and a viewing tower (accessible by elevator) that is open by day. ⊠ *Büyük Hendek Cad.,* ☎ *212/245– 1160.* ⌑ *$1.* ☉ *Daily 9–8.*

Galata Tower Neighborhood. The area around the Galata Tower was a thriving Italian settlement both before and after the fall of Constantinople. In 1492, when the Spanish Inquisition drove the Sephardic Jews from Spain and Portugal, many of the refugees settled here. For centuries after, there was a large Jewish population in Galata. Although most of them have moved to residential areas, they retain their traditions. Today, 16 active synagogues, one of which dates from the Byzantine period, serve a Jewish community of 25,000. The Neve Shalom synagogue, on Büyük Hendek Sokak near the Galata Tower, was where 22 Sabbath worshipers were shot by Arabic-speaking gunmen in September 1986. A visit to the now high-security location requires a show of identification. Some older Turkish Jews still speak a dialect of medieval Spanish called Ladino or Judeo-Spanish.

İstiklal Caddesi (Independence Street). One of European Istanbul's main thoroughfares heads north and east to Taksim Square from Tünel Square. Consulates in ornate turn-of-the-century buildings and 19th-century apartments line the route, along with bookstores, boutiques, kebab shops, and movie theaters. To appreciate the architecture, look toward the upper stories of what was once the most fashionable street in the Orient. Return your gaze to eye level and you will see every element of modern Istanbul's vibrant cultural melting pot. A trolley runs along İstiklal every 10 minutes or so, all the way to Taksim Square. The fare is about 50¢. If you have the time and energy, walk one way and take the trolley back.

㉒ Taksim Square. The square at the northern end of İstiklal Caddesi is the not particularly handsome center of the new town, especially since municipal subway digging turned its belly into a deep concrete crevasse. It's basically a chaotic traffic circle with a bit of grass and a *Monument to the Republic and Independence* featuring Atatürk and his revolutionary cohorts. Around the square are Istanbul's main concert hall, Atatürk Kültür Merkezi (Atatürk Cultural Center), the high-rise Marmara Hotel, and, set back into a grassy promenade, the 23-story former Sheraton Hotel that was at press time being refurbished prior to its rebirth as the Continental Hotel. On the main street headed north from the square, Cumhuriyet Caddesi, are shops that sell carpets and leather goods. Also here are the entrances to the Hyatt, Divan, and Istanbul Hilton hotels; several travel agencies and airline ticket offices; and a few nightclubs. Cumhuriyet turns into Halâskârgazi Caddesi, and when this street meets Rumeli Caddesi, you enter the city's high-fashion district, where Turkey's top designers sell their wares.

NEED A
BREAK?

The **Patisserie Café Marmara** in the Marmara Hotel on Taksim Square serves a selection of hot and cold drinks and snacks, ice creams, and excellent homemade cakes. Despite the turbulence, and often downright chaos, of Taksim Square itself, the café somehow retains an air of unhurried calm. A duo usually plays soothing classical music in the late afternoon or early evening. In the summer one can observe the bustle of the square from the shaded refuge of the café's terrace. ⊠ *Marmara Istanbul, Taksim Sq.,* ☎ *212/251–4696. AE, DC, MC, V.*

⓴ **Tünel Square.** The northern terminus of the city's mini-underground is at the southern end of İstiklal Caddesi. Nearby is the Pera Palace, one of the most famous of Istanbul's hotels, where Agatha Christie wrote Murder on the Orient Express and Mata Hari threw back a few at the bar.

⓲ **Voyvoda Caddesi.** Considering all the trouble he's said to have caused, it's a tad ironic that the street named after the 15th-century *voyvode* (prince) of Transylvania, Vlad the Impaler—better known as Count Dracula—is a nondescript commercial strip. As a child, Vlad was sent to the Ottoman sultan as ransom, and though he was finally released, he grew up despising the Turks. He devised elaborate tortures for his enemies, and at length drove the Turks from Romania. Killed near Bucharest in 1476, his head was sent to Constantinople, where Mehmet II the Conqueror displayed it on a stake to prove to all that the hated Vlad was finally dead. Some say the street is the site of his grave.

OFF THE
BEATEN PATH
RAHMI KOÇ INDUSTRIAL MUSEUM – A restored foundry once used to cast anchors for the Ottoman fleet now houses this museum that traces the development of technology. Exhibits include medieval telescopes and the great engines that powered the Bosporus ferries. A special section devoted to transportation includes planes, bicycles, motorbikes, and some well-crafted maritime instruments. ⊠ *27 Hasköy Cad., Hasköy,* ☎ *212/ 256–7153 or 212/256–7154,* 🖷 *212/256–7156.* 🎫 *$1.50.* ☽ *Tues.–Sun. 10–5.*

Beşiktaş

The shore of the Bosporus became the favorite residence of the later Ottoman sultans as they sought to escape overcrowded Old Stamboul. Eventually they too were engulfed by the noise of the ever-expanding city.

A Good Walk
Start at the extravagant 19th-century **Dolmabahçe Palace** ㉓. Exiting the palace, continue northeast along tree-lined Dolmabahçe Caddesi onto Beşiktaş Caddesi and the **Naval Museum** ㉔. From here continue on the main coast road past the Beşiktaş ferry terminal into Çırağan Caddesi and the **Çırağan Palace** ㉕, now a luxury hotel. Directly opposite the hotel's main door is the entrance to the wooded slopes of **Yıldız Park** ㉖, probably the most romantic place in Istanbul. Follow the road up the hill through the park and take a right at the top of the slope to get to **Yıldız Şale,** the chalet of the last of the Ottoman sultans.

TIMING
Allow approximately two hours from leaving Dolmabahçe Palace to the entrance to Yıldız Park, including 45 minutes in the Naval Museum and 30 minutes in the Çırağan Palace. There are numerous paths in Yıldız Park. Allow another two to three hours for walking in the park, including 45 minutes to an hour for a visit to Yıldız Şale. Dolmabahçe Palace is closed Monday and Thursday, and the Naval Museum Wednesday and Thursday. Yıldız Park is open daily, but Yıldız Şale is closed Monday and Tuesday.

Sights to See

㉕ **Çırağan Palace.** Istanbul's most luxurious hotel was built by Abdül Mecit's brother and successor, Sultan Abdül Aziz (ruled 1861–76), in 1863. That the palace is about a third the size of Dolmabahçe, and much less ornate, says a good deal about the declining state of the Ottoman Empire's coffers. The vacuous Abdül Aziz was as extravagant as his brother; having begun his reign by ordering an 8-foot-long bed, wide enough to accommodate himself and a concubine, he was soon attempting to emulate the splendors he had seen on travels in England and France. Today the restored grounds, with their splendid swimming pool at the edge of the Bosporus, are worth a look, and the hotel bar provides a plush, cool respite with a view. You won't find much from the original palace, as a major fire gutted the place; the lobby renovations were done with a nod to the 19th-century design, though the color scheme is decidedly gaudier. ⊠ *Çırağan Cad. 84, Beşiktaş,* ☎ *212/258–3377.*

㉓ **Dolmabahçe Palace.** The last sultans of the Ottoman Empire resided at this palace, which was erected in 1853. After the establishment of the modern republic in 1923, it became the home of Atatürk, who died here in 1938. The name, which means "filled-in garden," predates the palace; Sultan Ahmet I (ruled 1603–17) had a little cove filled in and an imperial garden planted here in the 17th century. The palace is an extraordinary mixture of Hindu, Turkish, and European styles of architecture and interior design. Abdül Mecit, whose free-spending lifestyle (his main distinction) eventually bankrupted his empire, intended the structure to be a symbol of Turkey's march away from its Oriental past and toward the European mainstream. He gave his Armenian architect, Balian, complete freedom and an unlimited budget. His only demand was that the palace "surpass any other palace of any other potentate anywhere in the world."

The result was a riot of Rococo—marble, vast mirrors, stately towers, and formal gardens along a facade stretching nearly ½ km (⅓ mi). His bed was solid silver; the tub and basins in his marble-paved bathroom were carved of translucent alabaster. Europe's royalty contributed to the splendor: Queen Victoria sent a chandelier weighing 4½ tons, Czar Nicholas I of Russia provided polar-bear rugs. The result is as gaudy and showy as a palace should be, all gilt and crystal and silk, and every bit as garish as Versailles. The nearby Dolmabahçe Mosque was founded in 1853 by Abdül Mecit's mother. You must join a guided tour, which takes about 80 minutes, or a short one that takes about 45 minutes and omits the harem. ⊠ *Dolmabahçe Cad.,* ☎ *212/258–5544.* 🎫 *$10 for long tour, $5.50 for short tour.* ☉ *Tues., Wed., and Fri.–Sun. 9–4.*

㉔ **Naval Museum** (Deniz Müzesi). The Ottoman Empire was the 16th century's leading sea power. The flashiest displays here are the sultan's barges, the long, slim boats that served as the primary mode of royal transportation for several hundred years. The museum's cannon collection includes a 23-ton blaster built for Sultan Selim the Grim. An early Ottoman map of the New World, cribbed from Columbus, dates from 1513. ⊠ *Beşiktaş Cad.,* ☎ *212/261–0040.* 🎫 *$1.* ☉ *Fri.–Tues. 9–11:30, 1:30–5.*

㉖ **Yıldız Park.** The wooded slopes of Yıldız Park once formed part of the great forest that covered the European shore of the Bosporus from the Golden Horn to the Black Sea. During the reign of Abdül Aziz, the park was his private garden, and the women of the harem would occasionally be allowed to visit. First the gardeners would be removed, then the eunuchs would lead the women across the wooden bridge from the palace and along the avenue to the upper gardens. Secluded from prying eyes, they would sit in the shade or wander through the acacias, maples, and cypresses, filling their baskets with flowers and figs. Today the park is still hauntingly beautiful, particularly in spring and fall.

Yıldız Şale (Yıldız Chalet) at the top of the park is yet another palace of Sultan Abdül Hamit II (ruled 1876–1909). Visiting dignitaries from Kaiser Wilhelm to Charles de Gaulle and Margaret Thatcher have stayed here. The chalet is often blissfully empty of tourists, which makes a visit all the more pleasurable. Forgotten is the turmoil of the era when the palace was occupied by the last rulers of the once-great Ottoman Empire. All were deposed: free-spending Abdül Aziz; his unfortunate nephew, Murad (who, having spent most of his life in the Harem, isolated in the Cage, was none too sound of mind); and Abdül Hamid, who distinguished himself as the last despot of the Ottoman Empire. ✉ *Çırağan Cad.*, ☎ *212/261–8460 (park)*, ☎ *212/258–3080 (chalet).* ▨ *Park 25¢ pedestrians, $1.50 cars; chalet $1.50.* ☉ *Park daily 9 AM–sunset. Chalet Wed.–Sun. 9–5.*

The Bosporus

There are good roads along both the Asian and the European shores, but the most pleasant way to explore the Bosporus is by ferry from the Eminönü docks in the old town (☞ Getting Around *in* Istanbul A to Z, *below*). Along the way, you will see wooded hills, villages large and small, modern and old-fashioned, and the old wooden summer homes called *yalıs* (waterside houses) that were built for the city's wealthier residents in the Ottoman era. When looking at ferry schedules, remember that *Rumeli* refers to the European side, *Anadolu* to the Asian.

A Good Ferry Tour

There are two ways to take a ferry tour of the Bosporus. One is to take one of the cruises that depart daily from Eminönü. These zigzag up the Bosporus, stop for a couple of hours near the Black Sea, then zigzag back down to Eminönü. The other way is to fashion your own tour, hopping on one of the regular Bosporus commuter ferries, stopping wherever you fancy, and then continuing your journey on the next ferry going your way. The advantage of the latter is that you have more freedom; the disadvantage is that you may end up spending considerable extra time waiting for ferries. During the middle of the day schedules can be erratic, and not all ferries stop at each quay.

After departing from Eminönü, the ferry heads north out of the Golden Horn and past the Dolmabahçe and Çırağan palaces on the European shore. As you approach the first Bosporus Bridge you pass **Ortaköy Cami** (Ortaköy Mosque) on the European shore and, just past the bridge on the Asian shore, the **Beylerbeyi Palace** ㉗. Back on the European side is the village of **Arnavutköy,** followed by the stylish suburb of **Bebek.** Just before the second Bosporus bridge (officially known as Fatih Sultan Mehmet Bridge) are two fortresses, **Anadolu Hisarı** ㉘, on the Asian side, and **Rumeli Hisarı** ㉙, on the European side. North of Fatih Sultan Mehmet Bridge on the Asian side lies the village of **Kanlıca** ㉚. Across the water are the wooded slopes of **Emirgan** ㉛. Still farther north on the European side are the fashionable resort area of **Tarabya** and the waterfront village of **Sarıyer,** the ferry stop for the **Sadberk Hanım Museum.** The organized cruises from Emonönü usually stop at either **Rumeli Kavağı** or **Anadolu Kavağı,** two fishing villages, for a couple of hours. Anadolu Kavağı is particularly fun; its sidewalk vendors sell deep-fried mussels and wickedly sweet waffles. The ferries begin their return trips to Istanbul from Rumeli Kavağı and Anadolu Kavağı.

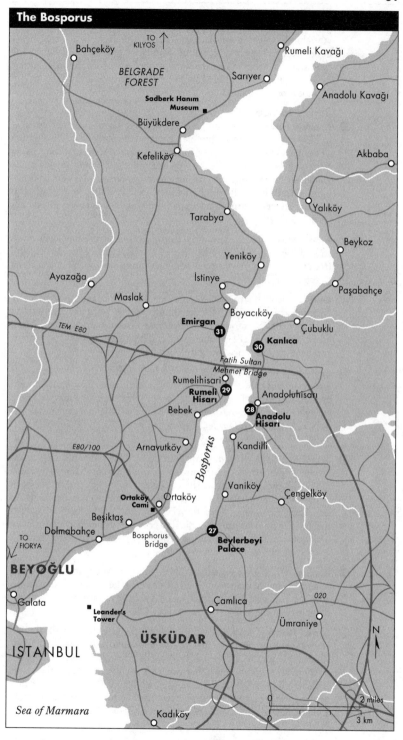

The Bosporus

TO KILYOS ↑

Bahçeköy

BELGRADE FOREST

Sarıyer

Rumeli Kavağı

Anadolu Kavağı

Sadberk Hanım Museum ■

Büyükdere

Kefeliköy

Akbaba

Tarabya

Yalıköy

Beykoz

Yeniköy

Ayazağa

İstinye

Paşabahçe

Maslak

Boyacıköy

Emirgan ③①

Çubuklu

③⓪ **Kanlıca**

TEM E80

Fatih Sultan Mehmet Bridge

Rumelihisarı

Anadoluhisarı

Rumeli Hisarı ②⑨

Bebek

②⑧ **Anadolu Hisarı**

E80/100

Arnavutköy

Kandilli

Bosporus

Vaniköy

Çengelköy

Ortaköy Cami ■ Ortaköy

Beşiktaş

Dolmabahçe

Bosphorus Bridge

②⑦ **Beylerbeyi Palace**

TO FIORYA

BEYOĞLU

Galata

Çamlıca

020

Ümraniye

Leander's Tower ■

ÜSKÜDAR

N ↑

ISTANBUL

Sea of Marmara

0 ——— 2 miles
0 ——— 3 km

Kadıköy

TIMING

Whether you take a Bosporus cruise or make your own way by ferry, you should allow a whole day. The cruises usually take about six hours. Add at least an extra hour waiting for ferries in addition to the time spent at stops along the way. Rumeli Hisarı is closed Monday. Beylerbeyi Palace is closed Monday and Thursday. Sadberk Hanım Museum is closed Wed.

Sights to See

㉘ Anadolu Hisarı (Anatolian Castle). Sultan Beyazıt I built this fortress in 1393 to cut off Constantinople's access to the Black Sea. At the mouth of the Göksu stream, known in Ottoman times as one of the "Sweet Waters of Asia," the castle is a romantic sight (especially at sunset), its golden stone blending into the surrounding forest and tiny boats bobbing beneath its walls (some of which are crumbling, so be careful if walking on them). An unmarked path leads up to the castle ruins; there's no admission fee.

Arnavutköy. This village on the European side of the Bosporus has a row of 19th-century wooden houses at the water's edge. Up the hill from the water, narrow streets contain more old wooden houses, some of them trailing vines.

Bebek. One of the most fashionable suburbs of Istanbul, particularly with the affluent expatriate community, Bebek has a shaded park on the waterfront next to the mosque, good restaurants and open air cafés, and a jazz club. Small rowing boats, and even sizable cutters with crew, can be rented for trips around Bebek Bay.

㉗ Beylerbeyi Palace. Built for Sultan Abdül Aziz in 1865, Beylerbeyi is a mini Dolmabahçe, filled with marble and marquetry and gold-encrusted furniture. The central hall has a white-marble fountain and a stairway wide enough for a regiment. You must join a tour to see the palace. ⊠ *Çayıbaşı Durağı, Beylerbeyi,* ☏ *216/321–9320.* ⊡ *$3.* ☉ *Tues., Wed., and Fri.–Sun. 9:30–4.*

㉛ Emirgan. This town on the European shore of the Bosporus was named after a 17th-century Persian prince to whom Sultan Murat IV (ruled 1623–40) presented a palace here. The woods above are part of a park with flower gardens and a number of restored Ottoman pavilions. In late April, the town stages a Tulip Festival. Tulips take their name from the Turkish *tulbend* (turban); the flowers were originally brought from Mongolia and, their cultivation refined by the Dutch, were great favorites of the Ottoman sultans.

㉚ Kanlıca. White 19th-century wooden villas line the waterfront of this village on the Asian shore. Kanlıca has been famous for its delicious yogurt for at least 300 years; it's served in little restaurants around the plane tree in the square by the quay.

㉙ Rumeli Hisarı (Thracian Castle). Mehmet the Conqueror built this eccentric-looking fortress in 1452, a year before his siege of Constantinople finally succeeded. Its crenellated walls and round towers are popular with photographers, though what you see from the water is about all there is to see. In the summer, Rumeli Hisarı is sometimes used for Shakespeare performances (usually in Turkish) and music and folk dancing. ⊠ *Rumeli Hisarı Cad., no phone.* ⊡ *$1.* ☉ *Tues.–Sun. 9:30–5.*

Sadberk Hanım Museum. An old waterfront mansion houses this museum named for the deceased wife of the late billionaire businessman Vehbi Koç. Though small, it houses an enviable collection of high-quality pieces. Half is dedicated to Islamic and Turkish arts (from İznik tiles

to Ottoman embroidery and calligraphy), and half to Anatolian archaeology (Hittite pottery and cuneiform tablets). ✉ *Piyasa Cad. 27–
29, Büyükdere,* ☎ *212/242–3813.* ▣ *$1.* ☉ *Summer, Thurs.–Tues.
10:30–6; winter, Thurs.–Tues. 10–5.*

DINING

For a chart that explains the cost of meals at the restaurants listed below,
see Dining and Lodging Price Categories at the front of this book.

South of the Golden Horn

$$$$ ✗ **Reşat Paşa Konağı.** A chic atmosphere prevails inside this pink and
white gingerbread-style villa. It's a little out of the way on the Asian
side, but the delicious Ottoman and Turkish dishes are well worth the
trip, which you can make with a taxi driver instructed by someone at
your hotel. Order à la carte and sample the mixed seafood cooked in
a clay pot, or let the waiter tempt you with the *Paşa Sofrasi,* a fixed
menu including 20 cold and hot appetizers, shish kebab as a main course,
and lemon helva for dessert, all accompanied by unlimited domestic
drinks. A band plays *fasil* (traditional Turkish music) on weekends. ✉
Sinan Ercan Cad. 34/1, Kozyatağı Mah., Erenköy, ☎ *216/361–3411.
AE, DC, V. Closed Mon. No lunch.*

$$$ ✗ **Develi Restaurant.** One of the oldest and best kebab restaurants in
★ Istanbul has views across the Sea of Marmara. The Develi specializes
in dishes from southeast Anatolia, which are traditionally more spicy
than those in the west of the country. Try the *patlıcan kebap* (kebab
with eggplant) or the *fıstıklı kebap* (kebab with pistachios). ✉
Balıkpazarı, Gümüşyüzük Sok. 7, Samatya, ☎ *212/585–1189. AE, DC,
MC, V.*

$$$ ✗ **Gelik.** This restaurant in a two-story l9th-century villa is usually
packed with people out to savor its delicious specialty: all types of meat
roasted in deep cooking wells to produce rich, unusual stews. ✉ *Sa-
hilyolu 68–70,* ☎ *212/560–7284. AE, DC, MC, V.*

$$$ ✗ **Sarniç.** It's not often one may dine deep down in an old Roman cis-
tern. Candlelight reflects off the arched yellow-brick walls, and a large
fireplace provides warmth in chilly weather. The service is fairly for-
mal, and the fare is a mix of Turkish and Continental, ranging from
duck à l'orange to *döner kebap* (meat roasted on a spit). ✉ *Sogukçesme
Sok., Sultanahmet,* ☎ *212/512–4291. AE, V.*

$$ ✗ **Borsa Lokantasi.** This unpretentious spot serves some of the best food
★ in the city. The baked lamb in eggplant puree and the stuffed artichokes
are highly recommended. But expect plain wood chairs and tables, paper
napkins, and a crowd of hungry Turks. ✉ *Yalıköşkü Cad., Yalıköşkü
Han 60–62, Eminönü,* ☎ *212/522–4173. No credit cards. Closed Sun.*

$$ ✗ **Fırat.** At this hopping Kumkapı fish house, you barely have time to
settle yourself in your chair before the food starts coming at you: sal-
ads, a savory baked liver dish, shrimp with garlic. In addition to the
usual grilled presentation, fish here is baked in a light cream or tomato-
based sauce to great effect. Just point at what you want, but try to pass
on a round or two to save room for dessert. ✉ *Çakmaktaş Sok. 11,
Kumkapı,* ☎ *212/517–2308. V.*

$ ✗ **Doy-Doy.** "Doy-doy" is a Turkish expression for "full," and one can
indeed fill up here for a reasonable sum. Kebabs and *pide* (Turkish pizza)
are served; vegetarians will appreciate the meatless pizzas and salad
options. Service is friendly and the menu's prices are unambiguous (some-
times a problem in Istanbul). ✉ *Şifa Hamamı Sok. 13, Sultanahmet,*
☎ *212/517–1588. No credit cards.*

Beyoğlu Area

$$ ✕ **Çatı.** This restaurant on a Beyoğlu side street serves hot and cold Turkish dishes and a good open buffet. Its seventh-floor location allows diners to appreciate the architectural splendors of İstiklal Caddesi. Open late, it presents live music in the evenings. ⊠ *Orhan Apaydın Sok. 20/7, İstiklal Cad., Beyoğlu,* ☎ *212/251–0000. MC, V. Closed Sun.*

$$ ✕ **Dört Mevsim** (Four Seasons). A handsome Victorian building on new
★ town's main drag houses this restaurant, noted for its blend of Turkish and French cuisine and for the Anglo-Turkish couple, Gay and Musa, who opened it in 1965. You'll find them in the kitchen overseeing the preparation of such delights as shrimp in cognac sauce and baked marinated lamb. ⊠ *İstiklal Cad. 509, Beyoğlu,* ☎ *212/293–3941. DC, MC, V. Closed Sun.*

$$ ✕ **Osmancık.** This Turkish restaurant on the 23rd floor of the Pullman Etap Hotel has a 360-degree view of the Bosporus, the Golden Horn, and the rest of Istanbul. The fixed menu includes starters such as *Osmancık Boreği* (cheese-filled pastries topped with a yogurt sauce) and grills, and all the domestic liquors you want to drink. Entertainment, which starts after 9 PM, comes in the form of traditional Turkish music, followed by a belly dancer. ⊠ *Meşrutiyet Cad., Tepebası,* ☎ *212/251–5074. AE, DC, MC, V.*

$ ✕ **Hacıbaba.** The menu at this large, cheerful place runs the gamut of Turkish specialties; the lamb kebabs are good, and there are so many mezes that you may never get around to ordering main courses. A shady terrace overlooks a Greek Orthodox churchyard. ⊠ *İstiklal Cad. 49, Taksim,* ☎ *212/244–1886. AE, DC, V.*

$ ✕ **Hacı Salih.** You may have to line up for lunch at this tiny, family-
★ run restaurant—it has only 10 tables. But the traditional Turkish fare is worth the wait. Lamb and vegetable dishes are specialties, and though alcohol is not served, you are welcome to bring your own. ⊠ *Anadolu Han 201, off Alyon Sok. (off İstiklal Cad.),* ☎ *212/243–4528. No credit cards. Closed Sun. No dinner.*

$ ✕ **Rejans.** Slightly down-at-the-heels, much as mother Russia is, this restaurant oozes atmosphere; even the waiters are an eccentric bunch. The walls are half wood-paneled, half covered in peeling wallpaper. The borscht and Stroganoff are sturdy and filling rather than haute. Try the chicken Kiev and sample the lemon vodka that will be plopped down on your table—you pay by the glass. ⊠ *Emir Nevrut Sok. 17, İstiklal Cad., Beyoğlu,* ☎ *212/244–1610. DC, MC, V. Closed Sun.*

$ ✕ **Yakup 2.** This cheery hole-in-the-wall is smoky and filled with locals rather than tourists, and it can get loud, especially if there is a soccer match on the television. From the stuffed peppers to the octopus salad, the mezes are several notches above average. ⊠ *Asmalı Mescit Cad. 35–37,* ☎ *212/249–2925. AE, V.*

Hasköy

$$$$ ✕ **Café du Levant.** Black and white floor tiles and turn-of-the century European furnishings lend this café next to the Rahmi Koç Industrial Museum the feel of a Paris bistro. Chefs Giles and Cyril serve superb French cuisine, including fillet of turbot with zucchini and tomatoes. For dessert, try the crème brûlée or the orange cake with ice cream. ⊠ *27 Hasköy Cad., Hasköy,* ☎ *212/250–8938 or 212/256–7163. Reservations essential. AE, DC, MC, V. Closed Mon.*

Taksim Square Area

$$$ ✕ **Divan.** The Divan is a rare exception to the rule that suggests avoiding hotel restaurants. The menu is a thoughtful blend of Turkish and

French cuisine, the surroundings are elegant, and the service is excellent. ⊠ *Cumhuriyet Cad. 2, Beyoğlu,* ☎ *212/231–4100. AE, DC, MC.*

Bosporus

$$$$ ✕ **Club 29.** Seafood is the specialty of this chic restaurant, which serves the "in" crowd in spring, fall, and winter in a suburb called Etiler and in summer on the Asian side of the Bosporus. The Etiler location is all silver and crystal and candlelight; the Asian premises recall a Roman villa, except for the view of the yachts bobbing in the harbor. After midnight, discotheques get going upstairs in both locations, and the action continues until 2 AM. The place can be pretty dead when the weather gets cold. ⊠ *Nispetiye Cad. 29, Etiler,* ☎ *212/263–5411 in spring, fall, and winter; Paşabahçe Yolu, Çubuklu,* ☎ *216/322–2829. Reservations essential. Jacket required. AE, DC, MC, V. No lunch.*

$$$$ ✕ **Körfez.** Call ahead and this restaurant in the picturesque Asian village of Kanlıca will ferry you across the Bosporus from Rumeli Hisar to your table. The decor is nautical, and the seafood fresh, superbly cooked to order. The menu includes flying-fish chowder, shrimp in béchamel sauce, and sea bass cooked in salt. ⊠ *Körfez Cad. 78, Kanlıca,* ☎ *216/413–4314. AE, DC, MC, V. Closed Mon.*

$$$$ ✕ **Tuğra.** In the historic Çırağan Palace, this spacious and luxurious restaurant serves the most delectable of long-lost and savored Ottoman recipes, including stuffed blue fish and Circassian chicken. Cookbooks from the Ottoman palace were used to re-create some of the dishes. But that's not all. The Bosporus view is flanked by the palace's marble columns, and ornate glass chandeliers hover above, all to make you feel like royalty. ⊠ *Çırağan Cad. 84,* ☎ *212/258–3377. Jacket required. AE, DC, MC, V. No lunch.*

$$$$ ✕ **Ziya.** Power lunchers and Turkish yuppies patronize this restaurant in a white, two-story mansion with a lovely garden. The cuisine is international, the decor elegant and modern, the atmosphere see-and-be-seen. The crepes with caviar and smoked sturgeon are not cheap, but you would pay a lot more in Paris or New York. ⊠ *Mualim Naci Cad. 109, Ortaköy,* ☎ *212/261–6005. AE, DC, MC, V.*

$$ ✕ **Dünya.** This restaurant is right on the Bosporus in the city's Bohemian quarter, Ortaköy, with a view of the Bosporus Bridge, the Ortaköy Mosque, and many a passing boat. As wonderful as these sights are, the food, which includes fresh and delicious appetizers such as eggplant or octopus salad, is even better. Ask for a table on the terrace as close to the water as possible. ⊠ *Salhane Sok. 10, Ortaköy,* ☎ *212/258–6385. DC, V.*

$$ ✕ **Hanedan.** The emphasis here is on kebabs, all kinds, all of them excellent. The mezes—tabbouleh, hummus, and the flaky pastries known as böreks—are much tastier than elsewhere. Crisp white linens set off the cool, dark decor of the dining room. Tables by the front windows offer the advantage of a view of the lively Beşiktaş ferry terminal. ⊠ *Çiğdem Sok. 27, Beşiktaş,* ☎ *212/260–4854. AE, MC, V.*

LODGING

For a chart that explains room rates at the accommodations listed below, *see* Dining and Lodging Price Categories at the front of this book.

South of the Golden Horn

$$$$ ▥ **Four Seasons Hotel.** A former Turkish prison instantly became one
★ of Istanbul's premier hotels when it opened in September 1996, steps from Topkapı Palace and the Hagia Sophia. Rooms and suites within the neoclassical building overlook either the Sea of Marmara or an in-

36

Dining

Borsa Lokantasi, **16**
Café du Levant, **18**
Çatı, **23**
Club 29, **37**
Develi Restaurant, **2**
Divan, **30**
Dört Mevsim, **22**
Doy-Doy, **8**
Dünya, **40**
Fırat, **5**
Gelik, **1**
Hacı Salih, **28**
Hacıbaba, **27**
Hanedan, **35**
Körfez, **41**
Osmancık, **19**
Rejans, **26**
Reşat Paşa Konağı, **17**
Sarniç, **15**
Tuğra, **36**
Yakup 2, **21**
Ziya, **38**

Lodging

Ayasofia Pansiyons, **14**
Berk Guest House, **13**
Büyük Londra, **25**
Büyük Tarabya, **39**
Çırağan Palace, **36**
Conrad International İstanbul, **34**
Divan, **30**
Four Seasons Hotel, **11**
Hotel Empress Zoë, **10**
Hotel Nomade, **9**
Hotel Zürich, **4**
Hyatt Regency, **31**
Ibrahim Paşa Oteli, **7**
Istanbul Hilton, **32**
Merit Antique Hotel, **3**
Pera Palace, **20**
Pierre Loti, **6**
Richmond Hotel, **24**
Sed Hotel, **29**
Swissôtel Istanbul, **33**
Yeşil Ev, **12**

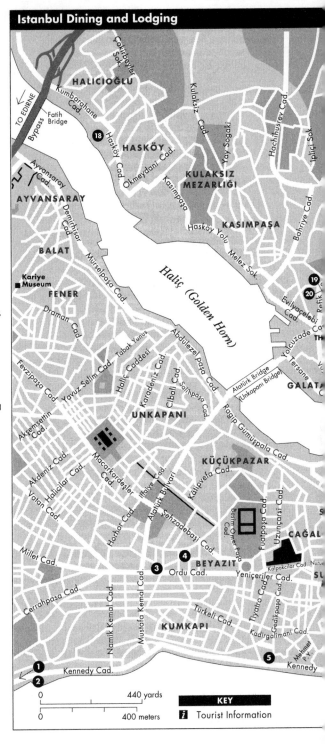

Istanbul Dining and Lodging

KEY

i Tourist Information

0 — 440 yards
0 — 400 meters

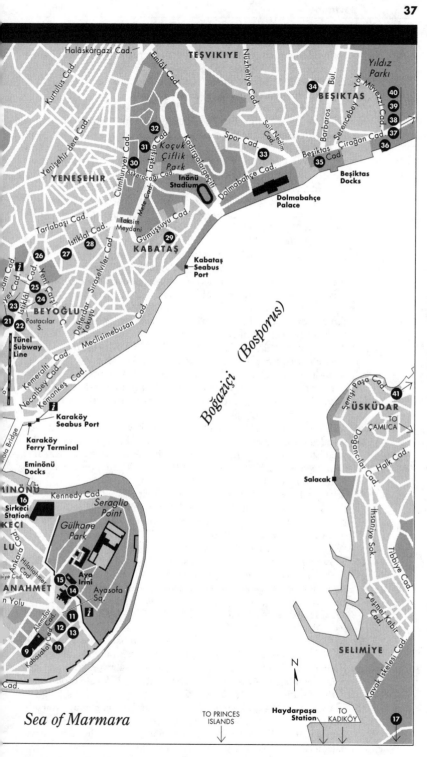

terior courtyard, and are luxuriously outfitted with reading chairs, original works of art, and bathrooms with deep soaking tubs. The glass-enclosed courtyard restaurant serves both international cuisine and local specialties. ⊠ *Tevkifhane Sok. 1, Sultanahmet,* ☎ *212/638–8200,* FAX *212/638–8210. 65 rooms with bath. Restaurant, bar, room service, health club, business services. AE, DC, MC, V.*

$$$ 🏨 **Ayasofia Pansiyons.** These guest houses are part of an imaginative
★ project undertaken by Turkey's Touring and Automobile Club to restore a little street of 19th-century wooden houses along the outer wall of Topkapı Palace. One house has been converted into a library and the rest into pansiyons, furnished in late Ottoman style with Turkish carpets and kilims, brass beds, and big European armoires. Front units have an incredible view of Hagia Sophia. During the summer, tea and refreshments are served in the small, white-trellised garden to guests and nonguests alike. ⊠ *Soğukçeşme Sok., Sultanahmet,* ☎ *212/513–3660,* FAX *212/513–3669. 57 rooms with bath. Restaurant, bar, café, Turkish bath. AE, MC, V.*

$$$ 🏨 **Merit Antique Hotel.** Four turn-of-the-century apartment buildings were combined to create this hotel. The rooms are generic and unimpressive, but the public spaces couldn't be grander, with their arched-glass canopies and reproduction furnishings in turn-of-the-century style. There's even a small stream, stocked with goldfish, running through the lobby. The only drawback is the neighborhood, on the old town side, which is full of cheap hotels and restaurants. ⊠ *Ordu Cad. 226, Laleli,* ☎ *212/513–9300,* FAX *212/512–6390. 275 rooms with bath. 4 restaurants, bar, pool, health club, casino. AE, MC, V.*

$$$ 🏨 **Yeşil Ev** (Green House). Another Touring and Automobile Club proj-
★ ect, this one is around the corner from the Ayasofia Pansiyons. The location is spectacular, on the edge of a small park between the Blue Mosque and Hagia Sophia. The hotel is decorated in Ottoman style with lace curtains and latticed shutters; rooms have brass beds and carved wooden furniture upholstered in velvet or silk (but they're small, with smallish baths and no phones or televisions). ⊠ *Kabasakal Cad. 5, Sultanahmet,* ☎ *212/517–6785,* FAX *212/517–6780. 20 rooms with bath. Restaurant. AE, V.*

$$ 🏨 **Hotel Zürich.** This 10-story hotel is efficient, well run, and one of the choicer options in Laleli; the lobby is highly polished and the rooms bright and carpeted, with little balconies. The higher floors are quieter. ⊠ *Harikzadeler Sok. 37, Laleli,* ☎ *212/512–2350,* FAX *212/526–9731. 132 rooms with bath. Restaurant, 2 bars, nightclub. MC, V.*

$$ 🏨 **Ibrahim Paşa Oteli.** This exquisitely renovated Ottoman house in the historic Sultanahmet neighborhood has a rooftop terrace with glorious views of the Bosporus and the Blue Mosque. The personable staff ensures a relaxing atmosphere. ⊠ *Terzihane Sok. 5, Sultanahmet,* ☎ *212/518–0394 or 212/518–0395,* FAX *212/518–4457. 19 rooms with bath. Restaurant, bar. MC, V.*

$$ 🏨 **Pierre Loti.** The tree-shaded terrace café and bar of this pretty little
★ hotel faces onto Divan Yolu. The property is centrally located in Old Stamboul, within easy walking distance of most sights. ⊠ *Piyerloti Cad. 5, Çemberlitaş,* ☎ *212/518–5700,* FAX *212/516–1886. 36 rooms with bath. Restaurant. No credit cards.*

$ 🏨 **Berk Guest House.** The cheerful Güngör and Nevin Evrensel run this clean and quite comfortable pansiyon in a converted private home. There are no real public spaces to speak of, though two of the rooms have balconies overlooking a garden. ⊠ *Kutlugün Sok. 27, Sultanahmet,* ☎ *212/516–9671,* FAX *212/517–7715. 9 rooms with bath. AE, V.*

$ 🏨 **Hotel Empress Zoë.** This small, unusual, and friendly hotel is conveniently near the sights in Sultanahmet. Named for the 11th-century empress who was one of the few women to rule Byzantium, it is decorated with murals and paintings in the style of that period. A terrace has a fine view over the old city. Rooms, accented with colorful textiles and paintings, have cool marble bathrooms. The American owner, Ann Nevans, helps guests fashion their itineraries. ⊠ *Akbıyık Cad., Adliye Sok. 10, Sultanahmet,* ☎ *212/518–4360,* 𝔽𝔸𝕏 *212/518–5699. 12 rooms with bath. MC, V.*

$ ★ ⊞ **Hotel Nomade.** The service is personal, the beds comfortable, and the prices low at this Sultanahmet pansiyon. The building is a restored, five-story Ottoman house decorated with kilims and folk crafts. The rooms are small, and those downstairs share a bath. The roof-garden bar and terrace have incredible views of Sultanahmet. ⊠ *Ticarethane Sok. 7, Sultanahmet,* ☎ *212/512–4753,* 𝔽𝔸𝕏 *212/513–2404. 12 rooms, some share bath. AE, MC, V.*

Beyoğlu Area

$$$ ⊞ **Pera Palace.** This hotel was built in 1892 to accommodate guests arriving on the *Orient Express*. The elevator looks like a gilded bird cage, the main stairway is white marble, and the lobby surrounding it has 20-foot-high coral marble walls. Unfortunately, though the hotel has been modernized, its facilities and rooms are not in the greatest shape. ⊠ *Meşrutiyet Cad. 98, Tepebaşı,* ☎ *212/251–4560,* 𝔽𝔸𝕏 *212/251–4089. 145 rooms with bath. Restaurant, bar, café. AE, DC, MC, V.*

$$ ⊞ **Büyük Londra.** This six-story establishment that was built in the 1850s as the home of a wealthy Italian family has grown old gracefully. Rooms are small and comfortably worn, and the current layout has the feel of an old apartment building. The dark woods and velvet drapes used in the high-ceilinged lobby and dining room exude an aura of the Ottoman Victorian era. ⊠ *Meşrutiyet Cad. 117, Tepebaşı,* ☎ *212/293–1619,* 𝔽𝔸𝕏 *212/245–0671. 54 rooms with bath. Restaurant. AE, MC, V.*

$$ ⊞ **Richmond Hotel.** On pedestrian İstiklal Caddesi and very close to the consulates, this hotel is a restored turn-of-the-century building with plush, clean rooms, some with views of the Bosporus. The sidewalk patisserie Lebon at the entrance is a remake of the original. ⊠ *İstiklal Cad. 445,* ☎ *212/252–5460,* 𝔽𝔸𝕏 *212/252–9707. 101 rooms with bath. Restaurant, bar, café, meeting room. AE, V.*

Taksim Square

$$$$ ⊞ **Istanbul Hilton.** Lavishly decorated with white marble, Turkish rugs, and large brass urns, this is one of the best Hiltons in the chain. The extensive grounds, filled with gardens and rosebushes, make the hotel a restful haven in a bustling city. Rooms are Hilton-standard, with plush carpeting and pastel decor; ask for one with a view of the Bosporus. ⊠ *Cumhuriyet Cad., Harbiye,* ☎ *212/231–4650,* 𝔽𝔸𝕏 *212/240–4165. 500 rooms with bath. 4 restaurants, bar, indoor pool, outdoor pool, spa, Turkish bath, 3 tennis courts, health club, squash, shops, casino. AE, DC, MC, V.*

$$$$ ⊞ **Hyatt Regency.** The massive but tastefully designed pink building here recalls Ottoman splendor. So does the interior, which has plush carpeting and earthy tones. Rooms have views of the Bosporus and the Taksim district. ⊠ *Taşkıla Cad., Taksim,* ☎ *212/225–7000,* 𝔽𝔸𝕏 *212/225–7007. 360 rooms with bath. 2 restaurants, bar, café, pool, beauty salon, health club, business services, baby-sitting. AE, DC, MC, V.*

$$$ ⊞ **Divan.** The staff at this quiet, modern hotel is thoroughly professional. The restaurant is excellent, and the public spaces and good-size rooms are comfortable. ⊠ *Cumhuriyet Cad. 2, Şişli,* ☎ *212/231–4100,* 𝔽𝔸𝕏 *212/248–8527. 180 rooms with bath. Restaurant, bar, tea shop. AE, DC, MC.*

Bosporus

$$$$ 🏨 **Çırağan Palace.** This 19th-century Ottoman palace (pronounced
★   "Chirahn") is the city's most luxurious hotel. The setting is exceptional,
right on the Bosporus and adjacent to lush Yıldız Park; the outdoor
pool is on the water's edge. The public spaces are all done up in cool
marble. The rooms are on the bland side, with gray walls and carpets,
but the views are exceptional. Be sure to specify old or new wing; the
new looks at the palace, and the old is in it. ⊠ *Çırağan Cad. 84, Beşiktaş,*
☎ *212/258–3377,* 𝔽𝔸𝕏 *212/259–6686. 312 rooms with bath. 4 restau-*
rants, bar, indoor pool, outdoor pool, Turkish bath, putting green, health
club, casino. AE, DC, MC, V.

$$$$ 🏨 **Conrad International Istanbul.** This big, round, showy, 14-story
tower has views over the Bosporus and terraced gardens. The lobby
has a domed ceiling and marble staircase, and rooms all around have
good views and contemporary Italian furnishings. ⊠ *Barbaros Bul. 46,*
Beşiktaş, ☎ *212/227–3000,* 𝔽𝔸𝕏 *212/259–6667. 627 rooms with bath.*
2 restaurants, 3 bars, indoor pool, outdoor pool, 2 tennis courts,
health club, shops, casino, business services. AE, DC, MC, V.

$$$$ 🏨 **Swissôtel Istanbul.** This bright hotel has a superb location just
★   above Dolmabahçe Palace. The building was controversial—nobody
liked the idea of such a big, modern structure towering over the palace.
But you'll appreciate its views—all the way to Topkapı Palace across
the Golden Horn. The vast, high-ceilinged lobby is usually filled by the
tinkling of a piano. The occasional Swiss-village mural strikes a jar-
ring note in Istanbul, but service is crisp and efficient. The rooms, done
in muted greens, have contemporary if undistinguished furnishings. ⊠
Bayıldım Cad. 2, Maçka, ☎ *212/259–0101,* 𝔽𝔸𝕏 *212/259–0105. 503*
rooms with bath. 4 restaurants, 2 bars, indoor pool, outdoor pool, health
club, business services. AE, DC, MC, V.

$$$ 🏨 **Büyük Tarabya.** This summer resort, less than an hour's drive up
the Bosporus from the center of Istanbul, is popular among the more
affluent locals. Though it has been around for years, it is well main-
tained and perfectly modern, with bright white walls and plenty of cool
marble. It has a private beach. ⊠ *Kefeliköy Cad., Tarabya,* ☎ *212/262–*
1000, 𝔽𝔸𝕏 *212/262–2260. 262 rooms with bath. Restaurant, bar, in-*
door pool, outdoor pool, health club. AE, MC, V.

$$ **Sed Hotel.** Tucked away on a side street, halfway down the hill from Taksim Square to Kabataş, the Sed makes up for being slightly off the tourist
track by providing superb Bosporus views from many of its rooms at
half the price of a five-star hotel. It also has a good restaurant. Insist on
a room with a view. ⊠ *Beşaret Sok. 14, Kabataş,* ☎ *212/252–2710,* 𝔽𝔸𝕏
212/252–4274. 50 rooms with bath. Restaurant, bar. MC, V.

NIGHTLIFE AND THE ARTS

For upcoming events, reviews, and other information, pick up a copy
of *The Guide,* a reliable bimonthly English-language publication that
has listings of hotels, bars, restaurants, and events, as well as features
about Istanbul. The English-language *Turkish Daily News* is another
good source.

Nightlife

Bars and Lounges

With views over the Bosporus, and a top-notch restaurant next door,
Bebek Bar (⊠ Bebek Ambassadeurs Hotel, Cevdet Paşa Cad. 113, Bebek,
☎ 212/263—3000) gets the dress-up crowd. **Beyoğlu Pub** (⊠ İstiklal
Cad. 140/17, Beyoğlu, ☎ 212/252–3842) sits off İstiklal Caddesi in
a pleasant garden and draws moviegoers and an expatriate crowd. At

Cuba Bar (✉ Vapur Iskelesi Sok. 20, Ortaköy, ☎ 212/260–0550), in the bohemian Ortaköy district, a band serves up Latin rhythms while the cook prepares a special Cuban soup and other dishes.

Memo's (✉ Salhane Sok. 10, Ortaköy, ☎ 212/260–8491), which has a great Bosporus location, hosts the showy crowd; the disco gets rolling around 11 PM.

Hayal Kahvesi (✉ Büyükparmakkapı Sok. 19, Beyoğlu, ☎ 212/224–2558) is a smoky, crowded late-night hangout for a mostly young crowd that likes live (and loud) rock and blues. **Orient Express Bar** (✉ Pera Palace Hotel, Mesrutiyet Cad. 98, ☎ 212/251–4560) is hard to beat for its turn-of-the-century atmosphere; you can't help but sense the ghosts of the various kings, queens, and Hollywood stars who have passed through its doors.

Local young professionals patronize **Zihni** (✉ Bronz Sok. 1A, Teşvikiye, Maçka, ☎ 212/246–9043) for lunch and for evening cocktails. In summer Zihni relocates to a terrace bar on the shores of the Bosporus (✉ Muallim Naci Cad. 19, Ortaköy, ☎ 212/258–1154).

Discos

Discos get rolling by about 10 and usually keep going until 3 or 4. **Regine's** is described in Nightclubs, *below.* **Juliana's** (✉ Swissôtel, Bayıldım Cad. 2, Maçka, ☎ 212/259–0940) is a popular disco with space-age styling. With its *Mad Max* decor, shoulder-high bursts of foam on the dance floor, and wild shows, **2019** (✉ Talimbane 19, Taksim, ☎ 212/235–6197) is one of the hottest scenes in town. **Memo's** (☞ Bars and Lounges, *above*) draws glossy types. **Cities** (✉ Sabancı Korusu, Yeniköy, ☎ 212/223-8424) is a posh and trendy bar that turns into a disco after 11 PM. The classy **Club 29** (✉ Paşabahçe Yolu, Çubuklu, ☎ 216/322–2829) holds forth in a faux-Roman villa by the Bosporus on the Asian side from mid-June through September (☞ Dining, *above*). **Samdan** (✉ Nisbetiye Cad., Etiler, ☎ 212/263–4898; Piyasa Cad. 101, Büyükada, ☎ 216/382–2654 in summer), which also has a fancy restaurant, is favored by fashionable Turks and the international expatriate crowd.

Nightclubs

Probably a good deal tamer than you would expect to find in the exotic East, Istanbul nightclub shows include everything from folk dancers to jugglers, acrobats, belly dancers, and singers. Some routines are fairly touristy but still fun. Typically, dinner is served after 8, and floor shows start around 10. Be aware that these are not inexpensive once you've totaled in drink, food, and cover. Reservations are a good idea; be sure to specify whether you're coming for dinner as well as the show or just for drinks.

Orient House (✉ Tiyatro Cad. 25, Beyoğlu, ☎ 212/251–4560) presents a floor show with belly dancers and Turkish folk dancing and good traditional Turkish food. The fixed prices are around $70 for the show and dinner, and $50 for the show and a drink. **Galata Tower** (✉ Kuledibi, ☎ 212/245–1160) is high atop the new town in a round room sheathed in windows; the ambience is strictly hotel lounge, and the Turkish dishes are only average. The fixed prices are around $70 for the show and dinner and $40 for the show and a drink. Comfortable, well-established **Kervansaray** (✉ Cumhuriyet Cad. 30, ☎ 212/247–1630) hosts a varied floor show, including two belly dancers, regional folk dances, and medleys of songs from around the world. It serves a range of Turkish dishes. Fixed prices are around $70 for the show and dinner and $50 for the show and a drink. The revue at **Regine's** (✉ Cumhuriyet Cad. 16, ☎ 212/247–1630) features some of Istanbul's best-known belly dancers, soft-core strippers, and big dance-production numbers; an adjacent upscale disco hops until 4 AM.

At the seedy strip-tease places off İstiklal Caddesi, the goal is to get customers to pay outrageous drink prices for questionable companionship. Those unwary enough to enter such places have reported being physically intimidated when questioning a drinks bill that has run into hundreds of dollars.

The Arts

The **Istanbul International Festival,** held from late June through mid-July, attracts renowned artists. To order tickets to the festival in advance, apply to the **Istanbul Foundation for Culture and Arts** (⊠ Kültür ve Sanat Concer Vakfi, Yıldız, Beşiktas, ☎ 212/261–3294 or 212/260–9072). Performances, which include modern and classical music, ballet, opera, and theater, are given throughout the city in historic buildings, such as Aya Irini and Rumeli Hisar.

In May, Istanbul hosts an **International Theater Festival,** which attracts major stage talent from eastern and western Europe. Because there is no central ticket agency, ask your hotel to help you get tickets or inquire at the box office or local tourist offices.

Concerts

Istanbul's main concert hall is **Atatürk Kültür Merkezi** (☎ 212/251–5600) in Taksim Square. The Istanbul State Symphony performs here from October through May, and ballet and dance companies do so year-round.

The **Cemal Reşit Rey Concert Hall** (⊠ Gümüş Sok., Harbiye, ☎ 212/248–5392 or 212/240–5012), close to the Istanbul Hilton, hosts recitals, chamber and symphonic music, modern dance, rock, folk, and jazz concerts performed by international talent. Tickets are often less than half the price they might be in the United States or Europe.

The **Aksanat Cultural Center** (⊠ Akbank Building, İstiklal Cad., Beyoğlu, ☎ 212/252–3500) shows classical and jazz concerts on a large laser-disc screen, presents films, and hosts exhibitions.

The Touring and Automobile Association (☎ 212/231–4631) organizes chamber music performances at **Beyaz Köşk** (in Emirgan Park) and **Hıdiv Kasrı** (in Çubuklu), two small 19th-century palaces. For information, contact the association.

Film

Some theaters on the strip of İstiklal Caddesi between Taksim and Galatasaray show the latest from Hollywood, with a few current European or Turkish movies thrown in. There are also plush, modern theaters at the Istanbul Princess Hotel in Maslak and Akmerkez Shopping Center in Levent, although it is advisable to purchase tickets in advance for the latter, particularly on weekends. Look for the words *Ingilizce* (English) or *Orijinal* (original language), or you will be seeing a film dubbed in Turkish. Films in languages other than English will have subtitles in Turkish. When in doubt ask at the ticket office whether the film is dubbed ("dublaj" in Turkish) or subtitled ("altyazılı" in Turkish). The annual **Istanbul International Film Festival,** which is held in the first two weeks of April, presents films from around the world; ask for a schedule at any box office and make sure to purchase tickets in advance. Seats are reserved.

OUTDOOR ACTIVITIES AND SPORTS

Beaches

The European shore of the Sea of Marmara is muddy and unpleasant, the Bosporus is famous for its dangerously strong currents, and either way, the water is pretty cold and heavily polluted. Stick with the hotel pool. If you must, the best bet is probably to make the hour-long drive to the area's best beach, at **Kilyos** on the Black Sea. Avoid the municipal beaches at Florya, a suburb on the European side, where bacteria have dangerously contaminated the waters.

Golf

Istanbul is not a noted golfing destination; you won't find Sawgrass or Pebble Beach, but the courses are perfectly fine if you need a fix. Itinerant players are welcomed at the **Golf Club** (⌧ Büyükdere Cad., Ayazağa, ☎ 212/264–0742). The **Kemer Golf & Country Club** (⌧ Kemerburgaz in the Belgrade Forest, 25 mins from Istanbul, ☎ 212/239–7913) has a nine-hole course.

Hiking and Jogging

If walking the city's streets leaves you wanting more exercise, try one of its parks. The wooded slopes of **Yıldız Park,** just north of the Çirağan Palace, are usually blissfully uncrowded. **Belgrade Forest** has enticing wooded paths and a 6.5-km (4-mi) walking and jogging track around the shores of old reservoirs. **Emirgân Park** is noted for its flower gardens and Bosporus views. **Gülhane Park** is conveniently located, right alongside Topkapı Palace.

Soccer

Turkish Division One is the country's Major Leagues. Matches take place from September through May at İnönü Stadium, Fenerbahçe Stadium, and Ali Sami Yen Stadium. You can get tickets at the stadiums or ask at your hotel for help.

SHOPPING

Shopping Districts

The **Grand Bazaar** (☞ Exploring Istanbul, *above*) is a neighborhood unto itself and a trove of all things Turkish—carpets, brass, copper, jewelry, textiles, and leather goods. The fashions are not bad either—not quite up to Italian style, but dramatically less expensive. **Nuruosmaniye Caddesi,** one of the major streets leading to the bazaar, is filled with some of Istanbul's most stylish shops, with an emphasis on fine carpets, jewelry, and made-in-Turkey fashions.

İstiklal Caddesi has everything from stores that sell old books and Levi's to the Vakko department store to a less stylish Turkish version of Saks Fifth Avenue. The **high-fashion district** centers on Halâskârgazi Caddesi and Rumeli Caddesi in Nişantaşı, 1 km (⅝ mi) north of İstiklal Caddesi. Here you will find the best efforts of Turkish fashion designers. **Bağdat Caddesi and Bahariye Caddesi** on the Asian side hold more suburban shopping venues. The **Galleria** mall in Ataköy near the airport has more than 100 stores selling foreign and local brand-name clothing. **Akmerkez,** in the Etiler district, is a large and luxurious mall whose stores stock recognized trademarks. The center has a movie theater, a restaurant, a fast food court, and cafés.

Markets

Don't miss the **Egyptian Bazaar,** also known as the Spice Market (☞ Exploring Istanbul, *above*). **Balıkpazarı** (Fish Market) sells, despite its name, anything connected with food, from picnic supplies to exotic spices and teas; it's in Beyoğlu Caddesi, off İstiklal Caddesi. A flea market is held in **Beyazıt Square,** near the Grand Bazaar, every Sunday. In recent years it has become a favorite with street traders from the former Eastern Bloc, who sell everything from cheap vodka and electronic goods to cast-off Red Army uniforms. **Sahaflar Çarşışı** is home to a bustling book market, with old and new editions; most are in Turkish, but English and other languages are represented. The market is open daily. Sunday finds more vendors here than other days. Along the Bosporus at **Ortaköy** is a Sunday crafts market with street entertainment.

Specialty Stores

Antiques

These are a surprisingly rare commodity in this antique land, perhaps because the government, to ensure that Turkish culture is not sold off to richer nations, has made it illegal to export most categories of antiques more than 100 years old. **Sofa** (✉ Nuruosmaniye Cad. 42), an exception, stocks a fascinating collection of old maps and prints, original İznik and Kütahya ceramics, vintage jewelry, and assorted other treasures. The friendly and informative **Ory & Ady** (✉ Serifagu Sok. 7–8, in the Bedestan section of the Grand Bazaar) specializes in Ottoman miniatures, illustrations, and prints. **Çığır Kitabevi** (✉ Sahaflar Çarşışı 17) has an impressive collection of old books, many of them illustrated.

Carpets and Kilims

There are carpet shops at nearly every turn, and all stock rugs at a variety of prices. Some of the better ones include **Adnan Hassan** (✉ Halicilar Cad. 90), **Celletin Senghor** (✉ Grand Bazaar), **Ensar** (✉ Arasta Bazaar 109), **Al-Dor** (✉ Faruk Ayanoglu Cad. 5–8), and the shops along Nuruosmaniye Caddesi, particularly **Çınar** at No. 6. Each shop has slightly different pieces, so you will have to look at several to get a feel for the market. On the other hand, there's nothing wrong with buying from the first shop you go into if you find something you love. For the best buys, look outside Istanbul.

Clothing

Angel Leather (✉ Nuruosmaniye Cad. 67) has kidskin suede and leather in skirts and jackets; the best of Turkish leather is on a par with Italian leather, quality-wise, though the designs are not as stylish. **Sube** (✉ Arasta Bazaar 131) sells handmade kilim slippers with leather soles and kilim boots for a fraction of their price in New York City. Turkish designer **Zeki Triko** sells his own bathing suits, completely up-to-date, at his eponymous boutiques (✉ Valikonagi Cad.). Fashionable **Beymen** (✉ Halâskârgazi Cad. 230) is Istanbul's version of Bloomingdale's. **Beymen Club** (✉ Rumeli Cad. 81) is casual, somewhat Polo in style.

English-Language Bookstores

Many of the larger hotels and souvenir shops in the old city stock some English-language newspapers and books, mostly guides to the more famous sights. A more comprehensive range can be found at specialist stores in Beyoğlu and the fashionable shopping districts of Nişantaşı and Levent. Books originally published outside Turkey carry markups of 15%–75%. Some of the larger bookstores include: **Robinson Crusoe** (✉ İstiklal Cad. 389, Tünel, Beyoğlu, ☎ 212/293–6968); **Remzi**

Kitabevi (⊠ Akmerkez Shopping Mall, Basement Floor No. 121, Levent, ☎ 212/282–0245; and ⊠ Rumeli Cad. 44, Nişantaşı, ☎ 212/234–5475); and **Pandora** (⊠ Büyük Parmakkapı Sok. 3, Beyoğlu, ☎ 212/245–1667). A number of stores specialize in secondhand books, from dog-eared thrillers to rare old texts about the city. These include **Librairie de Pera** (⊠ Galip Dede Sok. 22, Tünel, ☎ 212/245–4998) and a cluster of antiquarian booksellers in the **Sahaflar Çarsısı** (⊠ Sahaflar Çarsı Sok., Beyazıt).

Jewelry

Specialties include amber necklaces and ethnic Turkish silver jewelry threaded with coral and lapis lazuli. **Venus** (⊠ Kalpakcilar Cad. 160) and **Georges Basoglu** (⊠ Cevahir Bedestan 36–37) have distinctive and original pieces. **Nasit** (⊠ Arasta Bazaar 111) often has vintage silver as well as new. **Urart** (⊠ Abdi Ipekçi Cad. 181) sells chic interpretations of ancient Anatolian designs.

SIDE TRIPS

Princes Islands

The nine islands in the Sea of Marmara, about 20 km (12 mi) from Sultanahmet, have proven a useful amenity for Istanbul. In the days when the city was known as Constantinople, religious undesirables sought refuge here; in the time of the sultans, the islands provided a convenient place to exile untrustworthy hangers-on. By the turn of the last century, well-heeled businessmen had staked their claim and built many of the Victorian gingerbread–style houses that lend the islands their charm. But the islands remained a place of refuge. In the 1930s Büyükada, the largest of the islands, was the home for several years of the exiled Bolshevik Leon Trotsky.

Today, the islands provide a leafy retreat from the noise and bustle of Istanbul. Restrictions on development and a ban on automobiles maintain the old-fashioned peace and quiet—transportation is by horse-drawn carriage or bicycle. Though there are no real sights and populations swell significantly on summer weekends, the Princes Islands are perfect for relaxed outings. Of the nine islands, only four have regular ferry service, and only the two largest, Büyükada and Heybeli, are of real interest. Both are hilly and wooded, and the fresh breeze is gently pine-scented.

Büyükada

To the left as you leave the ferry you will see a handful of restaurants with names like Monte Carlo, Capri, and Milano. They are pleasant dives, somewhat overpriced, and there's little difference among them. **Yörük Ali Plaj,** the public beach on the west side of the island, an easy walk from the harbor, has a little restaurant.

To reach splendid, old Victorian houses, walk to the clock tower and bear right. Carriages are available at the clock tower square. The carriage tour winds up hilly lanes that are lined with gardens filled with jasmine, mimosa, and imported palm trees. After all of Istanbul's mosques and palaces, the frilly, pastel houses come as something of a surprise. But it is quite easy to imagine men in panama hats and women with parasols having picnics out in the garden. You can have your buggy driver wait while you make the 20-minute hike up Yücetepe Hill to the **Greek Monastery of St. George,** where there are three chapels and a sacred fountain believed to have healing waters. As you walk up the path, you'll notice the pieces of cloth, string, and paper that visitors have tied to the bushes and trees, in hope of a wish coming true. This is a popular pilgrimage site, especially at Greek Easter, when hundreds take the hike barefoot. If you're lucky, the monastery will be serving its homemade wine.

DINING AND LODGING

There is little difference from one spot on Büyükada's restaurant row to the next. The best bet is to look at a menu and ask to see the dishes on display. If a place is crowded with Turks, it is usually good.

$$$ 🏨 **Splendid Hotel.** For character, it's hard to beat this wooden, turn-of-the-century hotel, with its old-fashioned furniture, large rooms, and Ottoman Victorian styling. The hotel is topped by twin white domes, copies of those at the Hotel Negresco in Nice. It's difficult to get a room on summer weekends unless you book ahead. ⊠ *23 Nisan Cad. 71,* ☎ *216/382–6950,* 🖷 *216/382–6775. 24 rooms with bath. Restaurant, outdoor pool, dance club. No credit cards. Closed Oct.–Apr.*

$$ 🏨 **Villa Rifat.** This hotel is smaller, less ornate, and cozier than the Splendid. Its primary advantage is its small strip of private beach. ⊠ *Yılmaztürk Cad. 80,* ☎ *216/351–6068. 6 rooms with bath. No credit cards. Closed Oct.–Apr.*

Heybeli

The big building to the left of the dock, the Deniz Kuvetler (Turkish Naval Academy), is open to visitors except on Sunday, though there's not really much of interest to see. To the right of Heybeli's dock, tea-houses and cafés stretch along the waterfront. You can take a leisurely carriage ride, stopping, if the mood strikes, at one of the island's several small, sandy, and rarely crowded beaches—the best are on the north shore at the foot of Değirmen Burnu (Windmill Point) and Değirmen Tepesi (Windmill Hill). You can rent a rowboat for a few dollars at these beaches and row out to one of the other Princes Islands across the way. You will also pass the ruined monastery of the Panaghia, founded in the 15th century. Though damaged by fires and earth-quakes, the chapel and several red-tile-roofed buildings remain. Carriages here do not climb the hills above the harbor, where the old mansions and gardens are. The walk, however, is none too strenuous.

Princes Islands A to Z

ARRIVING AND DEPARTING

Ferries ($1.50) make the trip from Sirkeci or Bostanci (Asian side) docks in half an hour to an hour, depending on where they depart. Go straight to Büyükada and catch a local ferry to Heybeli later. Ferry tickets are round-trip and are collected on return. During the summer the early-evening ferries returning to the mainland are often very crowded on Saturday and Sunday. Much quicker, though less romantic, is the sea bus, departing from Kabatas near the Dolmabahçe Mosque and from Bostanci sea-bus terminals on the Asian side. Buy tokens for the sea bus at the terminals.

GETTING AROUND

Since no cars are allowed on the islands, you'll do most of your exploring on foot. Horse-drawn carriage tours cost $10 to $15. The other, perhaps more strenuous, but definitely fun, option, is to rent a bicycle ($2 per hour) from one of the shops near the clock tower on Büyükada. To get from one of the Princes Islands to the other, hop aboard any of several daily ferries.

Edirne

Unlike Istanbul, which every conqueror and pretender within marching distance hoped to have as his capital, Thrace was the sort of country that most warriors passed on through. The climate is harsh—sizzling in summer, bitter in winter—and the landscape unexceptional. For the modern visitor, however, there are some worthy sights, particularly Edirne, founded in the 2nd century AD as Hadrianopolis by the Roman emperor Hadrian. The city has been fought over by Bulgars, crusaders, Turks, Greeks, and Russians through the centuries, though once the Ottoman capital was moved to Istanbul, it became something of a picturesque backwater. The overhanging balconies of traditional Ottoman wooden houses shade Edirne's still-cobbled lanes, and its rich collection of mosques and monuments remains mostly unspoiled by the concrete towers so prevalent in Turkey's boomtowns.

Exploring

Hürriyet Meydanı, the central square, should be your starting point. Then walk east along Talat Paşa Caddesi to the Eski Cami (old mosque). Follow Mimar Sinan Caddesi to the striking Selimiye Cami. The other great mosque in Edirne, Beyazıt Cami, is on the outskirts of the city, across the Tunca River. The immense complex is about a 20-minute walk northwest from Hürriyet Meydanı via the fine-hewn, six-arched Beyazıt Bridge, which dates from the 1480s, as does the mosque. You can also take a *dolmuş* (shared taxi) from the square.

In the middle of **Hürriyet Meydanı,** Edirne's central square, stands the monument to the city's great passion: Two enormous wrestlers steal the spotlight from the obligatory Atatürk statue. Just off the north side of the square is the **Üç Şerefeli Cami** (Mosque with Three Galleries), built between 1437 and 1447. The galleries circle the tallest of the four minarets, which are notable for their fine brick inlay. On the mosque grounds is the 15th-century **Sokurlu Hamam,** built by Sinan, and one of the country's more elegant baths. It is open to the public from about 8 AM until 10 PM ($4 for bath, $10 with massage).

The **Eski Cami** (old mosque) is well named: Completed in 1414, it is the city's oldest. The huge-scale calligraphy illustrating quotes from the Koran and naming the prophets is exceptional in its grace and intricacy. Adjoining is the **Rüstempaşa Kervansaray,** restored and reopened as a hotel, just as it was in the 16th century. Also alongside the mosque is the 14-domed Bedestan, and one block away, the **Ali Paşa Bazaar.** Both are more authentic than Istanbul's Grand Bazaar, as the wares sold here—coffeepots, kilims, soap shaped like fruits and vegetables, towels—are meant for locals rather than tourists. ⊠ *Talat Paşa Cad., east from Hürriyet Meydanı, no phone.* 🔁 *Free.* ⊙ *Daily 9–7.*

The **Selimiye Cami,** not Istanbul's Süleymaniye, is the mosque Sinan described as his masterpiece, and it is certainly one of the most beautiful buildings in Turkey. Today a statue of the architect stands in front, but it is hardly necessary; the mosque remains his greatest monument. The architect was 85 years old when it was completed. The central dome, more than 100 feet in diameter and 148 feet high, rests on eight pillars, set into the walls so as not to disturb the interior space. External buttresses help support the weight of 999 windows; legend has it that Sultan Selim thought 1,000 might be a bit greedy. The marble mimber is exquisitely carved, and the mihrab is set back in an apse adorned with exceptional İznik tiles. The *medrese* (mosque compound) houses Edirne's Türk-İslâm Eserleri Müzesi (Museum of Turkish and Islamic Art), which displays Islamic calligraphy and photos of local wrestlers, as well as collections of weapons and jewelry from ancient Thrace, folk costumes, kilims, and fine embroidery. ⊠ *Hürriyet Meyd.* 🔁 *Free.* ⊙ *Daily sunrise to sunset; usually closed to tourists at prayer times, particularly Friday noon prayers.*

The **Beyazıt Cami** was built by the Sultan Beyazıt, hence its name, at the end of the 15th century. The complex includes both the mosque it-self—with a remarkable indented dome and a beautifully fretted mihrab—and two schools, a hospital, a kitchen, and storage depots. Out-side the city on the banks of the gently flowing Tunca River, the mosque is rarely used for worship. Apart from visiting tourists or a handful of young boys from the neighboring village playing soccer in the shadow of its walls, the complex is usually deserted by all but the custodian and fluttering pigeons, making it not only one of the most peaceful spots in Edirne but also a poignant reminder of the city's imperial past. ⊠ *Head northwest from Hürriyet Meydanı, across Beyazıt Bridge, no phone.* ☏ *Free.* ☉ *Daily sunrise to sunset during summer. Mosque is often locked during the winter, but custodian will sometimes open it up.*

Sarayiçi is the site of Edirne's famous wrestling tournament. Usually held in June, it is the best known of those held in villages throughout the country: Its burly, olive-oil-coated men have been facing off an-nually here for more than 600 years. Thousands of spectators turn out. Sarayiçi is a 20-minute walk up the Tunca River from Benazıt Cami.

DINING AND LODGING

$ ✕ **Aile Restaurant.** This locally popular restaurant serves stewed meat and vegetable dishes at lunch and switches to grilled fare in the evening. On the second floor above a bank, next to the post office, it has clean, modest seating, and the food is good and fresh. ⊠ *Belediye İşhanı, Kat 2,* ☎ *284/225–1250. No credit cards.*

$ ✕ **Çatı.** Typical but delicious Turkish dishes are served here, such as *tas kebap* (diced and stewed meat and vegetables with rice or bread) and *islim kebap* (a tender chunk of roast lamb covered with strips of eggplant). It's a clean place, if a little shabby, with views of the main square and the market. ⊠ *Hürriyet Meydanı,* ☎ *284/225–1307. No credit cards.*

$ ✕ **Doruk.** The meat dishes are a notch above the competition. About a mile outside the city center on a woody roadside, Doruk has both indoor and outdoor seating. Locals go there for the *tandir kebap* (lamb baked in a clay pot). If that's too heavy for you, try the lamb or chicken shish kebab or the *kasarli köfte* (meatballs stuffed with cheese). The inside of the restaurant is filled with plants and trees. Marble steps and a fountain dominate the entrance outside. ⊠ *Karaağaç Yolu, be-tween the Bunca and the Meriç bridges,* ☎ *284/213–8865. V.*

$$ ▦ **Hotel Rüstem Paşa Kervansaray.** The Kervansaray was built in the 1500s, reputedly by the celebrated architect Sinan, and today is the most impressive hotel in Edirne, at least from the outside. The rooms have high ceilings and decorative fireplaces, plain furniture, and low, single beds. The building sprawls around a pleasant courtyard full of flow-ers and shaded by a huge plane tree. Rooms near the nightclub are noisy. ⊠ *İki Kapılı Han Cad. 57, Sabuni Mah.,* ☎ *284/212–6119 or 284/225–2125,* ℻ *284/212–0462. 100 rooms with bath. Restaurant, nightclub. No credit cards.*

$ ▦ **Açıgöz Oteli.** Modest and nondescript, the Açıgöz Oteli is efficient, clean, and well located just off the main square and opposite the Ker-vansaray. The hotel does not have the charm of its neighbor, but its rooms are functional with all the basic amenities. A small restaurant serves breakfast, but no midday or evening meals. ⊠ *Tahmis Meydanı Çilingirler Cad. 9,* ☎ *284/213–1404 or 284/213–0313,* ℻ *284/213–4516. 34 rooms with shower. Restaurant. No credit cards.*

Edirne A to Z

ARRIVING AND DEPARTING

There are frequent **buses** from Istanbul's Esenler Terminal. The ride lasts four hours and costs $4.

By **car,** Edirne is about 235 km (150 mi) northwest of Istanbul. The new toll road, the E80 TEM (the toll from Istanbul to Edirne costs $3.50), is faster and much easier than Route 100.

Three **trains** daily leave Istanbul's Sirkeci Station for the painfully slow six- to 10-hour trip; the cost is about $5, so you are better off taking the bus or driving.

GETTING AROUND

The bus and train stations are on the outskirts of town, too far to walk to comfortably. Take a taxi into the center, asking for Hürriyet Meydanı. The sights within town can all be reached on foot.

CONTACTS AND RESOURCES

Edirne's **tourist information office** (⊠ Talat Paşa Cad., near Hürriyet Meydanı, ☎ 284/213−9208) is open every day during summer.

ISTANBUL A TO Z

Arriving and Departing

By Bus

Buses arrive at the Esenler Otogar (☎ 212/658−0036), outside the city near Bayrampaşa. This terminal is accessible by the **Hızlı Tren** (Rapid Train) system, which leaves from Aksaray. However, the train is often very crowded, particularly at rush hour. A few buses from Anatolia arrive at Harem Terminal, on the Asian side of the Bosporus (☎ 216/333−3763). Most bus companies have minibus services from the bus terminals to the area around Taksim Square and Aksaray, which is close to many hotels. Private **taxis** cost about $12 from Esenler Terminal to Taksim or Sultanahmet and about $10 from the Harem terminal. Customers also pay the Bosporus Bridge toll when crossing from Asia to Europe, or vice versa.

By Car

E80 runs between Istanbul and central Anatolia to the east; this toll road is the best of several alternatives. You can also enter or leave the city on one of the numerous car ferries that ply the Sea of Marmara from the Kabataş docks. There's an overnight ferry to İzmir from the Eminönü docks.

By Plane

All international and domestic flights arrive at Istanbul's **Atatürk Airport** (☎ 212/663−6400). The main airlines flying into the airport include (☞ Air Travel *in* the Gold Guide for phone numbers) **Delta, Air France, British Airways, Lufthansa,** and **Turkish Airlines.**

BETWEEN THE AIRPORT AND CENTER CITY

Shuttle buses (☎ 212/245−4208 or 212/245−4238) make the 30- to 40-minute trip from the airport's international and domestic terminals—which are some distance apart—to the Turkish Airlines terminal in downtown Istanbul at Şişhane Square near the Galata Tower; buses to the airport depart from the Şişhane Square every hour from 6 AM until 11 PM and as demand warrants after that. Allow at least 45 minutes for the bus ride in this direction, and plan to be at the airport two hours before international flights to allow for the time-consuming security and check-in procedures. **Taxis** charge about $15 to Taksim Square and $11 to Sultanahmet Square.

By Train

Trains from Europe and the west arrive at **Sirkeci Station** (☏ 212/527–0051) in Old Stamboul, near the Galata Bridge. Trains from Anatolia and the east come into **Haydarpaşa Station** (☏ 216/336–0475) on the Asian side.

Getting Around

The best way to explore the magnificent monuments in Old Stamboul is to walk. The setting shifts frequently, from narrow, cobbled streets to wide, tree-lined boulevards. To get to other areas, you can take a bus or one of the many ferries that steam between the Asian and European continents. Dolmuşes and private taxis are plentiful, inexpensive, and more comfortable than city buses.

By Boat

You would expect a sprawling city surrounded by water to be well served by ferries, and Istanbul does not disappoint. The main docks are at Eminönü, on the Old Stamboul side of the Galata Bridge; Karaköy on the other side of the bridge; Kabataş, near Dolmabahçe Palace; and, across the Bosporus on the Asian shore, at Üsküdar and Kadiköy. **Commuter ferries** of various sizes crisscross between these points day and night, and, like New York's Staten Island Ferry, provide great views of the city at a most reasonable price (usually $1 or less round-trip). Information on all city ferries is available 9 to 5 from the Istanbul Ferry Lines Office (☏ 212/244–4233). One of the most practical and speedy innovations on Istanbul's waterways has been the *deniz otobüsü* (sea buses), which are large and powerful catamarans painted blue, red, and white, operating to and from Karaköy, Kadiköy, Kabataş, Bostancı, the Princes Islands, Yalova, and Bakırköy. The interiors are air-conditioned and reminiscent of a large aircraft. Schedules are available at docks marked Deniz Otobüsü Terminalı and are also available on a 24-hour, Turkish-language telephone service (☏ 216/362–0444).

The **Anadolu Kavağı** boat makes all the stops on the European and Asian sides of the Bosporus and is best for sightseeing. It leaves year-round from the Eminönü Docks, Pier 5, next to the Galata Bridge on the Old Istanbul side, at 10:35 AM and 1:35 PM, with two extra trips on weekdays and four extra trips on Sunday from April through August. Unless you speak Turkish, have your hotel call for boat schedules, as English is rarely spoken at the docks (☏ 212/522–0045). The round-trip fare is $6; the ride each way lasts one hour and 45 minutes. You can disembark at any of the stops and pick up a later boat, or return by taxi, dolmuş, or bus.

By Bus

The city's buses (mostly vermilion-and-blue, although an increasing number are now completely covered in brightly colored advertising) are crowded and slow, but they are useful for getting around and—at about 50¢ per ride—inexpensive. The route name and number are posted on the front of each vehicle; curbside signboards list routes and itineraries. Buy tickets before boarding; they're available individually and in books of 10 at newsstands around the city, and, for a few cents above face value, can also be purchased from shoeshine boys and men sitting on wooden crates at most bus stops. London-style double-deckers operate between Sultanahmet and Emirgan on the Bosporus, and Taksim and Bostancı on the Asian side. Unlike the older city buses, these are clean and offer a panoramic ride. A bus attendant collects fares of three individual tickets ($1.50).

By Taxi or Dolmuş

Taxis are metered and inexpensive. Most drivers do not speak English and may not know every street, so write down the name of the one you want and those nearby, and the name of the neighborhood you're visiting. Although tipping is not automatic, it is customary to round off the fare to the nearest 5000 TL. Fares are 50% more expensive between midnight and 6 AM. Avoid taxi drivers who choose roundabout routes for more money by having your hotel's attendant, or a Turkish speaker, talk to the driver before you get in. The vast majority of Istanbul taxi drivers are scrupulously honest. But it is always advisable to check that the taxi has a working meter and that it is switched on. It is inadvisable to agree on a fare with a driver unless you know for certain that it is cheaper than the metered fare.

Dolmuşes, many of them classic American cars from the '50s, run along various routes. You can sometimes hail a dolmuş on the street, and as with taxis, dolmuş stands are marked by signs. The destination is shown on either a roof sign or a card in the front window. Dolmuş stands are placed at regular intervals, and the vehicles wait for customers to climb in. Though the savings over a private taxi are significant, you may find the quarters a little too close for comfort.

Contacts and Resources

Consulates

U.S.: (⊠ Meşrutiyet Cad. 104, Tepebaşı, Beyoğlu, ☎ 212/251–3602). **Canada:** (⊠ Büyükdere Cad. 107/3, Bengün Han, Gayrettepe, ☎ 212/272–5174). **U.K.:** (⊠ Meşrutiyet Cad. 34, Tepebaşı, Beyoğlu, ☎ 212/293–7540).

Emergencies

Ambulance (☎ 112; International Hospital Ambulance, ☎ 212/663–3000). **Hospitals:** American Hospital, (⊠ Güzelbahçe Sok. 20, Nişantaşı, ☎ 212/231–4050); International Hospital (⊠ Istanbul Cad. 82, Yeşilköy, ☎ 212/663–3000); and German Hospital (⊠ Siraselviler Cad. 119, Taksim, ☎ 212/293–2150) are good sources for an English-speaking doctor. **24-hour pharmacies** (☎ 111). There's a pharmacy in every neighborhood, and all Istanbul pharmacies post the name and address of the nearest one open around the clock. **Taksim** (⊠ İstiklal Cad. 17, ☎ 212/244–3195) is centrally located in the Taksim district. **Tourism police** (☎ 212/527–4503).

Guided Tours

Guided tours are arranged through travel agencies, and their offerings are all pretty similar, though names may change. "Classical Tours" take in Hagia Sophia, the Museum of Turkish and Islamic Arts, the Hippodrome, Yerebatan Sarayı, and the Blue Mosque in their half-day versions ($25); the Topkapı Palace, Süleymaniye Cami, the Grand or perhaps the Egyptian Bazaar, and lunch in addition to the above sights in their full-day version ($50; $60–$80 by private car). "Bosporus Tours" usually include lunch at Sarıyer and visits to the Dolmabahçe and Beylerbeyi palaces. A "Night Tour" ($50) includes dinner, drinks, and a show at either the Kervansaray or the Galata Tower nightclub.

Travel Agencies

Most travel agencies are along Cumhuriyet Caddesi, off Taksim Square, in the hotel area: **American Express** (⊠ Istanbul Hilton, Cumhuriyet Cad., Harbiye, ☎ 212/241–0248 or 212/241–0249); **Intra** (⊠ Halâskârgazi Cad. 111/2, Harbiye, ☎ 212/234–1200), **Setur** (⊠ Cumhuriyet Cad.

107, Harbiye, ☎ 212/230–0336) and **Vip Turizm** (⊠ Cumhuriyet Cad. 269/2, Harbiye, ☎ 212/241–6514).

Visitor Information

Turkish Ministry of Tourism: Atatürk Airport (☎ 212/663–6363); Istanbul Hilton (⊠ Cumhuriyet Cad., Harbiye, ☎ 212/663–0793); International Maritime Passenger Terminal (⊠ Karaköy Sq., ☎ 212/249–5776; in the Sultanahmet district (⊠ Divan Yolu Cad. 3, ☎ 212/518–1802); and in the Beyoğlu district (⊠ Meşrutiyet Cad. 57, ☎ 212/243–3472). Hours are usually from 9 until 5, though some close for an hour around noon.

3 The Southern Marmara Region

Whether you are heading out from Istanbul for the Aegean or for Ankara and central Anatolia, you would do well to take two or three days to explore this region near the southern shore of the Sea of Marmara. Termal remains a singularly Turkish spa, and both Bursa and İznik have rich histories.

Updated by
Gareth Jenkins

TERMAL IS NOTABLE FOR ONE and only one reason—its natural hot springs. A popular spa since Roman times, the springs were used by the Ottomans, refurbished in 1900 by Sultan Abdül Hamid II, and regularly visited by Atatürk during breaks from the frenzied business of running the country in the 1920s and '30s. Termal retains something of that 1930s air, and its restored baths, shady gardens, and piney woods are time-proven restoratives. There is little evidence today of Termal's ancient history, but the waters continue to attract the weary.

İznik, known as Nicaea in ancient times, was put on the map in 316 BC when one of Alexander the Great's generals claimed the city. Six years later it was conquered by another general, Lysimachos, who renamed it Nikaea after his wife. In AD 325 and again in 786, Nicaea hosted international ecumenical councils, which had profound effects on the practice of Christianity. The Seljuks made the city their capital for a brief period in the 11th century; Byzantine emperors in exile did the same in the 13th century, while Constantinople was in the hands of Crusaders. Orhan Gazi captured it in 1331.

Following the Ottoman conquest of Istanbul, İznik became a center for the ceramics industry. To upgrade the quality of native work, Sultan Selim I (ruled 1512–15), known as "The Grim," imported 500 Persian potters from Tabriz after he conquered it. The government-owned kilns were soon turning out tiles with intricate motifs of circles, stars, and floral and geometric patterns, executed in lush turquoise, green, blue, red, and white. Despite their costliness, their popularity spread through the Islamic world. Today original İznik tiles can be found in museums in Europe and the United States, as well as in Turkey.

Bursa became the first capital of a nascent Ottoman Empire after the city was captured in 1326 by Orhan Gazi (ruled 1326–61), the empire's first sultan. It was here that Ottoman architecture bloomed, laying the foundation for more elaborate works to be found in the later capitals, Edirne and Istanbul. More than 125 mosques here are on the list kept by the Turkish Historical Monuments Commission, and their minarets make for a grand skyline. Present-day Bursa is one of Turkey's more prosperous cities, a pleasing mix of bustling modernity, old stone buildings, and wealthy suburbs with vintage wood-frame Ottoman villas. Residents proudly call their city Yeşil Bursa (Green Bursa)—for the green İznik tiles decorating some of its most famous monuments, and also for its parks and gardens and the national forest surrounding nearby Mt. Uludağ. Uludağ, at 8,300 feet, is a popular ski resort.

Pleasures and Pastimes

Bird-Watching
Western Turkey lies on one of the main bird migration routes between Africa and Europe. Millions of birds pass through the region each spring and fall. One of the best places to bird-watch is the Kuşcenneti ("Bird Paradise") National Park on the shore of Lake Kuş west of Bursa. More than 239 different species of migrants and year-round residents have been recorded in its marshland and forests.

Dining and Lodging
Restaurants in the area near the Sea of Marmara's southern shore are not generally up to Istanbul standards, but there are some good choices, the fanciest being those at the Çelik and Dilmen hotels. Many establishments in Uludağ, except for those in hotels, are open only in winter. Bursa is the best place to use as a center for exploring the southern

Marmara region. There are also hotels in Yalova, Termal, and İznik for those looking for a one-night stopover. For charts that explain meal and room rates at the establishments in this chapter, *see* Dining and Lodging Price Categories at the front of this book.

Skiing

The mountain of Uludağ, which towers above Bursa, is usually covered with 6 to 10 feet of snow from December into May. Facilities are good, although less elaborate than in Europe or North America. The latest details of snow cover and facilities can be obtained from the tourist office in Bursa (☞ Visitor Information *in* The Southern Marmara Region A to Z, *below*).

Spas

Turkish baths can be found throughout the country, but south of the Marmara at spas such as Termal you can do your soaking in thermal water piping hot from the depths of the earth. Rich in minerals, the waters are said to cure a variety of ills from rheumatism to nervous complaints.

Exploring the Southern Marmara Region

Great Itineraries

IF YOU HAVE 3 DAYS
Numbers in the text correspond to numbers in the margin and on The Sea of Marmara map.

Leave Istanbul early enough to be in Yalova by midday. From Yalova either catch a minibus or drive to ☷ **Termal** ①. Spend the afternoon wandering in the gardens and soaking in the thermal water before staying overnight at one of the spa's hotels. On the morning of the second day return to Yalova and head toward ☷ **İznik** ②. If you leave Termal soon after breakfast you should be in İznik by mid-morning. In İznik head west along Kılıçaslan Caddesi and have lunch at a lakefront restaurant. Retrace your steps into the center of the town to the old Byzantine Church, **Sancta Sophia**, at the junction of Kılıçaslan Caddesi and Atatürk Caddesi. Continue east along Kılıçaslan Caddesi, past the **Belediye Sarayı** (Town Hall), the tourist office, and the **Hacı Özbek Cami** to **Yeşil Cami**, a mosque with a striking tiled minaret. The **İznik Museum** across the street exhibits artifacts from Greek to Ottoman times.

If you are traveling by private car, return by Route 150 as far as Orhangazi and head south along Route 575 to ☷ **Bursa** ③. If traveling by public transport either take a minibus to Bursa or one of the much more frequent minibuses returning to Yalova and then catch a bus from there to Bursa. Spend the night in Bursa.

Begin your day-three sightseeing in the town square at the intersection of Atatürk Caddesi and İnönü Caddesi, which is dominated by a statue of Atatürk. Head east from the statue, turn left onto Yeşil Caddesi, and walk another few blocks to the beautiful **Yeşil Cami** (Green Mosque) and its **Yeşil Türbe** (Green Tomb) complex. From here, hop into a taxi for a drive to the **Muradiye Complex,** which includes a mosque and 12 tombs around a fountain. Across from the mosque's park is the fascinating **17th-Century Ottoman House.** After viewing the house, either walk on west along Çekirge Caddesi to Bursa's **Archaeological Museum,** in **Kültür Park,** or catch a cab back into the city center to the **Bedestan,** Bursa's ancient bazaar.

When to Tour the Southern Marmara Region

The southern Marmara region is considerably cooler than the Aegean and Mediterranean coasts. For all except winter-sports enthusiasts the

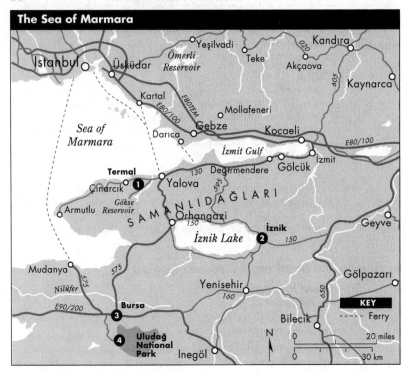

The Sea of Marmara

best time to visit the area is May through October; the national park at Uludağ remains refreshingly cool even in midsummer. But the region is still accessible during the cooler seasons, and soaking in one of the thermal baths (such as at Termal) is a fine antidote to the winter blues.

TERMAL, İZNIK, AND BURSA

Many of those arriving from Istanbul by car will head straight for Bursa, but if time permits, visit Termal or İznik before moving on to Bursa. It is possible to "do" Termal or İznik in one day from Istanbul, but attempting to see both, or trying to travel to and explore Bursa in a single day, will make for a less than satisfying tour.

Termal

❶ *12 km (8 mi) southwest of Yalova. Head west from Yalova, following signs to Çınarcık. Termal is signposted about 3 km (2 mi) outside of Yalova.*

Termal is a self-contained resort with two hotels, exotic gardens, and three public thermal baths with rich mineral waters. All have lockers where you can store your clothes and towels for use after a soak. If you stay overnight, you can also soak at either of the hotels, whose baths are open to guests only.

The grand **Sultan** baths is an Ottoman institution with Baroque decor and hot mineral waters. You can rent your own cabin and soak to your heart's content in a deep, gray marble tub. 🖂 *$3.50 per person, $5 for 2 people.*

★ The less imposing **Valide** baths—the Valide being the mother of the reigning sultan in Ottoman times—also has ornate decor and individual cabins and tubs. ⌘ *$2 per person for 90 mins.*

★ The **Kurşunlu** (Lead-Roof Bath) has a large outdoor thermal pool, an indoor pool, and a sauna. ⌘ *$2.50 for outdoor pool, $2 for enclosed pool and sauna, $2.50 per person for private cubicle, $3.50 for 2 people.*

Atatürk liked Termal so much he had a house built for himself here. From the path from the Kurşunlu pool you can see **Atatürk's Cottage** and a white house with gingerbread trim that was used by his guests. When you're finished soaking, make a quick stop at the museum devoted to him, a plain, modern structure built in 1929. It contains little more than some heavy wood furniture but has a delightful tea garden on one side. ⌘ *$1. ⊙ During daylight hrs.*

Dining and Lodging

$$ ✕🔲 **Turban Yalova Termal Çamlık Oteli.** This pleasant hotel adjoining
★ the baths sits on a ridge overlooking the resort's grounds and dates from Termal's modern heyday in the 1930s. It has a good Turkish restaurant and modern, white-tile tubs filled with thermal waters. Guest rooms in the back are less expensive, and in the off-season rates drop significantly. ☎ *226/675–7400,* 🖷 *226/675–7413. 83 rooms with bath. Restaurant. AE, DC, MC, V.*

$$ ✕🔲 **Turban Yalova Termal Çınar Oteli.** This hotel has the same ownership, management, accommodations, and phone number as the nearby Çamlık. It is a bit less atmospheric because it doesn't have as good a view, but is still comfortable. Its thermal baths have old-fashioned gray-marble tubs like those at the Sultan baths. ☎ *226/675–7400,* 🖷 *226/675–7413. 18 rooms with bath. Restaurant. AE, DC, MC, V.*

İznik

❷ *60 km (38 mi) from Yalova. Take Rte. 575 south from Yalova for approximately 25 km (15 mi) to Orhangazi, head east at the sign for İznik, and follow Rte. 150 around the northern shore of Lake İznik.*

Lakeside İznik is rather run-down today, but it has an incredible past. This is the place where the famed İznik tiles were made, although the ceramic industry went into decline in the 18th century. Its artisans are only now making a comeback by reproducing the rich colors of the original tiles, though on a small scale and without great success so far.

Sancta Sophia (Church of the Holy Wisdom) was built in the center of İznik in the 6th century, during the reign of Justinian. Its primitive mosaic floor is believed to date from that time. The wall mosaics were added as part of a reconstruction in the 11th century, after an earthquake toppled the original church. There are some fine fragments of Byzantine fresco and mosaic work, including a mural of Jesus with Mary and St. John the Baptist. It was here that the great ecumenical councils of the 4th and 8th centuries were held. ✉ *Atatürk Cad. and Kılıçaslan Cad., no phone.* ⌘ *$1. ⊙ Daily 9–noon and 2–5. If closed, ask for key at İznik Museum a few blocks away.*

The Ottoman style of **Hacı Özbek Cami** is very primitive. The small-scale mosque, which dates from 1332, lacks the ornamentation of later buildings in Bursa and Istanbul. ✉ *Kılıçaslan Cad., east of the Belediye Sarayı (town hall), no phone.* ⌘ *Free. ⊙ Daily sunrise–sunset.*

★ **Yeşil Cami** near İznik's east wall is known as the Green Mosque because of the color of much of its tile work. The Seljuk style is simpler than the Ottoman: Seljuk mosques usually have just one room under a single dome and borrow Persian and Indian architectural and decorative traditions; Ottoman mosques, as exemplified by Bursa's Ulu Cami, draw on Byzantine structures such as Istanbul's Hagia Sophia. Ironically, the Green Mosque's blue and green tiles are not the original İznik work, which was damaged by various earthquakes and replaced during the last century. ⊠ *Teke Sok., off Kılıçaslan Cad., no phone.* ☏ *Free.* ☉ *Daily sunrise–sunset.*

The building that houses the **İznik Museum** is interesting itself—it was built in 1388 as a soup kitchen. Such kitchens were often constructed by the wealthy near mosques to serve free food to the poor as examples of Muslim charity. Today the museum contains artifacts—Greek tombstones, Ottoman perfume bottles, and İznik tiles. If you have time, ask at the museum about a visit to the Byzantine Tomb, Yeraltı Mezar, on the outskirts of town. Discovered in the 1960s, this 5th-century burial place of an unknown family has well-preserved painted murals of peacocks, flowers, and abstract patterns in the Byzantine style. ⊠ *Kılıçaslan Cad., opposite Yeşil Cami,* ☏ *224/757–1027.* ☏ *$1.* ☉ *Daily 9–noon and 1–5.*

The gray stone **Lefke Kapısı,** the eastern gate to the ancient city, was built in honor of a visit by the Roman Emperor Hadrian in AD 120. Its old inscriptions, marble reliefs, and friezes remain intact. You can scramble up onto the old city walls for a good view. Thick, sturdy fortifications like these were what saved many a town from ruin. Outside the gate is the city graveyard and Muslim tombs belonging to a nobleman named Hayrettin Paşa and lesser luminaries. The oldest is 600 years old.

Dining and Lodging

$–$$ ✕ **Balıkçı Restaurant.** The specialties at this lakeside eatery include fish dishes, grilled meatballs, and mezes. ⊠ *Göl Kenarı,* ☏ *224/757–1152. No credit cards.*

$–$$ ✕ **Kırık Çatal.** Open since 1964, this restaurant is run by the same people who manage the Motel Burcum. No one knows why or how it got its name, which means "broken fork." Fresh appetizers and hot main dishes, including local eel, are served on an open-air terrace. ⊠ *Göl Kenarı,* ☏ *224/757–2990. Reservations essential for large groups. V.*

$ ⌂ **Çamlık Motel.** In this quiet and newly expanded lakefront establishment, rooms are sparsely furnished and unadorned, but the garden on the lake is pleasant and doubles as a café. ⊠ *Göl Kenarı,* ☏ *224/757–1362,* FAX *224/757–1631. 33 rooms with bath. V.*

$ ⌂ **Motel Burcum.** This is another lakeside hotel with sparsely furnished rooms. The loudspeakers in the adjacent café could be a bother for those who like it quiet, but the staff is friendly and the restaurant prepares fresh vegetable and meat dishes. ⊠ *Göl Kenarı,* ☏ *224/757–1011,* FAX *224/757–1202. 25 rooms with bath. V.*

Bursa

❸ *247 km (155 mi) from Istanbul via Rte. 100 or E80 to İzmit, Rte. 130 to Yalova, and Rte. 575 south from Yalova to Bursa. Alternatively, take Rte. 100 from Istanbul to Darıca, the ferry across to Yalova ferry terminal, Rte. 130 for 10 km (6 mi) into Yalova and Rte. 575 for 63 km (40 mi).*

Bursa, set along the slopes of Uludağ, suffers a bit from the sprawls. It stretches along an east–west axis, and its main street winds and changes names many times between the city center and the neighborhood known as Çekirge, several kilometers (a couple of miles) to the west. The town square, at the intersection of Atatürk Caddesi and İnönü Caddesi, is a logical starting point. The area, officially Cumhuriyet Alanı (Republic Square) is popularly called **Heykel** (Statue), after its imposing equestrian statue of Atatürk. Head east from here, turn left onto Yeşil Caddesi, and walk another few blocks.

An incredible juxtaposition of simple form, inspired stone carving, and spectacular İznik tile work, the **Yeşil Cami** is among the finest mosques in Turkey. Work on the mosque began in 1421, during the reign of Mehmet I Çelebi (ruled 1413–21). Its beauty starts in the carved-marble entryway, where feathery patterns in the stone create a complex design. Inside is a sea of blue and green İznik tiles, many with floral designs. The central hall rests under two shallow domes; in the one near the entrance, an oculus sends down a beam of sunlight at midday, illuminating a fountain delicately carved from a single piece of marble. The *mihrab* (prayer niche) towers almost 50 feet, and there are intricate carvings near the top. On a level above the main doorway is the sultan's loge, lavishly decorated and tiled; if you are lucky, a caretaker will take you up to see it. ⊠ *Yeşil Cad., no phone.* ☎ *Free.* ☉ *Daily sunrise–sunset.*

The **Yeşil Türbe** is Mehmet I Çelebi's tomb, built in 1424. The "green" tomb is actually covered in blue tiles, added after an earthquake damaged the originals in the 1800s. Inside, however, are incredible, original İznik tiles, including those sheathing Mehmet's immense sarcophagus. The other tombs belong to his children. ⊠ *Eastern end of Yeşil Cad., opposite Yeşil Cami, no phone.* ☎ *Free.* ☉ *Daily 8:30– noon and 1–5:30.*

The **Bursa Etnoğrafya Müzesi** (Bursa Ethnographic Museum) is on the site of a former theological school that is part of the complex that includes Yeşil Cami and Yeşil Türbe (☞ *above*). The collection is a good one, with tile work, inlaid wood, jewelry, books and almanacs, pottery, and bits of Seljuk architectural decoration. ⊠ *Yeşil Cad., on west side of Yeşil Cami, no phone.* ☎ *$1.* ☉ *Tues.–Sun. 8:30–noon and 1–5:30.*

NEED A BREAK?

Several **tea gardens** on the west side of the Yeşil Mosque and Yeşil Tomb are pleasant places to have a sandwich or pastries and take in views of the city and distant plains. The two mosques in the distance, the Emir Sultan (1431, to the right) and Yıldırım Beyazıt (1391, to the left), are not worth visiting, as earthquakes have damaged their interiors.

The **Orhan Gazi Cami,** set back from Atatürk Caddesi, was built for Sultan Orhan Gazi in 1335. This is the first truly Ottoman mosque. Although small, it has a graceful porch and fountain. The mosque is open from sunrise to sunset; admission is free. The Turks generally favor modern, practical concrete in their civic buildings, but Bursa's **City Hall** (⊠ Cumhuriyet Cad., opposite Orhan Gazi Cami) is constructed out of timber and brick and feels more rustic.

★ The **Covered Bazaar** was built in the 1300s by Yıldırım Beyazıt I (ruled 1389–1402), but was flattened by a massive earthquake in 1855. It has been lovingly restored, and many of the old Ottoman *hans* (markets) inside still provide the flavor of the 16th century. By and large, the Bedestan is less touristy and more atmospheric than Istanbul's Grand Bazaar. Best buys include silver and gold jewelry, thick Turkish cotton towels (for which Bursa is famous), and silk goods (☞ Shopping, *below,* for additional details about the bazaar). ⊠ *Cumhuriyet Cad., near its intersection with Maksem Cad.*

The striking **Ulu Cami** (Grand Mosque) dates from 1396. Sultan Beyazıt had it built after vowing to build 20 mosques if he was victorious in the battle of Nicopolis in Macedonia; this one mosque with 20 domes was something of a compromise. Its interior is decorated with an elegantly understated display of quotations from the Koran in fine Islamic calligraphy. ⊠ *Near the intersection of Atatürk and Maksem Cads.*

The neighborhood known as **Hisar** (Fortress) is where Bursa started, like so many cities of old: within the walls of a fortress. Pınarbaşi Caddesi is the main street through this part of town; make a detour on Kale Caddesi, an atmospheric block lined with wood-frame houses dating from the 17th to 19th centuries. In a small park not far from the citadel walls, overlooking Cemal Nadir Caddesi, are the tombs of Osman and Orhan, considered founders of the Ottoman Empire. The word Ottoman derives from Osmanli, the people led by Osman. Osman—the son of a warrior chieftain named Ertuğrul Gazi, who had taken control over an area near Bursa—sought to expand the boundaries of his father's state and eventually laid siege to Bursa. But it wasn't until 1326, several years after he died, that the city fell and the Ottomans, under Orhan, claimed the victory. The tombs date from the 19th century; the originals were destroyed in an earthquake.

The **Sultan Murat II Cami** and surrounding complex, Bursa's Muradiye neighborhood, were built in 1425–26, during the reign of Mehmet the Conqueror, in honor of its namesake, Mehmet's father. The mosque is unexceptional, perhaps because Mehmet's attentions were so firmly focused on Constantinople, which he would soon win. The mihrab is decorated in plain blue-and-white tiles; the exterior has some highlights of blue tile. Outside, next to the mosque in what is surely the city's most serene resting place, there is a fountain ringed by 12 tombs. Among those buried here are Murat himself, Mehmet, and Mustafa, the eldest son of Süleyman the Magnificent, who was strangled in his father's tent. The Sultan's ambitious wife, Roxelana, had persuaded her husband that Mustafa was a traitor. ⊠ *Kaplıca Cad., no phone.* ▨ *Free.* ☉ *Sunrise to sunset.*

The **17th-Century Ottoman House,** built on what is believed to have been the site of a pavilion belonging to Sultan Murat II, is one of the oldest and best-preserved of Bursa's historic homes, complete with authentic period carpets and furniture. The main room on the upper floor has wooden cupboards covered with painted floral motifs and an intricately carved wooden ceiling. For a glimpse into another era's "Lifestyles of the Rich and Famous," take a look. ⊠ *Kaplıca Cad., opposite Sultan Murat II Cami complex, no phone.* ▨ *$1.* ☉ *Tues.–Sun. 8:30–noon and 1–5.*

Dominating the view on Çekirge Caddesi is the refreshingly green **Kültür Park** (Culture Park). Many Turkish towns have such a park, with restaurants, tea gardens, a pond with paddleboats, a sports stadium, and a Ferris wheel. This park is quite large, stretching for about a dozen city blocks and containing Bursa's **Arkeoloji Müsezi** (Archaeological Museum). The museum, which is open Tuesday–Sunday 8:30–noon and 1–5 (admission $2), is pleasant enough, with its Roman coins and other artifacts, but there are better ones in Istanbul, Ankara, and elsewhere. The same goes for the nearby **Atatürk Museum,** with old-fashioned furniture and a few exhibits on the great leader's life. ⊠ *Kültür Park: Çekirge and Stadyum Cads.*

The affluent suburb called Çekirge starts at Kültür Park and continues west. Bursa has been a spa town since Roman times; the thermal springs run along these slopes, and mineral baths are an amenity at many hotels here.

Dining and Lodging

$$ ✕ **Cumurcul.** This old house converted into a restaurant in the Çekirge section of town is a local favorite. Grilled meats and fish are attentively prepared; ask the waiters to show you what's freshest. In addition to the usual cold mezes are hot starters, including a tasty *börek* (deep-fried or oven-baked pastry filled with meat or cheese). ⊠ *Çekirge Cad.,* ☎ *224/235–3707. Reservations essential on weekends. AE, MC, V.*

$ ✕ **Hacı Bey.** Arguments never end over where to find the best Bursa kebab, but this downtown stop is always a contender. The setting is basic cafeteria-style, but the food is what counts. ⊠ *Ünlü Cad., Yılmaz Iş Han 14C,* ☎ *224/221–6440. DC, MC, V.*

$ ✕ **Kebapçı Iskender.** Bursa is famous for the main dish served here: Iskender kebab, skewer-grilled slivers of meat and pita bread immersed in a rich tomato sauce topped with butter and yogurt. ⊠ *Ünlü Cad. 7, Heykel,* ☎ *224/221–4615. No credit cards.*

$ ✕ **Özömür Koftecisi.** *Köfte,* a rich, grilled patty of ground beef or
★ lamb, is a regional specialty, and that's pretty much the thing to get here. The restaurant gets the nod over others thanks to its charming location in the covered market, by the Ulu Cami. ⊠ *Ulucami Cad. 7, no phone. No credit cards.*

$ ✕ **Selçuk.** Another Kültür Park restaurant with the usual Turkish specialities, this one offers a shady terrace and slightly lower prices than its neighbors. ⊠ *Kültür Park,* ☎ *224/220–9695. No credit cards.*

$$$$ ▥ **Çelik Palas.** This is quite the poshest hotel in Bursa. Its main attraction
★ is its domed, Roman-style pool fed by hot springs; you will find your fellow guests constantly traipsing through the hallways in their robes en route. The pool, by the way, was where the late king of Libya was when he learned that Colonel Mu'ammar Qaddafi had taken over his country. The hotel has a lively 1930s design scheme, and some rooms have balconies. ⊠ *Çekirge Cad. 79,* ☎ *224/233–3800,* ℻ *224/236–1910. 173 rooms with bath. Restaurant, bar, dance club. AE, MC, V.*

$$$ ▥ **Hotel Dilmen.** The lobby in this fancy, modern hotel in the Çekirge section is accented by gleaming brass and stained-glass windows. Rooms, however, are simply furnished. There are the requisite thermal baths, a pleasant garden terrace and bar, and views of the valley. ⊠ *1 Murat Cad. 20,* ☎ *224/233–9500,* ℻ *224/235–2568. 98 rooms with bath. Restaurant, bar, exercise room. MC, V.*

$$ ▥ **Ada Palas.** The thermal pool of this hotel near the Kültür Park is inviting, and the price tag is lower than that at the nearby Çelik. Rooms are unexceptional but in good condition. ⊠ *1 Murat Cad. 21,* ☎ *224/233–3990,* ℻ *224/236–4656. 39 rooms with bath. V.*

$$ ▥ **Hotel Dıkmen.** This hotel is not to be confused with the Dilmen (☞ *above*). Although less grand than Çekirge hotels, the Dıkmen is conveniently located downtown. It has large, plain guest rooms, a spacious lobby, and a sunny garden with a marble fountain. It is often filled by tour groups. ⊠ *Fevzi Çakmak Cad. 78,* ☎ *224/224–1840,* ℻ *224/224–1844. 53 rooms with bath. Restaurant, bar. No credit cards.*

Nightlife

The **Kervansaray Termal Hotel** (⊠ Çekirge Meyd., ☎ 224/233–9300) has a fine floor show, with noted local singers and belly dancers. The presentation is more traditional and less touristy than similar offerings in Istanbul, although there is no skimping on the glitz. The price tag is substantial, too—about $30 per person with dinner. The **Çelik Palas** (☞ Lodging, *above*) has a somewhat more refined lounge act.

Shopping

In Bursa the **Bedestan** (Covered Bazaar) behind the Ulu Cami is where the action is from 8 to 5 Monday through Saturday. As is traditional, each section is dominated by a particular trade: jewelers, silk weavers, antiques dealers. The Koza Han section, in a historic courtyard by the eastern entrance, is the center of the silk trade. The Emir Han, in the southwestern section, is another silk market and has a fountain and a courtyard tea garden. These hans are lively in June and September, the silk harvesting months, when buyers swarm in from around the country to place orders. Bursa has been a center of the silk industry since the coming of the Ottoman sultans and remains a good place to buy silk scarves, raw-silk fabric by the yard, and other silk products.

Antiques are to be found in the small Eski Aynalı Carşı section of the bazaar. Of note is a shop called Karagöz, which has a fine collection of old copper and brass, kilims, jewelry, and the translucent, vividly colored shadow puppets from which the store takes its name.

OFF THE BEATEN PATH
KUŞCENNETI NATIONAL PARK – If you're heading on from Bursa to Çanakkale and the Aegean Coast, consider taking a break at Kuşcenneti ("Bird Paradise") National Park, beside Lake Kuş. There are benches and tables for picnics, a viewing tower for bird-watching, and a small information center with exhibits describing the more than 200 species of birds that visit the park. ⊠ *Take Rte. 200 west about 100 km (62 mi) from Bursa; signs for the park appear before the city of Bandırma.*

Uludağ

4 *33 km (21 mi) southeast of Bursa; start from Çekirge Cad. heading west and follow the signs for Uludağ.*

Bursa is the jumping-off point for excursions to Uludağ, where you will find a lush national park and Turkey's most popular ski resort. To appreciate fully why the town is called Green Bursa, take the 30-minute ride up the *teleferik* (cable car) from Namazgah Caddesi in Bursa to the mountain's summit for a panoramic view. You can also make the hour-long drive; heading west on Çekirge Caddesi, the turnoff to Uludağ is about 4 km (2½ mi) from the city center. The road is narrow and winding and sometimes passable in rough-terrain vehicles during winter. All Uludağ resort hotels are in an area near the highest peak, called Oteller. From here you can reach undeveloped spots for hiking during the summer, at blissfully cool temperatures. ⊠ *Teleferik,* ☎ *224/221–3635.* ☞ *$8 round-trip. Admission to park: $2.50 per car.* ☉ *Teleferik operates year-round, every 30 or 40 mins during daylight.*

Lodging

$$–$$$ 🏨 **Grand Hotel Yazıcı.** This slant-roof, seven-story hotel is probably the most luxurious of the resorts, with the most facilities. The rooms are pleasant, the lobby huge and showy. Your lasting impressions will probably involve acres of marble and the boisterous noise from the hotel's Greek taverna. ⊠ *Oteller Mevkii,* ☎ *224/285–2050,* ℻ *224/285–2048. 162 rooms with bath. Restaurant, bar, café, pool, sauna, 2 tennis courts, basketball, exercise room, dance club. MC, V.*

$$–$$$ 🏨 **Otel Beceren.** This Turkish version of an alpine ski lodge gets the nod for service, and its chalet decor certainly makes sense in the area. The hotel is not as well equipped as the Yazıcı, however. ⊠ *Oteller Mevkii,* ☎ *224/285–2111,* ℻ *224/285–2119. 80 rooms with bath. Restaurant, bar. No credit cards.*

$$ 🏨 **Büyük Otel.** The Büyük was the first lodge on the mountain when it was built 30 or so years ago, and despite its small rooms it remains popular. If your taste runs to the more old-fashioned, you'll prefer this low-slung property to its modern neighbors. ⊠ *Oteller Mevkii,* ☎

224/285–2319, FAX 224/285–2318. *98 rooms with bath. Restaurant, bar, outdoor pool, dance club. V.*

Nightlife
The **Büyük Otel** and **Grand Hotel Yazıcı** (☞ Dining and Lodging, *above*) have lively discos. The settings are far from flashy, but there are usually plenty of people out for fun.

Outdoor Activities and Sports
Uludağ is Turkey's largest ski resort. It has 30 intermediate and beginner trails, with five chairlifts and six T-bars. There are ski-rental shops at the base of the mountain. Prime season is January–April, and the resort is packed on weekends.

THE SOUTHERN MARMARA REGION A TO Z

Arriving and Departing

By Boat
Sea buses and express ferries operate daily between Istanbul's Kabataş docks and Yalova. A sea bus from Kabataş costs only about $4 and takes just under an hour; the express ferry costs about $2 and takes two hours. Sea buses also travel to Yalova from Kartal and Bostancı docks on the Asian side, but Kartal is difficult and time-consuming to reach by public transportation. There is a car ferry from Darıca to Yalova that also accepts passengers, although the dock isn't served by public transportation.

By Bus
Several buses daily make the trip from Istanbul's terminal at Esenler to Yalova and Bursa. The journey takes about four hours to Yalova and an extra hour on to Bursa, including the ferry trip from Darıca to Yalova. By bus, the trip costs about $3.50. A better option is to take the sea bus to Yalova. Near the sea bus quay in Yalova are buses to Bursa and minibuses to İznik.

By Car
From Istanbul take dreary Route 100, lined with factories and slowed by heavy truck traffic headed for Ankara. At İzmit take Route 130 to Yalova, a small transportation center east of Termal; Route 575 connects Yalova and Bursa. Alternatively, take the TEM toll road (E80) as far as İzmit, before linking up with Route 130 to Yalova.

Better still, take Route 100 only as far as the car ferry from Darıca, 45 km (28 mi) east of Üsküdar on the Asian side of Istanbul, to Yalova. The ferry trip costs about $10 one way, but lops 140 km (87 mi) off the journey. From Bursa, Route 200 runs west toward Çanakkale and the Aegean, east toward Ankara. There are often huge lines for ferries from Darıca at the beginning and end of local religious holidays, and there may be a wait of up to an hour on summer weekends as the ferries become crowded leaving Darıca on Friday evenings and leaving Yalova on Sunday evenings.

By Plane
AIRPORTS AND AIRLINES
Sönmez Holding Hava Yolları (☎ 212/663–0671), a domestic airline, operates two flights daily Monday–Saturday from Istanbul to Bursa. The trip takes roughly 20 minutes. You can take a shuttle bus or taxi into the city.

Getting Around

By Bus and Dolmuş

Just off the sea-bus quay in Yalova you will find minibuses headed for İznik and Bursa, both 90 minutes and a $2 bus fare away. Make sure not to mistake the İznik bus for those headed for İzmit. Dolmuşes (shared taxis) also wait off the docks; they cost a bit more than the bus and offer comparable comfort and speed. Between Bursa and İznik, service is by bus (about $2) and dolmuş ($2–$5).

To get from Yalova to Termal, walk from the ferry dock straight ahead to the traffic circle with the big statue of Atatürk, turn right, and walk one block. Bus 4 (marked TAŞKÖPRÜ–TERMAL) departs from here; the fare is about 50¢ for the 20-minute ride. Minibuses are more frequent but cost slightly more. The telephone number for the Bursa bus station is 224/254–9330.

By Car

From Yalova, Termal is 12 km (7½ mi) west via the road marked ÇI-NARCIK; Bursa is 60 km (37 mi) south via Route 575; İznik is 62 km (38 mi) southeast (via Route 575 south and Route 150, which loops around İznik Lake).

Contacts and Resources

Emergencies

Police (☎ 155).

Guided Tours

Yöntur Turizm (✉ İnönü Cad., Hüzmen Plaza Çarsısı 20 B 13, Bursa, ☎ 224/220–9132) arranges tours of Bursa and İznik.

Visitor Information

Bursa: (✉ Ulu Cami Park, Atatürk Cad. 1, ☎ 224/223–8307 and 224/223–8308). **İznik:** (✉ Belediye Ishanı, 2nd Floor, Kılıçaslan Cad., ☎ 224/757–1933). **Termal:** (☎ 226/675–7400).

4 The Aegean Coast

Along the turquoise Aegean Coast are long stretches of sandy beaches and pine-clad hills punctuated by old port villages—Foça, Çeşme, Kuşadası, Bodrum—some reincarnated as modern resorts. Reconstructed Greek and Roman cities can be found here, including the 3,000-year-old ruins of Troy, made famous by the poet Homer; Pergamum on its windswept hilltop; and the magnificent temples, colonnaded streets, and theater at Ephesus.

N THE 2ND CENTURY **AD,** the Greek travel writer Pausanias wrote glowingly of the Aegean Coast, lauding its climate and magnificent buildings. Not all the wonders Pausanias mentioned are visible today, but enough are left to give you a good idea of what life was like when this part of the world could fairly have been called the center of the universe.

Updated by
Gareth Jenkins

Pleasures and Pastimes

Beaches

Alluring white-sand beaches ("plajlar" in Turkish) are among the Aegean Coast's big draws. The most notable are the ones at Akçay (on the Gulf of Edremit); Sarmısaklı, outside Ayvalık; those along Akburun (the White Cape) and Ilıca, 5 km (3 mi) south and north of Çeşme, respectively; deserted Gümüssu, down the hill from the ancient city of Colophon; and the long strand at Pamucak, 2 km (1 mi) west of Selçuk. The beach within Bodrum proper is not one of the reasons people flock to the town. You'll find better in the outlying villages on the peninsula—Torba, backed by a big holiday village and casino; Türkbükü, quiet and family-oriented; Turgutreis, more of a scene; Akyarlar, which is rarely crowded; Ortakent, backed by old wooden town houses; Bitez, on a small bay; Gümbet, popular for windsurfing and diving; and Gümüşük, rimming a perfect bay with the half-submerged ruins of ancient Mindos. At all these, the water is clear and outdoor restaurants abound; all are easy to reach from Bodrum by minibus or *dolmuş* (shared taxi). Sedir Island, in the Gökova Gulf, is delightful when not overrun with day-trippers.

Cruises

One of the most enjoyable ways to see the coast is from the water. Bodrum is the main harbor for chartering a yacht, either with crew or bare. You can take a one- or two-week blue-voyage cruise—as the locals call almost every boat trip in the area. Many of these are on *gulets,* converted wooden fishing craft with full crew. Alternatively, you can arrange a cruise on the spot and do your own negotiating at the docks and save up to 25%, depending on the season.

Dining

Eating along the Aegean Coast is a pleasure, especially if you like seafood. The main course is often whatever was caught that day, though there are always beef and lamb kebabs. Regional specialties generally begin with the sea—mussels stuffed with rice, pine nuts, and currants (one of the many stuffed dishes that fall under the heading of dolma); *ahtapot salatası,* a cold octopus salad, sometimes with shrimps thrown in, tossed in olive oil, vinegar, and parsley; and grilled fish, including *palamut* (baby tuna), *lüfer* (bluefish), *levrek* (sea bass), and *kalkan* (turbot). Your standard eatery might have sturdy wood tables and chairs, paper napkins on the tables, and maybe a fishnet draped on the wall, but especially in the resort towns you'll find classier restaurants with crystal and linens. Because the Aegean is the most heavily visited region of the country, prices are higher than in the interior or on the Mediterranean but are still reasonable. For a chart that explains the cost of meals at restaurants in this chapter, *see* Dining and Lodging Price Categories at the front of this book.

Diving and Snorkeling

The warm, placid bays along the coast are ideal for snorkeling, and many of the big beach resorts have gear. However, Turkish authorities frown on exploring near archaeological ruins without a permit. To obtain permits, contact the local tourist information office (☞ The Aegean Coast A to Z, *below*). Specialized three-night blue-voyage trips are available for scuba divers and snorkelers.

Lodging

If you want something fancy and upscale, you'll have to stay in İzmir or Bodrum. Elsewhere, accommodations are much more modest. Expect clean, simply furnished rooms, with low wooden beds, industrial carpeting or Turkish rugs, and maybe a print on the wall. As many hotels are near the water, don't forget to ask for a room with a view—you'll pay little or sometimes nothing extra. For a chart that explains room rates for the accommodations listed in this chapter, *see* Dining and Lodging Price Categories at the front of this book.

Exploring the Aegean Coast

The Aegean Coast can be divided into three main regions: the northern coast from Çanakkale to the northern outskirts of İzmir; the city of İzmir itself; and the southern coast down to Bodrum, including a detour inland to the ruins at Aphrodisias and the natural hot springs of Pamukkale.

Great Itineraries

The distances and wealth of sights of interest mean that you should allow eight to 10 days to explore the region thoroughly. If you are pressed for time it is best to head straight for İzmir and use it as a base from which to take in some of the main sights nearby.

IF YOU HAVE 4 DAYS

Numbers in the text correspond to numbers in the margin and on the Aegean Coast, İzmir, and Ephesus and Selçuk maps.

Take an early-morning flight from Istanbul to **İzmir** ⑫–⑱. Head by bus or rental car to explore **Ephesus** ㉑ and ⚏ **Selçuk** ㉒. On the second day visit the ruins of **Priene** ㉗, **Miletus** ㉘, and **Didyma** ㉙ before looping back to ⚏ **Kuşadası** ㉖. On the third day move on to ⚏ **Pamukkale** ㉓, stopping off at **Aphrodisias** ㉔ on the way. Early the next day, soak in one of Pamukkale's hot springs and visit **Hierapolis** before returning to İzmir, where, if you have time, you can stroll the city's waterfront promenade, the **Kordonboyu** ⑰.

IF YOU HAVE 10 DAYS

Arrive by car, bus, or ferry from Istanbul, book into a hotel in ⚏ **Çanakkale** ①, and tour the Army and Navy Museum if time permits. On day two, take the ferry back across the Dardanelles to the battlefields of **Gallipoli** ②. Early on day three stop briefly at the ruins of **Troy** ③ and the **Apollo Smintheon** ⑤ on the way to **Assos** ⑦, where you'll spend the bulk of the day exploring the ruins. Overnight in ⚏ **Behramkale,** near Assos. The next morning head south along the coast, stopping for lunch in **Ayvalık** ⑧ and taking a detour to the hilltop ruins of **Pergamum** ⑩ before continuing on to ⚏ **Foça** ⑪ or ⚏ **İzmir** ⑫–⑱. If you stay in İzmir, be sure to stroll the **Kordonboyu** ⑰, the city's waterfront promenade. On day five visit **Ephesus** ㉑ and ⚏ **Selçuk** ㉒—the Ephesus Museum in Selçuk is definitely worth a stop. Swim and catch the sunset at deserted Gümüssu, down the hill from the ancient city of Colophon on the way to ⚏ **Kuşadası** ㉖.

On the following morning visit the ruins of **Priene** ㉗, **Miletus** ㉘, and **Didyma** ㉙. Return to Kuşadası. On day seven head for ⚏ **Pamukkale** ㉓ stopping off at **Aphrodisias** ㉔ on the way. Early the next day, soak in one of Pamukkale's hot springs and visit **Hierapolis** before moving on to ⚏ **Çeşme** ⑲, where you can either tour the nearby Genoese castle

The Aegean Coast

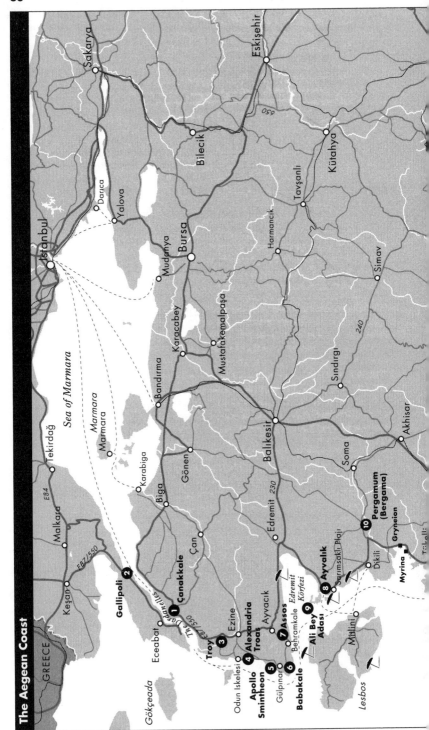

GREECE

Sea of Marmara

Marmara
Marmara

Istanbul

Sakarya

Eskişehir

Darıca

Yalova

Bilecik

Kütahya

Tekirdağ

Mudanya

Bursa

Tavşanlı

Karacabey

Mustafakemalpaşa

Harmancık

Simav

Malkara

Bandırma

Gönen

Balıkesir

Sındırgı

Keşan

Karabiga

Biga

Çan

Soma

Akhisar

Gökçeada

Eceabat

Çanakkale

Edremit

Pergamum
(Bergama)

Gallipoli

The Dardanelles

Ezine

Ayvacık

Edremit
Körfezi

Ayvalık

Sarımsaklı Plajı

Dikili

Gryneion

Odun İskelesi

Troy

Alexandria
Troas

Assos

Behramkale

Ali Bey
Adası

Apollo
Smintheon

Gülpınar

Babakale

Myrina

Mtilini

Lesbos

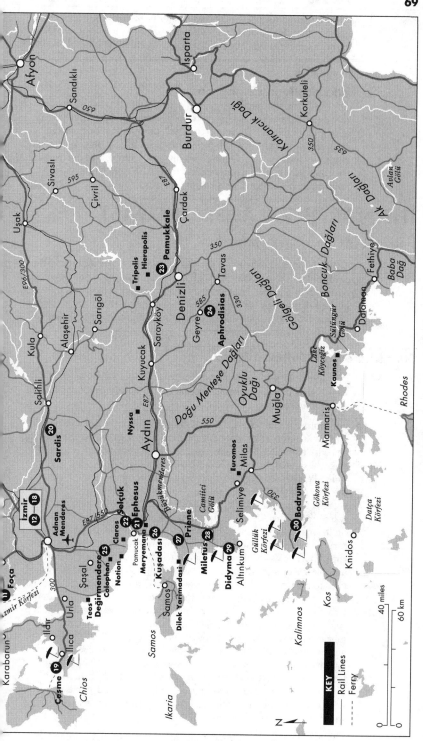

or hang out on the beaches at **Akburun** or **Ilıca.** Spend day nine and as much of day 10 as you can along the beach. If you have a rental car, you can drop it off in İzmir and return to Istanbul by plane. If you've been taking the bus, you might consider taking the ferry back to Istanbul from İzmir.

When to Tour the Aegean

The best time to tour the Aegean is probably in May when the countryside is still swathed in spring flowers and before the more popular tourist destinations become too crowded. Bodrum in particular can become very hot and crowded during July and August. But crowds can also bring their benefits. During high summer several of the towns along the coast host open-air concerts and plays, the most famous of which are held in the old Greek theater at Ephesus.

THE NORTHERN AEGEAN COAST
From Gallipoli to İzmir

This tour starts at the tip of the Çanakkale peninsula and the battlefields of Gallipoli, passing through legendary Troy. A detour along one of Turkey's grandest back-country drives ends at the clifftop ruins of ancient Pergamum. Back on the main road south is İzmir. You will need at least two overnights to cover the ground comfortably, though you could easily spend a whole week.

Çanakkale and Gallipoli

320 km (200 mi) southwest of Istanbul, E80 to Tekirdağ, E84 to Keşan, and E87 to Eceabat, from where an hourly ferryboat crosses the Dardanelles to Çanakkale.

❶ For centuries, **Çanakkale** has been the guardian of the Dardanelles, the narrow straits that separate Europe from Asia and connect the Aegean Sea with the Sea of Marmara. This strategic point has been fought over since the days of the Trojan War. En route to Greece, the invading armies of the Persian conqueror Xerxes used a bridge made of boats to cross the straits in 480 BC; the Spartans crushed the Athenians here in 404 BC, effectively ending the Peloponnesian War. A century later, the straits were crossed by Alexander the Great (356–323 BC, ruled 336–323) on his march from Macedonia to conquer Asia, and, in the 14th century, provided the nascent Ottoman Empire with its first access to Europe. During World War I, Britain (including soldiers from Australia and New Zealand, which were then still British colonies) and France tried to breach Çanakkale's defenses in the Gallipoli campaign, devised by the young Winston Churchill, then Lord of the Admiralty. The goal was to capture Istanbul and control the entire waterway from the Aegean to the Black Sea and open up a supply channel to Russia. After nine months and bloody fighting that left more than 50,000 Allied and an unknown number of Turks dead, the Allies admitted defeat and evacuated their forces, beaten by the superior strategy of Lieutenant-Colonel Mustafa Kemal—the man who would later be called Atatürk. Nowadays, Çanakkale is an agricultural center and garrison town with drab, utilitarian architecture and few frills, but it serves as the gateway to historic Gallipoli.

The **Askeri Ve Deniz Müzesi** (Army and Navy Museum) occupies the imposing Çanak Kale (Fortress of Çanak), built in the 15th century under the aegis of Mehmet the Conqueror. Inside the high, sturdy, gray walls, much weaponry is on display, including dozens of cannons, ancient and modern. But the real reason to come here is for the sweeping view of the mouth of the Dardanelles and the Aegean. ⊠ *Waterfront, 3 blocks south of ferry dock.* ☎ *Free.* ☉ *Museum Tues.–Thurs. and Sat.–Sun. 9–noon and 1:30–5; fortress grounds daily until 10.*

② **Gallipoli** lies to the north of the Dardanelles. Thirty-one beautifully tended military cemeteries of the Allied dead from World War I line the Gallipoli battlefields. The major battles were in two sections—along the coast between Kabatepe and Suvla Bay, and at Cape Helles.

If you don't have a car, either hire a taxi for the day (about $20) or sign up for the half-day excursion to Gallipoli from **Troy-Anzac Tours** (⊠ İskele Meyd., south side near clock tower, Çanakkale, ☎ 286/217–5849 or 286/217–5847, ℻ 286/217-0196; about $15 per head, including breakfast). The ferry from Eceabat leaves from the main square.

From where the ferry from Eceabat lands, it's a 20-minute drive east via the single road skirting the coast. A major forest fire in 1994 destroyed many of the region's trees. Start with the small but poignant exhibit of photographs at Kabatepe. There are several cemeteries here,
★ all with long, mesmerizing rows of austere white crosses. The **Anzac Memorial at Lone Pine Cemetery** bears the names of the Australian and New Zealand troops killed during the battle.

Farther along the same road is the French cemetery and the Turkish trenches where Atatürk's men dug themselves in. You can also look down on Sulva Bay as the Turkish defenders did and imagine the coming onslaught. At Cape Helles, there is a massive, four-pillared memorial to Turkey's war dead. No one knows how many there were; estimates vary from 60,000 to 250,000. When returning on the ferry to Çanakkale, look for the memorials to the campaign carved into the cliffs on the European side. The large one at Kilitbahir reads: "Stop, O passerby. This earth you tread unawares is where an age was lost. Bow and listen, for this quiet place is where the heart of a nation throbs."

Dining and Lodging

$–$$ ✕ **Sehir Restaurant.** This waterside eatery has spacious indoor seating dominated by a painting of the siege of Troy, wooden horse and all, though you might prefer the terrace, out front, if it's not windy. Try the octopus salad followed by a grilled version of whatever looks freshest. Top it off with a sample of the local dessert, *höşmerim* (a pastry made with semolina and cheese). ⊠ *Yalı Cad. 24,* ☎ *286/217–1070. No credit cards.*

$ ✕ **Trakya Restaurant.** Run by six brothers who prepare the food daily, this popular restaurant has three branches in the main square. The oldest branch is where you'll find kebabs, moussaka, and the ever-present *kuru fasulye and pilav* (beans and rice). The two other locations specialize in doner kebabs (meat roasted on a spit) and grilled meats. Neither the landlocked setting nor the decor is remarkable, but the food is worth the trip. ⊠ *Cumhuriyet Meyd. 32,* ☎ *286/217–3152. No credit cards.*

$ ✕ **Yalova Liman.** The menu at this waterfront restaurant with white starched tablecloths includes appetizers and grilled fish or meat. Ask the chef which fish is in season and order it grilled or fried. The best part of eating here is the evocative setting of the Dardanelles and the hum of locals discussing the latest soccer match. ⊠ *Gümrük Sok. 7,* ☎ *286/217–1045. MC, V.*

$$ ▦ **Akol.** In this modern hotel on the Çanakkale waterfront, the lobby is bright, full of cool white marble and brass fixtures. The rooms resemble the better roadside motels in the United States, complete with green carpeting, wooden café table and chairs, and TV on the low wooden dresser. But if you've been staying in guest houses, what you will appreciate most is the good water pressure in the showers. Ask for a room with a terrace overlooking the Dardanelles; you'll be able to see the memorials to World Wars I and II in the distance. ⊠ *Kordonboyu,* ☎ *286/217–9456,* ℻ *286/217–2897. 137 rooms with bath. Restaurant, bar, pool. AE, MC, V.*

$$ 🏨 **Grand Truva Oteli.** This establishment is a training school for aspiring young hotel professionals, and the students in charge are solicitous, only partly because their grades depend on it. The older section has views of the Dardanelles; the modern section in back, which lacks the views, is spiffier. The location near Çanakkale's center makes the hotel an excellent base for sightseeing. ⊠ *Kayserili Ahmet Paşa Cad., Yalıboyu,* ☎ *286/217–1024,* ℻ *286/217–0903. 69 rooms with bath. Restaurant, bar. MC, V.*

$ 🏨 **Hotel Bakır.** This small hotel near the clock tower in Çanakkale is acceptable if you're on a tight budget. The accommodations are unexceptional, but some rooms have views and the prices are low. Request a room overlooking the water when booking. ⊠ *Rıhtım Cad. 12,* ☎ *286/217–2908,* ℻ *286/217–4090. 35 rooms with bath. Restaurant, bar. MC, V.*

$ 🏨 **Tusan Güzelyalı.** A pine forest on the beach at Intepe, 14 km (8½ mi) south of Çanakkale on the road to Troy, surrounds this popular hotel. The draw is the setting, as the two-story, stucco-and-brick structure holds the usual nondescript rooms: low wooden beds, no real decor. Be certain to reserve well in advance. ⊠ *Güzelyalı,* ☎ *286/232–8210 or 286/232–0646,* ℻ *286/232–8226. 64 rooms with bath. 2 restaurants, bar, exercise room, beach, dance club. MC, V. Closed Oct.–Feb.*

Troy

3 *32 km (20 mi) south of Çanakkale on Rte. E87.*

Troy, known as Truva to the Turks and Ilion to the Greeks, is one of the most evocative names in literature. Long thought to be the figment of the Greek poet Homer's imagination, depicted in his epic *Iliad,* the site was excavated in the 1870s by Heinrich Schliemann, a minister's son and German businessman who had struck it rich in California's gold rush. While scholars scoffed, he poured his wealth into the excavations and had the last laugh: He found the remains not only of the fabled Troy but also of nine successive civilizations, one on top of the other, dating back 5,000 years (and now known among archaeologists as Troy I–IX). Subsequent excavations during the 1930s revealed 38 additional layers of settlements. A new dig by a German team, meanwhile, has revealed the footings of a late Bronze Age wall; the find enlarges the supposed Troy by fivefold.

Still, it is Homer's Troy that fascinates most. Archaeologists believe that the Troy of the Trojan War represents the seventh layer (1300 BC–900 BC), though no one is quite certain. Schliemann found a hoard of jewels that he believed were those of the mythological King Priam, but they have more recently been dated to the much earlier Troy II (2600 BC–2300 BC). Adding to the controversy that surrounded his discoveries even then, Schliemann smuggled the jewels out of the country and his wife was seen wearing them at fashionable social events. Schliemann later donated them to Berlin's Pergamonmuseum; they disappeared during World War II. They reappeared in 1993, when Moscow announced that their State Pushkin Museum of Fine Arts housed the lost "treasure of Priam," which had disappeared during the Red Army's sack of Berlin. Although Germany, Greece, and Turkey all have pressed claims to the treasure, recent custom dictates that archaeological finds belong to the country in which they were originally found.

As Homer's story was written 500 years after the war—generally believed to have taken place around 1250 BC—it is hard to say how much of it is history and how much is invention. Nonetheless, it makes for a romantic tale. Paris, the son of King Priam, abducted the beautiful Helen, wife of King Menelaus of Sparta, and fled with her to Troy. Menelaus enlisted the aid of his brother, King Agamemnon, and launched a thousand ships to get her back. His siege lasted 10 years and involved such ancient notables as Achilles, Hector, and the crafty Odysseus, King of Ithaca. It was Odysseus who ended the war, after ordering a huge wooden horse to be built. When it was completed, the Greeks retreated to their ships and pretended to sail away. The Trojans hauled the trophy into their walled city and celebrated their victory. Under cover of dark, the Greek ships returned, and the attackers at last gained entry to Troy, after soldiers hidden inside the horse crept out and opened the city's gates. Hence the saying "Beware of Greeks bearing gifts."

What you will see today depends on your imagination. Some find the site highly suggestive, with its remnants of massive, rough-hewn walls, paved chariot ramp, and strategic view over the coastal plains to the sea. Others consider it an unimpressive row of trenches with piles of earth and stone. Considering Troy's fame (and the difficulties involved in conquering it), the city is surprisingly small. The best-preserved features are from the Roman city, with its *bouleuterion* (council chamber), the site's most complete structure, and small theater. An exhibit space has little to see (the impressive artworks are in Istanbul and Ankara); a site plan shows the general layout and marks the beginning of a signposted path leading to key features from several historic civilizations. Labeling is cursory, so to appreciate Troy's significance fully, it's best to come prepared with a detailed history like scholar George Bean's *Aegean Turkey* (W. W. Norton, 1978) or to take a guided tour. English-speaking guides may or may not be available at the site; if you don't want to take your chances, arrange a tour in advance with a travel agent. As for the oft-debated horse, well, he's there, a giant wooden fellow stuck out near the parking area, duly entertaining to children, who climb up inside for a look around. ⊠ *Follow signs from Rte. E87. No phone.* 🖃 *$2.50.* ⊗ *Daily 8–7.*

Alexandria Troas

❹ *32 km (20 mi) from Troy on Rte. E87.*

Alexandria Troas was built at the behest of Alexander the Great in approximately 330 BC. It became a wealthy commercial center and the region's main port. The city, called at one point Antigonia, surpassed Troy in its control over the traffic between the Aegean and the Sea of Marmara and was even considered as a capital for the Roman and Byzantine empires. The seaside location that won it prosperity also invited plundering by raiders, which led to its demise. Saint Paul visited twice on missionary journeys in the middle of the 1st century AD, proceeding by land to Assos at the end of the second trip. In the 16th and 17th centuries, when the city was called Eski Stamboul (Old Istanbul), Ottoman architects had stones hauled from here to Istanbul for use in the building of imperial mosques, the Blue Mosque in particular. Visit today not so much to see the scanty remnants of the city's monumental baths and its aqueduct as for the setting, tucked away in a deserted stretch of wilderness. Shrubs and weeds cover the pottery-strewn ruins, which have patches of cultivated land between them. You can often have it all to yourself.

The Apollo Smintheon

❺ *20 km (12 mi) south of Alexandria Troas via the coast road.*

The Apollo Smintheon is, as the name suggests, a temple dedicated to the god Apollo. It dates from the 2nd century BC. Smintheus—one of the sun god's many names, meaning "killer of mice"—alludes to a problem that Teucer, the town's founder, had with mice eating his soldiers' bowstrings. The temple is just a trifle, but it has some interesting carved pillars and is surrounded by wild pomegranate trees.

Babakale

❻ *10 km (6 mi) from the Apollo Smintheon on the coast road, south from Gülpınar.*

Babakale is a minuscule, sleepy fishing village at the southern tip of the Çanakkale peninsula. No one is sure who built the 16th-century castle above the harbor, only that it was a haven for pirates until a Turkish naval officer named Mustafa Paşa routed them out in the late 18th century. Mustafa Paşa went on to build a small mosque and *hamam* (Turkish bath). Babakale is not the place to visit for monuments, which are decidedly minor, but for its wholly unspoiled flavor.

Behramkale (Assos)

20 km (12 mi) southeast of Gülpınar on coast road.

The lofty ruins of Behramkale, known in ancient times as Assos, provide a panoramic view over the Aegean. As you approach, the road forks, one route leading to the ancient village atop the hill and the other twisting precariously down to the tiny modern port (it's harrowing at night, so arrive before dark). The port is a marvel, pressed against the sheer cliff walls. There are a few small hotels, built of volcanic rock, that seem much older than they are, a fleet of fishing boats, and a small, rocky beach. The crowd at this low-key resort is an interesting mix of Turkish elite, artists, and intellectuals.

★ **❼** The ruins of **Assos,** on a site measuring about five square city blocks, lie at the top of a hill. Founded about 1000 BC by Aeolian Greeks, the city was successively ruled by Lydians, Persians, Pergamenes, Romans, and Byzantines, until Sultan Orhan Gazi (1288–1360) took it over for the Ottomans in 1330. Aristotle is said to have spent time here in the 4th century BC, and Saint Paul stopped en route to Miletus, where he visited church elders in about AD 55. The old stone village just under the ruins is unpretentious and little changed in the last century, though the carpet and trinket sellers have grown more aggressive of late. Abandon your car on one of the wider streets and make your way up the steep, cobbled lanes to the top of the acropolis, where you will be rewarded with a sensational view of the coastline and, in the distance, the Greek island of Lesbos, whose citizens were Assos's original settlers.

At Assos are a gymnasium, theater, agora (marketplace), and, carved into the hillside below the summit of the acropolis, the site of the **Temple of Athena** (circa 530 BC), which has splendid sea views and is being reconstructed. A more modern addition is the **Murad Hüdavendigâr Mosque,** built in the late 14th century. It is very simple, a dome atop a square, with little decoration. The Greek crosses carved into the lintel over the door indicate that the Ottomans used building material from an earlier church, possibly one on the same site. Back down the slope, on the road toward the port, are a parking area for the **necropolis** and city walls stretching 3 km (2 mi). Assos was known for its sarcophagi, made of local limestone, which were shipped throughout the Greek world. Unfortunately, most of the tombs here are broken into pieces.

Dining and Lodging

$$ ✕⊞ **Assos Kervansaray.** The best-situated of the trio of Assos hotels,
★ right at the farthest edge of the harbor, the Kervansaray has an aura of antiquity, probably because of the gray lava stone of which it was built just a few years ago. The rooms are small and functional, but most have terrific views of the Aegean. The restaurant serves dressed-up versions of traditional Turkish dishes. There is a swimming pier, though the beach itself is rocky. ⊠ *Behramkale, Ayvacık,* ☎ *286/721–7093 or 286/721–7199,* ℻ *286/721–7200. 48 rooms with bath, 4 suites. Restaurant, windsurfing. AE, MC, V.*

$$ ✕⊞ **Hotel Assos.** This blocky hotel between the Kervansaray and the Behram draws a decidedly international crowd. Built in Mediterranean-style gray lava stone, it has burnished wood paneling inside and a refined Turkish restaurant that opens up to the bay in good weather. Rooms are done in the same minimalist style as those of its neighbors. ⊠ *Behramkale, Ayvacık,* ☎ *286/721–7017 or 286/721–7034,* ℻ *286/721–7249. 36 rooms with bath. Restaurant, bar. AE, MC, V.*

$$ ✕⊞ **Hotel Behram.** This is the third in the line of hotels in Assos, the first one you reach when driving into town, and the one to book if the other two are full. The rooms are tidy and simple, with whitewashed walls and Scandinavian-style furniture; not all have a view, however, so ask for one when you book. The restaurant has a cozy fireplace and stone walls, and turns out standard Turkish fare. ⊠ *Behramkale, Ayvacık,* ☎ *286/721–7016 or 286/721–7328,* ℻ *286/721–7044. 17 rooms with bath. Restaurant. AE, MC, V.*

Ayvalık

★ ❽ *131 km (81 mi) from Assos, east on coast road to Rte. E87 south.*

Ayvalık first appears in Ottoman records at the late date of 1770, when an Ottoman naval hero, Gazi Hasan Paşa, was aided by the local Greek community after his ship sank nearby. Soon after, the town was granted autonomy, perhaps as a gesture of gratitude, and the Muslim population was moved to outlying villages, leaving the Greeks to prosper in the olive oil trade. In 1803, an academy was founded following Plato's instructions, with courses in Attic Greek, physics, logic, philosophy, rhetoric, and mathematics. Nothing remains of the school today. At the close of World War I, the Greeks invaded Turkey and claimed the Aegean Coast. The Turks ousted the Greek army in 1922, and the entire Greek community of Ayvalık was deported.

This rapidly growing town holds some of the finest 19th-century Greek-style architecture in Turkey. Unlike the typical Ottoman house (tall, narrow, and built of wood, with an overhanging bay window), Greek buildings are stone, with classic triangular pediments above a square box. The best way to explore is to turn your back to the Aegean and wander the tiny side streets leading up the hill into the heart of the old residential quarter (try Talat Paşa Caddesi and Gümrük Caddesi). Several historic churches in town have been converted into mosques. St. John's is now the **Saatli Cami** (Clock Mosque). St. George's is now the **Çinarlı Cami** (Plane Tree Mosque). The **Taxiarchis Church,** a museum, displays a remarkable series of paintings on fish skin depicting the life of Christ. After wandering through town, take Talat Paşa Caddesi or Gümrük Caddesi back down the hill, cross İnönü Caddesi, and keep going (you will be on the spit of land behind the harbor) until you reach Mareşal Cakmak Caddesi (it's only a block or two past İnönü Caddesi). Amid several old buildings here you will find the 19th-century French Embassy, just behind the post office. It still carries the sign "L'Union de Paris" atop its door, a reminder of Ayvalık's importance in an earlier day.

❾ **Ali Bey Adası** (also known as Cunda Island) lies just off the coast at Ayvalık. Like Ayvalık it was once predominantly Greek, and some Greek is still spoken here. The fishing town has good seafood restaurants lining its atmospheric quay; they're noted for their grilled *çipura* (a local fish) and dishes made with octopus, served grilled, fried, or in a cold seafood salad.

The island's Greek houses are well preserved and varied, and the 19th-century **St. Nicholas Church** in the middle of town is a must-see. Though the frescoes have been defaced—the eyes of the apostles have been gouged out—there is an amusing depiction of Jonah with a whale that looks a lot like the grouper you could order for lunch. With its large cracks, caused by an earthquake in 1924, and the birds flying around its airy domes, the whole place has a ghostly air. If the church is closed, wait by the front door and someone will eventually come by to let you in.

NEED A
BREAK?
Take the main street, Atatürk Caddesi, west along the coast to reach the fine 10-km (6-mi) stretch of beach called **Sarmısaklı.** The resorts a few kilometers down provide a good place to stay overnight before tackling the ruins at Pergamum, southeast from Ayvalık.

Dining and Lodging

$$ ✕ **Canlı Balık.** This fish restaurant at the end of Ayvalık pier is a cut
★ above most other small-town dining options. It delivers excellent food in a romantic setting—with local fishing boats swaying in the water a few feet away and the Aegean stretching to the horizon. Mezes range from fried squid to mussel salad in local olive oil. Then move on to fresh, grilled local fish, perhaps *barbunya* (red mullet). No alcohol is served here (unless a disputed ban by the governor has been lifted). ⊠ *2nd bldg. north of Inönü Cad., on harbor, no phone. No credit cards.*

$$ 🏨 **Büyük Berk.** This modern hotel is on Ayvalık's best beach, about 3½ km (2 mi) from the center of town. All rooms have balconies, most looking out over the Aegean. Rooms are functional, with low wooden beds and whitewashed walls. ⊠ *Sarmısaklı Plaj,* 🕾 *266/324–1045,* 🖷 *266/324–1194. 189 rooms with bath. Restaurant, pool, tennis court, exercise room, dance club. AE, DC, MC, V.*

$$ 🏨 **Grand Hotel Temizel.** Set away from the other hotels along Sarmısaklı beach, the Temizel is a fairly plush luxury hotel, with a private beach, a casino, a diminutive Turkish spa, and an elegant lobby, all cool marble and gleaming brass. The guest rooms are also a cut above the usual, with bigger beds, wooden dressers, and minibars. Most have Aegean views. ⊠ *Sarmısaklı Plaj,* 🕾 *266/324–2000,* 🖷 *266/324–1274. 164 rooms with bath. Restaurant, bar, pool, sauna, Turkish bath, tennis court, exercise room, soccer, windsurfing, casino, dance club. AE, DC, MC, V.*

$ 🏨 **Ankara Oteli.** Another hotel with a great location on Sarmısaklı beach, just a few feet from the surf, this is the least expensive option. Although rooms are nondescript, they do have balconies; book ahead to get one facing the beach. ⊠ *Sarmısaklı Plaj,* 🕾 *266/324–1195 or 266/324–1048,* 🖷 *266/324–0022. 108 rooms with bath. Bar, café, recreation room. No credit cards. Closed Nov.–Mar.*

Pergamum (Bergama)

★ **⑩** *54 km (34 mi) from Ayvalık; take Rte. E87 south approximately 44 km (28 mi), then follow signs to Bergama.*

The windswept ruins of Pergamum, about 8 km (5 mi) from the modern city of Bergama, are among the most spectacular in Turkey. The attractions here are spread out over several square miles, so if you don't have a car, negotiate with a taxi driver in Bergama (you have to pass through the town anyway) to shuttle you from site to site—this shouldn't cost more than $10 or $20, depending on how long you plan to spend looking around. All told, you will probably want to spend half a day.

Pergamum was one of the ancient world's major powers, though its moment of glory was relatively brief. Led by a dynasty of maverick rulers, it rose to prominence during the 3rd and 2nd centuries BC. Impressed by the city's impregnable fortress, Lysimachus, one of Alexander the Great's generals, here stowed the booty he had accumulated while marching through Asia Minor. When Lysimachus was killed in 281 BC, Philetaerus (circa 343 BC–263 BC), the commander of Pergamum, claimed the fortune and holed himself up in the city. After defeating the horde of invading Gauls that had been sacking cities up and down the coast in 240 BC, the Pergamenes were celebrated throughout the Hellenic world as saviors. The dynasty established by Philetaerus, known as the Attalids, ruled from then until 133 BC, when the mad Attalus III (circa 170 BC–133 BC) died and bequeathed the entire kingdom to Rome. By a liberal interpretation of his ambiguous bequest, his domain became the Roman Province of Asia and transformed Rome's economy with its wealth.

The city was a magnificent architectural and artistic center in its heyday—especially under the rule of Eumenes II (197 BC–159 BC), who lavished his great wealth on it. He built Pergamum's famous library, which contained 200,000 books. When it rivaled the great one in Alexandria, Egypt, the Egyptians banned the sale of papyrus to the city. Pergamum responded by developing a new paper—parchment—made from animal skins instead of reeds. This *charta pergamena* was more expensive but could be used on both sides; because it was difficult to roll, it was cut into pieces and sewn together, much like today's books. Nothing remains of either collection.

The most dramatic of the remains are at the acropolis. Signs point the way to the 6-km (4-mi) road to the top, where you can park your car and buy a ticket and perhaps one of the reasonably good picture books containing site maps on sale here, then begin to explore. Broken but still mighty triple ramparts enclose the Upper Town, with its temples, palaces, private houses, and gymnasia (schools). In later Roman times, the town spread out and down to the plain, where the Byzantines subsequently settled for good.

After entering the **acropolis** through the Royal Gate, you can follow a couple of different paths. To start at the top, pick the path to the far right, which takes you past the partially restored **Temple of Trajan,** at the summit. This is the very picture of an ancient ruin, with burnished white marble pillars high above the valley of the Oç Kemer Çayi (Selinos River). On the terraces just below, you can see the scant remains of the **Temple of Athena** and the **Altar of Zeus;** once among the grandest monuments in the Greek world, the latter was excavated by German archaeologists who sent Berlin's Pergamonmuseum every stone they found, including the frieze, 400 feet long, that vividly depicted the battle of the gods against the giants. Now all that's left is the altar's flat stone foundation. The **Great Theater,** carved into the steep slope west of the terrace that holds the Temple of Athena, is another matter; it can seat some 10,000 spectators and retains its astounding acoustics. You can test them by sitting near the top and having a companion do a reading at the stage area. ☎ 232/632–6663. ⊡ *$2.* ⊙ *Apr.–Oct., daily 8:30–5:30; Nov.–Mar., daily 8:30–5.*

The **Kızıl Avlu** (Red Courtyard) in Bergama is named for the red bricks from which it is constructed. You will pass it on the road to and from the acropolis—it's right at the bottom of the hill. This was the last pagan temple constructed in Pergamum before Christianity was declared the state religion in the 4th century. At that time it was converted into a basilica dedicated to Saint John. The walls remain, but not the roof. Most interesting are the underground passages, where it is easy to imagine how concealed pagan priests supplied the voices of "spirits" in mystic ceremonies. ☎ *232/633–1096 at Archaeological Museum for information.* ⊡ *$1.* ⊙ *Apr.–Oct., daily 9–noon and 1–7; Nov.–Mar., daily 9–noon and 1–5.*

Bergama's **Arkeoloji Müzesi** (Archaeological Museum) is one of Turkey's better provincial museums. It houses a substantial collection of statues, coins, and other artifacts excavated from the ancient city. ✉ *Hükümet Cad.,* ☎ *232/633–1096.* ⊡ *$2.* ⊙ *Apr.–Oct., daily 8:30–5:30; Nov.–Mar., Tues.–Sun. 9–noon and 1–5:30.*

The **Asklepieion** is believed to be the world's first full-service health clinic. The name is a reference to Asklepios, god of medicine and recovery, whose snake and staff are now the symbol of modern medicine. In the heyday of the Pergamene Asklepieion in the 2nd century AD, patients were prescribed such treatments as fasting, colonic irrigation, and running barefoot in cold weather. The nature of the treatment was generally determined by interpretation of the patient's dreams. You enter the complex at the column-lined **Holy Road,** once the main street connecting the Asklepieion to Pergamum's acropolis. Follow it for about a city block into a small square and through the **propyleum,** the main gate to the temple precinct. Immediately to the right are the **Shrine of Artemis,** devoted to the Greek goddess of chastity, the moon, and hunting, and the **library,** a branch of the one atop Pergamum's acropolis. Patients also received therapy accompanied by music during rites held in the intimate theater, which is now used each May for performances of the Bergama Arts Festival. Nearby are pools that were used for mud and sacred water baths. A subterranean passageway leads down to the sacred cellar of the **Temple of Telesphorus,** where the devout would pray themselves into a trance and record their dreams upon waking; later, the dreams would be interpreted by a resident priest. ✉ *Follow Hükümet Cad. west to Rte. E87; near the tourist information office, follow sign pointing off to right 1½ km (1 mi),* ☎ *232/633–1096.* ⊡ *$2.50.* ⊙ *Daily 8:30–5:30.*

Dining and Lodging

$ ✕ **Bergama Restaurant.** The food at this spot, on the main street and not far from the Archaeological Museum, is basic Turkish. The kebabs are good, as is the spicy, cold eggplant salad. The interior is airy and simple; if the weather is nice, you can sit outside under the awning. ✉ *Cumhuriyet Cad. 13,* ☎ *232/632–0601. No credit cards.*

$$ 🖾 **Hotel Iskender.** Rooms at this plain-looking hotel in the center of town are comfortable and air-conditioned for the hot summers. An outdoor restaurant serves typical Turkish food. ✉ *İzmir Cad., Ilıca Önü Mev. P.K. 35,* ☎ *232/633–2123,* 🖷 *232/633–1245. 60 rooms with bath. 2 restaurants, bar. No credit cards.*

$$ 🏨 **Tusan Bergama Moteli.** If you can't get to someplace more picturesque, like Ayvalık or Foça, this serviceable, two-story motel is a good bet. The rooms are simple and well maintained. The location on the main route leading into Bergama, a short drive from town, means that it's quiet, though not terribly convenient if you don't have a car. ⊠ *İzmir Yolu, Yolaçtı Mev.,* ☎ *232/633–1938,* FAX *232/633–1938. 44 rooms with bath. Restaurant, pool. No credit cards.*

Foça

⑪ *70 km (42 mi) from Bergama, south on Rte. E87 and west on Rte. 250.*

Foça is a typical Aegean fishing village with good restaurants, a few cozy *pansiyons* (guest houses), and a big Club Med nearby. Odysseus is said to have lost six men in the straits between Scylla and Charybdis, but these islands, rather more tame today, have the best beaches in the area; you can hire a boat in the village for $10 or $20 for the ride out. If it's late in the day, or you just prefer staying in a small town instead of big-city İzmir, Foça is a good spot to stay overnight.

Dining and Lodging

$ ✗ **Restaurant Foça.** The restaurants along Foça's little harbor usually prepare an appropriately dizzying array of fresh fish. In this one, the best of a good bunch, you can have your palamut, lüfer, or levrek grilled to perfection. ⊠ *Küçükdeniz, Belediye Altı,* ☎ *232/812–1307. No credit cards.*

$$$$ 🏨 **Club Méditerranée.** This fishing village seems an unlikely spot for one of these all-inclusive vacation resorts, but the French vacation operation does a creditable job here. Red-tile-roofed bungalows are grouped into two small hamlets, one atop a hill overlooking the Aegean, the other in an olive grove. ⊠ *In Eski Foça, 12 km (7 mi) north of Foça,* ☎ *232/812–1607 or 232/812–2176,* FAX *232/812–2175; in U.S.,* ☎ *212/750–1687. 376 rooms with bath. Restaurant, bar, pool, tennis court, dive shop, windsurfing, waterskiing. AE, DC, MC, V.*

$$ 🏨 **Hanedan.** This unassuming four-story hotel in what looks like a town house is right on the harbor. Public areas are scattered with Turkish rugs and kilims; guest rooms are small and simple. ⊠ *Büyükdeniz Sahil Cad. 1,* ☎ *232/812–1515,* FAX *232/812–1609. 30 rooms with bath. Restaurant. No credit cards.*

İzmir

70 km (42 mi) from Foça, east on Rte. 250 and south on Rte. E87.

Turkey's third-largest city, population 2 million, was called Smyrna until 1923. A vital trading port, though one often ravaged by wars and earthquakes, it also had its share of glory. Many believe that Homer was born in Old Smyrna sometime around 850 BC. Alexander the Great favored the city with a citadel atop its highest hill.

The city fell into assorted hands after the Romans, starting with the Byzantines and Arabs. From 1097 on, Smyrna became a battlefield in the Crusades, passing back and forth between the forces of Islam and Christendom. Destroyed and restored successively by Byzantines and Seljuks, Smyrna was held by the Knights of Rhodes in 1402 when the Mongol raider Tamerlane came along, sacked it yet again, and slaughtered its inhabitants. Thirteen years later Sultan Mehmet I Çelebi incorporated it into the Ottoman Empire.

Toward the end of the 15th century, Jews driven from Spain settled in Smyrna, forming a lasting Sephardic community. By the 18th and 19th centuries, Smyrna had become a successful, sophisticated commercial port with an international flavor. Its business community included sizable Italian, Greek, Armenian, British, French, and Jewish contingents. This era came to an end with World War I, when Ottoman Turkey allied itself with Germany. In 1918, the Greek army, encouraged by the British and French, landed at the harbor and claimed the city. The occupation lasted until 1922, when Turkish troops under Atatürk defeated the Greek forces and forced them to evacuate. On September 9, 1922, Atatürk made a triumphant entry into the port. The joy of the local Turks was short-lived; a fire shortly thereafter blazed through the city. Fanned by the wind, it burned wooden houses like matches while hidden stores of munitions exploded.

İzmir was quickly rebuilt—and given a Turkish name. Like the name, much of the city dates from the '20s, from its wide boulevards to the office buildings and apartment houses, painted in bright white or soft pastels. This important industrial center is not particularly pretty, though it has a pleasant, palm-lined harborfront promenade and peaceful green Kültür Park at its center.

The sweeping view of the city and its harbor from the windy restored **⑫** ramparts of the **Kadifekäle** (Velvet Fortress), built by Alexander the Great, make it a good spot to orient yourself to İzmir. The name, according to romantics if not to scholars, alludes to the resemblance of the present-day citadel's walls to rubbed velvet. Rebuilt after various mishaps and enlarged and strengthened by successive conquerors, the structure looks like a childhood fantasy of a medieval castle, with solid stone blocks (some dating from Alexander's day), Byzantine cisterns, and Ottoman buttresses jutting out to support the walls.

⑬ The **Agora** at the foot of Kadifekäle hill, just off 816 Sokak (816 Street), was the Roman city's market. The present site is a large, dusty, open space surrounded by ancient columns and foundations. There are well-preserved Roman statues of Poseidon, Artemis, and Demeter in the northwest corner. To get there from Kadifekäle, exit from the fortress's main gate and take the road that descends to the left; when you see steps built into the sidewalk, turn right and go down. ⊟ $1. ⊙ *Daily 8:30–5:30.*

⑭ **Konak Square,** at the water's edge, is one of the two main squares in the city (the other, Cumhuriyet Meydanı, or Republic Square, is to the north along Atatürk Caddesi). Konak marks the start of the modern-day marketplace, a maze of tiny streets filled with shops and covered stalls. Unlike Istanbul's Grand Bazaar, İzmir's is not covered. Anafartalar Caddesi is the bazaar's principal thoroughfare, but try the smaller side streets, too, where you'll find minimarkets dedicated to musical instruments, songbirds, clothing, blankets, and many other treats. If you have a problem finding a particular market, just ask a vendor for directions. ⊙ *Mon.–Sat. 8–8.*

⑮ The **Arkeoloji Müzesi** (Archaeological Museum) contains the 2nd-century statues of Demeter and Poseidon found when the Agora was excavated, as well as an impressive collection of tombs and friezes, and the memorable, colossal statue of Roman emperor Domitian (AD 51–96, ruled 81–96). ⊠ *Cumhuriyet Bul., Bahribaba Parkı,* ☎ *232/484–8324.* ⊟ *$2.* ⊙ *Tues.–Sun. 8:30–5:30.*

⑯ The **İzmir Etnoğrafya Müzesi** (Ethnographic Museum) focuses on folk arts and daily life, housing everything from period bedrooms to a reconstruction of İzmir's first Turkish pharmacy. ⊠ *Cumhuriyet Bul., Bahribaba Parkı,* ☎ *232/484–8324.* ⊟ *$1.* ⊙ *Tues.–Sun. 8:30–5:30.*

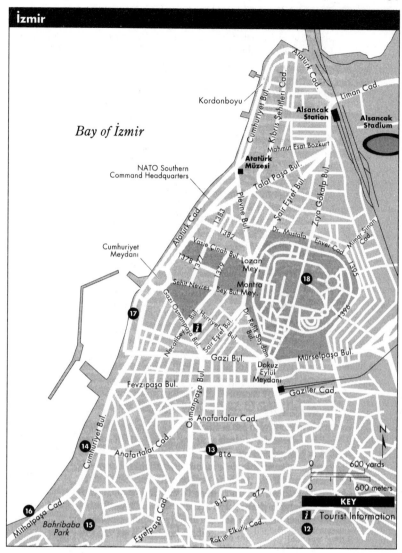

İzmir

Bay of İzmir

Kordonboyu

Alsancak Station

Alsancak Stadium

Liman Cad.

Atatürk Cad.

Cumhuriyet Bul.

Kıbrıs Şehitleri Cad.

Mahmut Esat Bozkurt

NATO Southern Command Headquarters

Atatürk Müzesi

Talat Paşa Bul.

Şair Eşref Bul.

Ziya Gökalp Bul.

Mimar Sinan Cad.

Plevne Bul.

Dr. Mustafa

Enver Cad.

1383

1382

Cumhuriyet Meydanı

Vasıf Cinah Bul.

1378 1377

1379

Lozan Mey.

Montra Mey.

Şehit Nevres Bey Bul.

1395

1396

Atatürk Cad.

17

18

Gazi Osmanpaşa Bul.

Necatibey Bul.

Hürriyet Bul.

Şair Eşref Bul.

Dr. Refik Saydam Bul.

i

Gazi Bul.

Dokuz Eylül Meydanı

Mürselpaşa Bul.

Fevzipaşa Bul.

Osmanpaşa Bul.

Gazler Cad.

Anafartalar Cad.

N

Cumhuriyet Bul.

14

Anafartalar Cad.

13

816

| 0 | 600 yards |
| 0 | 600 meters |

KEY

i Tourist Information

810

877

12

16

Mithatpaşa Cad.

Bahribaba Park

15

Eşrefpaşa Cad.

Rakım Elkutlu Cad.

⑰ The **Kordonboyu** (Cordon), the waterfront promenade, is the most fashionable section of town. It starts at the museum complex in Bahribaba Parkı and stretches north along the busy harbor, past the 19th-century Ottoman **Saat Kulesi** (Clock Tower), the **NATO Southern Command Headquarters,** and the small **Atatürk Müzesi** (Atatürk Museum; ✉ Atatürk Cad., Alsancak 248, ☎ 232/421–7026). The museum, housed in a pale-yellow Levantine building, is open Tuesday–Sunday 8:30–noon and 1–5:30. There are several good seafood restaurants along this strip, all with a few tables outside, overlooking the water.

⑱ **Kültür Park** (Culture Park), İzmir's central park, has gardens, a zoo, amusement rides, and nightclubs. It is the site of a major industrial fair from late August to late September. ✉ *East of Lozan and Montrö Meyds.*

Dining and Lodging

$$ ✗ **Altınkapı.** Probably the best of the many kebab houses on 1444 Sokak, this has the distinction of being the only one to have received the Turkish Standards Institute seal of approval. Its specialties include an excellent İnegöl *köfte* (ground, grilled lamb patties) and a fine selection of *pide* (Turkish pizza). ✉ *1444 Sok. 9, Alsancak,* ☎ *232/422–5687. MC, V.*

$$ ✗ **Deniz.** Befitting its bayside location, the main event in this attractive spot on the ground floor of the İzmir Palas hotel is the seafood. Options range from sole to sea bass, mussels to mullet. *Kılıç şiş* (grilled swordfish kebab) is a house specialty. ✉ *Atatürk Cad. 188, Alsancak,* ☎ *232/422–0601. DC, MC, V.*

$$ ✗ **Ömür Balık Lokantası.** Open only at lunchtime, this pleasant restaurant in a restored Ottoman building serves all sorts of seafood, including fresh fish, octopus, and shrimp. ✉ *902 Sok. 44, Hisarönü,* ☎ *232/425–6839. No credit cards.*

$ ✗ **Ilif Iskender.** Everybody in İzmir has a favorite kebab place, and this one is on a lot of lists. It's a lively sidewalk café in the center of the city, a block in from the water, with tasty doner kebabs and budget-wise prices. ✉ *Cumhuriyet Bul. 194, no phone. No credit cards.*

$$$$ 🏨 **İzmir Hilton.** At 34 stories, the Hilton is one of the tallest buildings on the Aegean coast. Striking and modern, it looms over the center of the city. From the 10-story atrium to the elegant rooftop restaurant, the public spaces are suitably grand. Guest rooms are plush, with thick floral comforters and matching drapes. About the only complaint that can be leveled is that there is nothing particularly Turkish about the place. ✉ *Gazi Osman Paşa Bul. 7,* ☎ *232/441–6060,* 🖷 *232/441–2277. 381 rooms with bath. 4 restaurants, 2 bars, pool, 2 tennis courts, health club, squash, shops, casino, business services. AE, DC, MC, V.*

$$$ 🏨 **Pullman Etap Konak.** Of İzmir's two hotels in France's Pullman chain, this is the better situated—right on the water. There's lots of cool marble and greenery, and the guest rooms have full-size beds, plush carpeting, and big windows with views. The city's museums are within easy walking distance. ✉ *Mithatpasa Cad. 128,* ☎ *232/489–1500,* 🖷 *232/489–1709. 76 rooms with bath. Restaurant, bar, meeting room. AE, MC, V.*

$$ 🏨 **Hotel Kilim.** Rooms here are comfortable, and some have bay views. Those close to the street can be noisy, so ask for one higher up. The hotel's nondescript restaurant serves seafood and traditional Turkish lamb dishes—in good weather at sidewalk tables with harbor views. ✉ *Kazim Dirik Cad. 1,* ☎ *232/484–5340,* 🖷 *232/489–5070. 90 rooms with bath. Restaurant, bar. MC, V.*

$$ ⚏ **Karaca Otel.** This mid-rise hotel is on a little side street; some rooms have a view of the gardens and some rooms have terraces. The decor is contemporary, with wall-to-wall carpeting and some Turkish touches. The location is convenient, and the rates are lower than at larger, neighboring properties. ⊠ *1379 Sok. 55, at Necatibey and Gazi Osmanpaşa Buls.,* ☎ *232/489–1940,* ⅁⅃⅂ *232/483–1498. 73 rooms with bath. Restaurant, bar, beauty salon, meeting room. AE, MC, V.*

$–$$ ⚏ **Kısmet.** The guest rooms and public spaces at the friendly, comfortable Kısmet are tastefully decorated, but since it doesn't have a great view and is an older property, you'll pay less. The side-street location makes it quieter than places on the main drag. ⊠ *1377 Sok. 9,* ☎ *232/463–3850,* ⅁⅃⅂ *232/421–4856. 68 rooms with bath. Restaurant. AE, DC, MC, V.*

$ ⚏ **Hotel Baylan.** This four-story property with a shiny marble facade is a good value. Its bright and pleasant rooms, on the small side, have unprepossessing Scandinavian-style furniture. ⊠ *Anafartalar Cad., Basmane, 1299 Sok. 8,* ☎ *232/483–1426,* ⅁⅃⅂ *232/483–3844. 33 rooms with bath. Restaurant, bar. No credit cards.*

Nightlife

Two open-air restaurant-nightclubs, the **Kubana** (☎ 232/425–4773) and the **Mogambo** (☎ 232/425–5488), are in Kültür Park. At the Boğaziçi Turistik İşletmeleri (☎ 232/368–8082), in the Karsiyaka ferry terminal, Turkish musicians perform for diners. **Charlie's Cocktail Bar** (⊠ 1386 Sok. 8/B, Alsancak, ☎ 232/421–4981) is popular with the expatriate crowd. The **Tempels Club Disco Bar** (⊠ Atatürk Cad. 390, ☎ 232/421–4981) attracts a young crowd. If you're into bar-hopping, 1469 Sokak is known as the bar strip and the favorite place to be seen is the **Punta Bar** (☎ 232/463–1504).

THE SOUTHERN AEGEAN COAST
Ephesus, Pamukkale, Priene, and Bodrum

Çeşme

⑲ *81 km (50 mi) west of İzmir on Rte. 300.*

Çeşme's honey-color Genoese castle and clean beaches have made it a popular resort. But life has not always been as peaceful. Two historic sea battles were fought off Çeşme's coast. The first, in 190 BC, ended with the defeat of Hannibal, the famed general of Carthage, at the hands of the Romans. Nearly 2,000 years later, in 1770, the Russian fleet utterly destroyed the Ottoman navy, a blow from which the empire never recovered. Things are quieter now and the only boats you will see today are yachts and pleasure craft tied up along the quay that curves around Çeşme Bay.

The 14th-century **Genoese castle** is more picturesque than of great architectural interest, its stone walls given over to basking lizards and its keep often deep in wildflowers. The castle's museum displays weaponry from the glory days of the Ottoman Empire. ⊡ *$2.* ⊙ *Daily 8:30–11:45 and 1–5:15.*

NEED A
BREAK?

Beaches are the main event in Çeşme. About 5 km (3 mi) south of town, out along Akburun (White Cape), are several nice stretches, including Pirlanta, as well as numerous unnamed coves. The same distance north of town is the popular Ilıca beach.

Dining and Lodging

$$ ✗ Körfez. With its chic terrace, upbeat pizza section, and indoor disco, this popular waterfront restaurant fills with vacationers in summer. At white-linen-covered tables on the terrace you can sample appetizers and order grilled or stewed fish—or allow the chef to send you his specialty, *sütlü balık* (baked fish in a special sauce topped with mushrooms and cheese). ⊠ *Yalı Cad. 12,* ☎ *232/712–6718 or 232/712–0901. Reservations essential in summer. V.*

$ ✗ Sahil. A waterfront eatery across from the Ertan Hotel, Sahil serves fresh, tasty appetizers like eggplant salad and typical Turkish dishes such as lamb kebabs and grilled fish. Seating is indoors or outdoors on a terrace, with red tablecloths. For scenery, you have the pretty but unremarkable bay of Çeşme as well as vacationers out for a promenade. ⊠ *Cumhuriyet Meyd. 12,* ☎ *232/712–8294. Reservations essential in summer. No credit cards.*

$ ✗ Sevim Café. Despite its location on an awkward corner at the edge of the main square by the sea, this establishment is charming and serves its dishes in a style that you won't find elsewhere. The owner, Ms. Zehra, hand-prepares the main dish for which the café is famous: *mantı* (meat-filled raviolis topped with garlicky yogurt and served with a speckle of hot pepper and saffron). The chef, whose expertise is enhanced by international experience, also juggles meats on the grill, and arranges beautiful salads on the side. Come early for a good seat. ⊠ *Hal Binası 5, opposite Kervansaray, no phone. No credit cards.*

$$$ ✗⊡ Kervansaray. Built in 1528 during the reign of Süleyman the
★ Magnificent, this old property in the town center, next to Çeşme's medieval castle, is largely decorated in traditional Turkish style with kilims, low wooden furniture, and brass fittings. The bathrooms are tiled, motel-modern affairs. The restaurant is excellent. Good choices for lunch or dinner include lamb kebabs with yogurt, cold eggplant salad, and *börek* (deep-fried pastry shells, here filled with goat cheese). In pleasant weather, you can dine outdoors in a courtyard surrounded by the ancient stone walls of the Kervansaray. ⊠ *Kale Yanı,* ☎ *232/712–7177 or 232/712–6491,* 𝔽𝔸𝕏 *232/712–2906. 34 rooms with bath. Restaurant, bar. AE, DC, MC, V. Closed Nov.–Mar.*

$$$ ⊡ Altın Yunus Tatilköyü. The low, bright-white cuboid buildings of this
★ big resort—whose name translates as "golden dolphin"—curve along an attractive white sand beach edging a cove dotted with sailboats. The rooms are done in Mediterranean style, with lots of white and pale ocean blue. You'll find thicker carpets, bigger beds, and a more plush feel than usual for Turkey. With almost every imaginable recreational facility, the resort is a destination unto itself. ⊠ *Kalemburnu Boyalık Mev., Ilıca,* ☎ *232/723–1250,* 𝔽𝔸𝕏 *232/723–2252. 526 rooms with bath. 4 restaurants, 2 bars, 2 indoor pools, 2 outdoor pools, beauty salon, Turkish bath, 5 tennis courts, exercise room, windsurfing, boating, dance club, nightclub, playground. AE, MC, V.*

$$$ ⊡ Şifne Hotel. As much a thermal resort as a hotel, the Şifne is named for the seaside hamlet near which it is located, 11 km (6 mi) out of Çeşme. The rooms are functional rather than luxurious, although most have fine sea views. What's special is the water in two large open-air thermal pools—it's reputed to cure numerous diseases. The hotel also has its own beach. ⊠ *Şifne,* ☎ *232/717–1099. 40 rooms with baths. Restaurant, bar. No credit cards.*

$$ ⊡ Ertan Oteli. The five-story, white stucco hotel, on the water on the north side of the main square, is modern and efficient. Many rooms have views of the Aegean, as does the terrace restaurant. ⊠ *Cumhuriyet*

Meyd. 12, ☎ 232/712–6795, telex 51980. 60 rooms with bath. Restaurant, bar. MC, V.

$ ⊞ **Tani Pansiyon.** A friendly retired couple runs this very modest pansiyon. The rooms are simple, with low wooden beds, and have views of the bay through crocheted lace curtains made by the wife. Be sure to ask for a room facing the bay. Bathrooms and showers are shared, as is a lace-decked kitchen upstairs on the terrace, where breakfast is served. ⊠ Çarşı Sok. 5, Musalla Mah., ☎ 232/712–6238. 6 rooms with shared baths. No credit cards.

Sardis

⓴ 171 km (106 mi) east of Çeşme on Rte. 300 (also called E96 east of İzmir).

The ancient city of Sardis was the capital of Lydia under King Croesus (ruled 560–546 BC), who put a lot of money into building temples, the most famous of which is the Temple of Artemis. The Lydians' main claim to fame comes from their invention of minted coinage at the end of the 7th century BC. Today it is possible to see the remains of the equipment that was used to melt and shape the gold they were so skillful in extracting. In 546 BC the city came under Persian rule, when Cyrus captured Sardis but spared Croesus's life. In Byzantine times it was the site of a diocese, and in the 14th century AD it was taken by the Turks. The older city was fairly well destroyed by a major earthquake in AD 17. Most of the remains date from the Roman Empire, which held sway in the area until the 3rd century AD.

The **Temple of Artemis,** slightly bigger than Athens's Parthenon, is unfortunately not as well preserved, but reerected columns with fine Ionic capitals and the one wall still standing hint at the temple's former grandeur. The acropolis behind it offers splendid views, but the hike up and down can take two hours. ⊠ South of the village of Sartmustafa; a sign points the way down an unpaved but passable road. No phone. ☜ $1. ⊙ Daily 8:30–dusk.

Other **Sardis ruins** are across the highway from the Temple of Artemis. At the **gymnasium complex,** bathers would enter through the colonnaded palaestra (exercise hall), continue through the row of changing rooms, and end up in the enormous caldarium (hot pool). The ornate **Marble Court,** where you can see the remains of Byzantine-era shops, has been reconstructed, revealing a multistory facade with carved reliefs. The **restored synagogue** dates from the 4th century AD and has some intact mosaic pavements. ⊠ On dirt road heading north, across highway from road to Temple of Artemis (10 mins on foot, less by car). No phone. ☜ $1 for each site. ⊙ Daily 8:30–dusk.

Ephesus and Selçuk

79 km (50 mi) south of İzmir on Rte. E87.

★ **㉑** **Ephesus** is the best-preserved and probably the most evocative ancient city in the eastern Mediterranean. The Delphi oracle led the Ionian Greeks here from their original home in central Greece in the 11th century BC with this advice to Androkles, the Ionian leader: "The site of the new town will be shown . . . by a fish; follow the wild boar." According to the legend, as Androkles and his men were traveling in the vicinity of what became Ephesus, they came across some people cooking fish. Soon after, as the story goes, a fish, about to be cooked over an open fire, jumped and knocked embers into nearby brush. The fire spread, and a boar fleeing the flames was hunted down and killed at Mt. Koressos, later called Bülbül Dağ, or Mount of the Nightingale, by the Turks. And that is where the Ionians settled.

Ephesus, on the sea at the time, quickly became a powerful trading port and sacred center for the cult of Artemis. Its fame drew the attention of a series of conquerors, among them Croesus of Lydia and 6th-century BC Cyrus of Persia. After a Greek uprising against the Persians failed, Ephesus managed to stay out of trouble, often by playing up to both sides of any conflict. Perhaps because the Temple of Artemis was consumed by fire on the day Alexander the Great was born, Alexander himself aided the city in its efforts to rebuild after his rise to power.

Like most Ionian cities in Asia Minor, Ephesus became a Roman city, and eventually a Christian one, though not without a struggle. In the Acts of the Apostles, Saint Luke writes at length about the popularity of the cult of Artemis, referring to the goddess by her Latin name, Diana. The city's silversmiths drove Saint Paul out of Ephesus for fear that his preaching would lessen the sale of the "silver shrines for Diana," claiming, "by this craft we have our wealth." When Saint Paul addressed the town in its amphitheater, saying that "there are no gods made with hands," the local silversmiths rioted; they were "full of wrath, and cried out, saying, 'Great is Diana of the Ephesians' " (Acts 19:24–40). Paul is believed to have written some of his Epistles here. Saint John visited between AD 37 and AD 48, perhaps with the mother of Jesus, and again, in 95, when he is supposed to have written his Gospel here and died. In AD 431, Ephesus was the scene of the Third Ecumenical Council, during which Mary was proclaimed the Mother of God.

Ephesus was doomed by the silting in its harbor. By the 6th century the port had become useless and the population had shifted to what is now Selçuk; today, Ephesus is 5 km (about 3 mi) from the sea. The new city was surrounded by ramparts and a citadel was built. In the year 1000, crusaders came from the West, Turks from the East. Ephesus became known as Hagios Theologos (Holy Word of God) and then by the Turkish version of that name, Ayasoluk. The first Seljuk invaders were fought off in 1090, and the Byzantines held out until 1304. The town was incorporated into the Ottoman Empire at the beginning of the 15th century.

Ephesus is the showpiece of Aegean archaeology and one of the grandest reconstructed ancient sites in the world. The extensive, remarkably preserved remains are especially appealing out of season, when the place can seem like a ghost town. In the summer it's packed with tourists, many of whom come off the Greek ships that cruise the Aegean and call at Kuşadası, 20 km (12 mi) to the south, so go early or late in the day, if possible. Site guides are available at the trinket stands ringing the parking lot.

The ruins of Ephesus were rediscovered in the late 19th century, and excavations have been going on for nearly a century. As a result, the site is a pleasure to explore: Marble-paved streets with grooves made by chariot wheels take you past buildings and monuments that have been partially reconstructed.

The road leading to the site parking lot passes a 1st-century AD **Stadium,** where chariot and horse races were held on a track 712 feet long and where gladiators and wild beasts met in combat before 70,000 spectators. On your left after you enter the site is the 25,000-seat **theater,** backed by the western slope of Mt. Pion. A huge semicircle, with row upon row of curved benches, it was begun by Alexander's general Lysimachus and completed by the emperors Claudius and Trajan in the 2nd century AD. There is a fine view from the top of the steps; higher still,

Ephesus and Selçuk

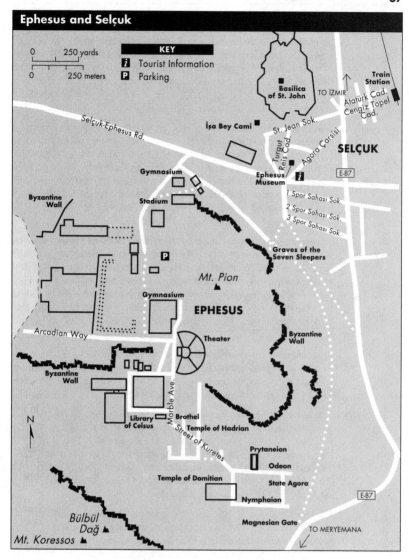

KEY
- **i** Tourist Information
- **P** Parking

0 — 250 yards
0 — 250 meters

Byzantine Wall

Basilica of St. John

İşa Bey Cami

TO İZMİR

Train Station

Atatürk Cad.
Cengiz Topel Cad.

St. Jean Sok.

Selçuk-Ephesus Rd.

Turgut Reis Cad.

Agora Carsisi

SELÇUK

Gymnasium

Ephesus Museum

i

E-87

1 Spor Sahası Sok.
2 Spor Sahası Sok.
3 Spor Sahası Sok.

Stadium

Graves of the Seven Sleepers

Mt. Pion

P

Gymnasium

EPHESUS

Arcadian Way

Byzantine Wall

Theater

Byzantine Wall

Byzantine Wall

Marble Ave.

Library of Celsus

Brothel

Temple of Hadrian

Street of Kuretes

Prytaneion

Odeon

Temple of Domitian

State Agora

E-87

Nymphaion

Bülbül Dağ

Magnesian Gate

TO MERYEMANA

Mt. Koressos

N

near the top of Mt. Pion, are vestiges of the city's Byzantine walls. The theater is used for music and dance performances each May during the Selçuk Ephesus Festival of Culture and Art. Leading away from the theater toward the ancient port, now a marsh, is the **Arcadian Way.** This 1,710-foot-long street was once lined with shops and covered archways. Only a long line of slender marble columns remains.

In front of the theater is Marble Avenue. Follow it to the beautiful, two-story **Library of Celsus.** The courtyard of this much-photographed building is backed by wide steps that climb to the reading room, where you can still see rolls of papyrus. The library is near Marble Avenue's intersection with the **Street of Kuretes,** a still-impressive thoroughfare named for the college of priests once located there. Strategically positioned at this corner is a large house believed to have been a **brothel.** Look for the floor mosaics of three women. To the right along the street are the multistoried houses of the nobility, with terraces and courtyards. To the left are public buildings. A block down from the brothel is the fine facade of the **Temple of Hadrian,** with four Corinthian columns and a serpent-headed hydra above the door to keep out evil spirits; beyond is a partially restored fountain dedicated to the emperor Trajan. The street then forks and opens into a central square, which once held the **Prytaneion,** or town hall; the **Nymphaion,** a small temple decked with fountains; and the **Temple of Domitian** on the south side of the square, once a vast sanctuary with a colossal statue of the emperor for whom it was named. All are now a jumble of collapsed walls and columns.

Returning to the Street of Kuretes, turn right to reach the **odeon,** an intimate semicircle with just a few rows of seats, where spectators would listen to poetry readings and music. Columns mark the northern edge of the **State Agora.** Beyond, the **Magnesian Gate** (also known as the Manisa Gate), at the end of the street, was the starting point for a caravan trail and a colonnaded road to the Temple of Artemis. ⊠ *Site entry 4 km (2½ mi) west of Selçuk on Selçuk–Ephesus Rd.,* ☎ *232/892–6402 or 232/892–6940.* ⌧ *$5.* ☉ *Daily 8–5:30.*

According to the legend attached to the **Graves of the Seven Sleepers,** seven young Christian men hid in a cave to avoid persecution by the Romans in the 3rd century AD. They fell into a sleep that lasted 200 years, waking only after the Byzantine Empire had made Christianity the official state religion. When they died, they were buried here, and the church that you see was built over them. The tombs in the large cemetery are largely from the Byzantine era. ⊠ *South of Sor Sahasi Sok. 3.* ⌧ *Free.*

22 Huddled under its crenellated, gray stone Byzantine fortress that, when floodlit at night, seems to float above the town, **Selçuk** has retained a special charm, despite the presence of its illustrious neighbor Ephesus. The fortress itself holds nothing of interest.

★ The **Ephesus Museum** has one of the best collections of Roman and Greek artifacts to be found anywhere in Turkey. Along with some fine frescoes and mosaics are two pale white statues of Artemis. In each, she is portrayed with several rows of what are alternatively described as breasts or a belt of eggs; in either case, they symbolize fertility. ⊠ *Agora Çarsısı, opposite tourist information office,* ☎ *232/892–6010.* ⌧ *$2.50.* ☉ *Daily 8:30–noon and 1–5:30.*

İsa Bey Cami is one of the oldest mosques in Turkey, dating from 1375. Its jumble of architectural styles suggests a transition between Seljuk and Ottoman design: Like later Ottoman mosques, this has a courtyard, something not found in Seljuk mosques. The structure is built out of "borrowed" stone: marble blocks with Latin inscriptions, Corinthian columns, black granite columns from the baths at Ephesus, and pieces from the altar of the Temple of Artemis. ⊠ *St. Jean Sok.* ☉ *Daily 9–5.*

The fragments of the Temple of Artemis on display at the İsa Bey Cami are about all you will see of the holy site that drew pilgrims from around the ancient world and was one of its Seven Wonders. Begun in the 7th century BC, greatly expanded by the wealthy Lydian king Croesus and redone in marble in the 6th century BC, it was burned down by a disgruntled worshiper in 356 BC. Alexander the Great had it rebuilt, but it was sacked by Goths in AD 263 and later stripped for materials to build Istanbul's Hagia Sophia and Selçuk's Basilica of St. John. Today a muddy field and a lone column drum on the Selçuk–Ephesus road are all that remain of a temple that was once four times larger than the Parthenon in Athens.

The emperor Justinian built the **Basilica of St. John** over a 2nd-century tomb on Ayasoluk Hill believed by many to hold Saint John the Evangelist. Eleven domes once topped the basilica, which rivaled Istanbul's Hagia Sophia in scale. The barrel-vaulted roof collapsed after a long-ago earthquake, but the church is still an incredible sight, with its labyrinth of halls and marble courtyards. ✉ *Entrance off St. Jean Sok., just east of İsa Bey Cami, no phone.* 🎫 *$2.* ☼ *Daily 8–5.*

NEED A BREAK?	Tea and samples of a wide array of excellent *lokum* (Turkish Delight candy) are offered to you at tiny **Tadim** (☎ 232/892–3999) in the Emlak Bankası arcade. Hikmet Çeliker's family has been making the confection for the last 250 years, shipping it to discriminating sweet tooths the world over.

Meryemana, the House of the Virgin Mary, is becoming an increasingly popular pilgrimage for Catholics. Many believe it to have been the place where Saint John took the mother of Jesus after the crucifixion and from which she ascended to heaven. Pope Paul VI visited the site in 1967 and confirmed its authenticity. ✉ *Off Rte. E87, 5 km (3 mi) south of Ephesus.* 🎫 *$1.50.* ☼ *Daily 7:30–sunset.*

Dining and Lodging

$ ✕ **Günhan Restaurant.** One of the few places to eat at the Ephesus ruins prepares a variety of foods, from sandwiches to traditional stewed Turkish dishes, kebabs, and grilled lamb chops and steaks. The spot, shaded by awnings, is perfect for a rest and cool drink before or after a trip to the ruins. ✉ *Efes Ruins,* ☎ *232/892–2291. No credit cards. No dinner.*

$ ✕ **Meryemana Restaurant.** This restaurant, which has sprawling outdoor seating under towering trees, is located on the grounds of Meryemana, the House of the Virgin Mary. Meat dishes, in particular *çöp şiş*, a smaller version of shish kebab cooked on thin wooden skewers, are the specialty here. In high season, it gets quite touristy, with busloads of visitors filling the seats and the shops nearby. ✉ *Meryemana, 5 km (3 mi) south of Ephesus,* ☎ *232/892–1422. Reservations essential for groups. No credit cards.*

$ ✕ **Seçil Restaurant.** This is a sidewalk restaurant in the summer. The appetizers are usually fresh, because there's a quick turnover in high season. Grilled meats are a better choice in summer, when there's a fishing ban and the price of fish goes up considerably. ✉ *Cengiz Topel Cad. 63, Atatürk Mah.,* ☎ *232/891–5384. No credit cards.*

$$ 🏨 **Hotel Pınar.** This four-story concrete hotel is the only one in town with a government three-star rating. But don't expect more than a modern motel, and a basic one at that, with small beds and industrial carpeting. On the other hand, the management is efficient, the location central, and there is always plenty of hot water—and good pressure in the showers, which you don't always find in a pansiyon. ✉ *Sehabettin Dede Cad., Selçuk,* ☎ *232/892–2561,* 🖷 *232/892–3033. 40 rooms with bath. Restaurant, bar. No credit cards.*

$$ 🏨 **Kale Han.** Designed to resemble an old stone inn, Kale Han is run by a friendly family. Antiques and old photographs create an air of eccentricity. The rooms are simple, with bare, whitewashed walls and dark timber beams. A building in the courtyard is reserved for private suites. The airy dining room has large windows and a big fireplace; better food, however, can be had in town. Ask for a room facing the castle behind the hotel. ✉ *Atatürk Cad. 49, Selçuk,* ☎ *232/892–6154,* 🖷 *232/892–2169. 50 rooms with shower. Restaurant, pool. V.*

$ ⊞ **Hotel Akay.** A quiet residential neighborhood by the İsa Bey Cami holds this relatively new hotel with old-Ottoman flourishes—white-washed walls inside and out, latticed balconies, arched windows and doors, kilims on the floor, copper and brass pots here and there. ⊠ *İsa Bey Camii Kar., Serin Sok. 3, Selçuk,* ☎ *232/892–3172,* ☏ *232/892–3009. 16 rooms with bath. Restaurant. MC, V.*

$ ⊞ **Hülya.** This pansiyon that looks like a small apartment building has lemon and tangerine trees in its courtyard. The rooms are simple, but the place does come with one special amenity: One member of the family that runs the place is a fisherman, and occasionally his day's catch is cooked to order for guests. This is probably the cheapest option in Selçuk. ⊠ *Özgür Sok. 15, at Atatürk Cad., Selçuk,* ☎ *232/892–2120. 8 rooms with bath. Restaurant. No credit cards.*

$ ⊞ **Tusan Efes Motel.** This white stucco compound next to the Ephesus archaeological site feels removed from the action, as it's surrounded by eucalyptus trees and next to a campground. Though the rooms are bare and unimpressive, the location is great: You can get to the site well ahead of the bus tours. The restaurant prepares delicious Turkish foods. ⊠ *Ephesus,* ☎ *232/892–6060,* ☏ *232/892–2665. 10 rooms with bath. Restaurant, pool. No credit cards.*

$ ⊞ **Victoria Hotel.** The name of this four-story hostelry in the heart of town recalls the owners' time in England. It's a tidy, cheerful little place with marble floors in the lobby and whitewashed walls set off by honey-color wood trim throughout. The restaurant is a good bet for traditional Turkish fare. Rooms have delightful views of storks nesting on the ancient columns of an aqueduct. ⊠ *Cengiz Topel Cad. 4, Selçuk,* ☎ *232/892–3203,* ☏ *232/892–3204. 24 rooms with bath. Restaurant. No credit cards.*

Pamukkale (Hierapolis)

㉓ *170 km (106 mi) from Selçuk on Rte. E87 (follow road signs after Sarayköy).*

Pamukkale first appears as an enormous, chalky white cliff rising 330 feet from the plains. Mineral-rich volcanic spring water cascades over basins and natural terraces, crystallizing into white curtains of solidified water seemingly suspended in air. The hot springs in the area are used today by people who believe that the water can cure rheumatism and other problems.

Hierapolis demonstrates how long the magical springs of Pamukkale have cast their spell over visitors to the region. There seems no doubt that the springs were the main reason for the first settlement here. The ruins that can be seen today date from the time of the Roman Empire, although there are references to a settlement here as far back as the 5th century BC. Because the sights here are spread over about ½ km (⅓ mi), prepare for some walking.

Between the theater and the Pamukkale Motel are the ruins of a **Temple of Apollo** and a bulky **Byzantine church.** The monumental fountain known as the **Nymphaion,** just north of the Apollo temple, dates from the 4th century AD. Near the northern city gates, a short drive or long walk, is another indication of the town's former popularity, a vast **necropolis** with more than a thousand cut-stone sarcophagi spilling all the way down to the base of the hill. The stone building that enclosed Hierapolis's baths is now the **Pamukkale Museum,** definitely worth a look for its display of marble statues found at the site. ☎ *258/272–2077 (tourism office for information) or* ☎ *258/272-2034 (museum).* ▣ *$1.* ◔ *Tues.–Sun. 8:30–noon and 1–5.*

Lodging

Though there are numerous pansiyons in Pamukkale village, the best bets are those clustered in one short strip at the top of the slope, overlooking the hot pools. They cost more than places down below but take advantage of Turkey's most famous spa waters and offer wonderful views over the calcified cliffs.

$$–$$$ 🏨 **Tusan Motel.** The pool of this white-stucco hostelry is one of the most enticing in the area, thanks to incredible views of the so-called cotton cliffs. Rooms are comfortable, if basic, with the usual bare walls and small, low wooden beds. The rectangular, one-story block of a building is at the top of a steep hill, with expansive views. ☎ *258/272–2010,* 𝐅𝐀𝐗 *258/272–2059. 47 rooms with bath. Restaurant, pool. AE, DC, MC, V.*

$$ 🏨 **Hotel Koru.** The rooms here are virtually indistinguishable from those at the nearby Tusan. The differences are that this white stucco box is larger, with two stories rather than one; attracts tour groups; delivers slightly less personal service; and costs less. ☎ *258/272–2429,* 𝐅𝐀𝐗 *258/ 272–2023. 132 rooms with bath. Restaurant, 1 indoor pool, 3 outdoor pools, dance club. AE, DC, MC, V.*

$$ 🏨 **Pamukkale Motel.** This otherwise unexceptional motel is celebrated for its pool, which has pieces of marble columns and statuary from Roman times scattered about. The rooms are fresh and pleasant. ☎ *258/272–2024,* 𝐅𝐀𝐗 *258/272–2026. 45 rooms with bath. Restaurant, pool, 2 tennis courts. MC, V.*

Aphrodisias

★ ㉔ *80 km (54 mi) from Pamukkale, west on E87 and south on Rte. 585 at town of Kuyucak.*

The city of Aphrodite, goddess of love, is one of the largest and best preserved archaeological sites in Turkey. Though most of what you see today dates from the 1st and 2nd centuries AD, archaeological evidence indicates that the local dedication to Aphrodite followed a long history of veneration of pre-Hellenic goddesses (such as the Anatolian mother goddess and the Babylonian Ishtar). Only about half the site has been excavated so far.

Aphrodisias, which was granted autonomy by the Roman Empire in the late 1st century BC, prospered as a significant center for religion, arts, and literature in the early 1st century AD. Imposing Christianity proved far more difficult than granting the pagan city autonomy, however, due to the cult of Aphrodite. One method that was used to mop up remnants of paganism was to rename the city, first Stavropolis (City of the Cross), then just Caria, which archaeologists believe is the origin of the name of the present-day village of Geyre. Excavations here have also led archaeologists to believe that this was a thriving haven of sculpture that found patrons beyond the borders of the city. The signatures of Aphrodisian artists on statues, fragments, and bases as far away as Greece and Italy attest to this.

The beauty of Aphrodisias is in its details. The towering Babadağ range of mountains to the east of the city offered ancient sculptors a copious supply of white and delicately veined blue-gray marble, which has been used to stunning effect in the statues you will see in the site museum: in the spiral, fluted, and other columns that sprout throughout and in the delicate reliefs of gods and men, vines, and acanthus leaves on decorative friezes.

Start your tour at the **site museum** (☎ 256/448–8084), just past the ticket booth. The museum's collection includes several impressive statues from the site, among them one of Aphrodite herself. Pick up a guide and a map (you'll need it, as the signage is poor).

From the museum, follow the footpath to the right, which makes a circuit around the site and ends up back at the museum. The **Tetrapylon,** recently restored, is a monumental gateway with four rows of columns and some of the better friezes here. The **Temple of Aphrodite** was built in the 1st century BC on the model of the great temples at Ephesus. Its gate and many of its columns are still standing; some bear inscriptions naming the donor of the column. Next to the temple is the fine **Odeon,** an intimate, semicircular concert hall and public meeting room. Farther on is the **stadium,** which once was the scene of foot races, boxing and wrestling matches, and other competitions—horse and chariot races were held in Greek cities' hippodromes. The stadium, which is one of the best preserved of its kind anywhere, could seat up to 30,000 spectators. The **theater,** built into the side of a small hill, is still being excavated. Its 5,000 lush white marble seats are simply dazzling on a bright day. The adjacent **School of Philosophy** has a colonnaded courtyard with chambers lining both sides where teachers would work with small groups of students. *No phone.* ▨ *Site $3, museum $3 additional.* ☉ *Site and museum daily 8:30–5.*

Değirmendere

㉕ *35 km (22 mi) from Selçuk, west to Pamucak, north on coastal road, and then north on marked road to Ahmetbeyli and Değirmendere.*

Less than 2 km (1 mi) west of the present-day village of Değirmendere is the ancient site of **Colophon,** the farthest inland of the Ionian cities. Colophon prospered in the 8th and 7th centuries BC, and the fine horses and fierce cavalry for which it was known were often enlisted as allies by foreign armies to finish off unending wars. The popularity of the nearby oracle at Claros, the fertility of their land, and their skill as mariners made the citizens of this city very wealthy—so wealthy that it was possible to find more than a thousand musk-scented men dressed in purple strolling through the agora. In Colophon's heyday, women musicians were paid an official salary by the government to play from dawn to dusk, and puppies were sacrificed to the Wayside Goddess of the underworld. A combination of extreme wealth and possibly decadence—and the founding of nearby Ephesus—brought about Colophon's decline. In the 3rd century, the population was moved by Lysimachus to fill his new-walled city of Ephesus, and according to Pausanias, those who resisted were "buried left of the road to Claros." Today, there is not much to see except the remains of a wall, though excavations have uncovered streets, a stoa (colonnaded porch), and a temple dedicated to Demeter.

Claros, 7 km (4 mi) south of Colophon, was the site of a highly regarded oracle and **Temple of Apollo,** now standing alongside the road. Claros is mentioned in Homer's verses as the site of an important cult as far back as the 7th and 6th centuries BC. Because the location, in a low-lying valley that was probably the site of a sacred spring and wood, is subject to flooding, the temple is often buried in mud, but ongoing excavations should be clearing that. Excavations have also revealed much information about how the oracles were performed in the temple. A mazelike corridor leads you to the sacred oracle chamber, where annually appointed male prophets would drink holy water and make predictions through a priest and *thespios,* a composer of poetry, who would versify the prophet's utterings. Fragments of colossal statues of Apollo, Artemis, and Leto are scattered about, with the statue of Apollo estimated as having been 24 to 25 feet high. Inscriptions of oracles from the temple have been found as far away as southern Russia, Algeria, Sardinia, and even Great Britain. According to one source, an oracle at this temple predicted the destruction of Europe and Asia in a war over the beautiful Helen.

The crumbling remains of **Notion,** Colophon's port, are scattered along a clifftop 2 km (1 mi) to the south of Claros along the same road. After Lysimachus depopulated Colophon to furnish Ephesus, Notion had a brief period of prosperity, when it was known as the New Colophon, but as Ephesus grew, Notion's population and wealth dwindled. You can make out the foundations of a temple, an agora, and a theater. Down below is a beach.

Kuşadası

㉖ *20 km (12 mi) southwest of Selçuk on Rte. 515.*

One of the most popular resorts in the southern Aegean is an ideal base from which to explore the surrounding area. A small fishing village as late as the 1970s, Kuşadası is now a sprawling, hyperactive town packed with curio shops and a population of around 55,000. The cheery holiday atmosphere is hugely popular with British tourists. Good hotels and restaurants are more plentiful than elsewhere along the coast; there's even a bit of nightlife. And it's the jumping-off point for the 2½-hour boat trip to the Greek island of Samos. Tickets, which should be obtained a day in advance, can be purchased at any travel agency in town (☞ Guided Tours *in* The Aegean Coast A to Z, *below*); the cost is about $35 each way, and departures are at 8 and 5 daily.

A causeway off of Kadınlar Denizi, just south of the harbor, connects Kuşadası to an old **Genoese castle** on Güvercin Adası (Pigeon Island). Today the site of a popular disco and several teahouses with gardens and sea views, the fortress was home to three Turkish brothers in the 16th century. These infamous pirates—Barbarossa, Oruc, and Hayrettin—pillaged the coasts of Spain and Italy and sold passengers and crews from captured ships into slavery in Algiers and Constantinople. Rather than fight them, Süleyman the Magnificent (ruled 1520–66) hired Hayrettin as his Grand Admiral and set him loose on enemies in the Mediterranean. The strategy worked: Hayrettin won victory after victory and was heaped with honors and riches.

Kuşadası's 300-year-old **caravansary** (⊠ Atatürk Bul. 1), now the Club Kervansaray (☞ Dining and Lodging, *below*), is loaded with Ottoman atmosphere. Its public areas are worth a look even if you're not staying there.

NEED A BREAK? If you're looking for beaches, either head north from Kuşadası to Pamucak or travel 33 km (20 mi) south to lovely, wooded **Samsundağ National Park** (also known as Dilek Peninsula National Park), which has good hiking trails and several quiet stretches of sandy beach. To get there, take the coast road, marked Güzelçanlı or Devutlar, from about 10 km (6 mi) south of Kuşadası. ▣ Park $2. ☉ Apr.–Dec.

Dining and Lodging

$$$ ✕ **Sultan Han.** This excellent restaurant is in an old house built around a courtyard whose focal point is a stately, gigantic palm tree. You can dine in the open-air courtyard or upstairs in small rooms piled with kilims, where you sit on cushions at low brass tables. Much of the seafood is grilled. Fish baked in salt is a local specialty. Sultan Han is in the heart of town, just off Barbaros Hayrettin Caddesi, the main shopping

street. ⊠ *Bahar Sok. 8,* ☎ *256/614–6380. Reservations essential. No credit cards.*

\$\$ ✕ **Ada Restaurant.** Choices from this spacious Pigeon Island restaurant's menu—among them local fish, appetizers, and kebabs—are conveniently displayed at the entrance along with their prices. ⊠ *Güvercin Adası,* ☎ *256/614–1725. AE, MC, V.*

\$\$ ✕ **Ali Baba Restaurant.** An appetizing and colorful mound of the day's catch meets you at the entrance to this waterside fish restaurant. The decor and the style are simple, but the view over the bay is soothing and the food fabulous. For starters, try the cold black-eyed bean salad, the marinated octopus salad, or the fried calamari, and follow it with a grilled meat dish or whatever fish is in season. It's worth reserving in advance at this spot, which fills up by 8 PM. ⊠ *Belediye Turistik Çarşısı 5,* ☎ *256/614–1551. Reservations essential. MC, V.*

\$\$ ✕ **Nil Restaurant.** The cook here prides himself on *bugulama* (stewed
★ fish with spices) and fish baked in salt; barbecued shrimp or chicken are also good, and you can choose appetizers from the many on display. The atmosphere, not as scenic as the seaside eateries, is nautical, with shells, fish, and garlic suspended with a ceiling fishnet. ⊠ *Yıl Cad. 3, Türkmen Mah. 50,* ☎ *256/614–8063. Reservations essential. MC, V.*

\$ ✕ **Çamtepe Restaurant.** This new and modest terrace restaurant across from the Club Kervansaray and the central market has views of the sea and the bustling pedestrian street below. The *pirzola* (grilled lamb chops) are particularly good here, as are the appetizers. The seafood is exhibited at the entrance in an artistic heap. ⊠ *Cephane Sok. 3,* ☎ *256/614–8348. Reservations essential in summer. MC, V.*

\$ ✕ **Özurfa.** The focus at this Turkish fast-food spot is on kebabs. The Urfa kebab—spicy, grilled slices of lamb on pita bread—is the house specialty, and the fish kebabs are tasty. The location just off Barbaros Hayrettin Caddesi is convenient to the market. ⊠ *Cephane Sok. 7,* ☎ *256/612–6070. No credit cards.*

\$\$\$ ▦ **Club Kervansaray.** A refurbished, 300-year-old inn that was once a way station for camel caravans, this hotel is decorated in the Ottoman style. The main entrance has massive, armor-plated doors. The central courtyard—where the camels once were kept—is paved with marble and planted with palm trees. Rooms are decorated with kilims and Turkish folk art. The hotel, in the center of town, has a dressy Turkish restaurant with live entertainment: singers, perhaps a belly dancer, and, later, a pop band. ⊠ *Atatürk Bul. 1,* ☎ *256/614–4115,* 🗏 *256/614–2423. 40 rooms with bath. Restaurant, bar, nightclub. AE, DC, MC, V.*

\$\$\$ ▦ **Kismet.** Although small, Kismet is run on a grand scale by a descendant
★ of the last Ottoman sultan. It's surrounded by beautifully maintained gardens. On a promontory overlooking the marina on one side and the Aegean on the other, it feels almost like a private Mediterranean villa with its low, white stucco cubes stepped up a hillside. Each room has a private balcony, most with sea views. Kismet's popularity makes reservations a must. ⊠ *Akyar Mev., Türkmen Mah.,* ☎ *256/614–2005,* 🗏 *256/614–4914. 96 rooms with bath. Restaurant, tennis court, beach. MC, V. Closed Nov.–Mar.*

\$\$ ▦ **Atınç Otel.** The Atınç, a mid-rise, has a good location: It's a walk from the center of town, but not so close that you're bothered by the noise. Other pluses include the Aegean views from the front rooms, and the rooftop pool that looks out on the whole town. Guest rooms have balconies, but not much style. ⊠ *Atatürk Bul.,* ☎ *256/614–7608,* 🗏 *256/614–4967. 75 rooms with bath. 2 restaurants, 2 bars, pool, exercise room. MC, V.*

$$ ⌖ **Efe Otel.** This mid-price hotel sits on the waterfront a little beyond the path to Pigeon Island. A four-story whitewashed box with dark wood trim, it's small but has a personable staff. Rooms are nondescript—the carpeting drab, the walls bare, and the beds low, with wooden frames—but many have balconies and views of Pigeon Island. ⌧ *Güvercin Ada Cad. 37,* ☎ *256/614–3661,* FAX *256/614–3662. 44 rooms with bath. Restaurant, bar. MC, V.*

$ ⌖ **Bahar Pansiyon.** Front rooms at this cozy hotel have balconies, and all rooms are quiet and easily affordable. The Bahar is a block from Hayrettin Barbaros Caddesi. ⌧ *Cephane Sok. 12,* ☎ *256/614–1191,* FAX *256/614–9359. 16 rooms with bath. Restaurant, bar. No credit cards.*

$ ⌖ **Liman Hotel.** Very close to the port in a whitewashed, narrow building with black cast-iron balconies, the Liman has basic but clean rooms with comfortable furniture. The service is attentive and sincere. Don't forget to ask for a room in the front of the building, facing the sea. ⌧ *Buyral Sok. 4, Kıbrıs Cad.,* ☎ FAX *256/612–3149. 16 rooms with bath. Indoor café, outdoor café, air-conditioning. No credit cards.*

Nightlife

The **Club Kervansaray** (⌧ Atatürk Bul. 1, ☎ 256/614–4115) has dining, dancing, and a show on most nights. The **Beebop** (⌧ Cephane Sok. 20, ☎ 256/614–7070) is in the market area. The **Orient Bar** (⌧ Kişla Sok. 8, ☎ 256/614–2249) usually presents pop or jazz music to a younger crowd. You can walk across the causeway to **Pigeon Island,** where today's young Turks dress up to mingle with the more energetic tourists at a boisterous disco—there's no name beyond the "Disco" on the sign but you can hear its music almost everywhere on this minuscule landfall. Several British-style pubs punctuate the street called **Eski Pazaryeri Sokak.** On **Barlar Sokak,** Kuşadası's bar strip, the spacious, popular **Queen Victoria** (☎ 256/614–1511) has live music in summer.

Priene

★ ㉗ *37 km (23 mi) from Kuşadası, southeast on Rte. 515, south on Rte. 525, west on Rte. 09–55 (follow signs).*

Priene sits in a spectacular location atop a steep hill above the flat valley of the Büyük Menderes (Maeander River). Dating from about 350 BC, the city you see today was still under construction in 334, when Alexander the Great liberated the Ionian settlements from Persian rule. At that time it was a thriving port. But as in Ephesus, the harbor silted over, commerce moved to neighboring Miletus, and the city's prosperity waned. As a result, the Romans never rebuilt Priene, and the simpler Greek style predominates as in few other ancient cities in Turkey. Excavated by British archaeologists in 1868–69, it's smaller than Ephesus and far less grandiose.

From the parking area, the walk up to the **Priene ruins** is fairly steep; because your routes through it are well marked, you won't need a map. After passing through the old city walls, you follow the city's original main thoroughfare; note the drainage gutters and the grooves worn into the marble paving stones by the wheels of 4th-century BC chariots. Continuing west, you come to the well-preserved **bouleterion** (council chamber) on the left. Its 10 rows of seats flanked an orchestra pit with a little altar, decorated with bulls' heads and laurel leaves, at the center. Passing through the doors on the opposite side of the council chamber takes you to the **Sacred Stoa,** a colonnaded civic center, and the edge of the **agora,** the marketplace. Farther west along the broad promenade are the remains of a row of **private houses,** typically two or three rooms on two floors; of the upper stories, only traces of a few stairwells remain. In the largest house, a statue of Alexander was found, a remnant that seemed to say "Alexander slept here."

A block or so farther along the main street is the **Temple of Athena.** Its design—the work of Pytheos, architect of the Mausoleum of Halicarnassus (one of the Seven Wonders of the Ancient World)—was repeatedly copied at other sites in the Greek world. It was not a place for worshipers to gather but a dwelling for the god; only priests could enter. Alexander apparently chipped in on construction costs. Earthquakes have toppled the columns; the five that have been reerected provide an evocative vision of the temple that once had a stunning view over the Menderes valley. A walk north and then east along the track leads to the well-preserved little **theater,** sheltered on all sides by pine trees. Enter through the stage door onto the orchestra section; note the five front-row VIP seats, carved thrones with lions' feet. If you scramble up a huge rock known as Samsun Dağı (behind the theater and to your left as you face the seats), you will find the scanty remains of a **Sanctuary of Demeter,** goddess of the harvest; a few bits of columns and walls remain, as well as a big hole through which blood of sacrificial victims was poured to the deities of the underworld. Since few people make it up here, it is an incredibly peaceful spot, with a terrific view over Priene and the plains. Above this, should you care to go farther, are the remnants of a Hellenistic fortress. *No phone.* ✉ *$1.50.* ✆ *Daily 8:30–6.*

Miletus

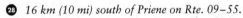 *16 km (10 mi) south of Priene on Rte. 09–55.*

Miletus was one of the greatest commercial centers of the Greek world before its harbor silted over. The first settlers were Minoan Greeks from Crete, who arrived between 1400 and 1200 BC. The Ionians, who arrived 200 years later, slaughtered the male population and married the widows. The philosopher Thales was born here in the early 6th century BC; he calculated the height of the pyramids at Giza, suggested that the universe was actually a rational place despite its apparent disorder, and coined the phrase "Know thyself." An intellectual center, the city was also home to the mathematicians Anaximenes, who held that air was the single element behind the diversity of nature, and Anaximander, whose ideas anticipated the theory of evolution and the concept of the indestructibility of matter. Like the other Ionian cities, Miletus was passed from ruling empire to ruling empire—being successively governed by Alexander's generals Antigonus and Lysimachus and Pergamum's Attalids, among others. Under the Romans the town finally regained some control over its own affairs and shared in the prosperity of the region. Saint Paul preached here before the harbor became impassable and the city had to be abandoned once and for all.

The **archaeological site** is sprawled out along a desolate plain. Well-marked trails make a guide or map unnecessary. The parking lot is right outside the city's most magnificent building—the **Great Theater,** a remarkably intact 25,000-seat amphitheater built by the Ionians and kept up by the Romans. Along the third to sixth rows, some inscriptions reserving seats for notables are still visible, and the vaulted passages leading to the seats have the feel of a modern sporting arena. Climb to the top of the theater for a look at the defensive walls built by the Byzantines and a view across the ancient city.

To see the rest of the ruins, follow the dirt track to the right of the theater. A stand of buildings marks what was once a broad processional avenue. The series begins with the **delphinion,** a sanctuary of Apollo;

a **Seljuk hamam** (bath) added to the site in the 15th century, with pipes for hot and cold water still visible; a **stoa** (colonnaded porch) with several reerected Ionic columns; the foundations of a **Roman bath** and **gymnasium;** and the first story of the **Nymphaion,** all that remains of the once highly ornate three-story structure, resembling the Library of Celsus at Ephesus, that distributed water to the rest of the city.

To the south, your dirt track becomes a tree-lined lane that leads to the **İlyas Bey Cami,** a mosque built in 1404 in celebration of its builder and namesake's escape from Tamerlane, the Mongol terror. The mosque is now a romantic ruin: The ceiling is cracked, dust covers the tiles, and birds roost inside. The path from the mosque back to the parking lot passes a small and underwhelming museum. *No phone.* ✉ *Ruins $1.50, museum $1.50.* ☉ *Tues.–Sun. 8:30–6.*

Didyma

❷❾ *20 km (12 mi) south of Miletus on Rte. 09–55.*

Didyma (Didim in Turkish) is famous for its magnificent **Temple of Apollo.** As grand in scale as the Parthenon—measuring 623 feet by 167 feet—the temple has 124 well-preserved columns, some still supporting their architraves; its oracles rivaled those of Delphi. Started in 300 BC and under construction for five centuries, it was never completed, and some of the columns remain unfluted. Beneath the courtyard is a network of underground corridors where the temple priests would consult the oracle. The corridor walls would throw the oracle's voice into deep and ghostly echoes, which the priests would interpret. The tradition of seeking advice from sacred oracles probably started long before the arrival of the Greeks; in all likelihood, the Greeks converted an older Anatolian cult based at the site to their own religion. The Greek oracle had a good track record and at the birth of Alexander the Great (356 BC) predicted that he would be victorious over the Persians, that his general Seleucus would later become king, and that Trajan would become an emperor.

The popularity of the oracle dwindled with the rise of Christianity, around AD 385. The temple was later excavated by French and German archaeologists; its statues are long gone, hauled back to England by Sir Charles Newton in 1858. Fragments of bas-relief on display by the entrance to the site include a gigantic head of Medusa and a small statue of Poseidon and his wife, Amphitrite. *No phone.* ✉ *$1.50.* ☉ *Daily 8:30–6.*

NEED A
BREAK?   For a rest after all this history, continue another 5 km (3 mi) south to **Altınkum.** The white sand beach, which stretches for a bit less than 1 km (½ mi), is bordered by a row of decent seafood restaurants, all facing the water, and some small hotels.

En Route Shortly before you reach Milas, along the road to Bodrum, Route 525 skirts the southern shore of **Çamiçi Gölü** (Bafa Gölü, or Lake Bafa). The lake is relatively small and largely undeveloped, especially away from the main road. For a real change of pace, hire a boat to take you across the lake, or drive the rough 10-km (6-mi) road along the eastern shore to the village of Kapikiri and the ancient ruins of Heracleia. Though a minor town in antiquity, Heracleia has a wonderful setting, surrounded by high mountains. The villagers are Türkilometersen, descended from the Turkish tribes that settled Anatolia in the 13th and 14th century. The ruins, a Temple of Athena and some city walls, are also unusual: They are Carian rather than Greek. The Carians were a native Asian people who adopted Greek language and culture. On an islet facing the village are the remains of a Byzantine monastery, and huge volcanic boulders are scattered about. The combination of elements is incredibly atmospheric.

Bodrum

 161 km (100 mi) from Kuşadası, southeast on Rte. 515 to Rte. 525 south to Rte. 330 heading southwest; 125 km (78 mi) from Didyma, northeast on town road to Rte. 525 south to Rte. 330 southwest.

Bodrum, known as Halicarnassus in antiquity, has a good claim to being Turkey's leading resort. The modern town stretches along the shore of two crescent-shape bays and has for years been the favorite haunt of the Turkish upper classes. Today thousands of foreign visitors have joined the elite, and the area is bursting at the seams with villas, hotels, guest houses, cafés, restaurants, and discos. Comparing it to Saint-Tropez on the French Riviera, some sniff that Bodrum is spoiled. But it is still beautiful, with its gleaming, whitewashed buildings covered with bougainvillea and unfettered vistas of the sparkling bays.

Founded around 1000 BC, Halicarnassus was one of the first Greek colonies in Asia. The northern cities of the Aegean formed the Ionian League, but those farther south joined the Dorian Federation, which included Kos, Rhodes, Knidos, Lalysos, Lindos, Camiros—and Halicarnassus. Halicarnassus reached its height under Mausolus, who ruled from 377 to 353 BC as a satrap (governor) of what was then a distant outpost of the far-flung Persian Empire. After his death, his wife (who was also his sister), Artemisia, succeeded him. Upon learning that a woman ruled Halicarnassus, Rhodes sent its fleet to seize the city, only to be promptly, and soundly, defeated.

Artemisia ordered the construction of the great white marble tomb at Halicarnassus that made the Seven Wonders list and gave us the word mausoleum. The **mausoleum** consisted of a solid rectangular base topped by 36 Ionic columns, surmounted by a pyramid and crowned with a massive statue of Mausolus and Artemisia riding a chariot. The site, two blocks north of the bay, indicated by signs on Neyzen Tevfik Caddesi, the shore road ringing the west bay, is not worth the price of admission. ☎ *252/316–1095.* ▨ *$2.* ☉ *Tues.–Sun. 8–noon and 1–5.*

The ancient **theater** is one of the few surviving pre-Hellenic theaters in Asia Minor, thus one of the oldest, and a popular place to take in a sunset. ⊠ *North of mausoleum.* ▨ *Free.*

The **Petronion** (Castle of St. Peter) is the most outstanding historic sight in modern Bodrum and one of the great showpieces of late-medieval military architecture. The European crusaders known as the Knights of St. John seized Bodrum in 1402 and dismantled the mausoleum, using many of the stones to build the Petronion. The castle and its beautiful gardens, visible from every part of town, look as if they belong in a fairy tale. On the ramparts, heraldry buffs may recognize prominent coats-of-arms—those of the Plantagenets, d'Aubussons, and others. The five turrets are named after the homelands of the knights, who came from England, France, Germany, Italy, and Spain. Inside is an unusual and interesting **Museum of Underwater Archaeology,** with treasures recovered from historic wrecks discovered off the Aegean Coast. ⊠ *Kale Cad.,* ☎ *252/316–2516.* ▨ *$3.* ☉ *Tues.–Sun. 8:30–noon and 1–5.*

Dining and Lodging

$$$ ✕ **Restaurant Han.** This restaurant benefits from a fine location, in an old 18th-century caravansary with a tree-shaded courtyard a block from the harbor. The decor is minimal—you eat at trestle tables in the open air. But the kebabs, köfte, and grilled fresh prawns are crowd pleasers. So is the belly dancer who performs most nights. ✉ *Kale Cad. 29,* ☎ *252/316–7951. Reservations essential in summer. No credit cards.*

$$ ✕ **Amphora.** The options are dazzling: 20 or so mezes (including eggplant pureed, sautéed with garlic, or in tomato sauce) and two dozen kinds of kebabs. Another plus is the setting, opposite the marina at the edge of town in an old stone building decorated with kilims and boating and fishing gear. ✉ *Neyzen Tevfik Cad. 172,* ☎ *252/316–2368. Reservations essential in summer. MC, V.*

$$ ✕ **Club Pirinç.** This restaurant is notable for its Turkish-French cuisine and pleasant bar. ✉ *Yenicarsi 8,* ☎ *252/316–1454. No credit cards.*

$$ ✕ **Kortan Restaurant.** This seaside fish house has outdoor seating with
★ views of Bodrum's castle and Chios. The better dishes include fish kebabs, octopus salad, and whatever the catch of the day happens to be, usually served grilled. ✉ *Cumhuriyet Cad. 32,* ☎ *252/316–1241. Reservations essential in summer. AE, MC, V.*

$$$ 🏨 **Çömça-Manzara Hotel.** Each of the 30 small, whitewashed two-story apartments in this group has a living room, kitchen, and terrace. The location on a hill facing Bodrum's castle across the bay makes the complex look like a little Mediterranean village. But don't expect high style in the furnishings—the interiors recall American motels of the 1950s. In peak season, half board may be required. ✉ *Kumbahçe Mah. Meteoroloji Yanı,* ☎ *252/316–2012 or 252/316–1719,* 📠 *252/316–1720. 30 apartment units and 60 rooms with bath. Restaurant, pool. AE, DC, MC, V.*

$$ 🏨 **Ayaz Hotel.** This hotel is on a small bay just east of the Bodrum harbor, away from the noise and bustle of town yet less than a five-minute drive from the center. It has its own gardens and its beach has a bar where you can listen to the waves and while away the hours. The guest rooms are contemporary and have balconies and sea views. ✉ *On Gümbet Bay,* ☎ *252/316–1174 or 252/316–2956,* 📠 *252/316–4751. 96 rooms with bath. Restaurant, bar, pool, waterskiing, playground. V.*

$$ 🏨 **Manastir Hotel Bodrum.** The bar in this comfortable, whitewashed stucco Mediterranean-style hotel was once the site of a monastery. Front rooms have balconies and look out on the Petronion. ✉ *Baris Sitesi Mev., Kumbahçe,* ☎ *252/316–2854,* 📠 *252/316–2772. 59 rooms with bath. 2 restaurants, bar, 2 pools, sauna, tennis court, exercise room. AE, V.*

$$ 🏨 **Maya Hotel and Pansiyon.** Though in the center of town, this hotel feels secluded, its private garden and swimming pool bordered by bright flowers. The rooms, in low white-stucco buildings, are utilitarian and nondescript, with Scandinavian-style furniture. In the associated pansiyon, on a tiny side street behind the marina, rooms are smaller and you have to walk over to the hotel for a dip in the pool, but the prices are lower. ✉ *Gerence Sok. 32, Gümbet,* ☎ *252/316–4741,* 📠 *252/316–4745. 72 rooms with bath. Restaurant, bar, pool, sauna, exercise room. MC, V.*

$ 🏨 **Mylasa Pansiyon.** An Australian archaeologist who found it hard to leave Bodrum runs this pansiyon in an attractive white-stucco building in the center of town. There is a comfortable lounge, and the roof deck has a view of the Aegean. Rooms are just what you find in most pansiyons—the beds are low, with wooden frames, and there's no decor to speak of. ⊠ *Cumhuriyet Cad. 34,* ☎ *252/316–1846,* FAX *252/316–1254. 16 rooms with bath. Bar, breakfast room. MC, V.*

Nightlife

The scene here is more sophisticated than anywhere else along the Aegean. The **Halikarnas Disco** (⊠ Cumhuriyet Cad. 178, ☎ 252/316–8000) bills itself as "probably the most amazing nightclub in the world." It is, in fact, rather like discos more commonly found in western Mediterranean resorts, complete with fog machines and laser lights. The **Mavi Bar** (⊠ Cumhuriyet Cad. 175, ☎ 252/316–3932) and **Hadigari** (⊠ Dr. Alım Bey Cad., ☎ 252/316–7121) are venerable meccas in Bodrum drinking circles, attracting Turkish artists, writers, and their numerous hangers-on. **MM Dancing** (⊠ Dr. Alım Bey Cad., 1025 Sok. 44, ☎ 252/316–2725) near the marina is a pleasant place to while away the night hours.

Outdoor Activities and Sports

CRUISES

The prime cruising ground at Bodrum is the mountain-rimmed **Gökova Körfezi** (Gökova Gulf), the body of water between the Bodrum peninsula and the Datça peninsula, 30 km (18 mi) or so to the south. This densely pine-forested region is punctuated by tiny farming and fishing settlements. Although there are many classical and Byzantine remains along the Datça peninsula, **Knidos,** at its tip, is the only major site (☞ Chapter 5, The Mediterranean Coast). **Sedir Island** (and the ancient city called Cedreae), due north of Marmaris, is delightful when not overrun with day-trippers attracted by the golden sands of the lovely "Cleopatra Beach," so called because Mark Antony is said to have sent for sand from the Sahara to please his love.

The cost of a cruise is about $600 a day for a boat with six double berths and crew. Agencies in Bodrum can provide information and make arrangements in advance, among them **Era Travel** (☎ 252/316–2054, FAX 252/316–5338), **Halikarnas Turizm** (☎ 252/316–2397), **Karya Tur** (☎ 252/316–1914, FAX 252/316–1759), and **Motif Travel** (☎ 252/316–2309, FAX 252/316–3522).

DIVING

The sea around Bodrum provides some of the best diving in the Aegean. For further details contact **Motif Diving** (⊠ Neyzen Tevfik Cad. 80, ☎ 252/316–6198) or **Bodrum Spor** (⊠ Yeni Çarşi 4, ☎ 252/313–2074).

THE AEGEAN COAST A TO Z

Arriving and Departing

By Boat

FROM ECEABAT

You can reach Çanakkale by car and passenger ferry across the Dardanelles, the straits dividing Europe and Asia. Boats depart on the hour from Eceabat, near the battlefields, about 330 km (200 mi) and a three- or four-hour drive from Istanbul. The crossing takes about 30 minutes, and the cost is $6 for a car and driver and 50¢ per additional passenger and those without a car.

FROM ISTANBUL

Turkish Maritime Lines (⊠ Rıhtım Cad. 1, ☎ 212/244–0207 for information or 212/249–9222 for reservations) operates passenger and car ferry services to İzmir. Boats leave in the afternoon and arrive the next morning. Fares range from $25 for a single seat to $110 for a suite accommodating from two to four. In summer there is also service between İzmir and Marseille, Genoa, Venice, and Piraeus, the port for Athens.

By Bus

Buses, typically modern and air-conditioned, operate between the larger and smaller towns and from there depart for the major archaeological sites. Typical travel times are: Istanbul to Çanakkale, six hours; Çanakkale to İzmir (via Bergama, Ayvalık, and Ayvacık), six hours; İzmir to Bodrum, 3½ hours.

By Car

A car is a plus for exploring this region, since it allows you to stop at will at picturesque towns and to track down lesser-known ruins and less-crowded beaches. However, it's a long haul from Istanbul to İzmir—565 km (353 mi), an exhausting seven- or eight-hour drive. To make this trip, pick up Route 200 heading west toward Çanakkale. From there, the E87 follows the coast south all the way to Kuşadası, where it turns inland toward Antalya. Route 525 continues along the coast, past Priene and Miletus; Route 330 branches off in Bodrum and connects with the main Mediterranean highways.

By Plane

The major airport serving the region is **Adnan Menderes Airport,** 25 km (16 mi) south of İzmir. **Turkish Airlines** (THY, ☎ 212/252–1106 in Istanbul for information or 212/663-6363 for reservations) and **Istanbul Airlines** (☎ 212/231–7526 or 212/231–7527) make the hourlong flight direct from Istanbul.

THY offers two other options in summer: Fly nonstop from London or Frankfurt into İzmir. Or connect through Istanbul to **Dalaman Airport** on the Mediterranean coast, near Marmaris, and drive north. Dalaman is 395 km (237 mi) from İzmir.

By Train

Trains to İzmir from Istanbul take a good 10 to 12 hours. You start out by taking a boat across the Sea of Marmara, and about four hours later you connect with a train at Bandırma. Take the morning, rather than night, departure if you want to enjoy the scenery of the cruise and the northern Aegean. Contact **Turkish Maritime Lines** (☞ *above*) in Istanbul for schedules and fares.

Getting Around

By Boat

The Aegean Coast is one of the more popular routes for the international yachting crowd. Usually, harbors are right in the city center, and the main archaeological sites are a cheap and easy cab ride away. Kuşadası and Bodrum are charter centers.

By Bus

Though it's slower and more restrictive than traveling by car, bus travel is a viable option if you don't want to rent a car. It's exceptionally inexpensive, as fares are rarely more than a few dollars, and all the towns and attractions are well served by bus. When you arrive at the main bus station for one town, simply ask about connecting service to the next town along the line.

By Car

Except around İzmir, where heavy and hectic traffic requires serious concentration to keep you from getting lost, the highways are generally in good condition, the traffic fairly light, and the main attractions relatively close together. As you head south, distances are: Çanakkale

to Bergama, 245 km (151 mi); Bergama to İzmir, 98 km (60 mi); İzmir
to Ephesus, 79 km (50 mi); Ephesus to Bodrum, 172 km (106 mi).

CAR RENTALS

İzmir has Avis (☎ 232/441–4417 or 232/441–4418), Budget (☎ 232/
441–9224), Europcar/National (☎ 232/441–5141 or 232/441–5521),
and Hertz (☎ 232/274–2193).

Contacts and Resources

Emergencies

Ambulance (☎ 112). **Police** (☎ 155). **Tourist Police** (☎ 252/316–1216
in Bodrum, ☎ 232/421–8652 in İzmir). Those answering the Tourist
Police telephone are unlikely to speak English. You are just as well off
using the standard Turkish emergency numbers (or, in rural areas, ☎
156 for the gendarme).

Guided Tours

Travel agencies in all the major towns offer tours of the historical sites.
At the harbor in Ayvalık, dozens of small tour boats operate two-hour
outings along the coast and to nearby islands (around $5, $10 including
a meal). **Egetur Travel** (✉ Talat Paşa Bul. 2/B, İzmir, ☎ 232/421–7925)
is the local American Express representative. In Kuşadası, **Akdeniz Turizm** (✉ Atatürk Bul. 26, ☎ 256/614–1140), **Toya Turizm Seyahat Acen-
tesi** (✉ Atatürk Bul. 60, ☎ 256/614–3344), and travel agencies along
Teyyare Caddesi offer escorted tours to Ephesus; to Priene, Miletus,
and Didyma; and to Aphrodisias and Pamukkale.

Visitor Information

Ayvalık (✉ Yat Limanı Karşısı, ☎ 266/312–2122). **Bergama** (✉ İzmir
Cad. 54, Zafer Mah., ☎ 232/633–1862). **Bodrum** (✉ Eylül Meyd. 12,
☎ 252/316–1091). **Çanakkale** (✉ İskele Meyd. 67, ☎ 286/217–
1187). **Çeşme** (✉ İskele Meyd. 8, ☎ 232/712–6653). **İzmir** (✉ Atatürk
Cad. 418, Alsancak, ☎ 232/422–1022; ✉ Gaziosmanpasa Bul. 1/C,
☎ 232/489–9278). **Kuşadası** (✉ İskele Meyd., ☎ 256/614–1103).
Selçuk (✉ Agora Çarsisi 35, Atatürk Mah., ☎ 232/892–6328).

5 The Mediterranean Coast

Mention the Mediterranean, and the first images that usually come to mind are of villas along the French Riviera, chic Italian resorts, or the white cuboid houses of the Greek Islands. Turkey's slice of the Med has elements of these and more. It has the country's best beaches, endless stretches of fine white sand, many of them seldom crowded. And, if you believe the endless references, Cleopatra and Mark Antony swam at almost every one of them while carrying on their torrid affair.

THE MODERN TURKISH MEDITERRANEAN is as noteworthy as the ancient. Unspoiled fishing villages,
among them Üçağiz on Kekova Sound, share the
shoreline with ultrasmart seaports such as Marmaris and Antalya.
The coast's bustling bazaars are stocked with bright, baggy trousers;
piles of halvah (a tasty candy made from sesame seeds); and jams
made of eggplant, rose, and other exotic ingredients. Turkish media
releases compare the Mediterranean Coast to the Greek Islands of 20
or 30 years ago. In a sense they're right. Tourism has not yet developed here to the point that restaurants serve up mainly fish-and-chips,
or that the natives think of you only in terms of the trinkets you might
buy. Here, if you ask a young man directions to the main highway, he
is apt to jump onto his motorcycle and lead you the 5 km (3 mi) or so
to find it.

Revised and
updated by
Paula S.
Bernstein

But the Turkish Riviera, as tourist brochures have begun to call it, isn't
just about untainted beaches and charming fishing villages. The region
also contains ancient cities of Greek, Roman, Arab, Seljuk, Armenian,
crusader, and Byzantine vintage. Termessos, known as the Eagle's
Nest, was the one fortress Alexander the Great deemed too strong to
take. The Roman theater at Aspendos rivals the Colosseum. Saint Paul
came here spreading the Gospel to the Seven Churches of Asia. Later
the might of Islam overcame the Byzantines, setting the foundation for
a great Muslim empire.

Turkey's Mediterranean Coast is not virgin territory. Though the big
tour buses that ply the Aegean are less common here, British and German travelers discovered the area long ago, and the requisite services
have been developed. Roads are mostly paved, there are gas stations
when you need them, and you can always find a clean, comfortable
place to stay.

Pleasures and Pastimes

Beaches

İstuzu beach, near Dalyan, and Patara, a bit farther east, are two of
the most exceptional beaches in all Turkey. Phaselis is the nicest place
to swim west of Antalya; east of the city are the splendid beaches at
Side and, even better, Alanya. Near Marmaris, head for İçmeler, Turunç, or Kumlubük. All are blissfully clean and uncrowded; most have
fine white sand, though the azure lagoon at Ölü Deniz and the beach
by the ruins of Olympos are pebbled. Beach umbrellas, lifeguards, and
changing rooms have yet to arrive—one or two tiny restaurants are
often the extent of the amenities.

Cruises

Perhaps the most romantic way to tour the coast is to cruise for several days in a *gulet,* the traditional wood sailboat that looks so graceful on the turquoise water. In this dreamy, private world, timbers
creak, brass fittings glint in the sun, hidden bays beckon off the bow,
and beaches and ancient cities not on landlubbers' maps become your
personal hideaways. The best time to go is on the edge of summer, in
May, September, and October, when the weather is cooler and the number of fellow travelers is low. Ask around at the harbor in any of the
seaside towns—even during the height of the season, boats will be available. Most follow a regular itinerary; a few are for hire and will put
together a trip to suit you.

Dining

Regional specialties along the coast include mussels stuffed with rice, pine nuts, and currants (one of the many stuffed dishes that fall under the general heading of dolma); *ahtopot salatası,* a cold octopus salad, tossed in olive oil, vinegar, and parsley; and grilled fish—*palamut* (baby tuna), *lüfer* (bluefish), *levrek* (sea bass), *kalkan* (turbot), and more. As in other parts of Turkey, the main difference between good inexpensive restaurants and good expensive restaurants is the setting: Higher tabs get you linen or cotton tablecloths and napkins rather than paper mats, crystal rather than glass. Unless otherwise noted, dress is casual at all restaurants described below, and reservations are not required. For a chart that explains the cost of meals at restaurants in this chapter, *see* Dining and Lodging Price Categories at the front of this book.

Diving and Snorkeling

The warm, placid bays along the coast are ideal, and many of the big beach resorts have snorkeling and diving gear. Sunken archaeological sites, where the ocean floor is littered with ancient columns and bits of stairways and tombs, put Turkey's Mediterranean Coast among the world's top diving experiences.

Lodging

Most of the upscale lodgings are in Marmaris, Kemer, and Antalya. Accommodations elsewhere are more modest. As a rule, expect clean, simply furnished rooms, with low, wooden beds, industrial carpeting or Turkish rugs, and maybe a print on the wall. As many establishments are near the water, be sure to ask for a room with a view. The rare surcharges are insignificant. For a chart that explains room rates at the accommodations in this chapter, *see* Dining and Lodging Price Categories at the front of this book.

Nightlife

Nightlife barely exists in the small towns and villages. However, you will find disco and bar action in the main resort areas, typically within hotels. In Kemer, for example, it's hard to find a place without a disco. Elsewhere, do as the locals do and let dinner in a waterfront setting be the evening's entertainment. Sometimes your meal will be accompanied by music; it will always be accompanied by raki—Turkey's distinctive anise–grape seed schnapps. It shouldn't be hard to strike up a conversation with residents and vacationing Turks; tourist traffic along the coast is not so heavy that they have lost interest in visitors. If you are headed for a disco, the action usually starts around 10 PM and ends around 2 AM.

Shopping

Shops pop up in the oddest spots, in places with no town for miles and sometimes no electricity. Some finds can be had in the bazaars at Antalya and Marmaris. Look for old jewelry, leather goods and sandals, local jams, honey, and spices. The smaller towns have outdoor markets, usually only once a week. Visiting on the right day is hard to plan, so accept fate and shop when the opportunity presents itself.

Exploring the Mediterranean Coast

Until the mid-1970s, Turkey's southwest coast was inaccessible to all but the most determined travelers—those intrepid souls in four-wheel-drive vehicles or on the backs of donkeys. Today well-maintained highways wind through the area. The countryside along the Turquoise

Coast, east from Marmaris, is uncrowded, and the ruins are unlike anything on the Aegean Coast. The beaten path peters out after Antalya and Side, although the adventurous (and those with plenty of time) can continue all the way to Antakya, near the Syrian border. The attractions below are listed roughly from east to west from Marmaris, with a loop to Loryma and the Datça Peninsula west from Marmaris.

Great Itineraries

If you have seven full days, you will have time to travel from Marmaris to Antalya, stopping at all of the highlights in between. You'll have to stick to the beaten path to cover all this ground in a week, but fortunately in Turkey the beaten path isn't all that beaten. Even if you have only three days, you will find time to comb the beaches, explore local villages, and visit ancient ruins. With a car, you will be able to pack more into each day, though taking the bus—a viable option since local service is so good—would give you time to rest between sights. Another option, outlined in the five-day itinerary below, is to fly into Antalya and work your way west by car or bus.

IF YOU HAVE 3 DAYS

Numbers in the text correspond to numbers in the margin and on the Western and Eastern Mediterranean Coast and Antalya maps.

On your first morning, proceed north and then east from **Marmaris** ① on Route 400. Relax for an hour or so in the sulfurous hot springs along the eastern shore of **Lake Köyceğiz** ⑤. In the afternoon, head to the intimate village of ⚑ **Dalyan** ⑥, where you can catch a boat to **Kaunos** ⑦. Explore the ruins in Kaunos before continuing on to İstuzu Beach. Return to Dalyan for a quiet riverside dinner. The next morning, head to ⚑ **Fethiye** ⑨ to view the town's famous rock tombs, then board a boat for a visit to **Gemiler Island** ⑩, which holds the ruins of several civilizations. Spend your third day on the beach at **Ölü Deniz** ⑫.

IF YOU HAVE 5 DAYS

Fly to ⚑ **Antalya** ㉖–㉝ on day one. Stroll around the **old harbor** ㉖, shop in the **covered bazaar** ㉚, and visit the **Antalya Müzesi** ㉝. The next morning, head west on Route 400, stopping for a picnic or a swim at **Phaselis** ㉔ before exploring the unexcavated remains of nearby **Mt. Olympos** ㉓. Arrive in ⚑ **Kaş** ⑲ in time for dinner. On day three, take a boat trip to **Kekova Sound.** Stay another night in Kaş. The next morning, head to ⚑ **Fethiye** ⑨ and **Ölü Deniz** ⑫. Dine in Fethiye and overnight there. On your final day, visit **Marmaris** ①.

IF YOU HAVE 7 DAYS

Begin your first day in **Marmaris** ①, and then drive north and east on Route 400, stopping at **Lake Köyceğiz** ⑤ on the way to ⚑ **Dalyan** ⑥. Have dinner along the waterfront in Dalyan. The next day, take a boat to **Kaunos** ⑦ and İstuzu Beach before returning to Dalyan. On day three stop in ⚑ **Fethiye** ⑨. Take a swim and have a late lunch or an early dinner at nearby **Ölü Deniz** ⑫. The following day, continue east on Route 400 to ⚑ **Kaş** ⑲, stopping en route at the Lycian cities of **Tlos** ⑬, **Pinara** ⑭, and **Xanthos** ⑯. In the evening, stroll along the harbor in Kaş. On day five, take a boat trip from Kaş to **Kekova Sound.** After spending a second night in Kaş, continue east on day six to **Mt. Olympos** ㉓ and **Phaselis** ㉔. Have dinner overlooking the harbor and overnight in ⚑ **Antalya** ㉖–㉝. On day seven, hit as many of Antalya's highlights as your schedule permits.

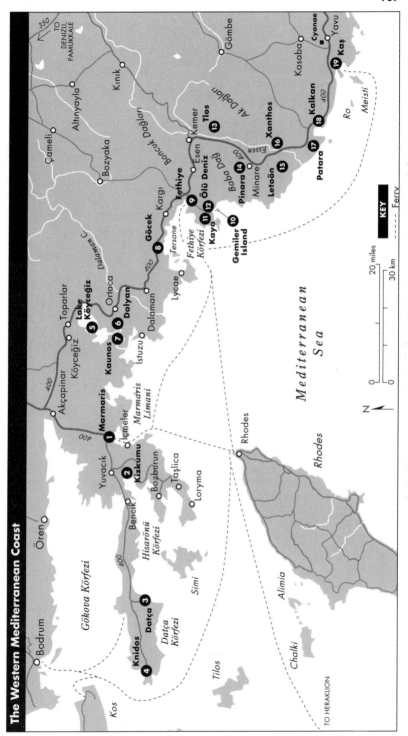

The Western Mediterranean Coast

TO DENIZLI, PAMUKKALE

350

Ören

Bodrum

Gökova Körfezi

Yuvacik

Toparlar

Köyceğiz

Akçapinar

400

Marmaris

İçmeler

Kizkumu

Bencik

Marmaris Limani

Bozburun

Taşlica

Hisarönü Körfezi

Loryma

Simi

Datça

Datça Körfezi

Knidos

Kos

Tilos

Chalki

Alimia

Rhodes

Rhodes

TO HERAKLION

Mediterranean Sea

N

20 miles
30 km

KEY
--- --- Ferry

Çameli

Altınyayla

Bozyaka

Kınık

Boncuk Dağları

Dalaman C

400

Ortaca

Lake Köyceğiz

Dalyan

Kaunos

İstuzu

Dalaman

400

Göcek

Tersane

Lycae

Kargı

Fethiye

Fethiye Körfezi

Kaya

Gemiler Island

Ölü Deniz

Esen

Kemer

Tlos

Ak Dağları

Esen

400

Baba Dağ

Pinara

Minare

Letoön

Xanthos

Patara

Kalkan

Gömbe

Kasaba

Kasaba

Cyanae

Yavu

Kaş

Ro

Meisti

400

1 Marmaris
2 Kizkumu
3 Datça
4 Knidos
5 Lake Köyceğiz
6 Dalyan
7 Kaunos
8 Göcek
9 Fethiye
10 Gemiler Island
11 Kaya
12 Ölü Deniz
13 Tlos
14 Pinara
15 Letoön
16 Xanthos
17 Patara
18 Kalkan
19 Kaş

The Eastern Mediterranean Coast

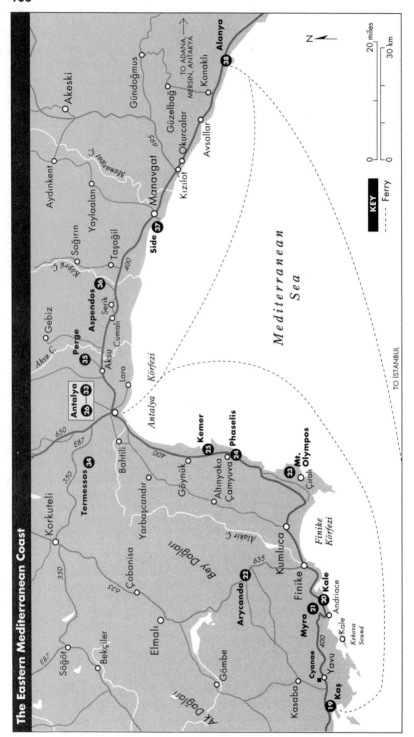

N

20 miles
30 km

TO ADANA, MERSIN, ANTAKYA →

Alanya 38

Konaklı

Güzelbağ

Gündoğmus

Okurcalar

Avsallar

Kizilöt

Akeski

Aydınkent

Manavgat 37

Yaylaalan

Side 37

Sağırın

Taşağil

Gebiz

Aspendos 36

Serik

Perge 35

Cumali

Aksu

Iara

Antalya 26–33

Termessos 34

Korkuteli

Bahtili

Göynük

Kemer 25

Phaselis 24

Altınyaka

Çamyuva

Mt. Olympos 23

Çıralı

Yarbaşçandır

Çobanisa

Kumluca

Finike Körfezi

Bey Dağları

Arycanda 22

Kumluca

Finike

Myra 21

Kale 20

Kale 19 Kaş

Cyanae

Yavu

Andriace

Kekova Sound

Elmalı

Gömbe

Kasaba

Bekçiler

Söğüt

Ak Dağları

Mediterranean Sea

Antalya Körfezi

TO ISTANBUL

KEY
--- Ferry

MARMARIS AND THE DATÇA PENINSULA

Modernity confronts antiquity in the westernmost portion of the Mediterranean Coast. The smart, international party crowd headquarters itself in Marmaris. Heading west from the town are several ancient ruins of note.

Marmaris

❶ *178 km (111 mi) from Bodrum northeast on coast road to Milas, and east and south on Rte. 330 to Rte. 400.*

A broad boulevard lined with eucalyptus trees leads into Marmaris, a fashionable resort area between two bays, backed by an old castle. The jumping-off point for some of the best sailing on the Mediterranean, it has sprouted the boutiques, restaurants, and nightlife that seem to be a requirement for the yachting set. The result is an attractive ensemble that is a far cry from anything in rural Turkey. Because of this, some will say it is not authentically "Turkish" and push on into the hinterland; others will be mesmerized and settle in for a long stay.

Until the growth of tourism, Marmaris was a sleepy little fishing village, but its origins go back more than 2,500 years. The modern town is built on the site of the ancient Greek city of Phryscus, the remains of which can still be seen on Asar Tepe, a hill 1½ km (1 mi) to the north of the modern town. Its fine natural harbor once attracted warships rather than today's yachts and pleasure boats. Süleyman the Magnificent launched his successful seaborne assault on the island of Rhodes from here in 1522, and the fleet of the British admiral Horatio Nelson sheltered in Marmaris before setting forth to defeat the ships of Napoléon Bonaparte at the battle of Aboukir in Egypt in 1798.

Modern Marmaris has a palm-lined waterfront promenade and a well-stocked bazaar where you can pick up delicious local honey and rose jam, frankincense, and other exotica. If you prefer more westernized shopping, visit the Netsel Shopping Mall next to the marina, which has coffee bars and Ralph Lauren and Lacoste stores. Urban sprawl—literally every block has a construction site—is making the city less attractive than in days gone by, but you can strike out for nearby beaches at İçmeler, Turunç, and Kumlubük.

NEED A
BREAK?

At the **Turunç Bar Yacht Club,** you can dine on traditional Turkish dishes on a small terrace built into a hill above a sandy cove, surrounded by mountains and pine forests. It's on the road toward Kumlubük beach, about a five-minute walk from the harbor, and is closed from November through mid-May.

Dining and Lodging

$$-$$$ ✕ **La Campagna.** This upscale restaurant, owned by an Italian chef and
★ her Turkish husband, is a real treat—it's probably the only place in Turkey where you can eat authentic homemade Italian pasta and tiramisu while watching boats head out to sea. There's also fresh fish, a full bar, an excellent wine list, and outdoor seating overlooking the Mediterranean during the summer. ⊠ *Netsel Marina,* ☎ *252/412–5557. MC, V.*

$-$$ ✕ **Birtat.** One of the best restaurants along the atmospheric waterfront promenade at the yacht harbor specializes in fish dishes and a good selection of starters. Depending on the weather, you can opt for either indoor or outdoor seating. ⊠ *Yat Limani,* ☎ *252/412–1076. No credit cards.*

$–$$ ✕ **Pineapple.** The menu is eclectic at this international restaurant in the Marmaris marina. The house specialty is roast lamb, but the chef also prepares Thai chicken, French onion soup, steak Diane, and fish-and-chips. Above Pineapple is its sister restaurant, My Marina English Pub. ⊠ *Netsel Marina,* ☎ *252/412–0976. AE, DC, MC, V.*

$ ✕ **Le Petit Café.** You're not in New York's East Village or Paris's Left Bank, but you'll sure feel far away from Turkey at this tiny waterfront café. Its limited menu includes salads, soups, sandwiches, pasta, and homemade cakes. On a nice day, you can sit outside, drink cappuccino, and watch the boats pass by. ⊠ *Yat Limani 231, no phone. No credit cards.*

$$$$ 🏨 **Mares Marmaris.** If you're looking for a first-class international resort, the Mares has so many activities and amenities that you may not find a need to leave during your entire stay. With 24-hour room service, plush bath towels, satellite TV, minibars, and bathroom telephones, you might not even want to go outside. You also have an option of staying in one of 159 villas on site or in a no-smoking room (a rarity in Turkey). ⊠ *Pamucak Mevkii,* ☎ *252/412–3617,* 𝔽𝔸𝕏 *252/412– 1214. 442 rooms with bath. 4 restaurants, 9 bars, minibars, no-smoking rooms, room service, 2 pools, Turkish bath, 2 tennis courts, health club, windsurfing, boating, shops, casino, dance club, children's programs. AE, DC, MC, V.*

$$–$$$ 🏨 **Hotel Elegance.** Rooms at this beach resort 3 km (2 mi) from the center of town are done in pastels, with floral-print curtains and bedspreads. All have terraces and some have sea views. The grounds are dotted with palm trees, and the beach is a long strip of white sand. There are more amenities here than in most Turkish hotels. ⊠ *Uzunyali Cad. 130,* ☎ *252/412–8101,* 𝔽𝔸𝕏 *252/412–2005. 190 rooms with bath. 2 restaurants, 4 bars, minibars, room service, 2 pools, Turkish bath, windsurfing, boating, waterskiing, shops, casino, dance club, babysitting. AE, DC, MC, V.*

$$ 🏨 **Hotel Lidya.** It's in no way intimate, but the Lidya has pretty gardens filled with jasmine and bougainvillea, and a full range of amenities, rather like a small-town Holiday Inn. It is also one of the few hotels in town with a private beach. The property is a long walk (or a fairly short drive) from the center of town, but its disco still manages to draw a crowd. ⊠ *Siteler Mah. 130, Uzunyalı,* ☎ *252/412–2940,* 𝔽𝔸𝕏 *252/412– 1478. 343 rooms with bath. 2 restaurants, 5 bars, indoor pool, beach, windsurfing, boating, dance club. AE, DC, MC, V.*

$$ 🏨 **Turban Marmaris Holiday Village.** One of the nicer all-inclusive resorts along the coast, the Turban Marmaris is on enchanting Turunç Bay, well away from the action of Marmaris itself. Families will like the place because accommodations are mostly in individual chalets in the pines and breakfast and dinner are included in the price. Guest rooms and public spaces are very plain; the beauty of the surroundings is the dominant feature. There's a good beach and plenty of water sports. ⊠ *Boynuzbuku, Marmaris,* ☎ *252/412–1843,* 𝔽𝔸𝕏 *252/412–3576. 234 bungalows with bath. Restaurant, 3 bars, beach, dive shop, windsurfing, boating, waterskiing, dance club, playground. AE, DC, MC, V. Closed Nov.–Apr.*

$–$$ 🏨 **Hotel Halici.** Because it is off Marmaris's waterfront promenade, the Halici doesn't have a view, but it does have quiet, something that you won't find right on the main drag. Extensive gardens filled with eucalyptus trees add to the sense of peace. Public areas and guest rooms are decorated with Turkish antiques and kilims, though the rooms could otherwise have come straight out of a 1950s roadside motel. At press time, the hotel was being renovated, so room decor may yet be brought up to date. ⊠ *66 Sok. 5,* ☎ *252/412–1683 or 252/412–3626,* FAX *252/412–9200. 131 rooms with shower. Restaurant, bar, pool. MC, V. Closed Nov.–Mar.*

$–$$ 🏨 **Otel 47.** This modern hotel on the waterfront in the center of town has comfortable rooms, many with double beds and wooden balconies overlooking the sea. ⊠ *Atatürk Cad. 10,* ☎ *252/412–4747,* FAX *252/412–4151. 51 rooms with bath. Restaurant, bar. DC, MC, V. Closed Nov.–Mar.*

Nightlife

Marmaris has the major nightlife scene on the Mediterranean Coast. The **Joy Club** at Içmeler beach is a dance club. The **Daily News** and **Sultan** bars are both on a little square by the caravansary in the historic district. **Physkos,** a bar at the yacht harbor, is big with the boating crowd.

Outdoor Activities and Sports

BOATS AND CHARTERS

You don't have to go far to escape the crowds that gather in Marmaris in season. The Marmaris and Datça peninsulas, which together form a sort of lobster claw at the far southwestern edge of the country, are blissfully untrammeled. The best way to see them is by boat; inquire at the Marmaris harbor about charters, both with crew and bare. In 1996 rates were about $500 a day for craft with six double berths and crew, but the exact fare is a direct reflection of your ability to haggle. Except in summer, which is high season here, you can simply present yourself on the quay and strike a deal on the spot; you'll get a far better price than if you book your cruise stateside and end up paying commissions on top of the fare. Alkor Yachting (☎ 252/412–4385, FAX 252/412–4384) and Yeşil Marmaris (☎ 252/412–6486, FAX 252/412–4470) are good sources.

Kizkumu

❷ *30 km (19 mi) from Marmaris, west on Rte. 400 and south on road to Bozburun.*

Pine-covered mountains surround this tiny village (known as Keci Buku on navigational maps) around an idyllic bay. You can get here by boat from Marmaris or by car. In the middle of the bay is a stretch of red sand just under the surface of the water. Legend has it that long ago a young girl was fleeing from marauding pirates. While running she gathered red dirt in her dress and cast it in front of her to form a path across the bay. She ran out of dirt, but her efforts were said to have created a coastal spit, which makes it possible to venture in the middle of the bay and look like one is walking on water. Just south of the spit are signs for Şekule waterfall. You've probably seen more spectacular falls, but the 15-minute walk to them through a forest complete with babbling brook is like a visit to Arcadia.

NEED A BREAK?   The fish couldn't be fresher than it is at the tree-shaded **Stone House Restaurant,** 3 km (1½ mi) south of Kizkumu at the entrance to the Şekule waterfall. Chicken wire partitions off a section of a nearby stream. Fish ordered here makes it from the stream to your plate in six minutes—and you can even catch it yourself.

OFF THE BEATEN PATH   **LORYMA –** A vast citadel stands guard over lonely Bozuk Bay in Loryma, one of the most beautiful spots on the coast. The citadel dates from Hellenistic times—the late 3rd through 1st centuries BC. Also along the coast are Amos, with its heavily fortified towers and gates, and Gerbekse, with the romantic ruins of several Byzantine churches. Approaching each of these cities from the sea (by boat from Marmaris or Kizkumu) is all the more dramatic. ⊠ *116 km (72 mi) from Marmaris, west on Rte. 440 and south on road to Bozburun.*

Datça Peninsula

76 km (47 mi) west of Marmaris (to town of Datça) on Rte. 400.

❸ Getting to **Datça** is easiest and quickest by sea: By land, the trip from Marmaris has startlingly beautiful views but takes as much as two hours on a winding road. The peninsula is heavily forested and lightly populated. Datça is more than the fishing village it once was, though not yet a real resort; the city's residents are refreshingly less obsessed with tourism than their counterparts elsewhere along the coast. There are a couple of antiques shops, simple restaurants, and a bar or two for the boating crowd.

❹ Windswept **Knidos** sits on a headland at the very end of the Datça Peninsula, 38 km (24 mi) west of Datça, where the Aegean meets the Mediterranean. A very primitive site, its ruins are strewn amid olive groves and few hints of modern civilization. The city was founded in the 7th century BC by Dorian Greeks; because of its prime location on shipping routes between Egypt, Rhodes, Ephesus, the Greek mainland, and other major ports, it later served as the meeting place for a federation of Dorian cities—including Rhodes, Kos, and Halicarnassus. Its main claim to fame was a temple to Aphrodite that housed a 4th-century BC statue of the goddess by Praxiteles, a realistic nude that the historian Pliny called the finest statue in the world. The statue became a tourist attraction, drawing travelers from afar, among them Cicero and Julius Caesar; eventually, it vanished.

Though Knidos is pretty much a do-it-yourself site, with few descriptive markers, the site custodian may be willing to show you around if the day is not too hot. As you approach, you will see the original stairway that led to the upper portion of the city to your right. Climb up and you will find the excavations of a **sanctuary to the goddess Demeter.** The British archaeologist Sir Charles Newton found a statue of her here in the 1850s and duly had it shipped to the British Museum.

To see the foundations of the unusual **circular temple** that housed the statue of Aphrodite, make your way to the trio of primitive restaurants by the harbor and follow the path leading uphill to the right. In 1970 a fragment of what may have been the original statue, inscribed *Prax*(iteles) and *Aph*(rodite), was found at the top of the hill. Back by the harbor, there is a small *odeon,* or concert hall. On the promontory with the lighthouse is the rectangular, stone **Lion Tomb**—the lion, however, has been removed and now resides in the British Museum.

Dining and Lodging

$$ ✗☷ **Hotel Mare.** Though the bright white building looks like a suburban corporate headquarters, this is the quintessential spot for getting away from it all, out on Datça's western beach, about 2 km (1 mi) from town. The rooms have balconies but are otherwise clean and simple. Modest suites make good choices for large families. The lawns and flower gardens are well manicured and quite pleasant. ⊠ *Datça,* ☎ *252/712–3397,* FAX *252/712–3396. 50 rooms with shower. Restaurant, bar, pool. MC, V.*

$ ✕ 🏠 **Olimpos Hotel.** Airy and clean, the Olimpos is decorated with old kilims and wood furniture. The staff is very accommodating, and the restaurant good. ✉ *Koru Mah., Datça,* ☎ *252/712–2001,* 🖷 *252/712–2653. 30 rooms with bath. Restaurant, bar, outdoor café. MC, V.*

THE TURQUOISE COAST
From Köyceğiz to Kemer

Lycia, a compact, mountainous, and isolated area that extends all the way to Antalya, begins just east of Köyceğiz. The first mention of the Lycians appears in Hittite records dating from the 14th century BC. Egyptian documents written a century later tell of a troublesome sea people called the Lukki, whom some historians believe to be the Lycians. The historian Herodotus, writing in the 5th century BC, said that the Lycians were descended from Sarpedon, who was exiled by his brother, King Minos of Crete, sometime around 1400 BC. Homer places them on the side of Troy in the Trojan War. The Lycians were considered an extraordinarily independent people, with their own language (even now not completely deciphered) and a fierce determination not to be conquered.

Like the rest of Anatolia, Lycia was ruled by a succession of overlords, starting with the Persians in the 6th century BC. It was the last region on the Mediterranean Coast to be incorporated into the Roman Empire (at the end of the 2nd century BC). The six major cities in the Lycian Union—Xanthos, Patara, Pinara, Tlos, Myra, and Olympos—grew wealthy from sea trade. Its citizens made an art of building monumental tombs. There were regal rock tombs carved directly into cliff walls, resembling everything from Ionic temples to rustic houses; pillar tombs, such as the one at Xanthos, with a massive, rectangular grave chamber 26 feet high; and giant sarcophagi, with arched lids.

Köyceğiz

63 km (39 mi) east of Marmaris on Rte. 400.

❺ The entire **Lake Köyceğiz** area is a wildlife preserve, inhabited by kingfishers, kestrels, egrets, and cranes. The peaceful market town of Köyceğiz has a lakeside promenade and broad, shady trees. The lion statues displayed in the town square, dredged out of nearby marshes, hint at the buried riches yet to be found in the region. Dotting the lake's eastern shore are the Sultaniye sulfurous hot springs, said to have medicinal value. Although their smell can be off-putting, the hot, muddy pools make for a bathing experience many pay good money for at posh spas. There are no facilities, so bring your own towels.

Dining and Lodging

$$ ✕ 🏠 **Panorama Plaza.** The lobby of one of the plusher hotels along the lakeside promenade is tastefully decorated with antiques and kilims. Every room has a terrace and a minibar, and the hotel will plan day trips for you. But since most of the guests are German, there's no guarantee that your guide will speak English. ✉ *Cengiz Topel Cad. 69, Ulucamii Mah.,* ☎ *252/262–3773 or 252/262–2642,* 🖷 *252/262–3633. 28 rooms with shower. Restaurant, 2 bars, minibars, pool. MC, V.*

$ ✕ 🏠 **Hotel Ozay.** On the shore of Lake Köyceğiz with views across to the mountains beyond, this family-run hotel is quiet and efficiently run. There is an outdoor café in a garden draped with vines, bougainvillea, and jasmine. The restaurant is above average. The hotel also organizes daily boat trips to nearby sites. ✉ *Kordon Boyu 11,* ☎ *252/262–4300 or 252/262–4361,* 🖷 *252/262–2000. 32 rooms with bath. Restaurant, bar, outdoor café, pool. MC, V.*

Dalyan

★ ❻ *12 km (7 mi) south of Köyceğiz on Rte. 400 to local road (follow signs).*

Carian tombs are carved into the cliff that rises from behind the reed-backed Dalyan River in the quiet fishing town of Dalyan. When the cliff is lit up at night, it's rather a grand sight. Dalyan has resisted development as a tourist destination, but its several restaurants and hotels make it a good base for exploring the ancient city of Kaunos, 10 km (7 mi) to the west. To reach Kaunos and İstuzu Beach, just downstream from Dalyan at Ekincik, rent a boat with a boatman at the harbor in Dalyan (they'll be lined up waiting for you; expect to pay about $20).

★ **İstuzu Beach** stretches for 5 unspoiled km (3 mi), with the Mediterranean on one side and a freshwater lagoon on the other. In June and July, carretta sea turtles lay their eggs here; signs along the beach mark possible nesting places and warn visitors not to stick umbrellas in the sand, which might damage nests. An international contingent intent on preserving the area for the turtle successfully fended off developers.

In his *Metamorphosis,* Ovid immortalized Kaunos, who fled from the amorous advances of his sister Byblis and founded the city that now bears his name; nymphs turned Byblis, who wept inconsolably at the ❼ loss, into a fountain. The remains at **Kaunos** include a crumbling Byzantine basilica, a massive Roman bath that is being restored as a site museum, and a well-preserved semicircular 4th-century BC theater cut into the hillside in the Greek style. The rock tombs here, although evocative and beautiful, are not strictly Lycian, as they appear to be. Instead it was the Carians, whose kingdom bordered Lycia, who carved these tombs in the 4th century BC in the Lycian style.

Dining and Lodging

$$–$$$ ✕ **Denizatı.** This is probably the best of Dalyan's riverside restaurants. The putter of caïques out on the water and the chirp of crickets in the evening set the tone. The service is thoroughly pleasant, and the gray mullet are caught locally and usually grilled to perfection. ⊠ *South of main sq. and statue of Atatürk,* ☎ *252/284–2268. MC, V. Closed fall–spring.*

$$–$$$ ✕ **Deniz Yılızı.** This fish restaurant lacks the view of its nearby sibling, Denizatı. Still, with its white table cloths, excellent service, and good selection of Turkish wine, it's a classy establishment that isn't so fancy you can't bring along the kids. ⊠ *Çarşi Içi,* ☎ *252/284–4183. MC, V.*

$$ ✕🏨 **Binlik Hotel.** Rooms at this family-run hotel are not luxurious, but ★ it does offer more amenities—such as blow-dryers and full-size beds— than most hotels its size. If you like meeting fellow travelers, this is the place to stay; guests generally gather in the comfortable common area after meals. Take the half-board option, as dinners here are satisfying. ⊠ *Sulungur Cad. 16,* ☎ *252/284–2148,* FAX *252/284–2149. 82 rooms with shower. Restaurant, 2 bars, minibars, 2 pools. MC, V.*

$$ ✕🏨 **Dalyan Hotel.** Comfortable, clean, and with views across the Dalyan River of ancient tombs, this hotel has an excellent restaurant. The attentive staff organizes bird-watching and moonlight excursions on Lake Köyceğiz and hiking, bicycling, and motorcycling trips on nearby mountain paths. ⊠ *Yali Sok., Maras Mah.,* ☎ *252/284–2239,* FAX *252/284–2240. 20 rooms with shower. 2 restaurants, 2 bars, pool, snorkeling, windsurfing, playground. MC, V.*

$$–$$$ 🏨 **Hotel Assyrian.** With modern bathrooms, 24-hour room service, and a large pool overlooking the Dalyan River, this relatively new property is a pleasant place to escape civilization without having to suffer

for lack of amenities. One km (½ mi) from the center of town, the hotel encourages long stays by offering reduced rates for extended visits. ☎ *252/284–3232,* ☏ *252/284–3244. 34 rooms with bath. Restaurant, outdoor café, bar, snack bar, air-conditioning, minibars, room service, pool. AE, DC, MC, V.*

$ 🏨 **Antik Hotel.** This hotel, 1 km (½ mi) from the center of Dalyan, is comfortable and well run, with air-conditioning in most rooms and balconies in all of them. ☎ *252/284–2136,* ☏ *252/284–2138. 42 rooms with shower. Restaurant, 2 bars, pool, playground, laundry service. No credit cards.*

Göcek

⑧ *40 km (24 mi) east of Dalyan on Rte. 400.*

Water-taxi service from Göcek, just east of Dalaman Airport, delivers visitors to any of the **Twelve Islands,** or one can hire yachts and gulets. These tiny dots of land lack exceptional ruins, but have coves with beaches. The most popular anchorages include Tersane, Kapi Creek, Cleopatra's Bay, and Tomb Bay. You can also take the water taxi to Kizilkuyruk Koyu, a village on a small, remote bay near ancient Lydae. Little is known about the history of this scenic but oft-deserted site with bits of ruined walls, foundations of ancient buildings, and fragments of decorative, carved marble. Katranci, in a rocky headland about halfway between Göcek and Fethiye, is a secluded cove and one of the prettiest spots in the area for a swim.

Fethiye

⑨ *52 km (32 mi) east of Göcek, 168 km (104 mi) east of Marmaris on Rte. 400.*

Fethiye was rebuilt after the original town was destroyed in an earthquake in 1957. Although it looks modern as a result, it's still an old-fashioned agricultural community where goats and sheep are herded along the main roads on their way to market. At night, residents promenade along the lighted harbor or relax, sipping tea, in their gardens. Daytimes lack charm, except for the spirited produce market where herbs, dried fruits, frankincense, and saffron are displayed and bartered. Saffron goes for a fraction of its price abroad. Fethiye was known in antiquity as Telmessus (not to be confused with Termessos near Antalya) and was the principal port of Lycia from the Roman period onward. In front of the town hall is the finest of several scattered tombs, representing a two-story Lycian house, with reliefs of warriors on both sides of its lid.

Fethiye's **museum** has some fine statues and jewelry from the glory days of Telmessus, and the English-language label interpretation is lively, even provocative, as in the following: "If you consider history as a period of time that has no significance for you, then it is only natural that you are indifferent to the destruction of cultural values." ⊠ *Off Atatürk Cad. (look for signs).* 🎟 *$1.50.* ☉ *Tues.–Sun. 8:30–5.*

Impressive **rock tombs** were carved into the cliff that looms above town. The largest is the **Tomb of Amyntas,** presumably a 4th-century BC ruler or nobleman. The portico imitates an Ionic temple; the door to the main grave chamber even has faux iron studs. Inside are the slabs where corpses were laid out. To reach the tombs you'll have to climb many steps—the stairway starts at Kaya Caddesi, near the bus station—but your effort will be well rewarded, particularly at dusk, when the cliffs take on a reddish glow. West via Kaya Caddesi is the requisite crusader castle, probably dating from the 12th century and attributed to the Knights of St. John.

The boats and water taxis in Fethiye's harbors take visitors on a variety of tours, some including meals, to Göcek, the Twelve Islands, Gemiler Island, and Ölü Deniz. Itineraries are posted, and there are people on hand to answer questions. Be sure to shop around, as packages vary widely. The cost ranges from $5 to $15 per person.

⑩ Gemiler Island is a scenic must, surrounded by an amphitheater of mountains and scattered with Byzantine remains, dating from the 7th to 9th centuries. There are also some Lycian tombs from the 2nd century BC, as well as a 19th-century Greek church with some intact mosaics dedicated to Saint Nicholas.

Dining and Lodging

$$ ✕ Meğri Restaurant. Stone walls, high-wood ceilings, and decorative kilims give this upscale fish restaurant the feel of a Swiss chalet as imagined by Turks. It's often crowded, so don't consider eating here if you're in a hurry. ⊠ *Eski Cami Geçidi Likya Sok. 8–9,* ☎ *252/614–4046. MC, V.*

$–$$ ✕ Yat. As its name suggests, this waterfront restaurant opposite the marina attracts the international yachting crowd. Fish (usually grilled), lamb (in stew and kebabs), and *bonfilé* (steaks) are the specialties. You can eat indoors or out in the garden. Some nights musicians and a belly dancer perform. ⊠ *Yat Limanı Karşısı (yacht harbor), near Hotel Likya,* ☎ *252/614–7014 or 252/614–9272. MC, V.*

$ ✕ Meğri Lokantasi. Away from the waterfront, this simple place has a good selection of typical local food. Vegetarian cuisine is also available. ⊠ *Çarşi Cad. 13/A,* ☎ *252/614–4047. No credit cards.*

$ ✕ Tepsi Restaurant. On a street parallel to the main thoroughfare, this no-frills restaurant serves standard Turkish dishes. ⊠ *Çarşi Cad.,* ☎ *252/614–2233. No credit cards.*

$–$$ ▦ Hotel Likya. If you've stayed in other small Turkish towns, you know what to expect—small rooms, small beds, simple wooden furniture. But there are compensations here. The gardens are attractively planted with flower beds, and rooms look out across them and toward the bay. At press time, the hotel's famous waterfront Chinese restaurant was closed for renovation but was expected to reopen. A Turkish restaurant remains on site. ⊠ *Yat Limanı,* ☎ *252/614–2234,* ℻ *252/614–1169. 40 rooms with shower. 2 restaurants, 2 bars, pool. MC, V.*

$ ▦ Otel Dedeoglu. This reliable old hotel has basic rooms with views over the bay. The location is convenient, near the yacht harbor and the tourist information office. ⊠ *İskele Meyd.,* ☎ *252/614–4010,* ℻ *252/614–1707. 44 rooms with bath. Restaurant, bar. AE, MC, V.*

Outdoor Activities and Sports

Med Diving (⊠ İskele Meyd., opposite Yacht Marina, ☎ 252/614–2587), and **Hotel Likya** (⊠ Yat Limanı, ☎ 252/614–2234, ℻ 252/614–1169) can provide information about local conditions and necessary permits.

Kaya

⑪ *From Fethiye, take the local road toward Ölü Deniz; as you head east, about 5 km (3 mi) before the turnoff to Ölü Deniz, look for signs to Kaya on the right side.*

Highly atmospheric Kaya is a ruin of an entirely different order from all others along the Mediterranean Coast. Turks assiduously avoid the place, a thriving Greek community until 1923, when all of the village's residents were repatriated to Greece after it unsuccessfully invaded Turkey in World War I. Spread across three hills, Kaya is eerily quiet and slowly crumbling. You can wander through small cuboid houses reminiscent of those in the Greek islands, some with a touch of bright Mediterranean blue or red on the walls. In the two basilicas, the murals have all been defaced, although Christ and the Apostles are visible in one. A few Turkish families that live near the ruins sell soda and trinkets to the occasional tourist. They may invite you inside their homes and serve you tea, after which you'll probably (they hope) feel obligated to buy something from them.

Ölü Deniz

★ ⑫ *15 km (9 mi) south of Fethiye.*

Ölü Deniz is one of Turkey's great natural wonders, an azure lagoon rimmed by white sand and pebble beaches. The area, a national park, can be reached by ferry, car, or *dolmuş* (shared taxi). The water is warm and the setting entirely delightful, even with the crowds. There's a single beachfront hotel, and campgrounds at the lagoon's edge with a handful of chalets are for rent. Opposite the beach are small restaurants with rooftop bars, many with live music.

Dining and Lodging

$$ ✕ **Beyaz Yunus.** Wicker chairs and wooden floors are set beneath a domed ceiling at the so-called White Dolphin, probably the nicest place in the Ölü Deniz area. It's on the adjacent bay of Belcekiz on a promontory near Padirali, a spot with fine views of the placid turquoise waters. Continental and Turkish dishes are imaginatively prepared and presented. ☎ *252/616–6036. No credit cards.*

$ ✕ **Asmali Restaurant.** On the road to the Meri Oteli, this family-run restaurant serves homemade dishes, which vary from day to day, and cold mezes, grilled meats, and fish. It has a beautiful garden terrace with overhanging vines. ☎ *No phone. No credit cards.*

$$$$ ✕🏨 **Robinson Club Likya.** The real plus of this huge, self-contained Turkish-owned/German-managed, Club Med–type resort village is a full array of water-sports equipment and sports facilities. The hotel's low, red-tile-roofed buildings cluster along a private beach and among green lawns and shady trees. The comfortable rooms are a few steps above those in town—about the equivalent of rooms in a modern motel in the United States. ⊠ *Ölü Deniz Kıdırak Mev.,* ☎ *252/616–6010 or 212/253–6200 in Istanbul;* ☎ *252/616–6011. 550 rooms with shower. 4 restaurants, 4 bars, 2 pools, 21 tennis courts, massage, sauna, health club, archery, volleyball, beach, windsurfing, nightclub, children's programs, playground. AE, DC, MC, V. Closed Nov.–Apr.*

$$$–$$$$ 🏨 **Meri Oteli.** This hotel's setting on a steep incline above the lagoon, alongside terraced gardens and overlooking one of Turkey's most beautiful bays, is a delight. Rooms are another story: Although perfectly clean, they're a bit down-at-the-heels and overpriced. But the area is short on accommodations, other than a few small guest houses. To get here, look for signs for Meri; this is the only hotel on its bay. ⊠ ☎ *252/616–6060,* ☎ *252/616–6456. 75 rooms with bath. Restaurant, bar, beach. AE, MC, V. Closed Nov.–Apr.*

Tlos

⑬ *About 20 km (12 mi) east of Fethiye; exit Rte. 400 and follow the local road north to Kemer, where a yellow sign marks the right turn that leads south for 15 km (9 mi) to Tlos.*

Tlos, an ancient Lycian city situated high above the valley of the Xanthos River, was called Tlawa in Lycian. Archaeologists believe it to be the Dalawa mentioned in 14th-century BC Hittite records. Park, pay your admission to the site custodian, and climb up to the **acropolis** for a stunning view of the Xanthos valley to the west and mountains—holding a Roman theater—to the east. The fortress at the summit is Turkish, from the 18th century, and was a popular haunt of the pirate Kanli ("Bloody") Ali Aga. Below the fortress, off a narrow track, is a cluster of rock tombs. Note the relief here of Bellerophon, son of King Glaucus of Corinth, mounted on Pegasus, the winged horse. The monster he faces is the dread Chimera—a fire-breathing creature with a lion's head, goat's body, and serpent's tail. (According to legend, Bellerophon won.) If you have time, hike over to the theater you saw from the fortress; among the ruins are carved blocks depicting actors' masks. Nearby, the old baths building provides a magnificent view of the Xanthos valley. This is a do-it-yourself site, but though there are no descriptive signs or maps, you should have little trouble finding the main sights. ⌂ *$1.* ☉ *Daily 8:30–sunset.*

Pinara

⑭ *40 km (24 mi) southeast of Fethiye on Rte. 400, 20 km (12 mi) south of Tlos.*

Pinara, an exceptionally romantic ruin atop a steep dirt road and backed by high cliffs, was probably founded as early as the 5th century BC. It eventually became one of Lycia's most important cities. You need time and determination to explore, as it is widely scattered, largely unexcavated, and overgrown with plane, fig, and olive trees.

Park down in the village of Minare and make the half-hour hike up the clearly marked trail. At the top, sitting on a chair in the shade, you will find the site steward, who will collect your admission and point you in the right direction—there are no descriptive signs or good site maps. The spectacular **Greek theater,** which has overlooked these peaceful hills and fields for thousands of years, is one of the finest in Turkey. It is perfectly proportioned, and unlike that of most other theaters in Turkey, its stage building is still standing, so you can get a clear picture of what it looked like in use. The site also contains groups of rock tombs with unusual reliefs, one showing a cityscape, and a cliff wall honeycombed with hundreds of crude rectangular "pigeonhole" tombs. Nearby villagers volunteer to show tourists this site; it's not a bad idea to accept the offer as they know the highlights. A tip is customary. ⌂ *$1.* ☉ *Daily 8:30–sunset.*

Letoön

⑮ *14 km (8 mi) south of Pinara off Rte. 400.*

Excavations have revealed **three temples** at Letoön. The first, closest to the parking area, was dedicated to Leto, the mother of Apollo and Artemis. It dates from the 2nd century BC. The middle temple, the oldest, is dedicated to Artemis and dates from the 5th or 4th century BC. The last, dating from the 1st century BC, belongs to Apollo and contains a rare Lycian mosaic depicting a bow and arrow (a symbol of Artemis) and a sun and lyre (Apollo's emblems). Compare the first and last temples: The former is Ionic, topped by a simple, triangular pediment and columns with scroll-shape capitals. The latter is Doric, with an ornate pediment with scenic friezes and detailing, and its columns have undecorated capitals. ⌂ *$1.* ☉ *Daily 8:30–sunset.*

Xanthos

🔞 *25 km (16 mi) south of Pinara on Rte. 400.*

Xanthos, perhaps the greatest city of ancient Lycia, earned the region its reputation for fierceness in battle. Determined not to be subjugated by superior forces, the men of Xanthos twice set fire to their own city, with their women and children inside, and fought to the death. The first occasion was against the Persians in 542 BC, the second against Brutus and the Romans in the 1st century BC. Though the site was excavated and stripped by the British in 1838 and most finds are now in London's British Museum, the remains are worth inspecting. Largely undeveloped, with no snack shop, no detailed signage, and no paved walk, Xanthos is nonetheless easily explored on the dusty paths around the ruins. Allow at least three hours, and expect some company: Unlike the other Lycian cities, Xanthos is on the main tour-bus route.

Start across from the parking area at the 2nd-century BC theater, built by Lycians in the Roman style. Inscriptions indicate that it was a gift from a wealthy Lycian named Opromoas of Rhodiapolis. Alongside are two much-photographed pillar tombs. The more famous of the pair is called the Harpies tomb after the half-bird, half-woman figures carved onto the north and south sides. Other reliefs show a seated figure receiving various gifts, including a bird, a pomegranate, and a helmet. The tomb has been dated to 470 BC, although the reliefs are plaster casts of originals in the British Museum. The other tomb consists of a sarcophagus atop a pillar, an unusual arrangement; the pillar section is probably as old as the Harpies tomb, the sarcophagus added later. On the side of the theater opposite the Harpies tomb, past the agora, is the Inscribed Pillar of Xanthos, a tomb dating from about 400 BC, etched with a 250-line inscription that recounts the heroic deeds of a champion wrestler and celebrated soldier named Kerei. Cross the road and walk past the parking area to see the large Byzantine basilica and its abstract mosaics. Along a path up the hill, you will find several sarcophagi and a good collection of rock-cut house tombs, as well as a spot of shade. Xanthos's center was up on the acropolis behind the theater, accessible by a trail. It was here that, when the battle turned against them, the Xanthian warriors rounded up their women and children, locked them into the fortress, set it aflame, and charged off to meet their death on the battlefield. 🎟 *$1.* ☉ *Daily 8:30–sunset.*

Patara

🔞 *18 km (11 mi) south of Xanthos, off Rte. 400.*

Patara was once Lycia's principal port. Cosmopolitan in its heyday—Hannibal, Saint Paul, and the emperor Hadrian all visited, and Saint Nicholas, the man who would be Santa Claus, was born here—the port eventually silted up. The ruins you'll find today are scattered among marshes and sand dunes. The city was famous for a time for its oracle and its temple of Apollo, still lost beneath the sands. Herodotus wrote that the oracle worked only part-time, as Apollo spent summers away in Delos (probably to escape the heat). While the sight of the 2,000-year-old theater half-buried in sand is unique, the real reason to come here is the **beach,** a superb 11-km (7-mi) sweep of sand dunes popular with Turkish families yet never so crowded you need to walk far to find solitude.

Kalkan

🔞 *16 km (10 mi) east of Xanthos on Rte. 400.*

Kalkan, another fishing village, has plenty of small hotels, guest houses, and restaurants with roof terraces where you can watch sunsets over the water. Seafood restaurants line the waterfront. To some, Kalkan is the perfect Mediterranean hideaway, with century-old houses topped by red-tile roofs, and blue waters lapping at the harbor. Others bemoan its rapid development and the lack of a beach. Most tourists take a water taxi to **Kapitaş,** a small strand of white sand set dramatically at the foot of a sheer cliff wall.

Dining and Lodging

$–$$ ✕ **Palanin Yeri.** As in most small seaside towns, the restaurant scene is down by the harbor. Palanin Yeri (Pala's Place) is on the waterfront with a vine-covered terrace and a good selection of fresh fish and meat dishes with salads and starters. There's one downside to eating outside: the town cats crowd around, waiting for leftovers. ☎ *242/844–3047. No credit cards.*

$$ ⌂ **Hotel Pirat.** Some complain that this large property, the first really modern addition to this resort full of old Greek houses, doesn't suit Kalkan. But the location is good, right on the harbor and a short walk from the swimming platform, and rooms are bigger than in local *pansiyons* (guest houses), with individual terraces. Ask for accommodations that overlook the water rather than the town. ⊠ *Kalkan Marina,* ☎ *242/844–3178,* FAX *242/844–3183. 136 rooms with bath. 2 restaurants, 2 bars, 3 pools. AE, MC, V.*

$–$$ ⌂ **Kalkan Han.** Near the back part of the village, the white, clean-lined Kalkan Han has a roof terrace with sweeping bay views; it's splendid at breakfast and perfect after dark, when the rooftop becomes the Star Bar. An old kilim decorates the small lobby, and dark wood accents add character inside and out. ⊠ *Köyiçi Mev.,* ☎ *242/844–3151,* FAX *242/844–2059. 16 rooms with bath. Restaurant, bar. MC, V. Closed Nov.–Apr.*

$ ⌂ **Balıkçı Han.** This delightful pansiyon, the only hotel on the small
★ street edging the waterfront, is in a converted 19th-century inn. The faded, Ottoman Victorian–style café-bar in the lobby is open to the sea, and some rooms have old brass beds, a nice change from the usual wooden platforms. This place is extremely popular, so book ahead. ⊠ *Yalı Boyu Mah.,* ☎ *242/844–3075,* FAX *242/844–3641. 10 rooms with bath. AE, MC, V.*

Kaş

⑲ *30 km (18 mi) east of Kalkan on Rte. 400.*

A few luxury hotels have replaced some of the tiny, traditional houses on the hills above the water in lively Kaş, yet there are still plenty of inexpensive, old-fashioned pansiyons in town. Kaş has a few ruins, including a monumental **sarcophagus** under a massive plane tree, up the sloping street to the left of the tourist information office. The tomb has four regal lion heads carved onto the lid. In 1842, a British naval officer counted more than 100 sarcophagi in Kaş—then called Antiphellus—but most have been destroyed over the years as locals nabbed the solid, flat, side pieces to use in construction of new buildings. This practice appears to have been halted. A few hundred yards west of the main square, along Hastane Caddesi, is a small, well-preserved theater, with a lovely view of the Greek island of Kaştellorizon (called Meis in Turkish).

Kaş makes a good base for boat excursions. The hour-long boat ride to **Kaştellorizon** yields a taste of Greece. Although immigration regulations limit your stay to a day, it's a good trip: The island is completely undeveloped and holds an impressive 12th- to 16th-century crusader castle with crenellated gray stone walls. Other excursion options include Kekova Sound, the 5th- to 14th-century Byzantine fortress at Kale, or Demre, site of St. Nicholas Basilica. Or head back toward Patara and Kapitaş beach.

To hire a boat, stop at the quay, survey the vessels and their posted itineraries, and strike a deal. Trips start at about $10 per person ($7 if you haggle a bit); boats with crew can be chartered for less than $100. Lunch—delicious grilled chicken, salad, and rice—is usually extra (around $4 per person, but be sure to ask the price in advance), or you can pack your own.

OFF THE BEATEN PATH

KEKOVA SOUND – Those who venture to Kekova Sound for more than a day trip often find the experience among the high points of their visit to Turkey. Most local transportation is by water, but a new road to Üçağiz off Route 400 has made the overland journey, which has magnificent views, more easy. Kekova Island lies close by the notched shore, whose many inlets create a series of lagoons. Anchoring each is a little fishing community. The apse of a Byzantine church backs **Tersane,** whose bay is a favorite swimming spot. **Üçağiz** has small pansiyons and waterside restaurants. **Kale,** the jewel of the sound, is a pleasing jumble of boxy houses built up a steep rocky crag alongside layers of history: Lycian tombs, a tiny Greek amphitheater and, atop the rocky hill, the medieval ruins of Simena Castle. As you cruise the waters between the villages, you can look overboard to see ancient Roman and Greek columns, buildings, stairways, and ubiquitous Lycian tombs, the last up to their lids in water—the sunken remains of a succession of ancient cities. Divers must obtain permits in advance (☞ Turkish Diving Federation *in* The Mediterranean Coast A to Z, *below*), but you don't need official papers to swim in the crystal-clear water of perfect, private little bays while your boatman naps. Accommodations on Kekova Sound are clean but basic, with plumbing, hot water, and some of the most incredible views $20 or so a night can buy.

Dining and Lodging

$$ ✕ **Eris.** Fifty yards north of Kaş's main square in a restored Ottoman house, the Eris prepares the usual Turkish grilled meats and appetizers but specializes in fresh seafood. The squid, lobster, octopus stew or kebab, and prawns are excellent. ✉ *Cumhuriyet Meyd., Orta Sok. 13,* ☏ *242/836–2134 or 242/836–1057. MC, V.*

$$ ✕ **Mercan.** On the eastern side of the harbor, the Mercan serves good, basic Turkish food in an attractive open-air setting. Prawns, sautéed in garlic or served cold tossed with lemon juice and olive oil, are usually on the menu, as well as grilled palamut, lüfer, levrek, kalkan, and the more exotic octopus salad. The water is so close you can actually hear fish jumping as you watch excursion boats head out to sea. ✉ *Cumhuriyet Meyd.,* ☏ FAX *242/836–1209. MC, V.*

$ ✕ **Derya.** Waiters bustle about this lively spot in "Restaurant Alley," near the governor's office (Kaymakamlik) northwest of the main square. All the activity makes for a great floor show. The options are more usual: kebabs, grilled fish, stuffed eggplant. ✉ *Orta Okul Cad. 7,* ☏ *242/836–1093. No credit cards.*

$$ ▦ **Hotel Club Phellos.** If you're looking for a break from simple pansiyons and are willing to pay a bit more, this hotel with a most gracious staff could be the answer. The building is modern, but old-fashioned wooden balconies in each room add a nice touch, as do marble floors and Turkish carpets in the public spaces. Rooms are decent in size, though most have the usual pair of single beds. ⊠ *Doğru Yol Sok.,* ☎ *242/836–1953 or 242/836–1326,* FAX *242/836–1890. 81 rooms with bath. Restaurant, 2 bars, pool, wading pool. MC, V.*

$$ 🖾 **Kaş Oteli.** The swimming is good off the rocks in front of this basic motel-style place, or you can laze in the sun with drinks and snacks from the bar or restaurant and enjoy the view of the Greek island of Kaştellorizon. Rooms are comfortable, if not memorable. ⊠ *Hastane Cad. 15,* ☎ *242/836–1271,* FAX *242/836–2170. No credit cards. Closed Nov.–Apr.*

$ 🖾 **Mimosa.** This hotel on a hill near the *otogar* (bus station) has a lobby pub-bar with darts and a pool table. Rooms, plain but adequate, have small balconies and some have water views. ⊠ *Elmalı Cad.,* ☎ *242/836–1272 or 242/836–1472,* FAX *242/836–1368. 26 rooms with bath. Restaurant, bar, pool. MC, V.*

En Route   Yellow signs on Route 400 mark the turnoff for Yavu, a short drive beyond the road to Kekova, where you can park and hike up to uncrowded ancient **Cyaneae** and perhaps the greatest concentration of tombs on the coast. The 45-minute trek to reach them—along a rough trail about 2 km (1 mi) long—takes in a theater, a bath, and a library, all from the Roman era, all heavily overgrown. The tombs vary in age, a few dating from as far back as the 3rd or 2nd century BC, most from the 2nd or 3rd century AD.

Kale (Demre)

⑳ *37 km (22 mi) east of Kaş on Rte. 400.*

The legend of jolly old Saint Nick started here, in Kale (not to be confused with the same-named town on Kekova Sound), also known as Demre. Born up the coast at Patara and made bishop of Myra in the first half of the 4th century, he was said to have made nocturnal visits to the houses of local children to leave gifts, including gold coins as dowries for poor village girls; if a window was closed, said the storytellers, he would drop the gifts down the chimney.

A church was built around the tomb of St. Nicholas in the 6th century but was later destroyed in an Arab raid. In 1043, the **St. Nicholas Basilica** was rebuilt with the aid of the Byzantine emperor Constantine IX and the empress Zoë near the center of town, a couple of blocks from the square. St. Nicholas's remains, however, were stolen and taken to Bari, Italy, in 1087, where the church of San Nicola di Bari was built to house them. The church that can be seen in Kale today is mainly the result of restoration work financed by 19th-century Russian noblemen. It is very difficult to distinguish between the original church, parts of which may go back to the 5th century, and the restorations, although the bell tower and upper story are clearly late additions. A service is held in the church every year on December 6, the feast day of St. Nicholas. 🎫 *$1.* ☉ *Daily 8:30–5:30 (times vary according to whim of guardian).*

㉑ The monuments of ancient **Myra**—a striking Roman theater and a cliff face full of Lycian rock tombs—are about 2 km (1 mi) north of Kale, well marked by local signs. The theater dates from the 2nd century BC and was used, for a time, for gladiator spectacles involving wild animals. There are some fine reliefs on the tombs (a stairway leads to a raised viewing platform so you can see them up close) and on the bits of pediments and statuary scattered about the grounds of the site. 🎫 *$2.* ☉ *8:30–5 or 5:30.*

In case you want to be welcomed there.

We're here to see that you're always welcomed at establishments everywhere. That's why millions of people carry the American Express® Card – for peace of mind, confidence, and security, around the world or just around the corner.

do more

Cards

In case you're running low.

We're here to help with more than 118,000 Express Cash locations around the world. In order to enroll, just call American Express before you start your vacation.

do more

Express Cash

And just in case.

We're here with American Express® Travelers Cheques and Cheques *for Two.*® They're the safest way to carry money on your vacation and the surest way to get a refund, practically anywhere, anytime.

Another way we help you...

do more

AMERICAN EXPRESS

Travelers Cheques

Lodging

$ 🏨 **Topçu Hotel.** On Route 400 at the turn to Kale is a typical, clean, whitewash-and-wood provincial hotel. The staff is very keen to be of assistance and serves an excellent breakfast of fresh bread, eggs, and cheese. ⊠ *Şehir Merkez Giriş,* ☎ *242/871–2200,* 𝖥𝖠𝖷 *242/871–2201. 42 rooms with shower. No credit cards.*

Arycanda

㉒ *48 km (30 mi) east of Kale on Rte. 400 to Rte. 635 north.*

By virtue of location, Arycanda remains one of Mediterranean Turkey's best undiscovered archaeological sites. The city first appeared in historical records in the 5th century BC, although it is probably considerably older. It passed through Persian hands, fell to Alexander, joined the Lycian League, and became a Roman province under the emperor Claudius in AD 43. Arycanda's setting is in an alluring valley punctuated by gorges, pine forests, and waterfalls, the first of which is right by the yellow sign, about 1 km (½ mi) from the site. There is a parking area and an easy-to-follow but unsigned trail up to the acropolis and across the little stream, which is dry in summer. It leads first to the monumental **Roman baths,** perhaps Turkey's best-preserved bathhouse with its intact mosaic floors, standing walls, and windows framing the valley. The tombs, farther east along the trail, are Roman rather than Lycian. North of the baths, toward the cliff face, you will come to a sunken agora, a market with arcades on three sides; the middle gate leads into an intimate odeon, a small concert hall topped by a Greek-style theater with a breathtaking view of the valley and the snow-covered mountains. Paved streets, mosaics, and an old church are scattered among these structures.

Mt. Olympos

㉓ *36 km (22 mi) from Kale on Rte. 400.*

Continuing east past the town of Kumluca, Route 400 ascends to dizzying heights, where, just past the summit, a sign points to Mt. Olympos, 9 km (5½ mi) south of the coast road. One of the 20 mountains to bear the name Olympos in antiquity, this one, known as Tahtali Dağ in Turkish, is the one where the hero Bellerophon is said to have defeated the legendary, fire-breathing Chimera. This is wild, undeveloped country—the first spot of civilization you reach is Çavus, where a fragment of wall here and there among the pink oleander and a crumbling temple to Marcus Aurelius mark the unexcavated remains of the ancient city of Olympos. Here, where a cool river reaches the sea, there is a pretty stretch of pebble beach, a coffeehouse, and little else.

You have to hike for about an hour from here up a dusty, rock-strewn mountain trail to discover the secret of the Chimera. From a gash in the rock, at a site known as the Sanctuary of Hephaistos, a natural gas produces a flickering flame, barely visible during the day but seen clearly by sailors far out at sea after dark since ancient times.

OFF THE
BEATEN PATH

ÇIRALI – A winding 7-km (4-mi) road off Route 400 leads to the coastal town of Çıralı. The Lycian ruins and sandy beach are striking, and from here it's only an hour's walk to the Sanctuary of Hephaistos on Mt. Olympos. Though Çıralı is small and out of the way, there are a dozen or so pansiyons (among them the Grand Aygün), most of them with restaurants. As the best time to visit the sanctuary is at dusk, it's not a bad idea to stay the night in Çıralı—or in the nearby town of Andrasan, which also has several pansiyons.

Phaselis

★ *56 km (35 mi) east of Finike on Rte. 400 to local road (look for yellow sign) through pine forest.*

For romantic ruins, it would be hard to beat Phaselis. There are substantial remains of the town founded in the 7th century BC by settlers from Rhodes, a successful trading post through the Roman era; but many of them lie buried under thick gorse on a knoll overlooking the sea. A broad, grassy lane cuts through the half-walls of the Roman agora; a small theater sits just behind that; and fine sarcophagi are scattered throughout a necropolis in the pine woods that surround the three bays. Overgrown streets descend to the translucent water, which is ideal for swimming. This is not so much an important place as a poetic one, ideal for a picnic or a day at the beach. ✉ *$2.* ☺ *Daily summer 8–6, other times 8–5.*

Kemer

㉕ *15 km (9 mi) east of Phaselis on Rte. 400.*

Kemer is a center of intensive tourist development, with hotels and restaurants, a well-equipped marina, and all-inclusive holiday villages that make you forget you're in Turkey.

Lodging

$$$$ 🏨 **Club Méditerranée.** The resort's white cube-shape buildings, set along a curve of beach and climbing up a hillside, recall a small town in Greece. As at other Club Meds, there are plenty of facilities; among water sports available, windsurfing is something of a specialty. The restaurants serve both traditional Turkish and Continental cuisine. Advance reservations are essential. ☎ *242/814–1009 or, in Istanbul, 212/246–1030;* 🖷 *242/814–1018. 462 rooms with shower. 3 restaurants, 3 bars, pool, Turkish bath, 8 tennis courts, beach, windsurfing, nightclub. AE, DC, MC, V.*

$$$–$$$$ 🏨 **Renaissance.** With 150 acres of gardens, pools, and sandy beach, and its nightclub, restaurants, and host of sports facilities, this resort is a world unto itself. It's more international than Turkish, and its reddish, seven-story buildings would be equally at home in Orlando or Phoenix. If you're tired of low wooden beds, you'll welcome the bigger, cushier mattresses, the hair dryers, the room service, and other amenities here. ✉ *Beldibi,* ☎ *242/824–8431,* 🖷 *242/824–8430. 338 rooms with bath. 3 restaurants, 3 bars, 2 pools, 5 tennis courts, health club, boating, windsurfing, waterskiing, casino, dance club. AE, DC, MC, V.*

Outdoor Activities and Sports

HORSEBACK RIDING

The **Erendiz Ranch** in Kemer (☎ 242/814–2504, 🖷 242/814–3742) organizes tours of various lengths, from an hour to a day, for about $3–$4 per hour, guide included.

En Route   Eastward along the Mediterranean Coast toward Antalya, the wild, mountainous terrain of Lycia gives way to the broad plains of Pamphylia ("land of all tribes" in Greek). More and more villas and motels have sprung up alongside the smooth-pebbled Konyalti Beach, where the big resorts rent horses for rides along the shore.

ANTALYA TO ALANYA

Alexander snapped up Pamphylia without much of a fight, although he simply passed around Termessos and its fortress stronghold high atop a mountain rather than wage a lengthy siege. Under the Romans, the major cities of Pamphylia—Attaleia (Antalya), Perge, Aspendos, Sillyon, and Side—were considered backwaters and left relatively free to run their own affairs. In about 67 BC, after Rome launched a naval campaign against pirates who had been raiding the coast, the cities prospered under the *pax romana*.

Antalya

35 km (22 mi) north of Kemer on Rte. 400.

The latecomer among Pamphylian cities, Attaleia, modern Antalya, was founded in about 160 BC by Attalus II, king of Pergamum, as his port on the southern coast. It has been the coast's major port ever since. Christian armies used it en route to the Holy Land during the Crusades, the Seljuk Turks held it for most of the 13th century, and the Ottomans kept a fleet here from the 1390s to the fall of their empire in the 20th century. Today the city is a booming resort center and a good base for excursions to the region's major archaeological sites: Perge, Aspendos, Side, and Termessos.

A big city, downright ugly on its outskirts, Antalya has a beautifully restored harbor area whose narrow streets are lined with small houses, restaurants, and pansiyons. On the hilltop above the harbor are tea gardens where the brew comes from old-fashioned samovars. The view extends beyond the bay to the Taurus Mountains, which parallel the coast. In response to an influx of tour groups from Germany and Israel, shop signs are often in Hebrew or German. Most locals are friendly and glad to help these new tourists find their way around town, but women of any nationality traveling alone should beware of overzealous men eager to "practice their English."

26 27 The **old harbor,** filled with yachts, fishing vessels, and tourist-excursion boats, is the place to begin any visit. **İskele Cami,** a mosque set on pillars, overlooks the harbor. Heading up any of the lanes leading north and east out of the harbor will bring you into the heart of old Kaleiçi ("Within the Citadel"), where you will find one of the purest examples of a traditional Ottoman neighborhood in Turkey. A restoration project launched in the 1980s has saved hundreds of houses, most from the 19th century and now being converted into pansiyons, rug shops, restaurants, and art galleries. Note the use of timber, brick, and stone, and the ornate bay windows. Behind each house is the center of Turkish family life, a shady garden punctuated by orange, fig, or palm trees and usually a little fountain.

NEED A
BREAK?
The **Hisar Café** and **Tophane** and **Mermerli** tea gardens along Cumhuriyet Caddesi all overlook Antalya's harbor and serve inexpensive snacks along with their priceless views. Stop for kebabs, baklava, or any of several varieties of pistachio-filled, honey-soaked shredded wheat. The three establishments are along the old city's walls, which surround the harbor in the section of town called Kaleiçi.

28 Several of the old town's cobbled lanes lead north from Antalya's harbor to the old stone **Clock Tower** (circa 1244) at Kalekapısı Square, the border between the old town and new.

29 Dark blue and turquoise tiles decorate the **Yivli Minare** (Fluted Minaret), a graceful 13th-century cylinder commissioned by the Seljuk sultan Alaaddin Keykubat. The adjoining mosque, named for the sultan, was originally a Byzantine church. Within the complex are two attractive *türbes,* or tombs, and an 18th-century *tekke,* or monastery, which once housed

Antalya

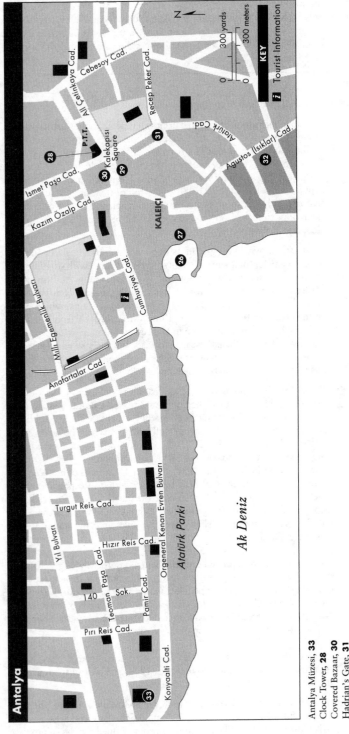

Antalya Müzesi, **33**
Clock Tower, **28**
Covered Bazaar, **30**
Hadrian's Gate, **31**
İskele Cami, **27**
Kara Ali Park, **32**
Old Harbor, **26**
Yivli Minare, **29**

a community of whirling dervishes. Of late, the monastery has been used as an art gallery. ⊠ *Cumhuriyet Cad., south side of Kalekapısı Sq.*

㉚ Antalya's **covered bazaar** was once the real thing, but is now for the most part a collection of tourist trinkets. Still, some merchants sell saddles, baggy trousers, old jewelry, kitchen utensils, and fragrant spices. A row of men work old sewing machines by an ancient wall; a one-stool barbershop is painted bright green. Back across the street is a row of shops purveying local honey, Turkish Delight candy, and pistachio and rose jam. ⊠ *Cumhuriyet Cad., north side of Kalekapısı Sq.*

㉛ **Hadrian's Gate** (⊠ Atatürk Cad., west of Cumhuriyet Cad.), constructed in honor of a visit by the Roman emperor in AD 130, has three arches, each with coffered ceilings decorated with rosettes.

㉜ Shady **Kara Ali Park** (⊠ Agustos Cad., at Atatürk Cad.) has a view of the Mediterranean and, at the north end, a stone tower 49 feet tall, called Hıdırlık Kulesi. It dates from the 2nd century AD, though no one really knows what it is—lighthouse, fortification, tomb? The Antalya Municipal Theater performs outdoors here, though unless you understand Turkish the nuances of the productions may be lost on you.

★ ㉝ The first-rate collection at the **Antalya Müzesi** (Antalya Museum) encompasses Turkish crafts and costumes and artifacts from the classical and Roman eras (including the notable statues of the gods, from Aphrodite to Zeus, in the Gods Gallery), with bits of Byzantine iconography and some prehistoric fossils thrown in. If you have the time, walk to the museum from the center of town along the coastline promenade. ⊠ *Konyaalti Cad., heading west out of town,* ☎ *242/241–4528.* 🎟 *$3.* ⊙ *Tues.–Sun. 9–6.*

Dining and Lodging

The fanciest places in town are the restaurants at the Talya and Sheraton Voyager hotels. The Marina Hotel, in the heart of the old town, is another option. **Eski Sebzeciler Sokak,** the misleadingly named "Old Greengrocer's Street," just before the crossroads where Cumhuriyet Caddesi intersects with Atatürk Caddesi, is now almost completely given over to inexpensive kebab restaurants. There are more than 20 of them, their tables spread out under plastic awnings, closing off the alley to all but pedestrian traffic. There is little to choose between them although a few, such as **Hüseyinin Yeri** (Huseyin's Place), which serves *guvec* (tomatoes, green pepper, onions, and lamb or fish, baked on a clay plate), provide an alternative to kebabs.

$$ ✗ **Yat.** Yachts bobbing in the gentle breeze and the soft light of dusk make a soothing backdrop for dining at this restaurant in an old stone building on the harbor. The lamb kebabs are good, and there are other grilled and skewered meats plus grilled fresh fish. If you need a break from Turkish cuisine, you can even find spaghetti here. ⊠ *Yat Limanı,* ☎ *242/242–4855. AE, DC, MC, V.*

$–$$ ✗ **Hisar.** Built into the 1500-year-old retaining walls of a former fortress, this wood-paneled restaurant with a view over the harbor is hard to beat for atmosphere. Above-average mezes include eggplant salad, hummus, and stuffed vine leaves. Fish kebabs and swordfish are also on the menu, as is *cordon bleu* (tenderized steak, rolled with cheese, mushrooms, and ham), a Hisar speciality. In summer, meals are served on the terrace. ⊠ *Cumhuriyet Cad.,* ☎ *242/241–5281. MC, V.*

$–$$ ✗ **Kirkerdiven Restaurant.** Once the barn of an Ottoman house, this **★** restaurant is in the heart of Kaleiçi, whose winding streets can make it difficult to find. Its gracious owner Ali, who speaks perfect English, serves high-quality meats, fishes, and a large selection of mezes and salads. You can eat inside the cozy restaurant or outside in the garden. ✉ *Musalla Sok. 2, Selçuk Mah.,* ☎ *242/242–9686. MC, V.*

$$$$ ✕🏨 **Sheraton Voyager Antalya.** West of town near the museum, this bright and shiny resort resembles a sleek cruise ship. Rooms are plush, with thick carpeting, minibars, and terraces (most with sea views). The restaurants—where Turks go to impress business associates and dates— serve Turkish and international cuisine. ✉ *100 Yil Bul.,* ☎ *242/243– 2432,* FAX *242/243–2462. 409 rooms with bath. 2 restaurants, 4 bars, outdoor café, air-conditioning, 2 pools, sauna, Turkish bath, 4 tennis courts, health club, windsurfing, boating, waterskiing, casino, dance club. AE, DC, MC, V.*

$$$–$$$$ ✕🏨 **Talya.** This luxurious resort curves around its own beach, which ★   is accessible via an elevator that runs up and down the side of the cliff. Rooms are spacious, with big beds, private terraces, and a view of the sea from every window. The restaurants have the same views and high standards as the rest of the hotel. One serves international cuisine, and the others traditional Turkish fare. Reserve early in high season, as this hotel is often completely full. ✉ *Fevzi Cakmak Cad. 30,* ☎ *242/248– 6800,* FAX *242/241–5400. 204 rooms with bath. 3 restaurants, 3 bars, minibars, pool, Turkish bath, tennis court, health club, casino. AE, DC, MC, V.*

$$–$$$ ✕🏨 **Marina Hotel.** Three vintage Ottoman houses, white stucco with bay windows and dark wood trim, were restored and connected to make this attractive hotel in the historic heart of Antalya. The staff is attentive, and the restaurant turns out imaginative nouvelle Turkish dishes. In- side, there are old carpets and kilims, and the rooms, though on the small side, are done in the same attractive white and dark wood as the facade. ✉ *Mermeli Sok. 15,* ☎ *242/247–5490,* FAX *242/241–1765. 42 rooms with bath. Restaurant, 2 bars, outdoor café, air-conditioning, minibars, room service, pool. AE, DC, MC, V.*

$$–$$$ ✕🏨 **Türk Evi Hotel.** A row of restored 120-year-old houses, just inside ★   the old wall of the citadel, forms this very fine hostelry. The lobby is tastefully decorated with antiques and the restaurant is good. Rooms at the back look out over a pretty little garden. The view of the an- cient yacht harbor from the Fortress bar at the rear of the hotel is breath- taking. ✉ *Mermerli Sok. 2,* ☎ *242/248–6591 or 242/248–6478,* FAX *242/241–9419. 18 rooms with shower. 3 restaurants, 3 bars, air- conditioning, pool, sauna. AE, MC, V.*

$–$$ 🏨 **Hotel Kişlahan.** The boxy exterior of the Kişlahan makes one think of Mondrian: It's bright white and blue, accented by thin red bands. Conveniently located next to the bazaar and a short walk from the old town, its rooms are more plain, but also considerably less expensive than those of its fancier competition. ✉ *Kazim Özalp Cad. 55,* ☎ *242/248–3870,* FAX *242/248–4297. 120 rooms with bath. Restaurant, 2 bars, outdoor café, minibars, pool. AE, DC, MC, V.*

$ 🏨 **Dedekonak Pansiyon.** This guest house in a traditional Old Antalya house has evocative Ottoman woodwork and a marble fountain in its courtyard. The only modern touch is in the plumbing—just where you'd want it. Rooms are small. ✉ *Hidirlik Sok. 13, Kilinçarslan Mah.,* ☎ FAX *242/247–5170. 15 rooms with bath. No credit cards.*

$ 🏨 **Ottoman House Pansiyon.** The facilities are well maintained and the staff highly accommodating at this modest establishment in the old town. The building is trimmed in honey-color wood and Turkish tiles are every- where, from the facade to the garden restaurant by the small pool. Try to get a room overlooking the garden, as rooms in the front tend to be noisy. ✉ *Mermerli Banyo Sok. 8,* ☎ *242/242–6630,* FAX *242/247– 6258. 14 rooms with shower. Restaurant, bar, pool. MC, V.*

Nightlife

Antalya's late-night scene runs to belly-dancing shows at the big hotels and gypsy bands and more belly dancers—some quite enticing—at a line of smoky clubs along Atatürk Caddesi, below Cumhuriyet Caddesi. Meals at these are overpriced, so come around midnight and stick to drinks. The restaurant **Club 29** (☎ 242/241–6260) on the marina is a disco in the late evening. **Karpiç** (⊠ Cumhuriyet Cad. 59, Sok. 6/A, ☎ 242/242–5662) is a bar with live pop music.

Outdoor Activities and Sports

BEACHES

Antalya's beaches—the pebbly Konyaalti to the west and the sandy Lara, to the east—are something of a letdown. Better to head to nearby Phaselis or Side, or stick to the tiny beach at the Talya Hotel (☞ Dining and Lodging, *above*). From Lara you can follow the signs to Düden Falls, where the Düden River plunges over a sheer cliff wall to pour into the sea. A tunnel behind the cascade (it's hard to find, so ask the locals for directions) leads to perhaps the coolest, and certainly one of the wettest, spots in Antalya.

DIVING

Antbirlik Spor (⊠ Antbirlik Genel Müdürlüğü, ☎ 242/321–2974) has information about permits and local conditions.

Shopping

Kaleiçi Art Center (⊠ Hamam Sok. 2, Kılıçarslan Mah., ☎ 242/242–2739) is a good source of local art. **Vakko** is a Turkish department store (⊠ Cumhuriyet Cad., ☎ 242/241–1190). **Beymen** is an upscale clothing store (⊠ Konyaalti Cad. 64, ☎ 242/248–7683).

Termessos

★ ㉞ *37 km (23 mi) northwest of Antalya; take road E87 north toward Burdur, bear left at fork onto Rte. 350 and follow signs to Korkuteli.*

Writers in antiquity referred to Termessos as the "Eagle's Nest," and it is not hard to see why. The city is impregnable, high in the mountains behind Antalya. The warlike people who made their home here launched frequent raids on their coastal neighbors. They were not Greek but a native Asian people who called themselves the Solymians, after ancient Mt. Solymus, which rises above the city. Termessos remained independent for much of its history and was quite wealthy by the 2nd century AD. Most of its remains date from this period. A massive earthquake in 567 leveled the city, and it never recovered.

The attractions in Termessos start right by the parking area, with a monumental gate dedicated to Hadrian. The steepness of the path that leads up to the craggy remains of the city walls soon makes it clear just why Alexander declined to attack. It is from here that the Termessans dumped boulders onto Alexander's soldiers. Next come a gymnasium and bath complex built of dark gray stone blocks, and the **5,000-seat theater,** whose perch at the edge of a sheer cliff garners many votes as the most spectacular setting in Turkey. From this staggering height you can view the Pamphylian plain, Mt. Solymus, and the occasional mountain goat or ibex. Termessos has one more wonder: a vast necropolis, with nearly 1,000 tombs scattered willy-nilly on a rocky hill. To get there, head back to the main trail and make a left. There is no restaurant at the site, so pack a picnic lunch. And wear your sturdy shoes! 🎟 *$1.* ⊙ *Daily 8–7.*

Perge

35 *22 km (14 mi) from Antalya, east on Rte. 400 to turnoff for Aksu and north (follow yellow signs).*

Perge suffers from comparison with more dramatic Termessos, and its 14,000-seat theater, though in good shape, is no match for its counterpart at nearby Aspendos. But a climb to the top of the theater rewards you with a panoramic view of the **Perge ruins,** including a stadium that is one of the best-preserved in the ancient world, just to the north, and beyond it the city's sturdy, 3rd-century BC garrison towers. The vaulted chambers under the stadium bleachers held shops; marble inscriptions record the proprietors' names and businesses.

The rest of the site is about 1 km (½ mi) north. You enter through the old gates, having parked just outside the old city walls. Directly ahead is a fine colonnaded avenue. The slender, sun-bleached columns that line the street once supported a covered porch filled with shops. You can still see floor mosaics in places, and delicate reliefs of gods and famous citizens decorate the entablatures between some columns. The long grooves in the paving are ruts worn by chariot wheels; the channel running down the center carried water from a fountain at the far end. Saint Paul, who sailed here from Cyprus, preached at the basilica near the end of the street, on the left. ⌨ *$1.* ☉ *Daily 8–7.*

Aspendos

★ **36** *31 km (19 mi) from Perge, east on Rte. 400 to turnoff past Belkis and north (follow yellow signs).*

Most experts agree that the **theater in Aspendos** is Turkey's best-preserved. Its quality rivals that of the Colosseum in Rome. A splendid Roman aqueduct that traverses the valley north of the acropolis, another superior example of Roman engineering, utilized the pressure of the water flowing from the mountains to supply the summit of the acropolis. The water tower here dates from the 2nd century AD; its stairway is still intact.

You pay your admission to the main site at what was once the actors' entrance to the theater. Built during the reign of Emperor Marcus Aurelius (ruled AD 161–180) by a local architect called Xenon, it is striking for the broad curve of seats, perfectly proportioned porticoes, and rich decoration. The Greeks liked open vistas behind their stages, but the Romans preferred enclosed spaces; the stage building you see today was once covered in marble tiles, and its niches were filled with statues, some now on view in the Antalya Museum (☞ *above*). The only extant relief depicts Dionysus (Bacchus) watching over the theater. The acoustics are fine, and the theater is still in use—though for music festivals and grease-wrestling matches rather than the wild-animal spectacles of ancient times.

Seeing the remainder of the site requires a hike up the zigzagging trail behind the theater, a trek of perhaps an hour or more. The rewards are a tall Nymphaion—a sanctuary to the nymphs built around a fountain decorated with a marble dolphin—and the remains of a Byzantine basilica and market hall. ⌨ *$1.* ☉ *Daily 8–7.*

Side

37 *22 km (14 mi) east of Aspendos on Rte. 400.*

The peninsular city of Side has an excellent museum, two long and beautiful beaches, and ancient ruins (some right by the water's edge). The downside is too much development and garish souvenir shops. Thousands *love* its jumbled mix of old and new, its energy and spirit, and its fun-in-the-sun hedonism. A vocal minority finds it honky-tonk and less deserving of their time than other Turkish destinations.

The name means "pomegranate" in some mysterious, pre-Greek language. The town's known history starts with Greeks fleeing Troy after its fall. Following Alexander's reign, the city was dominated by the Seleucids of Syria and the Ptolemies of Egypt; after the demise of the Seleucids in 129 BC, pirates overran the coast and Side became a major slave-trading center. A naval expedition in 67 BC cleaned things up, and for the next couple of centuries Side was a thriving Roman provincial town. By the 10th century it had been abandoned, most likely as a result of earthquakes and Christian and Arab raids.

Its beaches need little explanation: The one on the west side of the peninsula runs for miles; the one on the east is smaller but usually emptier. Ruins are all around: a lovely theater in the dead center of town, with city and sea views from the top row, and 2nd-century AD temples to Apollo and Athena, a few blocks south, on the tip of the peninsula.

Side Müzesi (Side Museum) in the center of town has a small but rich collection of Roman statues: the Three Graces, various cherubs, a brilliant satyr, and a bust of Emperor Hadrian. The sculpture garden behind the museum is larger than the museum itself and overlooks the Mediterranean. ⊠ *Selimiye Köyü,* ☎ *242/753–1006.* ✏ *$2.50.* ☉ *Tues.–Sun. 8–noon and 1–5.*

Dining and Lodging

$$ ✕ **Aphrodite Restaurant.** If you come to this restaurant on the square next to Side's waterfront during summer, ask for *kuzu baligi* (mutton fish), a local specialty that tastes something like swordfish. The kitchen prepares a good range of fish and meat dishes. ⊠ *İskele Cad.,* ☎ *242/ 753–1171. MC, V.*

$–$$ ✕ **Nergis Restaurant and Bar.** On the waterfront just to the east of the square, the Nergis is convenient yet far enough from the throng on the main street to allow for a quiet drink or meal at sunset. Fish and meat are both on the menu, but people come here for the view and not the food. ⊠ *İskele Meyd.,* ☎ *242/753–1467. MC, V.*

$–$$ ✕ **Sur Restaurant.** Close to the waterfront, Sur has a first-floor terrace overlooking the square and a panoramic view. Fish dominates the menu and varies according to what is in season. Kebabs and good salads are also served. ⊠ *İskele Cad.,* ☎ *242/753–1087. MC, V.*

$$–$$$ 🏨 **Hotel Acanthus.** The modest four-story Acanthus is done in Mediterranean style, with whitewashed walls, dark wood trim and terraces, and a red-tile roof. Rooms are comfortable if unimpressive. They are also air-conditioned—a rarity here. ⊠ *Side Köyü, Box 55,* ☎ *242/753– 3050,* ⅏ *242/753–1913. 104 rooms with bath. 2 restaurants, bar, air-conditioning, minibars, tennis court, beach, windsurfing, boating, waterskiing. MC, V.*

$ 🏨 **Subaşi Motel.** You'll be hard-pressed to decide which view here you prefer: the sunrise over the eastern beach and the ruins or the sunset behind the western beach and the rolling hills. The motel itself is less impressive, as its rooms have twin beds and cheap wooden furniture. Still, the place is on the beach and only a short walk from town. ☎ *242/753– 1215,* ⅏ *242/753–1855. 18 rooms with shower. Bar. MC, V.*

Nightlife

Ambience Bar, beside the post office, has a disco. **Deniz-ati** is another disco near the post office.

Alanya

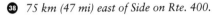 *75 km (47 mi) east of Side on Rte. 400.*

Ancient sources had a hard time deciding exactly where on their maps to place Alanya, known to the Greeks as Korakesion. The rocky peninsula on which it is set forms a natural boundary between Pamphylia, to the west, and Cilicia, to the east, which Mark Antony gave to Cleopatra as a gift. Though the lovers are said to have enjoyed the fine beaches, it was Cilicia's forests that Cleopatra was after; lumber was one of Egypt's major imports, and the queen had a mind to build a navy. The city of Alanya, which Mark Antony included in the package, was fairly insignificant until the arrival of the Seljuk Turks in 1220. Several amusing stories explain the Seljuk sultan Alaaddin Keykubat's conquest: One says he married the commander's daughter, another that he tied torches to the horns of thousands of goats and drove them up the hill in the dark of night, suggesting that a great army was attacking. Most likely, he simply cut a deal; once settled, he renamed the place and built defensive walls to ensure that he would never be dislodged.

The road into Alanya passes through an area of modern resorts and affords splendid views of Keykubat's **Kale** (citadel). The outer wall is 8 km (5 mi) long and took 12 years to build; through the battlement crenellations and 150 towers, arrows could be sent down on attackers. Up the hill, past another wall, is the **İç Kale** (Inner Fortress), where you can park and strike out on foot along tree-shaded lanes into the old city's residential area. Many a crumbling building here dates from Seljuk times. At its center are the remains of the original *bedestan* (bazaar) and caravansary. A path leading west from these buildings takes you to the attractive tomb of Sultan Akşabe, the **Akşabe Sultan Tekke,** now the quarters of the local order of whirling dervishes. The exterior is stone; the interior, the dome, and truncated minaret are redbrick. Continue up the path to the top of the promontory, where you will find a third wall, around the **İç Kale** (Keep). Inside lie the foundations of Keykubat's palace and the ruins of a Byzantine church, with some 6th-century frescoes of the evangelists. Steps ascend to the battlement on the summit. From there, the panorama takes in the Mediterranean's Technicolor blue-green, the two beaches, and a seemingly unending succession of cliffs jutting into the sea from the foothills of the Taurus Mountains. This, apparently, was the spot where condemned prisoners and unfaithful wives were tossed to their death. ☎ *242/512–3304.* ✉ *$3 for İç Kale and Byzantine church; admission free to other sites.* ◷ *Tues.–Sun. 8–7.*

Kızıl Kule (Red Tower), built in 1225 by an architect known as Abu Ali, was patterned on other Mediterranean-coast crusader castles. Bricks are used inside; archers manned the many loopholes, and a series of troughs conveyed boiling tar and melted lead that was dumped onto attackers. A short walk south along the water, a second defensive tower rises above a 13th-century shipyard; a guardroom is to the left of the entrance, a mosque to the right. ✉ *Eastern harbor at south end of İskele Cad.*

Alanya Müzesi (Alanya Museum) has some Greek and Roman pieces, including a bronze statue of Hercules and a big collection of Seljuk and Ottoman artifacts—beautiful old kilims, illustrated Korans and other religious books, silver and gold jewelry. ✉ *Azaklar Sok., south of*

Atatürk Cad., Sekerhane Mah., ☎ *242/513–1228.* 🖃 *$1.* ☉ *Tues.–Sun.*
8–noon and 1:30–5:30.

Damlataş Magarası (Weeping Cave) is named for the dazzling, multi-
hued stalactites and stalagmites inside. Many Turks while away the hours
here in the belief that the high humidity and cool temperature allevi-
ate asthma, bronchitis, and other respiratory illnesses. The cave encourages sick people to visit in the four hours prior to the official opening
time every morning. 🖃 *At the southern end of west beach, 2 blocks*
south of Alanya Museum. 🖃 *$1.25.* ☉ *Daily 10–8.*

Dining and Lodging

$–$$ ✕ **Canus Restaurant.** This restaurant close to the harbor is famous for
its fish dishes. The menu varies depending on what is available, but
ask for levrek or *barbunya* (red mullet). 🖃 *Rıhtım Meyd.,* ☎ *242/513–*
2694. MC, V. Closed fall–spring.

$–$$ ✕ **İskele Restaurant.** An agreeable view, outdoor seating, and a fully
stocked bar are among the draws at this restaurant close to the harbor. It serves fish and a range of mezes, plus European dishes such as
chicken Kiev, Wiener schnitzel, filet mignon, and lasagna. 🖃 *İskele Cad.,*
☎ *242/513–1822. MC, V.*

$ ✕ **Dimçayi Mangal Tesisleri.** This tree-shaded open-air restaurant near
the water makes a pleasant lunch stop on your way east from Alanya.
You choose your meat (chops, shish kebab, or köfte) and then grill it
yourself over a barbecue while the waiters bring salads and drinks. 🖃
Mersin Yolu, Dimçayi, 3 km (2 mi) east of Alanya on Rte. 400, ☎ *242/*
514–0141. No credit cards.

$$$–$$$$ ▦ **Club Hotel Alantur.** Like most of the other big seaside resorts here,
this is a bright, white, mid-rise complex with many facilities. The
beach is exceptional and the garden is cool and well tended. The com-
fortable rooms recall Holiday Inns; you can choose to stay in the main
hotel or in one of 252 bungalows. 🖃 *20 Dimçayı Mev., Çamyolu Köyü,*
☎ *242/518–1740,* 🖷 *242/518–1756. 352 rooms with bath. Restau-*
rant, 4 bars, 4 pools, miniature golf, 4 tennis courts, beach, windsurfing,
jet skiing, dance club. MC, V.

$–$$ ▦ **Alaiye Hotel.** A pool bar, modern rooms with balconies (some with
sea views), and a bright, clean lobby are among the recent renovations
to this property. The restaurant has a magnificent view of the water.
The beach is just a short walk away. 🖃 *Atatürk Cad. 228,* ☎ *242/513–*
4018, 🖷 *242/512–1508. 98 rooms with shower. Restaurant, 4 bars,*
pool, parasailing, waterskiing. No credit cards.

$–$$ ▦ **Kaptan Hotel.** If you want to stay in town rather than on the beach,
this is the place. The building, which overlooks the harbor, is small and
modern, in a minimalist vein. It's well located near the Red Tower and
has a lively poolside café. The view from the rooftop restaurant—
which serves good, traditional Turkish dishes—is delightful. Rooms are
comfortable. 🖃 *İskele Cad. 70,* ☎ *242/513–4900,* 🖷 *242/513–2000.*
48 rooms with shower. Restaurant, 3 bars, air-conditioning, 2 pools.
MC, V.

Nightlife

Alanya has a beer hall, **Ali Bey's Biergaste** (🖃 Keykubat Cad. 16, ☎
242/512–0819), with German food and live music.

Outdoor Activities and Sports

Alanya continues to develop, but its main beach remains relatively uncrowded. In the coming years, however, hotels will line the waterfront
and a free, accessible beach will be a rarity. It's easy to reach other nearby
beaches, coves, and caves by boat. Legend has it that buccaneers kept
their most fetching maidens at Korsanlar Mağarası (Pirates' Cave)

and Aşıklar Mağarası (Lovers' Grotto), two favorite destinations. Tour boats charge $5 to $10 per person; hiring a private boat, which you can do at the dock near the Red Tower, should cost less than $20—don't be afraid to haggle.

En Route   Because of the distances involved and the declining caliber of accommodations, few tourists venture east of Alanya. But if you have time and an adventurous spirit, the trip can be rewarding. The coastal plain narrows as you travel the 55 km (34 mi) on Route 400 to Gazipaşa, where you come to a fine beach, then a long stretch reminiscent of the Amalfi Coast or the French Riviera. For most of the 267 km (165 mi) from Gazipaşa to Mersin, precipitous pine-forested slopes march down to red cliffs or to long stretches of powdery white sand bordering the turquoise sea; now and then, coastal plains break up stretches of luxuriant banana plantations and orange groves. Everywhere there are medieval castles—Byzantine, Armenian, crusader, Seljuk. The occasional Hellenistic or Roman ruin adds to the spectacle. Silifke has a basilica and tomb dedicated to Saint Thecla, Saint Paul's first convert and the first female Christian martyr, and a decent museum with Hittite artifacts. Cicero resided in Korykos when he was governor of Cilicia, from 52 to 50 BC. The fallen temples, palace, theater, and aqueduct and the vast necropolis are overshadowed by the imposing Armenian twin castles dating from the 13th century.

Mersin

322 km (200 mi) from Alanya on Rte. 400.

A commercial center, Mersin is none too attractive but has good hotels. On the outskirts of town, bear right at the fork to Viransehir, a colony settled by Rhodes and later a pirate stronghold. There you will find a long row of Corinthian columns and, in winter, the goatskin tents of Turkoman nomads known as the yörük.

Lodging

$$$ 🏨 **Mersin Hilton.** Sometimes when you head off the beaten track, it's nice to see a familiar name, and that can be the case here. The hotel is thoroughly modern, efficient, more luxurious than the competition, and well equipped. At 12 stories, it's one of the taller buildings on the coast. Rooms are good-sized, and all have views of the Mediterranean. ⊠ *Adnan Menderes Bul. 3310,* ☎ *324/326–5000,* 🖷 *324/326–5050. 188 rooms with bath. Restaurant, bar, minibars, pool, sauna, 2 tennis courts, health club, shops, casino. AE, DC, MC, V.*

$$ 🏨 **Mersin Oteli.** The Mersin, which rates four stars on the rating system devised by the Turkish government, aspires to be like the nearby Hilton but doesn't quite succeed. Though it, too, is a big, white, modern box of a hotel, it's older and its public and private spaces are less grand. Of course, it costs less, too. ⊠ *Gümrük Meyd. 112,* ☎ *324/238–1040,* 🖷 *324/231–2625. 105 rooms with shower. Restaurant, bar, sauna, exercise room, casino, nightclub. AE, DC, MC, V.*

En Route   Saint Paul was born in Tarsus, 28 km (17 mi) east of Mersin on Route 400, some 2,000 years ago. From **Adana,** Turkey's fourth-largest city, you cross the plain of Issos, where Alexander the Great defeated Darius III of Persia in 333 BC. Alexander founded a city that still bears his name, though translated now into Turkish: İskenderun.

Antakya

211 km (131 mi) from Mersin, east on Rte. E90, south on Rte. E91.

Antakya is better known by its old name, Antioch. Founded around 300 BC by Seleucus Nikator, one of Alexander's generals, the city grew quickly, thanks to its strategic location on the trade routes between Asia, the Middle East, and the Mediterranean. After the Roman occupation began in AD 64, Antioch became the empire's third most important city, after Rome and Alexandria. Famed for its luxury and notorious for its depravity, it was chosen by Saint Paul as the objective of his first mission to the Gentiles. After enduring earthquakes and Byzantine and Arab raids, it fell to the crusaders in 1098; Egyptian raiders nearly leveled it in 1268. A late addition to the Turkish Republic, it was occupied by France after 1920 as part of its mandate over Syria. Though it reverted to Turkey just before World War II, it still maintains a distinctive character. The people of Antakya are all bilingual, speaking both Turkish and a local dialect of Arabic. In the cobbled streets of the old quarter, on the east bank of the River Orontes, one can also hear Syriac (Aramaic), the language spoken by many of Turkey's Christians.

At the northern edge of town is **Senpiyer Kilisesi** (the Church of Saint Peter), a tiny cave high up on a cliff, blackened by centuries of candle smoke and dripping with water seeping out of the rock. It is here that the apostle preached to his converts and where they first came to be called Christians. The present facade to the cave dates from the 11th and 12th centuries. Mass is celebrated here on the first Sunday of every month. ⊠ *Off Kurtuluş Cad.*

The River Orontes (Asi in Turkish) divides Antakya in two. In the old town you will find the 17th-century **Habib Neccar Cami,** a mosque on Kurtuluş Caddesi, due south of Saint Peter's, and just north, the bazaar quarter, a real change of pace: The feel here is more Syrian and Arab than Turkish. On Hürriyet Caddesi, several winding blocks southwest of the mosque opposite the Atahan Hotel, is the fine loggia of a derelict **Latin monastery**; enter its cloister from the side street.

★ Experts consider the exceptional Roman mosaics of **Hatay Müzesi** (Hatay Museum)—portraying scenes from mythology and figures such as Dionysus, Orpheus, Oceanus, and Thetis—among the highest achievements of Roman art. ⊠ *Gündüz Cad. 1, in the central sq. on the right bank of the Orontes,* ☎ *326/214–6167.* ⊒ *$1.* ☉ *Tues.–Sun. 8:30–12:30 and 1:30–5:30.*

Most of the mosaics at the Hatay Museum come from villas at **Harbiye,** originally called Daphne, a beautiful gorge of laurel trees and tumbling waterfalls, that was said to have been chosen by the gods for the Judgment of Paris and which contained one of the ancient world's most important shrines to the god Apollo (7 km [4 mi] south of Antakya on Rte. E91). Mark Antony chose it as the venue for his ill-fated marriage to Cleopatra in 40 BC. Daphne was also a favorite resort for wealthy Antiochenes and developed such a reputation for licentiousness that it was put off limits to the Roman army.

OFF THE **SAMANDAG AND SELEUCEIA AD PIERIA** – You will find a beach at
BEATEN PATH Samandag, 28 km (17 mi) south of Antakya, as well as ruins of Antioch's old port, Seleuceia ad Pieria, which includes an underground water channel, 1,400 meters (1,526 yards) long, that was built entirely by hand. Nearby rock tombs are still used by the local villagers to stable their donkeys.

Dining and Lodging

\$\$–\$\$\$ ✕⊞ **Büyük Antakya.** If you've made it this far, almost to the Syrian border, you deserve the best hotel available, and this is it: a giant, white pyramid of a building with cool marble in the lobby and bright rooms with big windows and nonstop sun. ⊠ *Atatürk Cad. 8,* ☎ *326/213–5860,* ℻ *326/213–5869. 72 rooms with shower. Restaurant, bar, dance club. No credit cards.*

THE MEDITERRANEAN COAST A TO Z

Arriving and Departing

By Bus

Service is plentiful. Routes are between Bodrum or İzmir and Marmaris; between Pamukkale's station in Denizli and Antalya; between Ankara and Antalya or Mersin. The trip from Ankara is a long, slow 12 hours, but fares are only \$10–\$15. From Marmaris to Istanbul takes a grueling 20 hours, with fares about \$15–\$20.

By Car

The main coast road from the Aegean becomes Route 330 at Milas and continues through Mugla toward Marmaris. From Marmaris, the coast road going east is Route 400, which continues all the way to Mersin. The drive to Marmaris is 287 km (177 mi) from İzmir, 178 km (110 mi) from Bodrum. To Antalya, the inland routes are E87 from Pamukkale (296 km, or 178 mi) and E90 to Polatli, joining up with Route 695 heading south to Aksehir and Route 330 from Ankara (552 km, or 341 mi).

By Plane

The main airports for flights between the coast and Istanbul, İzmir, or Ankara are in Dalaman and Antalya. Service to far eastern Turkey is from Adana. Charter flights, some direct from Europe, predominate in Dalaman, which also has summer service by **Turkish Airlines** (☎ 212/663–6363 in Istanbul, 242/243–4381 in Antalya) from Istanbul and Ankara. Antalya has several daily flights from Istanbul by Turkish Airlines and **Istanbul Airlines** (☎ 212/231–7526 in Istanbul, 242/243–3893 in Antalya), and less frequent service from Ankara and İzmir.

BETWEEN THE AIRPORTS AND CENTER CITY

There is frequent bus service between Antalya's airport and the city center, 10 km (6 mi) away; the cost is \$2. Taking a taxi to the city bus station (⊠ Kazım Özalp Cad., ☎ 242/241–6231) should cost about \$5.

From Dalaman Airport(☎ 252/692–5899), buses travel frequently between Fethiye and Marmaris, 50 km (31 mi) east and 60 km (37 mi) west, respectively; the trip costs about \$5. In Marmaris the city bus station (☎ 252/412–3037) is two blocks north of İskele Meydanı, the main square. In Fethiye, it is just off Atatürk Caddesi, about 1 km (⅔ mi) east of the town center (☎ 252/614–3531).

By Train

There is no service along the Mediterranean Coast. To reach Mersin or Adana in the east, the nearest trains leave from Ankara.

Getting Around

By Boat

This is the best way to see the many otherwise inaccessible coves and picnic areas. Local fishermen will transport you for a small fee, or you can hop on one of the many water taxis. You will see both types of transport lined up along the harbor in every seaside town. Many people charter boats and join the small flotillas that leave the Bodrum and Marmaris marinas daily for sightseeing in the summer.

By Bus

Every city has an intercity bus terminal. Routes connect Antalya (bus station, ☎ 242/241–6231) with Marmaris (bus station, ☎ 252/412–3037) and Mersin (bus station, ☎ 324/238–1648), and Adana (bus station, ☎ 322/428–2047), with stops in between.

By Car

Although the highways between towns are well maintained, the smaller roads are usually unpaved and very rough, and the twisty coast roads require concentration. Some sample distances: Marmaris to Fethiye, 168 km (104 mi); Fethiye to Antalya, 318 km (196 mi); Antalya to Alanya, 115 km (71 mi). To estimate drive times, figure on about 70 km (42 mi) per hour.

Contacts and Resources

Car Rentals

Renting a car in Turkey tends to be expensive. Try to make advance reservations from home. Although you can get a better deal at a smaller, Turkish rental agency, you're better off sticking to the well-known American companies since their safety regulations are more stringent and their insurance is more dependable. On the Mediterranean, you'll find international car-rental offices at the major tourist centers and in airports. Or you can make reservations when you first arrive at Atatürk Airport in Istanbul at **Avis** (☎ 212/573–4403), **Budget** (☎ 212/574–1635), or **Hertz** (☎ 212/573–5987).

Diving

Turkish Diving Federation (⊠ Gençlik Ve Spor Genel Mürdürlüğü, Sualtı Sporları, Can Kurtarma ve Su Kayağı Federasyonu, Ulus İşhane, A. Blok. 303–304, Ulus, Ankara, ☎ 312/310–4136, FAX 312/310–8288).

Emergencies

Police, ☎ 155. **Ambulance,** ☎ 112.

Travel Agencies

Kahramanlar Turizm (⊠ Cumhuriyet Meyd. 9, Kaş, ☎ 242/836–1062 or 242/836–2400, FAX 242/836–2422). **Pamphylia Travel** (⊠ İstiklal Cad., Antalya, ☎ 242/243–1500, FAX 242/242–1400). **Sardes Tourism** (⊠ Kordon Cad. 26, Dalyan, ☎ 252/284–2050, FAX 252/284–2189). **Tantur** (⊠ Emre Oteli, K Evren Bul., Marmaris, ☎ 252/412–4616, FAX 252/412–6921).

Visitor Information

Tourist offices: **Adana** (⊠ Atatürk Cad. 13, ☎ 322/359–1994, FAX 322/352–6790); **Alanya** (⊠ Damlataş Cad. 1, ☎ 242/513–1240, FAX 242/513–5436); **Antakya** (⊠ Vali Ürgen Alanı 147, ☎ 326/216–0610, FAX 326/213–5740); **Antalya** (⊠ Cumhuriyet Cad., Özel Idare Altı 2, ☎ 242/241–1747 and ⊠ Mermerli Sok., Selçuk Mah., ☎ 242/247–5042, FAX 242/247–6298); **Dalaman** (⊠ at the airport, ☎ 252/692–5220); **Datça** (⊠ Hükümet Binası, İskele Mah., ☎ 252/712–3163, FAX 252/712–3546); **Fethiye** (⊠ İskele Karşısı 1, ☎ FAX 252/614–1527); **Kaş** (⊠ Cumhuriyet Meyd. 5, ☎ FAX 242/836–1238); **Marmaris** (⊠ İskele Meyd. 2, by the marina, ☎ 252/412–1035, FAX 252/412–7277); **Mersin** (⊠ İsmet İnönü Bul. 5/1, Liman Girişi, near the docks, ☎ 324/238–3271, FAX 324/238–3272); **Side** (⊠ Side Yolu Üzeri, Manavgat, ☎ 242/753–1265, FAX 242/753–2657); **Silifke** (⊠ Veli Gürten Bozbey Cad. 6, Gazi Mah., ☎ 324/714–1151, FAX 324/714–5328).

6 Ankara and Central Anatolia

The civilizations that have inhabited Central Anatolia have bequeathed a richly textured region. Where else can you tread the same ground as the ancient Hattis, Hittites, Luwians, Phyrgians, Cimmerians, Lydians, Persians, Macedonians, Bithynians, Galatians, Romans, Byzantines, Seljuks, and Ottomans? Many sights here are utterly unique: churches carved into volcanic rock, underground cities, and the dance of the whirling dervishes. Here also is the political and cultural center of Ankara, which has attained Atatürk's ideal of a modern Turkish city.

HISTORY HAS A WAY OF COMING FULL CIRCLE. In the 2nd millennium BC, Central Anatolia was the center of one of the earliest empires—that of the Hittites. In the 13th century AD, long after the Hittites had disappeared, the Seljuks built a new empire in the center of Asia Minor. By the 19th century, the region had become a backwater province in a failing Ottoman Empire, but after founding the modern Turkish Republic in 1923, Kemal Atatürk chose Ankara to be the seat of his government. Tens of thousands of Turks streamed into the town, mostly on foot, to undertake the building of the new capital. The population has swelled to well over 3 million today, and Central Anatolia is once again a political center.

Revised and
updated by
Paula S.
Bernstein

Ankara is the natural base for exploring the ancient Hittite cities of Hattuşaş, Alacahöyük, and Yazılıkaya; the wild lunar landscapes of Cappadocia; and the old Seljuk capital at Konya, home of the whirling dervishes (members of a Muslim religious order known for their mystic dance). But while Ankara may be physically close to these regions, its spirit is elsewhere. Atatürk was determined to westernize Turkey, and nowhere has that objective been more fully realized than in Ankara. In the 1930s, the neo-Ottoman architectural style popular in Turkey was scrapped in favor of a symbolic and stark modernism influenced by Walter Gropius and the German Bauhaus school. A master plan for the city was devised by Hermann Jansen, Berlin's city architect. Today's Ankara is thoroughly modern, very much imbued with the spirit that Atatürk envisioned. It is the haunt of politicians and civil servants, and its social calendar is studded with cocktail parties and diplomatic receptions. Ankara is also the home of Turkey's finest museum, the Museum of Anatolian Civilizations.

The mood changes in the historic towns of Central Anatolia. Çatal Höyük, settled around 7000 BC, quickly grew to become one of the world's first cities. Since then, Central Anatolia has been the homeland of numerous tribes and nations and has served as a historical battleground as well as a melting pot of East and West. Frontiers remained nebulous, as even the Taurus mountain chain, to the south, and higher chains to the southeast proved ineffective as natural boundaries of the interminable Anatolian plateau.

Pleasures and Pastimes

Dining

Central Anatolia's restaurants serve food similar to what you'll find throughout Turkey: kebabs, kebabs, and more kebabs. Other common dishes include mezes (appetizers), grilled fish and meat (especially lamb), and vegetarian dishes. Most restaurants serve wine, beer, and raki, the ouzo-like Turkish liqueur. Dress is casual, and unless otherwise noted, reservations are not necessary—in fact, you will seldom need them except in Ankara, where dining is more sophisticated. For a chart that explains the cost of meals at the restaurants in this chapter, *see* Dining and Lodging Price Categories at the front of this book.

Lodging

Because Ankara is the nation's capital and host to many foreign embassies, hotels here tend to be grander, more Western, and much more expensive than in the rest of the country. Hotels in the surrounding region have fewer amenities but much more charm—especially the cave hotels around Cappadocia. For a chart that explains room rates at the accommodations in this chapter, *see* Dining and Lodging Price Categories at the front of this book.

Nightlife

In the provincial towns of Central Anatolia, you'll have to comb through the hotel listings for a place with a bar or disco if you're hungry for nightlife. Ankara, on the other hand, has discos and nightclubs with live bands and singers at the Büyük Ankara, Hilton SA, Sheraton, and Dedeman hotels. You can also head for the Luna Park Aile Gazinosu (Family Nightclub) in Gençlik Parkı. Here you'll find a stage where Turkey's top pop singers perform nightly. Though the good seats go early, the best acts come on late—about 11 PM. Tickets are available at the door.

Shopping

The best bazaars can be found in Ankara, Kayseri, and Konya. Rugs and kilims are everywhere. In Ankara, look for products made from angora, a local specialty (which may have been named after the city); but check to see where it has come from, as much of the angora now on sale in the city has been imported. You'll find reasonably priced yarns and sweaters here; government-run stores called *dosim* are smart places to shop for indigenous handicrafts. There is one in Ankara and another one in the Göreme Open-Air Museum.

Exploring Ankara and Central Anatolia

If you are coming from the temperate Aegean or Mediterranean coasts, Central Anatolia provides a change of pace. The climate is harsh and temperatures can be extreme, especially in the north. Much of the plateau is an arid plain, slashed by ravines, centered on a huge salt lake, and scattered with mountains (often extinct volcanoes) and rivers dammed up into artificial lakes. In Cappadocia, volcanic eruptions long ago covered the ground with tuff, a thick layer of mud and ash, over which lava spread. Erosion by rain, snow, and wind created "fairy chimneys"—surrealistic cones, needles, pillars, and pyramids. To the infinite variety of forms, oxidation added an improbable range of colors, from the off-white of Göreme through yellow, pink, red, and russet to the violet-gray of Ihlara.

Great Itineraries

You can cover the whole of Ankara in a day or two. From here, the Hittite cities to the east can easily be done as a day trip. Ankara, Cappadocia, and Konya form something of a triangle; base your decision as to what to see first on where you are headed next or where you are coming from. Konya is en route to Antalya and the Mediterranean Coast, or, if you stay inland, to Pamukkale and then to İzmir on the Aegean Coast. Cappadocia, to the southeast, is on the way to Diyarbakır and the far east. You'll need at least two days to explore the wonders of Cappadocia, but Konya requires only a day.

IF YOU HAVE 3 DAYS
Numbers in the text correspond to numbers in the margin and on the Central Anatolia and Ankara maps.

You can easily cover Ankara and the Hittite cities in three days. Spend your first day exploring 🏛 **Ankara** by foot. Walk up Hisarparkı Caddesi to the **Hisar** ①, where you can visit **Alaaddin Cami,** the city's oldest mosque. From there, it's just a short walk south on Kadife Sokak to the **Ankara Anadolu Medeniyetleri Müzesi** ②, the Museum of Anatolian Civilizations. Visit the **Samanpazarı** neighborhood outside the outer citadel walls. Here you'll find the city's covered bazaar and numerous mosques. Head north on Çankırı Caddesi to the heart of the old town and the entrance to the **Roma Hamamları** ⑥, the Roman Baths, and afterward reverse south on Çankırı Caddesi until it turns into Atatürk Bulvarı. In fine weather, stroll around the green expanses of **Gençlik Parkı** ⑩ and visit the fine **Etnoğrafya Müzesi** ⑪ across from the park's entrance.

From here walk or take a cab south on Atatürk Bulvari to the **Kavaklıdere** neighborhood. On day two, head to the Hittite city of **Hattuşaş** ⑯. Continue 2 km (1 mi) northeast of Hattuşaş to view the rock carvings of **Yazılıkaya** ⑱. Return to Ankara in time for dinner. On your last day in Ankara, visit **Anit Kabir** ⑭, the Atatürk mausoleum, and the **Atatürk Museum.**

IF YOU HAVE 7 DAYS

Spend days one and two in 🔛 **Ankara** ①–⑮. On day three, head to **Hattuşaş** ⑯ and **Yazılıkaya** ⑱. In the afternoon, drive south on the road to **Yozgat.** Take Route E88 west and Route 785 heading south to Route 260, which eventually meets up with Route 765. Continue south on 765 to 🔛 **Nevşehir** ㉒. The morning of day four, drive 21 km (13 mi) south of Nevşehir on the road to Niğde, stopping at the underground city of **Kaymaklı** ㉓. Farther south toward Niğde is the underground city of **Derinkuyu** ㉔. Break for lunch in **Ürgüp** ㉕ before heading northwest to the vineyard-filled valley of 🔛 **Göreme** ㉖. The town's Open-Air Museum holds many rock churches. On day five, visit **Zelve** ㉗ and stop by **Avanos** ㉘ to shop for onyx jewelry and pottery before breaking for lunch. Take a scenic drive south on Route 300 until you reach **Ihlara** ㉝, where the Melendiz River has carved a rift into the sheer tuff cliffs. Spend another night in Göreme.

Early on day six, continue on Route 300 to Konya, stopping along the way at Anatolia's largest and best-preserved caravansary, **Sultan Hanı.** Have lunch when you arrive in 🔛 **Konya** ㉞. Then head out to **Mevlana Türbesi,** the tomb of Mevlana Celaleddin, the 13th-century poet and philosopher who founded the mystic order of the Mevlana dervishes. From here, you can easily walk to the rest of the sights in Konya. Opposite the Mevlana Museum is the **Selimiye Cami** (Selim Mosque). About 1 km (½ mi) past the museum on Alaaddin Caddesi is **İplikçi Cami,** Konya's oldest mosque. On your last day in Central Anatolia, make your way to the ancient acropolis, now called **Alaaddin Tepe,** which is crowned by the beautiful **Alaaddin Cami.** Enjoy the park on top of the hill and have lunch at the scenic-view café. In the afternoon, walk around the **bazaar** near the intersection of Selimiye Caddesi and Karaman Caddesi.

When to Tour Ankara and Central Anatolia

Ankara is always bustling, so there's no off-season when restaurants or hotels close. Elsewhere in Central Anatolia, outdoor activities slow during the winter season, and some sites close. It is especially difficult to explore the Hittite cities, even as late as April, because ice blocks some roads. Regardless of season, try to visit the temple at Yazılıkaya around noon since that is when the stone reliefs are the most visible. As elsewhere in Turkey, prices in winter are often cheaper than in summer, so bargain travelers (or those who hate crowds) might opt to visit then or at least in the spring or fall.

ANKARA AND THE HITTITE CITIES

The world-class city on the eastern edge of the high Anatolian Plateau may be physically close to the rest of the region, but in every other way Ankara feels a world apart from the surrounding steppe land. Turkey's capital provides a logical base for exploring the great sites of the Hittite Empire, which are contained within a triangle in northeastern

Central Anatolia

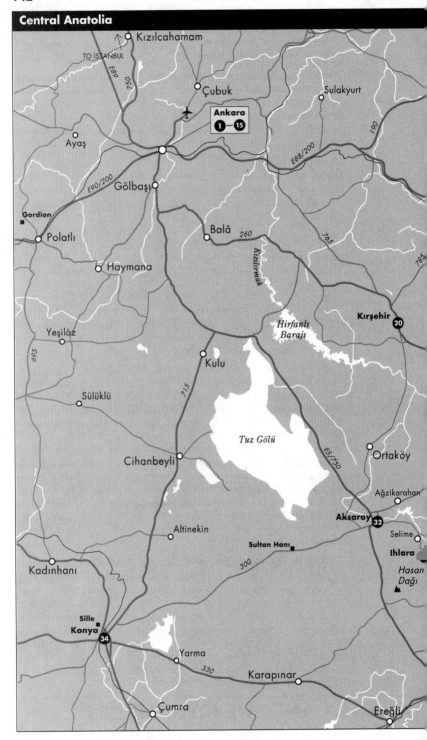

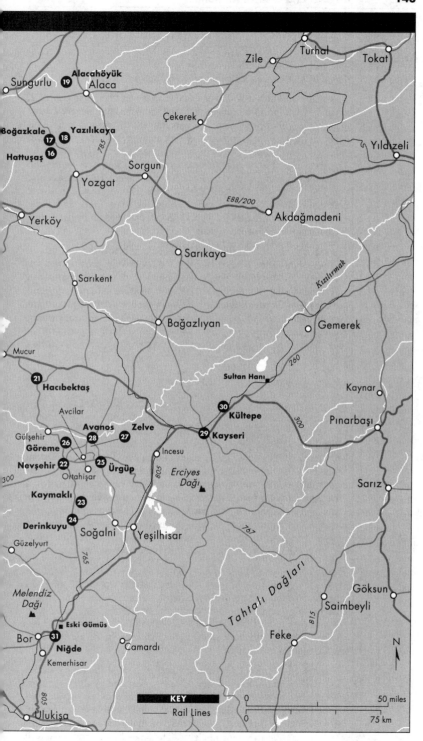

Central Anatolia bound by Hattuşaş, Yazılıkaya, and Alacahöyük. All of the Hittite cities can be seen in a day trip if you have a car.

Ankara

454 km (282 mi) east of Istanbul, Rte. E80 to Rte. E89.

Although Ankara is a young city, it has an ancient heart. It was here, at the dawn of the 15th century, that the Ottoman sultan Beyazıt I came face to face with the dread warrior Tamerlane, a descendant of Genghis Khan. Tamerlane came to Anatolia with an impressive record. He had subjugated Asia east of the Caspian Sea, invaded Persia, laid waste the Kirghiz plain, marched on Russia, turned south and attacked India, driven the Egyptians from Syria, and destroyed Baghdad, all in the course of 30 years. Beyazıt, called Yıldırım ("the Thunderbolt"), had not done badly himself. He had wrested Bulgaria, Macedonia, and Thessaly from their Christian rulers and had slaughtered an army of crusaders at the battle of Nicopolis.

The clash took place in July 1402, in the plain below the small town that was then called Ancyra. Beyazıt lost, decisively, providing much useful material for future poets. The Thunderbolt was taken prisoner, and some say the ruthless Tamerlane took pleasure in humiliating and torturing him, scenes depicted with relish by the 16th-century playwright Christopher Marlowe in *Tamburlaine the Great*. Most authorities, however, agree that the prisoner was treated with the regard due his rank. Beyazıt died after eight months of captivity, probably of a stroke, and Tamerlane, instead of continuing his march into Europe, turned his horse around and led his men back to the Mongol plains. He died the following year.

Before that epic battle, Ankara suffered a succession of Lydian, Persian, and Macedonian conquerors. Legend attributes the city's foundation to the redoubtable Amazons, but many archaeologists have identified it with the Hittite city of Ankuwash, which is thought to have been founded in around 1,200 BC and taken over by the Phrygians in around 700 BC. It was later taken by Alexander the Great, the Seleucids, and the Galatians before being annexed to Rome by Augustus in 25 BC. Ankara retained its strategic significance through the Byzantine Empire—as evidenced by the battle mentioned above—but under the Ottomans its importance gradually declined. By the early 20th century it was little more than a dusty provincial town with an illustrious pedigree, the perfect site for Atatürk to build his new capital.

Traffic moves smoothly along modern Ankara's wide, tree-lined avenues—except in the old town, the Ulus district, where narrow lanes surround the main sights of Ancyra, some untidy Roman remains, several mosques, and the citadel. Reminders of Atatürk are everywhere, from statues in his likeness to streets bearing the honorific name bestowed by his countrymen: Atatürk, the Father of the Turks; and Gazi, the Conqueror.

To understand Ankara's layout, it's best to start at the top; walk up ❶ Hisarparkı Caddesi to the **Hisar** (Citadel). Fortified by the Galatians, strengthened by the Romans, rebuilt by the Byzantines, and maintained by the Seljuks and Ottomans, the Hisar and its double walls are now crumbling away. Of the 20 towers that once guarded the structure, 15 are still standing to various heights. The citadel gates are fairly well intact; the best-preserved sections of the fortifications are near the Parmak Kapısı (inner gate). The Hisar Kapısı (outer gate) is topped by an inscription. Within the walls is a rambling, old-fashioned Turkish town. The ramshackle houses in the warren of narrow, cobbled lanes gain a touch of elegance from incorporated bits of broken marble columns and slabs taken from Roman ruins. The city's oldest *cami* (mosque) is also here, the small **Alaaddin Cami,** originally built in 1178, although much of what you see today was added later. To the south and west rise the skyscrapers of modern Ankara; the plains on which Tamerlane defeated Beyazıt stretch to the northeast; and the neighborhoods of Ankara's urban immigrants sprawl to the east.

★ ② The superb **Ankara Anadolu Medeniyetleri Müzesi** (Museum of Anatolian Civilizations) is housed in a restored 15th-century *bedestan* (covered bazaar) and inn. Though the museum itself is relatively small, the collection is world-class. Masterpieces from the Neolithic and Bronze ages and the Assyrian, Phrygian, Urartu, Hellenistic, and Roman eras are carefully displayed, all with explanations in English. (The freelance "guides" who offer their services tend to overcharge and add little to your visit.) The heart of the museum is its comprehensive collection of Hatti and Hittite art and crafts, dating from the dawn of the 2nd millennium BC. Here you will find the graceful, stylized deer statues that pop up on postcards throughout Turkey, as well as a bronze statuette of a bull (circa 2400 BC), a limestone Cappadocian idol with two heads (3rd millennium BC), a ram's-head vase (19th century BC), and a large bull's-head cauldron. Another huge cauldron, with clean, precise lines, is held up by four figures; it was found in Gordion, where a prophecy predicted Alexander the Great's rise to glory. There are small statues, jewels worked in gold and iron, combs, and needles as well as wonderful bas-relief carvings in stone, which display an incredible mastery of movement. This is best shown in a small bas-relief whose warriors, brandishing lances under cover of their shields, still bear faint traces of color. Another bas-relief depicts the Gilgamesh legend, which includes the Babylonian version of the Flood. ⊠ *Kadife Sok.,* ☎ *312/324–3160.* ▦ *$2.* ☉ *Sun.–Tues. 8:30–5.*

Outside the outer citadel walls is the neighborhood known as Samanpazarı. Along Kadife Sokak is the city's **bedestan,** where wide canvas tarps offer shade over piles of fruit, vegetables, and rice. Three mosques, all open during daylight hours and with no admission charge, lie south of the bedestan. The smallest of them, Ahi Elvan Cami, dates from the early 1400s and has Roman columns and a fine *mimber* (pulpit). ③ **Aslanhane Cami** (⊠ Atpazar Sok., south of citadel hill) took its name (Lionhouse Mosque) from the lion relief on a wall in front. It was built in 1289 by Emir Şeref Eddin.

④ The 16th-century **Yeni Cami,** or New Mosque (⊠ off Ulucanlar Cad.), was built by Süleyman's grand vizier, Çenabi Ahmet Paşa, supposedly after plans by the master architect Sinan, and executed by one of the great architect's pupils. The dark red porphyry of its walls is enhanced by the white marble mimber and *mihrab* (prayer niche).

⑤ The **Cumhuriyet Müzesi** (Republic Museum) is considered to be the birthplace of the Turkish Republic. It was here in 1920 that Atatürk was elected chairman of the Grand National Assembly, which would organize the new nation and galvanize the counterattack against the Greek troops occupying the Aegean. The early history of the parliament is given in photographs and documents. Most of the labels are in Turkish only. ⊠ *Cumhuriyet Cad., off Ulus Meyd. (Nation Sq.),* ☎ *312/310–5361.* ▦ *50¢.* ☉ *Tues.–Sun. 8:30–noon and 1–5.*

⑥ In the heart of Ankara's old town at the 3rd-century **Roma Hamamları** (Roman Baths), you can still see the oval soaking pool as well as the *frigidarium* and *caldarium* (cold and hot rooms). The steam rooms have raised floors; hot air once circulated below them from the furnace. A

146

Anıt Kabir, **14**
Ankara Anadolu
Medeniyetleri
Müzesi, **2**
Aslanhane Cami, **3**
Atatürk Orman
Çiftliği, **15**
Çankaya Köşkü, **13**
Cumhuriyet Müzesi, **5**
Etnoğrafya Müzesi, **11**
Gençlik Parkı, **10**
Hacı Bayram Cami, **8**
Hisar, **1**
Jülyanüs Sütunu, **7**
Kocatepe Cami, **12**
Roma Hamamları, **6**
Temple of Augustus, **9**
Yeni Cami, **4**

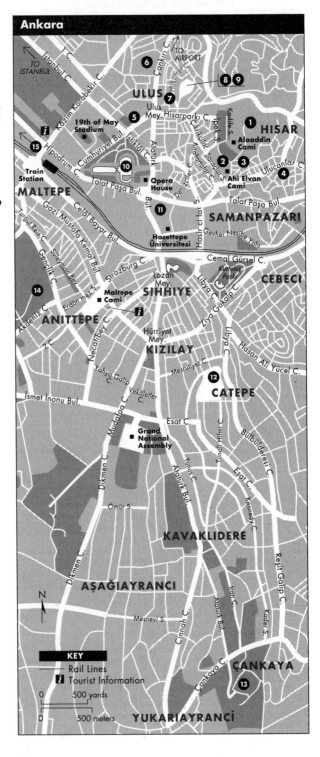

colonnaded palaestra, for sports and exercise, is part of the site. ⊠ *Çankırı Cad. 43, no phone.* ☞ *35¢.* ☉ *Daily 8:30–noon and 1–5.*

❼ The **Jülyanüs Sütunu** (Column of Julian) was erected in honor of the Roman Emperor Julian the Apostate (ruled AD 361–63), so-called because he attempted to reverse his father's decision to make Christianity the Empire's official religion. The column has 15 fluted drums topped by a Corinthian capital and commemorates a visit by the emperor in 362, when he was headed for battle with the Persians. Unfortunately, Julian didn't get to enjoy it; he died a year later. Storks often build their nests here now, gallantly withstanding the pollution. Facing the column across a fountain is the former Ministry of Finance; it is white with pointed arches and blue glazed tiles above big windows. ⊠ *Hükümet Meyd., a few blocks south of the Roman Baths.*

❽ At the end of a street lined with religious bookshops and stalls selling prayer beads is the **Hacı Bayram Cami,** built in the early 15th century of yellow stone and brick, with lavish touches of marble from the nearby Roman ruins and an unusual tiled roof. The glazed Kütahya tiles on the interior walls were added 300 years later. Hacı Bayram was a founder of an order of dervishes, and his tomb is near the entrance to the mosque. ⊠ *Bayram Cad., north of Hisarparkı Cad.,* ☎ *312/310– 8297.* ☞ *Free.* ☉ *During prayer times.*

❾ The **Temple of Augustus** was built in the 2nd century BC as a shrine to Cybele, a nature goddess of Asia Minor, and dedicated to Augustus after a Roman law deified dead emperors. Augustus, who was opposed to this concept, nonetheless requested that a summary of the achievements of his rule (known today by its Latin title *Res Gestae* or "Things Done") be carved into the walls of all his temples. The inscription discovered here in 1555 by a Flemish diplomat named Ghislain de Busbecq is the longest Latin inscription ever found and the only complete version of Augustus's text in the world. Fortunately Busbecq copied it down, as time has crumbled the stone and worn away most of the writing. Today you can make out only a few words here and there and only occasionally an entire line. ⊠ *Behind Hacı Bayram Cami.*

❿ The welcome green expanse of **Gençlik Parkı** is in Ankara's new town. Known as the Youth Park, it is filled with shady walks, tea gardens, and band shells, and has a small amusement park with a Ferris wheel and rides for children as well as a small lake where rowboats can be rented. ⊠ *Entrance west of İtfaiye Meyd.* ☞ *Free.* ☉ *Daily sunrise–sunset.*

⓫ The **Etnoğrafya Müzesi** (Ethnographic Museum) houses a rich collection of Turkish carpets, folk costumes, Anatolian handcrafts, and weapons. The building is done in Ottoman Revival style and includes a big oriental dome and marble decoration. Atatürk lay in state here from 1938 to 1955, when his mausoleum was finished. ⊠ *Talat Paşa Bul., Opera,* ☎ *312/311–3007.* ☞ *75¢.* ☉ *Tues.–Sun. 8:30–12:30 and 1:30–5.*

The **Resim ve Heykel Müzesi** (Painting and Sculpture Museum) displays works by contemporary Turkish artists. The building was built in 1925 as the Halk Evi (People's House) and was converted into a museum in the mid-1970s. South of the museum is the huge campus of Hacettepe University, modern Turkey's educational showpiece. Above the campus is the Karacabey Cami, built in 1428 on a T-shape plan; it has a thick minaret striped with colored tiles. ⊠ *Talat Paşa Bul., at Ocaği Sok.,* ☎ *312/310–2094.* ☞ *Free.* ☉ *Tues.–Sun. 9–noon and 1–5.*

The radial lobes surrounding the monumental replica of a Hatti Sun Disk on the principal shopping street of the **Sihhiye district** represent the planets, a rather impressive notion for 2000 BC. Many of the better hotels are located along the area's main drag, Atatürk Bulvari. In the distance, you might be able to see the **Maltepe Cami** (⊠ Gazi Mustafa Kemal Bul.), a handsome building whose large brass-plated dome is topped by slender minarets. Also in the neighborhood is **Kurtuluş Park** (⊠ Ziya Gökalp Cad., at Cemal Gürsel Cad.), which has a pond, clothing shops, and a Turkish Airlines ticket office.

The heart of Ankara's new town is in **Kizilay** (Crescent), named after the curving intersection of Atatürk Bulvari at Hürriyet Meydanı. You will find the high-rise Gima department store, once the city's tallest building, here.

⑫   The vast **Kocatepe Cami** opened to the faithful in 1982. The city's largest mosque, it was funded by the Saudi government; one has to wonder what Atatürk would have thought of such a gift in his secular capital city. The mosque is built in a classical Ottoman style reminiscent of the grand old mosques in Istanbul. ⊠ *Near intersection of Tunalı Hilmi Cad. and Bülbüldere Cad.*

Bakanliklar, the government district, begins with the **Grand National Assembly Hall,** the parliament building, which is west of Atatürk Bulvari at the intersection of Ismet Inönüu Bulvari and Dikmen Caddesi. Within walking distance in the Kavaklıdere neighborhood is Embassy Row, with gardens, fine restaurants, and world-class hotels.

⑬   The **Çankaya Köşkü** (Çankaya Pavilion), built for Atatürk after he moved the capital to Ankara, is in a city suburb. The little house is within the grounds of the Cumhurbaskanlığı Köşk (Presidential Mansion), which also has formal flower gardens and a fine view, though you can't visit the mansion itself. ⊠ *Atatürk Bul., south of Çankaya Cad., Çankaya.* ⊡ *Free.* ☉ *Sun. 1:30–4:30.*

★ ⑭   The most physically imposing of all of Ankara's attractions is the **Anit Kabir** (Monumental Tomb), which is the Atatürk mausoleum. Perched on a hilltop, it is reached by a marble-paved path lined with Hittite-style lions. To each side are pavilions with remarkable bas-relief carvings. At the entrance to the mausoleum are carved the words "Beyond all doubt, government belongs to the people." Sailors in white ducks and soldiers in olive drab mount the guard. The mausoleum itself is a vast, soaring hall lined with brilliant gold mosaics and marble, pierced by seven tall windows looking out over the city Atatürk built. The immensely impressive solitary marble sarcophagus is symbolic, as Atatürk's actual remains rest in the vault below. The **Atatürk Museum,** with personal belongings, objects associated with his life, and mementos from the War of Liberation (1919–22), is in an arcaded wing. ⊠ *Anit Cad., southern end,* ☎ *312/310–7140 (museum).* ⊡ *25¢.* ☉ *Daily 8:30–noon and 1–5.*

⑮   When Turks want to get away from the heat of the city, many head for **Atatürk Orman Çiftliği,** a model farm Atatürk had built on the city's western outskirts. In 1981, for the centenary of Atatürk's birth, a replica of his family home, the comfortable pink house of a merchant in Thessaloniki, was opened to visitors in the large park at the site. Pack a picnic lunch or try the on-site restaurant. You can also buy farm products here, including ice cream, yogurt, and milk. ⊠ *Hipodrom Cad., west from Talat Paşa Bul.,* ☎ *312/211–0170, ext. 285.* ☉ *Tues.–Sun. 9–12 and 1–5.*

Dining and Lodging

$$–$$$ ✗ **RV.** As befits a restaurant in the embassy quarter, RV is both elegant and costly. It's one of the few places men will feel more comfortable in a jacket. The menu covers both traditional Turkish specialties and

European dishes, a boon for homesick diplomats. ⊠ *İlbank Blok. 243, Atatürk Bul., Kavaklıdere,* ☎ *312/427–4344. Reservations essential. AE, DC, MC, V.*

$$ ✕ **Kale Washington.** This restaurant in Kale, the ancient heart of the city, serves a superb selection of grilled fish, kebabs, and *imam bayildi* (eggplant stuffed with ground lamb). ⊠ *Doyran Sok. 5, Kaleiçi, Ulus,* ☎ *312/311–4344 or 312/324–5959. Reservations essential. AE, DC, MC, V.*

$$ ✕ **Mest.** Ankara may seem an unlikely place to find northern Italian
★ cuisine, but you will come across it here. The Turkish chef, who is French-trained and who worked in Manhattan for years, openly disdains Turkish cuisine. Mest, nestled in a restored two-story villa, has an upstairs terrace for cocktails, a summer garden, and a bar. If you want to fraternize with ambassadors, this is the place to go. ⊠ *Attar Sok. 10, Gaziosmanpaşa,* ☎ *312/468–0743 or 312/468–6029. DC, MC, V.*

$$ ✕ **Nenehatun Washington.** This sibling of Kale Washington is in the upscale residential area of Gaziosmanpasa. The menu is similar to the Kale establishment's but also includes Russian dishes and very fine crepes. ⊠ *Nenehatun Cad. 97, Gaziosmanpaşa,* ☎ *312/445–0212 or 312/436–4353. DC, MC, V.*

$–$$ ✕ **Göksu.** Black Sea cuisine is the specialty of Göksu. The restaurant imports all its fish and cheese from the region, thus making it a popular hangout for Black Sea businessmen and their families. Rather incongruously, the walls are decorated with Hittite reliefs, but the food is excellent. ⊠ *Bayindir Sok. 22/A, Kizilay,* ☎ *312/431–2219 or 312/431–4727. Reservations essential. MC, V.*

$–$$ ✕ **Zenger Paşa Konaği.** The Mansion of Zenger Paşa, a traditional old
★ house within the citadel, has been restored and is now a fine restaurant. The food is traditional, too, from the *mantı* (Turkish ravioli) served at lunchtime to the *saç kavurma* (sautéed lamb) at dinner. The fine city view is an added attraction. ⊠ *Doyran Sok. 13, Ankara Kalesi,* ☎ *312/311–7070 or 312/311–4060. Reservations essential. MC, V.*

$ ✕ **Akman Boza ve Pasta Salonu.** This spot has been serving tasty breakfasts, sandwiches, desserts, and snacks since the 1930s. Tables are set out in a courtyard with a small fountain. ⊠ *Ulus Işhani G, Blok. 1,* ☎ *312/311–8755. MC, V.*

$$$$ ▥ **Ankara Hilton SA.** This luxurious 16-story hotel in a quiet hilly neigh-
★ borhood on Embassy Row provides many amenities and a view to boot. ⊠ *Tahran Cad. 12, Kavaklıdere,* ☎ *312/468–2888,* FAX *312/468–0909. 324 rooms with bath. 2 restaurants, 2 bars, minibars, no-smoking rooms, room service, indoor pool, sauna, Turkish bath, health club, casino, baby-sitting, dry cleaning, laundry service, business services. AE, DC, MC, V.*

$$$$ ▥ **Büyük Ankara.** This high-rise across from the Grand National Assembly was long Ankara's poshest hotel. Now competition from the international chains has relegated it to second place. Then again, it's slightly less expensive than the Hilton or Sheraton and has Turkish, rather than international, charm. ⊠ *Atatürk Bul. 183, Kavaklıdere,* ☎ *312/425–6655,* FAX *312/425–5070. 192 rooms with bath. 3 restaurants, bar, pool, casino. AE, DC, MC, V.*

$$$$ ▥ **Sheraton Ankara.** The splashiest of Ankara's luxury hotels is hard to miss; it's tall, white, and round. It is also well run, fashionable, and thoroughly international in style. Atatürk would have approved. ⊠ *Noktali Sok., Kavaklıdere,* ☎ *312/468–5454,* FAX *312/467–1136. 311 rooms with bath. Restaurant, bar, pool, health club, squash. AE, DC, MC, V.*

$$$ ▥ **Dedeman Oteli.** The Dedeman is the best bargain among the upper-echelon hotels. It has a rooftop nightclub with belly dancing, and other facilities you would find at higher-price hotels. The hotel has two wings, one more modern (and expensive), the other with older, smaller rooms. ⊠ *Büklüm Sok. 1, Akay,* ☎ *312/417–6200,* ℻ *312/417–6214. 292 rooms with bath. 2 restaurants, bar, pool, sauna, health club, casino, nightclub. AE, DC, MC, V.*

$$$ 🏨 **Kent.** A pleasant, helpful staff distinguishes this hotel in the heart of the city, near the main shopping and business areas. The restaurant is above average for a hotel. ⊠ *Mithatpaşa Cad. 4,* ☎ *312/435–5050,* ℻ *312/434–4657. 117 rooms with bath. Restaurant, bar. AE, DC, MC, V.*

$$ 🏨 **Tunali.** In the center of town, just across from the Kuglu Park, the Tunali is unspectacular and clean; the staff is very friendly. ⊠ *Tunali Hilmi Cad. 119, Kavaklıdere,* ☎ *312/467–4410 or 312/427–8100,* ℻ *312/427–4082. 52 rooms with shower. Restaurant, bar. AE, DC, MC, V.*

$–$$ 🏨 **Seğmen Hotel.** Near the Dedeman, the Seğmen is relatively new; interiors are done up in natural wood. The hotel is well located and reasonably priced. ⊠ *Büklüm Sok. 13, Kavaklıdere,* ☎ *312/417–5374,* ℻ *312/417–2859. 98 rooms with bath. Restaurant, bar. AE, DC, MC, V.*

$ 🏨 **Hotel Sultan.** This hotel is not fancy, but it's a perfectly acceptable place to stay and very inexpensive. Though there's no decor to speak of, the hotel does have clean sheets, hot water, and a friendly staff. The location is near Kızılay on a quiet side street in a residential area. ⊠ *Bayındır Sok. 35,* ☎ *312/431–5980,* ℻ *312/431–1083. 40 rooms with bath. Restaurant. MC, V.*

$ 🏨 **Otel Karyağdi.** Good hotels on the Ulus side of town are rare; this is the exception. The exterior is a purplish gray and looks a bit like a fortress. The interior is well furnished, though in a no-nonsense style. It is not far from Itfaiye Meydanı (Opera Square). ⊠ *Sanayi Cad., Kuruçeşme Sok. 4, Ulus,* ☎ *312/310–2440,* ℻ *312/312–6712. 40 rooms with bath. Restaurant, 2 bars, recreation room, playground. AE, DC, MC, V.*

OFF THE **GORDION** – The city made famous by King Midas, he of the golden
BEATEN PATH touch, is only about 100 km (62 mi) southwest of Ankara, but it lies in the opposite direction from the main tourist routes to Cappadocia and Konya. This was the capital of Phrygia, whose population most likely emigrated from Macedonia and Thrace about 3,000 years ago. After a crushing defeat in 695 BC, Midas apparently committed suicide. There are a few remains of the royal palace, but more interesting is the Great Tumulus on the edge of town, including what is believed to be the tomb of King Midas. A well-lit tunnel, 70 meters (230 feet) long, has been cut through the mound to the burial chamber, which is framed with cedar and juniper beams. When the tomb was opened, the skeleton of a short man, about age 60, lay on a large table. The funeral artifacts and bronze fibulae were taken to the Museum of Anatolian Civilizations in Ankara; the small local museum displays only a minor miscellany of pottery and copper objects. ⊠ *Take Rte. E90 to Polatlı; then look for the road to Gordion branching off to the right, approximately 12 km (8 mi) west of Polatli.*

Hattuşaş

★ ⑯ *158 km (98 mi) from Ankara, east on Rte. E88 and northeast on Rte. 190 until past Sungurlu; then follow road signs.*

There is old and then there is *old.* The Greek and Roman ruins you may have seen elsewhere in the country are mere yearlings compared to Hattuşaş. The city dates from the Bronze Age and the sophisticated culture of a people called the Hatti, who were thriving here by 2300 BC. From about 2000 BC on, the Hatti princes ruling the main city-states of Hattuşaş, Kaneş, Kushara, and Zalpa were doing brisk trade with the great Mesopotamian towns, from which they derived considerable wealth. Around 1800 BC, Anitta, king of the lost city of Kushara, formed an Anatolian confederacy and took for himself the title *Rabum Rabum* (King of Kings). His glory was short-lived.

At about that time, a mysterious people known as the Hittites came to dominate the Hatti. The Hittites, of Indo-European origin, apparently entered Anatolia after crossing the Caucasus and the steppes beyond the Black Sea. They claimed Hattuşaş as their capital and soon built an empire of their own. Labarna, who ascended to the throne in 1680 BC, is considered the founder of the Old Kingdom. Royal intrigue and invasions by new tribes from the east sent the empire into decline, and the Old Kingdom was followed by the New Kingdom. A series of battles with the Egyptians in about 1296 BC appears to have favored the Hittites, but a pattern of family strife reemerged. In decline for a second time, the reign of the Hittites finally came to an end in 1200 BC, when Hattuşaş was sacked and burned by tribes from the north.

As mysteriously as they arrived, the Hittites suddenly dispersed, disappearing from history for almost three millennia. Then, in 1812, a German traveler named Burckhardt found at Hamath, in Syria, a stone tablet bearing hieroglyphics different from the Egyptian ones previously encountered. In subsequent years ruins of some of the cities were discovered, but it wasn't until 1879 that Englishman Henry Sayce suggested that the Hittites of the Bible had at last been located. Thirty thousand cuneiform tablets have since been dug up and deciphered, covering everything from marriage contracts to treaties between ancient nations. From an unknown people, the Hittites have emerged as one of the best-documented cultures of early antiquity.

Though of small physical stature (probably under 5 feet), the Hittites were muscular and strongly built. Society was sharply divided into free people and serfs, and the sovereign who ruled over the federation of principalities was also its high priest, becoming a god after death. Their religion was a tolerant polytheism, and subsequent cultures may well have borrowed from the Hittite creed. Many of the Hittites' gods bear striking similarities to Etruscan, Greek, and Anatolian gods.

The first thing to notice is the city's location—an excellent defensive position in a valley framed on both sides by rivers. The second item of note is the city's incredible size. Its walls, made of brick on stone foundations, reinforced by large cut stones, and surmounted by towers, were 6 km (4 mi) in circumference.

After investigating the ramparts of the lower city, **walk in the direction of the citadel.** The first ruins to the right as you ascend are those of the **Temple of the Storm God** (Temple I). Hattuşaş had five temples, all patterned on the same model. Like Babylonian temples, they consisted of small rooms arranged around a paved courtyard roughly 700 feet by 1,700 feet. Near the entrance to this complex are pieces of a ceremonial basin made from limestone and carved with trademark Hittite lions. Within the temple, you should be able to make out the main courtyard and two large rooms, which housed statues of the storm god and a sun goddess. The rooms opening out from the courtyard were probably administrative offices and archives. The temple stands on a terrace overlooking some public buildings; to the north and east once lay private residential buildings, parts of which have been excavated.

The ruins of **Büyükkale** (great fortress) are reached by a modern stairway that has replaced the ancient ramp. On the terrace atop the sheer cliff stood the royal palace, probably several stories high. The citadel's outbuildings include the **State Archive**, where, in 1906, thousands of stone tablets were found, mute but eloquent survivors of the plundering Phrygians. Among them was a copy of the Treaty of Kadesh, signed in 1279 BC after the war with the Egyptians. Continuing up the hill, you come first to the eastern side of the upper city's fortified wall. The ramparts here are the most impressive. They consist of two parallel walls connected by two main gates (one of which is the **Kral Kapısı,** or Royal Gate), which are themselves formidable bastions.

Follow along the ramparts. The ruins of **Temples II, III,** and **V** lie to your left. Beyond is the entrance to the **Yerkapı** (Earth Gate). Though only its foundations remain, it is still impressive, set on a man-made ridge some 30 feet high. In its day, the gate was decorated with finely carved sphinxes; to see one, you'd have to visit museums in either Istanbul or Berlin. Directly underneath the gate is an odd tunnel, 61 meters (200 feet) long and paved. No one is really sure of its purpose, although it may have led to a postern gate for sallies against besieging forces. The ruins of **Temple IV** are to the north. Beyond, at the end of the pathway that runs the length of the ramparts, rises the well-preserved **Gate of the Lions.** The lions themselves are reproductions. ⌨ *$1 (includes Yazılıkaya).* ⊙ *Daily 8-7 (according to sunlight).*

Boğazkale

🔼 *5 km (3 mi) north of Hattuşaş.*

In 1839, a Frenchman, Charles Texier, stumbled on the ruins of Boğazkale, which included stone carvings and bas-reliefs. (*A Guide to Boğazköy,* in English, is helpful; it's available at the archaeological museums in Ankara, Alacahöyük, and the nearby village of Boğazkale, as Boğazköy is also known.) Today there is a museum here, but if you've been to the Museum of Anatolian Civilizations in Ankara, you've already seen the best finds from the Hittite sites. ⌨ *75¢.* ⊙ *Daily 8–5:30.*

Yazılıkaya

🔼 *2 km (1 mi) northeast of Hattuşaş, 2 km (1 mi) west of Boğazkale.*

Yazılıkaya is thought to have served the capital city of Hattuşaş as a religious sanctuary or temple complex. The name means "rock with writing," a fitting title, as the natural rock walls here are covered with the carvings of Hittite artists dating from about 1300 BC. At the site, a large entrance portal opens onto a natural crevice that forms a narrow passageway through the rocks and ends at a small, circular open space. The rocky walls of the passageway are decorated with bas-reliefs illustrating various Hittite gods and kings. Within the **main shrine** are depicted 42 gods marching from the left to meet 21 goddesses coming from the right. The largest section portrays the most important deities, including the carved figures of **Teshub,** the weather god (the fellow with the most horns on his cap), and his consort, the goddess **Hepatu,** astride a leopard. Her son **Sharruma,** also riding a leopard, is directly behind her. Sharruma is believed to be a god of death and rebirth, like the Egyptian Osiris. On the opposite wall is a king with a major ego, **Tudhaliya IV.** Not only did he have his likeness placed among the gods, he also ordered that it be larger than any of them. If size alone is not enough to pick him out, look for a man with a rounded skullcap, earring, and curved scepter.

Next to the main shrine, a second, smaller passageway leads to a small gallery. Here again is King Tudhaliya, this time alongside a particularly fine and well-preserved image of Sharruma. The **frieze of the twelve gods** opposite is another exceptional work. Another gallery figure is the so-called **Sword God,** shown with the head of a god attached to a body made up of four lions; he carries a sword with its point aimed downward. Funeral rites for recently departed kings were probably held here. There are no official guides, but pamphlets are available at the ticket kiosk. ✉ *$1 (includes ruins at Hattuşaş).* ⊘ *Daily 8–7 (according to sunlight).*

Alacahöyük

⑲ *28 km (17 mi) from Boğazkale, 20 km (12 mi) north of the Sungurlu–Boğazkale Road.*

The site of Alacahöyük was settled as early as 4000 BC and not discovered until the 19th century AD by Englishman John Hamilton. Some scholars assert that it might be King Anitta's lost city of Kushara. Continuing excavations have brought to light 15 levels of four different cultures, beginning with 13 **rectangular burial chambers** belonging to Hatti kings. In the tombs were golden diadems, belts, necklaces and other jewelry, silver combs, mirrors, drinking vessels, and other funerary artifacts, all now in the Museum of Anatolian Civilizations in Ankara. A later Hittite temple was entered through the Gate of Sphinxes, likewise now in Ankara, with concrete replicas in situ. The double-headed eagle, an emblem of the Hittites as well as many succeeding empires, appears on the inside wall. Concrete casts of original bas-reliefs depict a royal couple before an altar with a bull on it, the sun goddess Arima, two musicians playing odd instruments, and a procession of animals. Next to the site is a small museum with sketches of what the city once looked like and paintings from the burial chambers. Though the museum and the rest of the site are officially closed on Mondays, the guards live next door and could easily be convinced to open up. ✉ *$1.* ⊘ *Tues.–Sun. 8–noon and 1:30–5:30.*

CAPPADOCIA AND KONYA
Kaymaklı, Göreme, Ihlara, and Konya

The story of the incredible kingdom of Cappadocia begins over 10 million years ago, when the three peaks that dominate the region—Erciyes Dağ, Hasan Dağ, and Melendiz Dağ (Mts. Erciyes, Hasan, and Melendiz)—were active volcanoes. Aeons worth of eruptions dumped layers of mud, ash, and lava on the area. Eventually the ground turned to tuff, a soft, porous rock. Rain, snow, and wind created a fantasyland of rock formations resembling chimneys, cones, needles, pillars, and pyramids, often topped by perfectly balanced, gigantic slabs of rock. Then came earthquakes to add vast valleys and oxidation to give the area the final artistic touch: rocks "painted" yellow, pink, red, russet, and gray-violet.

No one is really sure when people came to inhabit Cappadocia. There are signs of Hittite occupation, and by 600 BC there are references to the Kingdom of Cappadocia, a loose confederacy of neighboring states. Its first capital was at Nissa; later it was moved to Mazaca (modern Kayseri). Alexander the Great never bothered with the region, and it wasn't annexed by Rome until Emperor Tiberius claimed it in AD 17 and changed the capital's name to Caesarea. Still a backwater, albeit now a Roman one, Cappadocia never gained much in the way of theaters and temples. It did, however, go over to Christianity with great zeal following a visit from Saint Paul. In 370, a local son named Basilius became bishop of Caesarea. A believer in spiritual perfection through monasticism, he was also noted for his good works. His considerable inheritance was spent on the establishment of a charitable institution that cared for the poor and the sick. Though himself in bad health, he personally looked after the poorest of the poor, the lepers, and still found time to preach and write doctrinal treatises. The Eucharist Liturgy of the Greek Church bears his name, and he is one of its Four Doctors. He died on January 1, 379, and, as Saint Basil, entered Christian tradition as a bringer of joy and gifts. His foundation became the nucleus of Byzantine Caesarea, and his rules for Orthodox monks are still followed today.

Long before the Arab raids, ascetics inspired by Saint Basil carved cave dwellings into the soft tuff. This quickly led to the formation of religious colonies that combined the individuality of meditation with communal work on fertile volcanic soil wherever there was a patch of level ground. Rock chapels proliferated, especially in the Göreme Valley. Later, churches were designed in contemporary Byzantine architectural styles and decorated with geometric paintings and increasingly ambitious frescoes. Ironically, ecclesiastical art climaxed in the 11th century, just when the Christian era in Turkey was drawing to a close. Yet Christian communities persisted here, under tolerant Seljuk and Ottoman rulers, up until the exchange of Greek (Christian) and Turkish (Muslim) populations following World War I.

Cappadocia has changed little over the centuries. People travel between their farms and villages in horse-drawn carts, women drape their houses with strings of apricots and paprika for drying in the sun, and nomads pitch their black tents beside sunflower fields and cook on tiny fires that send smoke billowing through the tent tops. In the distance, a minaret pierces the sky. Recently, however, the spellbinding tuff rocks have been revealed to be no less dangerous to their inhabitants than the most ruthless invaders of old. For generations, villagers at Karain have suffered painful deaths, known throughout the area as "the Karain agony." These have finally been diagnosed as cancer, caused by prolonged exposure to the pale yellow rock. Karain and a similarly affected village nearby have been declared natural disaster areas, and the villagers have been evacuated, a fate that seems to them no less an evil than the disease. Only a few villages carved from the rocks are still inhabited, while the holes that riddle the nearby cliff bases shelter the occasional anachronistic troglodyte.

Today Cappadocia forms a rough triangle, starting about 272 km (169 mi) southeast of Ankara, between Nevşehir, Kayseri, and Niğde. The main sights are within an even smaller triangle, marked by Ürgüp, Göreme, and Avanos. Ürgüp is the center from which to explore the monastic villages of Cappadocia and the best place to shop and to arrange tours; Nevşehir is a good base for exploring the underground cities of Kaymaklı and Derinkuyu.

After visiting Cappadocia, many travelers continue on to Konya. As befits what was the capital of the Seljuk Empire for two centuries, Konya has Turkey's largest concentration of Seljuk architecture. The Seljuks chose their capital wisely; the combination of altitude and setting provides Konya with cool breezes from the surrounding mountain chains and a more moderate climate than in the rest of Anatolia.

Kırşehir

❷ *203 km (126 mi) from Ankara, east on Rte. E88 and south on Rtes. 765 and 260; 166 km (103 mi) from Boğazkale, west on Rte. E88 and south on Rtes. 785 and 260.*

Kırşehir, an important agricultural center, has several Seljuk monuments. The Alaaddin Cami is one of many mosques in the region named after

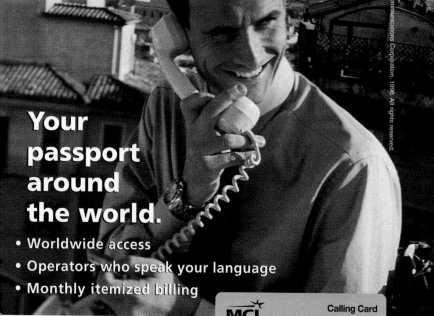

Your passport around the world.

- Worldwide access
- Operators who speak your language
- Monthly itemized billing

Use your MCI Card® and these access numbers for an easy way to call when traveling worldwide.

MCI ✦ Calling Card

415 555 1234 2244
J.D. SMITH

Austria (CC)✦†	022-903-012
Belarus	
From Gomel and Mogilev regions	8-10-800-103
From all other localities	8-800-103
Belgium (CC)✦†	0800-10012
Bulgaria	00800-0001
Croatia (CC)★	99-385-0112
Czech Republic (CC)✦	00-42-000112
Denmark (CC)✦†	8001-0022
Finland (CC)✦†	9800-102-80
France (CC)✦†	0800-99-0019
Germany (CC)†	0130-0012
Greece (CC)✦†	00-800-1211
Hungary (CC)✦	00▼800-01411
Iceland (CC)✦†	800-9002
Ireland (CC)†	1-800-55-1001
Italy (CC)✦†	172-1022
Kazakhstan (CC)	1-800-131-4321
Liechtenstein (CC)✦	155-0222
Luxembourg†	0800-0112
Monaco (CC)✦	800-90-19

Netherlands (CC)✦†	06-022-91-22
Norway (CC)✦†	800-19912
Poland (CC)✛†	00-800-111-21-22
Portugal (CC)✛†	05-017-1234
Romania (CC)✛	01-800-1800
Russia (CC)✛✦	747-3322
For a Russian-speaking operator	747-3320
San Marino (CC)✦	172-1022
Slovak Republic (CC)	00-42-000112
Slovenia	080-8808
Spain (CC)†	900-99-0014
Sweden (CC)✦†	020-795-922
Switzerland (CC)✦†	155-0222
Turkey (CC)✦†	00-8001-1177
Ukraine (CC)✛	8▼10-013
United Kingdom (CC)†	
To call to the U.S. using BT■	0800-89-0222
To call to the U.S. using Mercury■	0500-89-0222
Vatican City (CC)†	172-1022

To sign up for the MCI Card, dial the access number of the country you are in and ask to speak with a customer service representative.

http://www.mci.com

It helps to be pushy in airports.

Introducing the revolutionary new TransPorter™ from American Tourister®. It's the first suitcase you can push around without a fight. TransPorter's™ exclusive four-wheel design lets you push it in front of you with almost no effort–the wheels take the weight. Or pull it on two wheels if you choose. You can even stack on other bags and use it like a luggage cart.

Stable 4-wheel design.

TransPorter™ is designed like a dresser, with built-in shelves to organize your belongings. Or collapse the shelves and pack it like a traditional suitcase. Inside, there's a suiter feature to help keep suits and dresses from wrinkling. When push comes to shove, you can't beat a TransPorter™. For more information on how you can be this pushy, call 1-800-542-1300.

Shelves collapse on command.

the great Seljuk sultan Alaaddin Keykubat (ruled 1219–1236). Caca Bey Cami was built in 1272 as an astronomical observatory. Ahi Evran Cami holds the *türbe* (tomb) of the founder of the Ahi brotherhood, a religious sect that exercised considerable influence in Anatolia for several centuries. Its precepts had much to do with hospitality and good fellowship, a likely reason for the group's popularity. Just before the junction with Route 260 stands the tomb of the poet Aşık Paşa, built during the Mongol occupation of the region.

Hacıbektaş

㉑ *44 km (27 mi) south of Kırşehir, Rte. 260 to Rte. 765.*

Hacı Bektaş Veli founded a religious sect in the 13th century in Hacıbektaş. His teachings were based on a synthesis of Sunnism and Shiism, two branches of Islam, blended with a touch of Christianity. Hacı Bektaş became the spiritual leader of the newly founded Janissary Corps, the fierce warriors of the Ottoman Empire, which gave him tremendous political as well as religious influence. The monastery that belonged to his disciples is now the **Hacıbektaş Müzesi** (☎ 384/441–1022) in the center of town; admission is 75¢. Hacı Bektaş is buried in a tomb behind a gilded door here.

En Route   South of Hacıbektaş, on your way to Nevşehir, you'll pass through **Gülşehir,** where Grand Vizier Kara Mehmet Paşa constructed a rare Ottoman Baroque complex with a mosque, *medrese* (mosque compound), *hamam* (Turkish bath), and six fountains next to some Byzantine ruins. Soon the scenery starts to change. Pink-and-white mushroom-shape rocks are scattered along the rest of the route to Nevşehir.

Nevşehir

㉒ *49 km (30 mi) south of Hacıbektaş on Rte. 765.*

Known in ancient times as Nissa, Nevşehir is the region's largest town. It clings to the slopes below a ruined Seljuk fortress and has a 13th-century Seljuk mosque, the Kaya Cami. The town owes its prosperity to Grand Vizier Damat Ibrahim Paşa, who endowed his birthplace with the **Kurşunlu Cami** (Lead-domed Mosque) and its medrese, hospice, and library in 1726. Solid square houses of light local stone often stand amid pleasant gardens.

Dining and Lodging

$ ✕ **Aspava.** The centrally located Aspava serves good-quality *hazir yemek* (food prepared earlier and kept hot), kebabs, and *pide* (Turkish pizza). Men eat downstairs; upstairs is a section reserved for women and families. ⊠ *Atatürk Bul.,* ☎ *384/213–1051. No credit cards.*

$$–$$$ ▥ **Hotel Cappadocia Dedeman.** This modern high-rise offers the closest thing to luxury in the area. It's about 2 km (1 mi) out of town along the road to Ürgüp. ⊠ *Ürgüp Yolu,* ☎ *384/213–9900,* FAX *384/213–2158. 349 rooms with bath. 2 restaurants, 2 bars, indoor pool, outdoor pool, sauna, Turkish bath, tennis court, billiards, casino, dance club. AE, DC, MC, V.*

$$ ▥ **Altinoz Hotel.** This modern hotel lacks the character and charm of many smaller establishments in the region, but it is clean and comfortable, with a helpful staff and passable restaurants. ⊠ *Ragip Uner Cad. 23,* ☎ *384/213–5305 or 384/213–9961,* FAX *384/213–2817. 120 rooms with shower. 2 restaurants, bar, sauna. MC, V.*

$–$$ ▥ **Hotel Orsan Kapadokya.** The Orsan is quite chic by Turkish provincial standards; it has fine Turkish carpets in the public areas, a smart bar, and a pool. ⊠ *Yeni Kayseri Cad. 15,* ☎ *384/213–2115 or 384/213–*

5329, ⓕⓐⓧ *384/213–4223. 95 rooms with bath. Restaurant, bar, pool, dance club. AE, MC, V.*

Kaymaklı

★ ㉓ *21 km (13 mi) south of Nevşehir on Route 765.*

From the 7th through the 10th century, the Christian Cappadocians were under siege from Arab raiders. They took refuge in about 40 underground cities. These were cities in the truest sense, some stretching as deep as 20 stories below the surface and able to house as many as 20,000 people. Each had dormitories, dining halls, sewage disposal systems, and ventilation chimneys, as well as a cemetery and a prison. Large millstones sealed off the entrances from enemies. Who actually built these cities is a mystery. Some exhibit traces of Hittite settlements. The Greek historian Xenophon mentions Cappadocian underground dwellings as early as 401 BC. The Christians probably expanded what they found; certainly the cities took centuries to complete.

The narrow entrance to the **ruins of Kaymaklı** was only uncovered in the 1950s. A central air shaft assures perfect ventilation throughout the 394 feet that have been opened up so far, but if you have claustrophobic tendencies, you might want to skip this experience entirely. Sloping corridors and steps connect the floors, self-contained but for cemeteries and kitchens, which are spaced on every second level. Smoke was not allowed to escape for fear of betraying the hideout. In some cases a hole is cut above the doorway; through it defenders could pour boiling oil down on their attackers. The impermeable tuff kept the stone dry, and interior wells provided water. Little arrows enable you to take a self-guided tour. A flashlight is helpful, and you'll want a sweater, even in summer. ☎ *384/218–2500. ⌨ $1. ☉ Daily 8–sunset.*

Derinkuyu

㉔ *30 km (19 mi) south of Nevşehir on Rte. 765, 9 km (6 mi) south of Kaymaklı on Rte. 765.*

Kaymaklı is believed to be connected by a 10-km (6-mi) tunnel to Derinkuyu, though this has not yet been unblocked. The layout here is similar to that of the other hideaway, but there is an unusual Greek church about halfway down. Some carvings and paintings are visible, but they are fading fast. ☎ *384/381–3194. ⌨ $1. ☉ Daily 8–sunset.*

Ürgüp

㉕ *23 km (14 mi) east of Nevşehir.*

Ürgüp is the logical base for exploring the surrounding towns, but it's not necessarily the most pleasant, as its lodgings are often booked up by tours. Ürgüp has some old, white Greek-style houses, converted now into hotels and carpet shops. In summer its streets are filled with tourists haggling in myriad languages over antique copper and old kilims. The Saturday town market is popular with tourists. Hotel windows open on breathtaking scenery. A serrated white cliff is riddled with man-made holes. Some of the fragile masonry walls have crumbled away, revealing the interiors of houses. These caves, as well as some giant cones and chimneys in nearby villages, are still inhabited by troglodytes, who simply remove any fallen walls and dig deeper into the rock.

Dining and Lodging

$$ ✗ **Hanedan.** From the terrace of this restaurant in an old Greek-style house you can watch the sun set across the plains toward the mountains. The traditional Turkish food, including fresh fish and meat, es-

pecially lamb, is very good and presented with flair. ⊠ *Nevşehir Yolu Üzeri,* ☎ *384/341–4266,* 🗷 *384/341–8866. V.*

$ ✕ **Han Çırağan.** The setting within an old caravansary gives the Çırağan some charm. The menu usually includes *sac tava* (small pieces of fried beef, onion, pepper, tomato, and rice), *güveç* (a lamb or beef stew in a jealously guarded secret sauce) as well as mantı. ⊠ *Nevşehir Yolu 31,* ☎ *384/341–2566,* 🗷 *383/341–4181. MC, V.*

$$–$$$ 🏨 **Perissia Hotel.** Probably the best of a string of good hotels along Kayseri Caddesi, the Perissia is clean and very comfortable, with a large outdoor pool and other amenities, including dry cleaning, that you won't find elsewhere in the area. The marble lobby is impressive, and each room has a satellite TV system and a stereo. ⊠ *Kayseri Cad.,* ☎ *384/341– 2930,* 🗷 *384/341–4524. 230 rooms with bath. 2 restaurants, 3 bars, minibars, room service, pool, 2 tennis courts, dance club. AE, MC, V.*

$–$$ 🏨 **Hotel Alfina.** If you really want to experience Cappadocia, why not
★ lodge troglodyte-style? In the Alfina, a hotel carved out of volcanic rock, you get the definite sensation of being in a cave—despite the small windows in every room. Bathrooms are modern, however, and the restaurant is quite good. ⊠ *İstiklal Cad., Ürgüp Girisi 25,* ☎ *384/341–4822,* 🗷 *384/341–2424 (Ankara representative 312/417–8425,* 🗷 *312/418– 6207). 27 rooms with bath. Restaurant, bar. MC, V. Closed Nov.–Mar.*

$–$$ 🏨 **Turban Ürgüp Motel.** Big rooms and good facilities (including a Turkish bath) make this state-run holiday village 1 km (½ mi) from the center of town a popular overnight spot for tour groups. ⊠ *Nevşehir Yolu, Esbeli Mah.,* ☎ *384/341–2290,* 🗷 *384/341–2299. 243 rooms with shower. Restaurant, pool. DC, MC, V.*

En Route South of Ürgüp, on the Yeşilhisar road, there are several towns with cave churches, including Mustafapaşa and Soğanlı. The citadel of Ortahisar is hewn out of a gigantic serrated heap of stone; you can climb to the top for a panoramic view.

Göreme

㉖ *7 km (4 mi) northwest of Ürgüp.*

★ The **Göreme Açik Hava Müzesi** (Göreme Open-Air Museum), in the vineyard-filled valley of Göreme, contains a wealth of rock churches. Signs provide information about the site, but bring a flashlight—the churches are only illuminated by the natural light that seeps in.

The oldest rock church dates from the 4th century. Frescoes first appeared around the 8th century, when the geometric designs applied directly to the rock face gradually gave way to scenes from the New Testament and the lives of the more popular saints painted on plaster. The steep rock to the left of the site's entrance housed a six-story **convent,** which had a kitchen and refectory on the lower levels and a cruciform chapel on the third; large millstones lay ready to block the narrow passages in times of danger. Opposite is a **monastery** on the same plan, close to the **Elmalı Kilise** (Church with the Apple), probably named after a now-vanished orchard. This church is relatively new, only 12th century. Like those in other main churches, its polychrome scenes from the life of Christ on a dark blue background have been restored under the auspices of UNESCO. To protect the frescoes, all the churches are kept locked and are opened only to groups or by special permission.

The **Barbara Kilise** (Church of Saint Barbara) is decorated with early red designs from the Iconoclastic period (726–842) and 11th-century frescoes of Saint Barbara above the baptistry font. The **Yılanı Kilise** (Serpent Church) might be named after Saint George's dragon, pictured here. A bevy of saints adorns the two sections of this church, one barrel-vaulted, the other flat-roofed. In one mural, Saint Thomas and Saint Basil flank a rather unusual half-female, half-male figure—probably an ancient image of the Anatolian mother goddess, transformed under Christianity into a saint. The 11th-century **Karanlık Kilise** (Dark Church) is lit only through a small orifice in the narthex, reached by a spiral staircase from a refectory. The frescoes are exceptionally fine, especially the Christ, who appears in vivid colors on a dark blue background in the center of the main apse. Unfortunately, it is only opened by special permission. The **Çarıklı Kilise** (Church of the Sandal) was named after the footprint below the Ascension fresco, which some experts believe to be a cast of Jesus's own footprint. ⊠ *Open Air Museum: Ürgüp Rd.* 🖼 *$4.* ☉ *Daily 8–6.*

The largest of Göreme's churches, the 10th-century **Tokalı Kilise** (Church of the Buckle), contains scenes from the life of Christ. Inside, you might be in any Byzantine church, as sunlight streams in from the barrel entry and turns the underground vaults into gold. It's also worth following the path to the **Madonna Kilise** (Church of the Madonna), and the 11th-century **El Nazar Kilise**. The price of Tokalı Kilise is included in the admission to Göreme's Open-Air Museum; the other churches are free, but have irregular hours. ⊠ *Down the hill from Göreme Open-Air Museum parking lot.*

The aptly named **Saklı Kilise** (Hidden Church), a 12th-century work, has fine frescoes, but is difficult to find. ⊠ *1 km (½ mi) past the Tokalı Kilise, on the left.*

If you haven't yet tired of rock churches, in the vicinity of the troglodyte village of **Avcılar,** a long walk or short drive away, there are five more. At Çavuşin the church is guarded by frescoes of the angels Michael and Gabriel; inside are scenes from the life of Christ.

Dining and Lodging

$$ ╳ **Harmandali.** This cavernous restaurant prides itself on serving more kinds of meze (30) than any place else in the region. Popular with tour groups, Harmandali also prepares a variety of main dishes, all for one price. The house specialty is chicken güveç. But the real reason for coming here is the folkloric and belly dancing that follow the meal. ⊠ *Uçhisar, near Göreme,* ☎ *384/219–2364,* 🖷 *384/219–2394. No credit cards.*

$$$$ ╳🖬 **Ataman.** Run by tourist guide Abbas and his wife Şermin, this hotel just a short walk from the bus station is built into the face of a rock. The rooms, decorated with kilims and native handicrafts, are built into caves. Some have fireplaces. The restaurant ($–$$) serves good Turkish and international cuisine. Room rates include breakfast and dinner. ⊠ *Orta Mah.,* ☎ *384/271–2310,* 🖷 *384/271–2313. 16 rooms with bath. Restaurant, bar, minibars. MC, V.*

$$$$ 🖬 **Cave Hotel Melek.** Though decidedly basic, the Melek is special for one reason: It's partially carved out of the rock. ⊠ *On the main street toward Uchisar Castle,* ☎ 🖷 *384/271–2463. 20 rooms, 12 with bath. Restaurant. AE, MC, V.*

$ 🖬 **Ottoman House.** For only $10 a night, or $20 including breakfast ★ and dinner, you can stay at this cozy hotel that feels like a bed-and-breakfast inn. As an added bonus, the accommodating managers run a top-notch carpet shop down the street, where they'll give you a free education in carpets. The rooms are simple but clean and are decorated with carpets from the shop. After a delicious dinner in the restaurant, stop by the wonderful Harem Bar, where you get the feeling that belly dancing could begin at any moment. ⊠ *Orta Mah. 36,* ☎ *384/271–*

2616 ⚏ *384/271–2351. 35 rooms with shower. Restaurant, bar, laun-dry service. MC, V.*

Zelve

㉗ *6 km (4 mi) northeast of the Göreme Open-Air Museum.*

At Zelve is another open-air museum with another canyon filled with fairy chimneys and churches; this time the stone is a deep red rather than white. At the mouth of the canyon rises a small minaret. The central ridge divided the valley into Christian and Muslim sectors, with a mosque and church hewn back to back out of the same rock. Rockfalls in the 1960s caused the town to be evacuated. At the far end of the left-hand valley is a narrow tunnel in the rocks; it leads to a canyon with a stream, a peaceful place to rest. ⚏ *$3.* ⊘ *Daily 8–5.*

Avanos

㉘ *8 km (5 mi) north of Zelve.*

Avanos, on the north bank of the Kızılırmak (Red River), is an attractive old town filled with shops selling onyx jewelry and pottery. The river is named for the local red clay, from which the pottery is made. The latest of the region's underground cities has been discovered at **Özkonak,** off a dirt road 20 km (12 mi) north of Avanos. Potentially the largest of all, this hidden city may have been able to shelter up to 60,000 people, although as yet only a small portion of it has been excavated. Somewhat off the main circuit and still in need of cleaning up, it is omitted by most guided tours. The **Sari Han,** a 13th-century Seljuk caravansary from the time of Sultan Alaaddin Keykubat, is also nearby, about 5 km (3 mi) east of Avanos. Caravansaries were major outposts on trade routes. They had stables, sleeping quarters, a mosque, and baths, and within their sturdy walls, the goods carried by merchants were kept safe from highway robbers.

Dining and Lodging

$ ✕🏠 **Sofa Motel.** The Sofa's manager estimates that the restored old stone houses that form the motel are at least 200 years old. The excellent restaurant serves local cuisine and there is also an outdoor tea garden. The only downside is that it's a bit of a hike to the rooms. ⊠ *Orta Mah. 13,* ☎ ⚏ *384/511–4489. 34 rooms with shower. Restaurant, breakfast room. MC, V.*

$–$$ 🏠 **Otel Altinyazi.** This hotel has little character, but it's clean and offers a fair number of amenities for a reasonable price. Built in the late 1980s, it has a modern, minimalist decor. ⊠ *Kapadokya Cad. 23,* ☎ *384/511–2010,* ⚏ *384/511–4960. 84 rooms with bath. Restaurant, 3 bars, sauna, Turkish bath, dance club. AE, MC, V.*

Kayseri

㉙ *79 km (49 mi) from Avanos, south on Rte. 767 and north on Rte. 805 north.*

The last of the major cities of Cappadocia is Kayseri, a conservative, historic town that is unfortunately now being rebuilt in International Concrete Modern. Still, there are some engaging Seljuk monuments here. On Cumhuriyet Meydanı, where Sivas Caddesi and Istanbul Caddesi meet at the center of town, are not one but two statues of Atatürk. The black basalt walls of the **old citadel** still watch over the square; inside is a modern Turkish shopping mall. The citadel was built by the Byzantines and patched up by Sultan Alaaddin Keykubat in 1224 and again by the Ottomans after the conquest by Sultan Selim I in 1515. Two Seljuk lions guard the gate in the thick ramparts. The fortress walls, sufficiently intact for a trip around the catwalk, provide a fine view of the city.

Within **Atatürk Parkı** is the **Kurşunlu Cami,** which has a fine, lead-covered cupola. It was completed in 1585 by Ahmet Paşa after a design by the 16th-century architect Sinan, who was born in a nearby village.

Sahabiye Medrese was established by the Seljuk vizier Sahipata in 1267. Set around an open courtyard, the seminary has some of the finest carvings of the late Seljuk period. ⊠ *Cumhuriyet Meyd., facing the old citadel.*

In a maze of back streets is the **Giyasiye Medrese,** the first medical school in Anatolia (and older than any in Europe). A passage joined it to the Şifahiye Medrese, a hospital. Both were built in 1206 from legacies left by the daughter of Sultan Giyassedin Keyhusrev I. Much restored, they are now museums of Islamic medicine. ⊠ *Mimar Sinan Parkı.* 🎫 *Free.* ☉ *Buildings usually locked; ask for watchman.*

The architectural detail of the **Hacı Kılıç Cami and Medrese,** built in 1249 by the Seljuk vizier Abdül Gazi, is quite good, especially the handsomely wrought portals. ⊠ *Off İstasyon Cad.* 🎫 *Free.* ☉ *Daylight hrs.*

★ The outstanding complex containing the **Huant Hatun Cami, Medrese, and Türbe** demonstrates the influence of Huant Hatun, the wife of the greatest Seljuk sultan, Alaaddin Keykubat. The title Noble Lady given to this Georgian princess refers, clearly, to birth rather than character, as it is suspected that she poisoned the sultan when he was about to disinherit their son. In 1237, once the lad was safely enthroned, the queen mother had the religious complex constructed, perhaps by way of atonement. The mosque has a finely decorated main gate and double arches. The first instructor at the medrese, which is now an ethnographic museum, was Burhaneddin Tirmizi, teacher of Mevlana Celaleddin. The octagonal tomb is encircled by a double band of elegant geometric designs. The austere interior is distinguished by a rare Seljuk stone mihrab and holds three sarcophagi; Hunat Hatun's is of white marble, decorated with fine calligraphy. The main hamam, next door, is still in use. ⊠ *Cumhuriyet Meyd.,* ☎ *352/232–4812.* 🎫 *$1 (museum).* ☉ *8–noon and 1–5:30.*

Kayseri's centuries-old jumble of a **covered bazaar** is noted, as you might expect, for its carpets—and there are plenty of exceptional pieces from which to choose. It also stocks all the other necessities of Turkish life. A word on Kayseri and its carpet salesmen: In Turkish folklore, the people of Kayseri are renowned for being crafty dealers. Freelance touts pick up commissions for each tourist they convince to stop in a shop. So keep your wits about you and remember: If you don't want to shop or buy, make it absolutely clear from the outset. If all else fails, use the Turkish word *yok,* the ultimate, highly effective, don't-argue-with-me version of "no!" ⊠ *West of the citadel.*

Double-domed **Ulu Cami** (Great Mosque) was begun in 1135 and completed in 1205 and contains a finely carved wooden mimber. A tile mosaic is the outstanding feature of its cylindrical minaret. ⊠ *Near Düvenönü Meyd. and the bazaar.*

In 1247 three rival viziers prepared for the uncertain future by constructing the cylindrical Sırçalı Kümbet (Crystal Mausoleum), named for decorative tiles that have since vanished; the Çifte Kümbet (Twin Vault Mausoleum), octagonal under a cone-shape roof; and the Ali Kafer Kümbet (Ali Kafer Mausoleum). Older still is the Kasbek Kümbet (Kasbek Mausoleum). All of these mausoleums are south of the citadel on Cumhuriyet Bulvari.

The **Doner Kümbet** (Turning Mausoleum) of Sultan Shah Cihan was built in 1276. The name is derived not from the popular kebab but from the tomb's conical roof, which fits upon the 12-sided structure so lightly that it might be turned by any breeze. All its panels are decorated with bas-reliefs, among others the Tree of Life and a double-headed eagle above lions. Unfortunately, signs are only in Turkish. ⊠ *Cumhuriyet Bul., south of the citadel.* ▤ *Free.* ⊙ *Daylight hrs.*

The best pieces at the local **Arkeoloji Müzesi** (Archaeological Museum) are finds from Kültepe, site of the ancient Hittite city of Kaneş, including many cuneiform tablets. Greek and Roman statuary are also exhibited. ⊠ *Kışla Cad.,* ☎ *352/331–1131 or 352/331–4941.* ▤ *$1.* ⊙ *8–noon and 1–5:30.*

Dining and Lodging

$ ✕ **Beyaz Saray.** If you want to eat with the locals, stop by this inexpensive restaurant where the specialty of the house is *oltu kebap,* a sandwich-like affair featuring spit-roasted meat. ⊠ *27 Mayis Cad. 16,* ☎ *352/222–3381. MC, V.*

$ ✕ **Iskender Kebab Salonu.** You'll find a good range of standard Turk-
★ ish fare at this place near the citadel. *Iskender kebab* (slices of lamb grilled on a spit and served with yogurt and a tomato sauce) is the specialty. The main dining area is on the first floor with views over the street, but there is a quieter, more pleasant *aile salonu* (family room) on the next floor up. ⊠ *27 Mayis Cad. 5,* ☎ *352/231–2769. MC, V.*

$ ✕🏨 **Hattat Hotel.** A business-type establishment, the Hattat has modern facilities and a good restaurant (among the best in town), which serves kebabs and the usual mezes. ⊠ *Park Cad. 21,* ☎ *352/222–6620,* ℻ *352/232–6503. 72 rooms with shower. Restaurant, bar, nightclub. MC, V.*

$ 🏨 **Hotel Turan.** This reliable old-fashioned hotel is right in the center of town. Though it is a bit worn, it has the advantages of a roof terrace and a decent restaurant that serves traditional Turkish cuisine. ⊠ *Turan Cad. 8,* ☎ *352/231–8214 or 352/231–1029,* ℻ *352/231–1153. 40 rooms with shower. Restaurant. AE, MC, V.*

En Route Past the archaeological museum in Kayseri, the boulevard narrows and climbs into the foothills of **Mt. Erciyes.** A suburb of villas has risen over the site of ancient Eusebeia, followed by barren slopes dotted with beehives, which supply the excellent honey sold along the roadside.

Kültepe

㉚ *20 km (12 mi) from Kayseri, north of Rte. 260 (Rte. 300 on some maps).*

Kültepe (Hill of Ashes) is the site of Kaneş, an important Hittite city. Inhabited from the 4th millennium BC, Kaneş became powerful around 2500 BC. Five hundred years later, Assyrian trade caravans passed through Anatolia, and the trade colony of Kaneş flourished behind its single wall, attached to the double fortifications of an upper town. Only the foundations are left, and most of the 15,000 cuneiform tablets, alabaster idols, statuettes, and painted pottery found here are now in Ankara and Kayseri museums.

OFF THE
BEATEN PATH
SULTAN HANı – Behind the thick, rectangular walls of this remarkable, handsome caravansary, built by Alaaddin Keykubat in 1236, travelers and their beasts found ample space for a rest. For a good view of the surroundings, take the stairway to the right of the main gate up to the roof.

⊠ *Rte. 260, about 30 km (18 mi) from Kültepe (head northeast on Rte. 260 when Rte. 300 forks to southeast).* ☎ *50¢.* ⊙ *Daily 9–1 and 2–5.*

Niğde and Environs

③① *126 km (78 mi) southwest of Kayseri on Rte. 805.*

The quiet provincial town of Niğde has Hittite roots, though it really flourished in the 13th century, when Sultan Keykubat built the Alaaddin Cami. The mosque proudly bears three domes, exquisitely pure in line. A century later, the Mongol Sungur Bay constructed a mosque of his own, with portals distinguished by unusual Gothic features. The inevitable fortress looks down from the heights; dating from the end of the 11th century, it's the town's earliest Seljuk monument. Subtle, lacy stone carvings adorn the Hudavent Hatun Türbe (1312) and the charming white **Ak Medrese** (1409), which is now a small regional museum with a Byzantine mummy that is something of a scene stealer. A 16th-century bedesten adds to the list of distinguished architecture here.

The 10th-century church of **Eski Gümüs** (Old Silver) houses exceptionally well-preserved frescoes of Christ, Mary, and the saints. The adjoining monastery is hollowed out of the rock. ⊠ *9 km (6 mi) northeast of Niğde.*

Bor has another Alaaddin Cami, as well as a 16th-century covered bazaar and bath. The town is 14 km (9 mi) southwest of Niğde along Route 330. Five km (3 mi) farther at Kemerhisar are a Roman aqueduct, pool, and hot springs. The sites in Bor and Kemerhisar are free and are open during daylight hours.

Aksaray

③② *121 km (75 mi) from Niğde, north on Rte. 805, west on Rte. 330, and north on E90 (or south on Rte. 805 to Ulukişla and north on Rte. E90).*

Especially if you're heading to Konya, you might consider stopping in Aksaray. Thanks to the Melendiz Çayı (Melendiz River), Aksaray is surrounded by an oasis in the baked plain. Though not quite up to the standards of Pisa's Leaning Tower, the Egri Minare (Crooked Minaret), a reddish brick structure, has leaned alarmingly over the low houses on the riverbanks for almost as long, since 1236. The main monuments date from the 15th century: the Ulu Cami, which dominates the main square, and the Ibrahim Bey and Zinciriye medreses.

Another old caravansary built under the aegis of Alaaddin Keykubat, **Ağzıkarahan,** 15 km (9 mi) east of Aksaray on Route 300, has been restored to a semblance of the splendor it had when opened in 1239.

En Route On your way back toward Aksaray, head east just after the Mamasın Reservoir on the road leading south to Selime. Once again, you're back in the fairyland of Cappadocia.

Ihlara

★ **③③** *42 km (26 mi) southeast of Aksaray (past Selime).*

At Ihlara, the Melendiz River has carved a rift into the sheer tuff cliffs, which rise up to 492 feet. They are pierced by thousands of churches, chapels, and caves. The best view can be obtained from the hilltop restaurant, from which 285 steps descend the wall-like rock to the bottom of the canyon, a green gash in the barren highland below Mt. Melendiz. Byzantine Peristrema, the ancient name for Ihlara, is still idyllic;

poplars and wild olive trees shade the slow-moving water, along which the 20 main churches are slowly crumbling away.

En Route It is hard to tell the difference between steppe and desert, at least in summer, along Route 300 heading southwest to Konya. Most travelers welcome a stop along the way: Sultan Hanı, 95 km (59 mi) northeast of Konya, is Anatolia's largest and best-preserved caravansary and in ancient times was a place of rest and shelter for travelers and their camels plying the trade routes. Hans were constructed every 30 km (19 mi) or so, so there are two others on this route, the Agizkara Han (Dark-mouthed Inn), dating from 1231, and the Sari Han (Yellow Inn), from 1249.

Konya

34 *258 km (160 mi) from Ankara, south on Rtes. E90 and 715; 142 km (88 mi) from Ihlara on Rte. 300, southwest from Aksaray.*

Konya, at an altitude of 3,336 feet in a large, well-watered oasis, is the home of the whirling dervishes. It's one of the fastest-growing cities in Turkey. When the Seljuks arrived in 1076, Konya was hardly new. Earlier there had been a Hittite settlement here and, later, an important Phrygian town. Saint Paul and Saint Barnabas delivered sermons in the years 47, 50, and 53. Konya was prosperous under the Romans and hosted one of the first ecumenical councils, in 235. After being invaded by Arab raiders from the 7th to 10th centuries, the city flourished again in the early 13th century, during the reign of Alaaddin Keykubat. It was a golden era that would last until the city fell to Mongol invaders in the early 1400s.

★ The most-visited site in Konya is the **Mevlana Türbesi** (Tomb of Mevlana Celaleddin), the 13th-century poet and philosopher who founded the mystic order of the Mevlana dervishes. Born in present-day Afghanistan in 1207, Mevlana Celaleddin was the son of a renowned theologian who fled with his family before Genghis Khan's hordes. Celaleddin came to Konya at the age of 22, during the reign of Sultan Alaaddin Keykubat. He studied philosophy and religion and, like his father, became famous as a teacher of canonical law. In 1244 he came under the influence of a Persian dervish named Şemseddin (or Sems), abandoned his profession, and devoted himself to philosophical discussions with his new mentor. When Sems disappeared, most likely murdered by Celaleddin's jealous followers, Celaleddin in his grief turned to Sufic mysticism and to poetry. His greatest work, the *Mesnevi*, consists of 25,000 poems that were read and taught in the countless *tekkes* (monasteries) of the order he founded. The *Mesnevi* is the only philosophical system formulated in poetry. It ranks close to the Koran in Islamic literature. Mevlana died in 1273, and was succeeded by Hüsamed-din Çelebi, followed in turn by Mevlana's son, Sultan Veled. ⊠ *Eastern end of Mevlana Cad.*

Mevlana was a firm believer in the virtues of music and dance as a means of abandoning oneself to God's love and freeing oneself from earthly bondage. He considered the whirling pattern of motion to be representative of the soul's state of agitation. In the early years of the republic all religious orders were banned and forced to go underground, although they have gradually been reemerging since the 1980s. Until recently very few read Mevlana's works, but the authorities did preserve the *sema,* the whirling dance of his order, as a folkloric spectacle. The sema is still held in Konya once a year, during the weeklong festival to mark the anniversary of Mevlana's death on December 17. When it came to communicating with God, Mevlana made no distinction between social class, race, or even religion; the sema was open to all.

The dancers one sees today are men of ordinary trades and, despite 60 years pretending to be merely a dance, the sema retains all its religious symbolism. The dancers' accelerated turning and position—right arm pointing up and left down—suggest their openness to divine grace. Their conical hats represent tombstones, their jackets the tombs themselves, and their skirts the funerary shrouds. Removing their jackets signifies their shedding of earthly ties and their escape from their graves. As they whirl, they also rotate around the room, as the universe rotates in the presence of God. Thus, in whirling away his earthly ties, the dervish effects a union with God.

Several travel agencies operate tours to the Mevlana festival; they are often fully booked weeks in advance. If you want to join a tour, book before you leave home. The Tourism Information Office in Konya (☎ 332/351–1074, ℻ 332/350–6461) will help individuals find tickets and make hotel reservations for the festival. Several of the staff speak English and are invariably delighted by foreign interest, but it is wise to call or fax several weeks in advance.

The monastery of Mevlana became the **Mevlana Müzesi** (Mevlana Museum) in 1927. Small, lead-topped domes set over the dervishes' cubicles form an honor guard around the garden leading up to the entrance. Inside, vivid reconstructions illustrate the dervishes' way of life in their former cells. The square room that you enter first is the **Koran reading room.** On the walls hang framed examples of distinguished calligraphy, including one specimen executed by a great devotee of this art, Sultan Mahmut. The translation of the quotation above the silver door is "He who enters incomplete here will leave complete." One showcase contains the first 18 verses of the *Mesnevi,* written in Mevlana's own hand. To the right and left of the reading room lie the tombs of the most illustrious disciples, 65 in all.

Continue on into the room where the enormous **tomb of Mevlana** rests on a pedestal. At its head are his black turban and the curious cylindrical headgear of the sect. Two silver steps lead up to the platform; they are the sacred stairway. Believers press their faces against it as a sign of devotion. A brocade cover, embroidered with gold thread and weighing almost 110 pounds, covers the biers of Mevlana and his eldest son; it was a gift from the Ottoman sultan Mehmet II (1451–81). At the foot of the tomb, the coffin of Mevlana's father stands vertically, his white funerary turban on top. Quotations from the Koran are embedded in the sarcophagus with the exquisite precision that characterizes Seljuk art at its best. The mausoleum dates from the 13th century; the rest of the monastery was built later. ⊠ *Mevlana Meyd., at eastern end of Mevlana Cad.,* ☎ *332/331–1215.* ◩ *$1.50.* ☉ *Tues.–Sun. 9–noon and 1–6; Mon. 10:30–noon and 1–6.*

The **Selimiye Cami** (Selim Mosque) was started by the heir to the throne in 1558, when he was governor of Konya, and finished after he had become Sultan Selim II. The style is reminiscent of that of the Fatih Cami in Istanbul, with soaring arches and windows surrounding the base of the dome. The surrounding streets, which contain some shops, have much character. ⊠ *Opposite the Mevlana Museum on Mevlana Meyd.*

On the way to Konya's ancient acropolis, heading west from Mevlana Meydanı, are a few mosques on or just off Alaaddin Caddesi. Şerefettin Cami, built in 1636, was started by the Seljuks and completed by the Ottomans. The Şemsi Tebrizi Cami and Türbe, north of Şerefettin Cami, off Hükümet Alanı, is dedicated to Mevlana's mentor and friend. Konya's oldest mosque, the İplikcı Cami (Thread Mosque), dates from 1202.

The beautiful **Alaaddin Cami,** completed in 1220 and recently restored, crowns the Alaaddin Tepe (Acropolis Hill). Designed by an architect from Damascus, the mosque is of the Syrian style, unusual for Anatolia. Its pulpit stands in a forest of 42 columns taken from Roman temples. Most of the hill is devoted to a park, which contains a café. Below are the scanty remains of a Seljuk palace, two venerable stumps of walls. The city has for some reason deemed it expedient to throw an unsightly concrete shelter over them.

The **Büyük Karatay Medrese,** a theological seminary, was founded by Emir Celaleddin Karatay in 1251, whose tomb is in a small room to the left of the main hall. The medrese is now a ceramics museum, the **Karatay Müzesi** (Karatay Museum), and it is easy to understand why this particular building was selected for that purpose. Its dome is lined with tiles, blue predominating on white, and the effect is dazzling. The frieze beneath the dome is in terrific shape, and the hunting scenes on the rare figurative tiles from the Kubadabat Palace at Beyşehir show the influence of Persia on Seljuk art. The soothing sound of a fountain spilling into a basin in the middle of the main hall sets just the right mood for meditation and study. The spectacular ceramics collection includes figures of almond-eyed women, animals, and vine leaves highlighted in shades of cobalt blue and turquoise. ⊠ *Alaaddin Cad., at intersection with Ankara–Istanbul Yolu.* ⌦ *$1.* ☉ *Daily 8:30–noon and 1:30–5:30.*

At the 13th-century **Ince Minare Medrese** (Seminary of the Slender Minaret) the minaret in question is bejeweled with glazed blue tiles. Unfortunately, it is now only half its original size, thanks to a bolt of lightning. The Ince Minare, now a museum, has a fine collection of stone and wood carvings. Be sure to note the ornate decoration of the building's entry portal. ⊠ *Alaaddin Cad., west side of Alaaddin Tepe.* ⌦ *50¢.* ☉ *Daily 8:30–noon and 1:30–5:30.*

The **Sırçalı Medrese** (Crystalline Seminary) opened in 1242 as a school for Islamic jurisprudence. The seminary's lavish tile decoration provides a dignified home for the Museum of Funerary Monuments. The small Catholic Church of Saint Paul next door proves that Konya has remained as tolerant as it was in its Seljuk heyday. On the opposite side of the Sırçalı are Roman catacombs and a mosaic. ⊠ *Mimar Muzaffer Cad., south of Alaaddin Bul.*

A magnificent portal marks the remains of the **Sahip Ata** complex, a group of structures dating from 1283. Mosque buildings here have been converted into an **Arkeoloji Müzesi** (Archaeological Museum). Though the collection begins with items from the Bronze Age, its most important artifacts are Greek and Roman; the 3rd-century BC marble depicting the 12 labors of Hercules is outstanding. ⊠ *Ressam Sami Sok., off Larende Cad.,* ☎ *332/351–3207.* ⌦ *$1.* ☉ *Daily 8:30–noon and 1:30–5:30.*

Facing the Sahip Ata complex is the **Etnoğrafya Müzesi** (Ethnographic Museum). It contains Islamic art, embroidery, carpets, and weapons. ⊠ *Larende Cad.,* ☎ *332/351–8985.* ⌦ *$1.50.* ☉ *Tues.–Sun. 8:30–noon and 1:30–5:30.*

Carpets and rugs still provide the main interest in Konya's **bazaar.** Though the rugs sold here today hardly justify Marco Polo's judgment as "the most beautiful carpets in the world," their colors and designs are pleasing enough. The bazaar is flanked by the **Aziziye Cami** (Sultan Abdül Aziz Mosque), dating from 1676, which has two short minarets topped off by a kind of loggia with a Florentine flavor. ⊠ *Market district, near intersection of Selimiye Cad. and Karaman Cad.*

Dining and Lodging

$–$$ ✕ **Horozlu Han Kervansaray.** A restored 700-year-old Seljuk caravansary on the old Silk Road has a cavernous interior where the old stone provides a cool refuge from the summer heat. There are often floor shows in the evening. Specialties include *ezo gelin* (lentil soup), *etli ekmek* (flat bread with ground lamb), and some excellent fish, which vary according to the season. There is also a prix-fixe menu. ⊠ *Konya–Ankara Yolu Üzeri, TNP Yani,* ☎ *332/248–3115 or 332/248–3130. MC, V.*

$ ✕ **Damla Restaurant.** Damla is owned and run by a woman who is famous for her kitchen wizardry, especially when it comes to her *piliç* (chicken, cheese, peas, and potatoes baked in a small clay pot) and *saç kavurma* (sautéed lamb). There's also a fully stocked bar. ⊠ *Hükümet Alani, near Sahin Oteli,* ☎ *332/351–3705. AE, MC, V.*

$ ✕ **Hanedan.** Kebabs are the order of the day at Hanedan, particularly the *tandir* (lamb baked in a bread oven and served with thick pita bread) or the *inegol köfte* (ground lamb with garlic, onion, pepper, and tomatoes). ⊠ *Mevlana Cad. 2/B,* ☎ *332/351–4546. No credit cards.*

$ ✕ **Konya Fuar.** The food at this outdoor dining spot is much the same as elsewhere: kebabs. Open only in the summer, the café tends to get very crowded. ⊠ *Luna Park, no phone. No credit cards.*

$ ✕ **Şifa 1, Şifa 2.** Opposite one another, both self-service restaurants serve basic Turkish fare, including pide, kebabs, rice and beans, and roast chicken. No alcohol is served. ⊠ *Mevlana Cad.,* ☎ *332/352–0519 (Şifa 1) and 332/353–3666 (Şifa 2). No credit cards.*

$$ ⌂ **Otel Selçuk.** The best in town, this hotel has many amenities, including satellite TVs and bathroom phones in all rooms. The annual lectures and the commemoration of the whirling dervishes are held here every December. ⊠ *Alaaddin Cad. 4,* ☎ *332/353–2525,* ⊞ *332/353–2529. 70 rooms with bath. 4 restaurants, minibars, barbershop, sauna. AE, MC, V.*

$$ ⌂ **Şifa Otel.** This comfortable new hotel is only a few minutes' walk from the Mevlana Museum. The rooms are simply decorated and clean. The hotel management also runs the Şifa 1 and Şifa 2 restaurants next door. ⊠ *Mevlana Cad. 11,* ☎ *332/350–4290,* ⊞ *332/352–9251. 30 rooms with shower. Restaurant, bar. MC, V.*

$ ⌂ **Konya Oteli.** The Konya is just a block from the Mevlana Museum. Its staff seems eager to please, and most guests give the place a strong endorsement. Though older than other hotels here, the building is well kept. ⊠ *Mevlana Meyd. 8,* ☎ *332/351–6677,* ⊞ *332/352–1003. 52 rooms with shower. Restaurant. No credit cards.*

OFF THE
BEATEN PATH

HOROZLU HAN – If you're heading out of Konya in the direction of Ankara, look for a fabulous Seljuk portal at the entrance to the ruined **Horozlu Han,** near the four-lane beginning of Route 715. At Sille, 8 km (5 mi) northwest, Saint Helena, mother of Constantine the Great, built a small church in AD 327. Nearby, frescoed rock chapels overlook the shores of a tiny artificial lake.

ANKARA AND CENTRAL ANATOLIA A TO Z

Arriving and Departing

By Bus

Few major town or cities are not connected to Ankara by bus. The nine-hour trip from Istanbul costs about $10, the 14-hour trip to Trabzon around $15. There are many bus lines, and, though there should always be seats available to major destinations, you may buy tickets in advance. The standard of buses is generally good, although some companies are better than others and cost a little more. The most comfortable is probably **Varan** (Ankara, ☎ 312/417–2525; Istanbul, ☎ 212/251–7474), followed by **Ulusoy** (Ankara, ☎ 312/418–3636; Istanbul, ☎ 212/547–7022) and **Bosfor Turizm** (Ankara, ☎ 312/425–7203; Istanbul, ☎ 212/251–7000). Ankara's *otogar* (bus station) is on Hipodrom Caddesi west of Talat Paşa Bulvari (☎ 312/310–4747).

By Car

There are good roads between Istanbul and the main cities of Anatolia: Ankara, Konya, and Kayseri. The highways are generally well maintained and lead to all the major sights, though truck traffic on the main highway from Istanbul to Ankara can be heavy. Two long stretches of toll road (*Ucretli gecis* in Turkish) linking Istanbul and Ankara—E80 to beyond Düzçe and E89 south from Dörtdivan—provide some relief from the rigors of the other highway. Minor roads are rough and full of potholes. On narrow, winding roads, look out for oncoming trucks—their drivers often don't seem to believe in staying on their side of the road. From Ankara, E90 (also known as Route 200) leads southwest toward Sívríhisar; continue southwest on E96 to Afyon, where you can pick up highways going south to Antalya or west to İzmir. Route E88/200 leads east out of Ankara and eventually connects with highways to the Black Sea Coast.

By Plane

Central Turkey is well served by Ankara's **Esenboga Airport,** 30 km (19 mi) north of the city. There are direct flights from Europe and New York, and many domestic flights. Carriers include THY Turkish Airlines (☎ 312/312–4900 or 312/309–0400) and Delta Airlines (☎ 312/468–2808 or, in the U.S., 800/221–1212). THY also has daily direct flights from Istanbul to the airport at Kayseri.

BETWEEN THE AIRPORT AND CENTER CITY
A taxi into Ankara can cost as much as $20. Less-comfortable shuttle buses operated by **Havas** cost $1. Board them in front of the terminal shortly after flight arrivals and call at the THY office in Kavaklidere on their way to the train station.

By Train

Regular rail service connects Ankara to both Istanbul and İzmir. On the Ankara–Istanbul route, the **Ankara Express** and **Anatolia Express** have sleeper compartments (about $30); the overnight trip takes about 11 hours in romantic, two-person compartments. The **Mavi Tren** (Blue Train) has no sleepers but takes only about eight hours ($12). The **Fatih Ekspres** costs a little more and is slightly faster at 7½ hours, but it runs only in the daytime, leaving at 10 AM, and is often airless and overheated. A Blue Train from İzmir ($12) leaves in the evening and arrives in Ankara early the next morning.

Getting Around

By Bus
Buses link most towns and cities, and fares are reasonable (less than $10 from Ankara to most anywhere in Central Anatolia, for instance).

By Car
Ankara is a big city with chaotic traffic, so you'll save yourself a lot of grief if you park your car and get around by public transportation. The center of the city is relatively compact, and it is possible to walk to most places. A car is useful for excursions to the Hittite cities and to Cappadocia. Boğazkale and Hattuşaş are about 125 km (78 mi) east of Ankara, Konya is 261 km (162 mi) to the south, and Kayseri is 312 km (194 mi) southeast.

By Taxi
The cost of traveling by taxi to historic sites outside Ankara is usually reasonable ($10–$30), but always agree on the fare in advance. Cabs can be hailed, or ask at your hotel.

By Train
Though there is Blue Train service between the region's main cities—Ankara, Konya, and Kayseri—trains are almost nonexistent between small towns. The one route that may be of use to tourists is Ankara–Kayseri, but it's generally much quicker to take a bus. For information, contact the train station (⊠ Talat Paşa Cad., at Cumhuriyet Bul., ☎ 312/311–0620 for information, 312/310–0615 for reservations).

Contacts and Resources

Car Rental
Avis (⊠ Esenboga Airport, ☎ 312/398–0315; ⊠ Ankara Hilton SA, Tahran Cad. 12, Kavaklıdere, ☎ 312/467–2313). **Hertz** (⊠ Esenboga Airport, ☎ 312/398–0535). **Budget** (⊠ Esenboga Airport, ☎ 312/398–0372; ⊠ Tunus Cad. 39, Kavaklıdere, ☎ 312/417–5952).

Emergencies
Ambulance (☎ 112). **Police** (☎ 155). **Balgat Amerikan Tesisleri** (American Hospital, Ankara, ☎ 312/425–9945). Your hotel is the best source of information on good hospitals elsewhere, as well as on doctors and dentists.

Guided Tours
If you are driving through Cappadocia, consider hiring a guide (about $15 to $30 a day). Local tourist offices and hotels can make recommendations. Ankara travel agencies arrange bus tours to Cappadocia and Konya as well as day trips within the city. In Ankara, **Setur Ankara** (⊠ Kavaklıdere Sok. 5/B, ☎ 312/467–1165, FAX 312/467–8775), **VIP Turizm** (⊠ Halici Sok. 8/3, Gaziosmanpasa, ☎ 312/467–0210), and **Türk Ekspres** (⊠ Cinnah Cad. 9, Çankaya, 312/467–7334 or 312/467–7335), the local American Express representative, are the major operations.

Visitor Information
Ministry of Tourism (⊠ Gazi Mustafa Kemal Bul. 121, ☎ 312/229–2631, FAX 312/229–3661; ⊠ Esenboga Airport, ☎ 312/398–0348). **Kayseri** (⊠ Kağni Pazari 61, ☎ 352/222–3903, FAX 352/222–0879). **Konya** (⊠ Mevlana Cad. 21, by the Mevlana Museum, ☎ 332/351–1074, FAX 332/350–6461). **Nevşehir** (⊠ Atatürk Cad., Hastane Yani, ☎ 384/213–3659, FAX 384/213–1137). **Ürgüp** (⊠ Park İi, ☎ 384/341–4059).

7 The Black Sea Coast

The Black Sea Coast harbors some of Turkey's wildest and most primitive districts, undeveloped regions that are far—in both distance and character—from the modern tourist resorts along the country's south and west coasts. With their old wooden Ottoman houses, cobblestone alleys filled with chickens and donkeys, and spare-looking mosques, the tiny villages here, many of them unmarked on maps, seem barely touched by the 20th century.

Revised and
updated by
Paula S.
Bernstein

THE HISTORY OF THE BLACK SEA COAST, like the rest of Turkey's, is long and complicated. When Greek colonists first settled in the area during the 8th century BC, the interior was dominated by feudal Persian nobility. In 302 BC, following the War of Succession sparked by the death of Alexander the Great, octogenarian Mithridates II Ktistes ("the Founder") established a dynasty in Amaseia, today's Amasya. During the next two centuries, his successors extended their rule over the petty Hellenistic and Anatolian states along the coast, making the kingdom of Pontus a power to reckon with in Asia Minor. Though superficially hellenized, the Pontic kingdom preserved a Persian religious and social structure, and the monarchs even claimed a spurious descent from Persia's Great Kings. Mithridates V's forces occupied the lands of Phrygia and Cappadocia to the southwest, and his son, known as Mithridates the Great (132–63 BC), expelled the Roman armies from Asia Minor, advanced into Greece, and seriously contested Rome's influence. It took Rome's greatest generals—Sulla, Lucullus, and Pompey—30 years to drive Mithridates VI back to his homeland, where he committed suicide. Julius Caesar incorporated the kingdom into the Roman Empire in 63 BC.

Things settled down for a long time, but the region had another brief moment of glory before all was said and done. In 1204, after the armies of the Fourth Crusade sacked Constantinople, a group of Byzantine aristocrats led by Alexius Comnene created the Trebizond Empire of the Grand Comneni. A lone Christian outpost in the Islamic East, the empire became a thriving city-state, with its capital at what is now Trabzon, surviving for two centuries. Then came the Ottomans, and the Black Sea Coast reverted to marginal status within a great empire.

Pleasures and Pastimes

Beaches

Şile and Akçako are beach resorts popular with Istanbulites. A number of fine beaches lie between Amasra and Inebolu; Kapısuyu beach near Kurucaşile is the nicest. Lovely Karakum beach at the tip of the Sinop peninsula is a good base for fishing trips or windsurfing. The Ünye bay area also has several fine beaches, particularly the one at Camlık.

Dining

The Black Sea supplies the seafood restaurants along the coast with many varieties of fresh fish. The specialties are *palamut,* which tastes like a cross between tuna and mackerel, and *hamsi,* anchovies prepared in countless ways. Delicious indigenous alternatives to fish include *pide,* a bread with meat or cheese that resembles Italian pizza, and *köfte,* tiny succulent meat balls. If these regional specialties don't appeal to you, there's always the standard kebab dish or rice and beans. For a chart that explains the cost of meals at the restaurants in this chapter, *see* Dining and Lodging Price Categories at the front of this book.

Lodging

Rooms are simple, even in the few modern hotels in the bigger towns. Many establishments boast "four-stars," but keep in mind that some adjust their star ratings as they see fit. If you're accustomed to satellite TVs, 24-hour room service, or chatting away on the bathroom telephone, you may come away disappointed with even some upscale hotels. In other words, consider yourself lucky if you find a hotel where your toilet flushes and the bathroom doesn't flood when you shower. Still, roughing it is a small price to pay for an unmediated glimpse of an ancient part of the world. For a chart that explains the room rates at accommodations in this chapter, *see* Dining and Lodging Price Categories at the front of this book.

Shopping

The best bazaars are in Trabzon, Amasya, and Kastamonu; each has a strong sense of history. In Ünye, hazelnuts are the thing to buy, and they will be almost everywhere you look (the Black Sea region produces 80% of the world's nuts). Chocolate lovers will want to stop in Ordu to visit the Sagra Special chocolate factory store in the center of town, which also sells nuts, tea, and coffee. Safranbolu is named after the costly spice saffron, which you can buy in this region for considerably less than what you'd pay at home. Several smaller towns clustered around Trabzon hold weekly markets where you can see mountain clanspeople coming down to trade, as they have for centuries.

Exploring the Black Sea Coast

Driving the twisty roads along the Black Sea coastline is not easy, but it is always dramatic. On the one hand lies a dark blue sea; on the other, surprisingly lush greens slowly give way to snowy white peaks. The course rolls over steep forested hills, dips down to dry plains, scuttles over rocky outcrops, skims past wheat fields, and plunges back into forest. Ancient stone bridges alternate with patches of road so narrow that drivers must pull over and stop to allow an oncoming vehicle to pass. Sometimes you'll see a huddle of Turkish men pushing a bus up a steep incline rather than riding inside. There aren't many towns along the way, and the going is slow. Gas stations can be few and far between; try to keep the gas tank well topped off.

Gone is the guaranteed sunshine you find elsewhere in Turkey. Though the coastal climate is temperate, skies are often overcast. It may rain for days on end, even in summer—especially in the eastern parts below the Giresun Dağları and the Karadeniz Dağları, a pair of gently curved massifs that link into the mighty Pontic Mountains, now called the Kusey Anadolu Sira Dağları (North Anatolian mountain chain), rising nearly 13,000 feet. Each mountain and valley along the chain seems to shelter a distinct culture. In some villages you will hear Greek spoken, while in others the locals speak Laz and a strong dialect of Turkish almost incomprehensible to some Turks.

Great Itineraries

Since the distances between the major sites on the Black Sea are so vast, if you're pressed for time you might do best by sticking to either the eastern or western end of the coast. If you think you'll be satisfied with just a glimpse of the sea, you can do as the Istanbulites and take a relaxing weekend excursion to Şile or a more ambitious short trip to Lake Abant, Safranbolu, or Kastamonu. But if you want to experience the region fully, you'll need at least five days to make your way East—even just as far as Amasya. Roads are incredibly scenic but demanding, so don't try to cover too much ground at one time. If you're dead set on seeing the entire coast and have only a week, you're best off renting a car in Istanbul, driving east to Trabzon and then flying back, or flying to Trabzon and driving west.

IF YOU HAVE 2 DAYS

Numbers in the text correspond to numbers in the margin and on the Black Sea Coast map.

If you're based in Istanbul and have only a couple days to sample the Black Sea, stick to the western end. Traveling on Route 20 from Istanbul, northeast from the Bosporus Bridge, you come first to the beach resort of ⊞ **Şile** ①, dominated by a ruined Genoese castle. With its picturesque harbor and lighthouse, Şile makes an ideal weekend getaway.

IF YOU HAVE 5 DAYS
On day one, relax at the beach in ⊞ **Şile** ①. The next day head inland on Route 20 until it meets Route 100 East, which you'll follow all the way to the unspoiled historic town of ⊞ **Safranbolu** ④. Spend the afternoon viewing the town's Ottoman houses and mansions. On the morning of day three, visit Safranbolu's Arasta bazaar. East of town, Route 30 climbs over two passes through the densely wooded Kře Mountains. After 95 km (59 mi), you'll reach the medieval city of **Kastamonu** ⑤. Drive up to the town's castle past 19th-century Ottoman mansions. From Kastamonu, head south on Route 775 and then southeast on Route 100 until you arrive at ⊞ **Amasya** ⑧. View the provincial city from atop the town's citadel. Drive or hire a car and have dinner and catch the sunset at Çakallar Aile Gazinosu, which overlooks the city. On day four, stroll along Amasya's tree-lined river and explore the city's marketplace and other sights. On your fifth day, visit the nearby towns of **Zile** ⑨ or **Tokat** ⑩.

IF YOU HAVE 7 DAYS
Stop in **Şile** ① on day one. The next day, explore ⊞ **Safranbolu** ④. On day three, visit **Kastamonu** ⑤ and stay overnight in ⊞ **Sinop** ⑥, the oldest city on the Black Sea Coast. On the fourth day, tour ⊞ **Amasya** ⑧. On day five, breeze through the small towns of **Ordu** ⑫ and **Giresun** ⑬ before overnighting in the ancient Byzantine city of ⊞ **Trabzon** ⑭. On day six, drive a short distance out of town and climb to the monastery at **Sumela** ⑮. On your last day, visit the Trabzon's museum and take a drive to the Rize tea plantations.

When To Tour the Black Sea Coast

The Black Sea Coast is mild and damp throughout the year, but to capture the region at its lushest, greenest, and sunniest, you're best off visiting between late April and late October. It's not a problem traveling along the coast in the winter, but many hotels and restaurants geared to tourists are closed then. Also, because of the snow, it's a difficult climb to the monastery at Sumela. Even during March and April, the path to Sumela can be slippery, though you'll have the monastery and its peaceful surroundings all to yourself; in summer, the area is packed. The best time to visit the Black Sea Coast is late spring, when the blossoms are out and the tour groups have only started to arrive.

ŞILE TO SAMSUN

The 662 km (411 mi) between the beach resort of Şile and Samsun, the largest and busiest port on the Black Sea, are easily accessible from Istanbul and Ankara. This region is more popular with tourists and cosmopolitan Turks than points farther east. All along the coastline you'll find sandy beaches, mosques, and Genoese castles.

Şile

❶ *71 km (44 mi) northeast of Istanbul on Rte. 20.*

With its picturesque harbor and lively nightlife, Şile, its skyline dominated by a ruined Genoese castle, is a regular getaway for residents of Istanbul. Try to avoid the town's beach during vacation times, when it becomes very crowded.

The Black Sea Coast

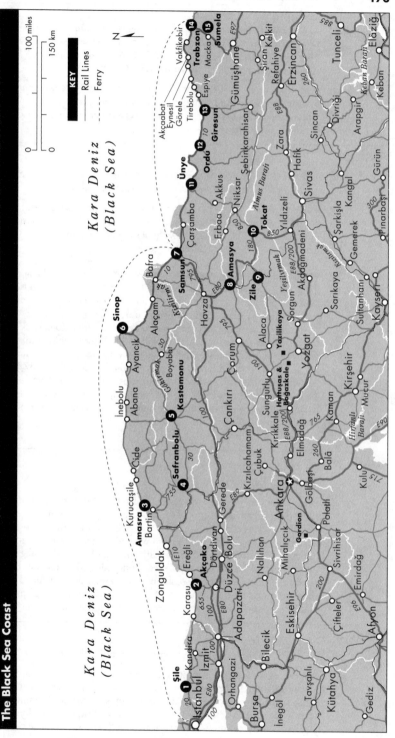

Kara Deniz
(Black Sea)

Kara Deniz
(Black Sea)

N

KEY
—— Rail Lines
- - - Ferry

0   100 miles
0   150 km

Lodging

$–$$ 🏨 **Değirmen Hotel.** An old standby among vacationing Istanbulites, the Değirmen has a beach and a nightclub and a good sense of fun. ✉ *Plaj Yolu 24,* ☎ *216/711–5048,* 🖷 *216/711–5248. 69 rooms with bath. Restaurant, bar, pool, windsurfing. AE, MC, V.*

En Route Winding east from Şile, Route 20 has a few rough patches along the 82 km (49 mi) to the fishing village of **Kandira.** Jason and the Argonauts supposedly saw a vision of Apollo near here during their quest for the Golden Fleece.

Akçako

❷ *169 km (105 mi) from Şile, east on Rte. 20 past Kandira to Adapazari, north on Rte. 650 to Karasu, and northeast on Rte. 10.*

The resort town of Akçako was named after an Ottoman general who conquered Bithynia between 1326 and 1330. Under the ruins of a Genoese castle stretches a long sweep of sand beach, popular with Turkish families. Nearby are hazelnut groves.

OFF THE BEATEN PATH   **YEDIGÖLLER NATIONAL PARK AND LAKE ABANT** – If you're hankering for the great outdoors, Yedigöller National Park, southeast of Akçako (south on Route 655, east on E80, and north on a marked access road from Bolu), has seven lakes; forests of beech, oak, and elm; and wolves, deer, and brown bears. The park is also accessible from Zonguldak, a coal-mining town and major port east of Ereğli. The magnificent Lake Abant resort area, southwest of Bolu, is renowned for its scenery and the best trout fishing in Turkey. The plush Abant Palace hotel (☎ 374/224–5012, 🖷 374/224–5011), perched on a sliver of land between the lakeshore and pine-clad hills, is a favorite getaway for wealthy Istanbulites, who enjoy its many amenities (among them satellite TVs in every room).

Ereğli

40 km (25 mi) from Akçako on Rte. 10.

Ereğli claims to have the largest steel mill in the Middle East, not something that will attract hordes of tourists. The town does, however, have significant classical connections. It was believed in antiquity to have been the location of the grotto from which Hercules descended to the underworld to accomplish the most difficult of his labors—fetching Cerberus, the god Hades's three-headed, hundred-eyed watchdog; here, also, an ancient Greek philosopher named Herecleides concluded that the earth turns on its axis every 24 hours. If you visit during spring, you'll notice the sweet aroma of strawberries in the air.

Amasra

❸ *212 km (131 mi) east of Ereğli on Rte. 10 to Rte. 750 to Rte. 10.*

Amasra is named after Amastris, a nephew of the great Persian king Darius I. Recognizing the advantage presented by the town's two harbors divided by a rocky promontory, Amastris promptly built his fortress here. A Byzantine church in the tiny old quarter within the fortress walls was converted into a mosque (Fatih Cami). The beach on the eastern side of the peninsula has good swimming.

OFF THE
BEATEN PATH

COASTLINE FROM AMASRA TO SINOP – The 166 km (103 mi) of Black Sea coastline leading up to Inebolu are a particularly untrammeled stretch, with ramshackle Mediterranean-style fishing villages and empty beaches. From Inebolu it's another 158 km (100 mi) to Sinop—a difficult drive, with the road perpetually under construction and few gas stations. The nearly deserted Inceburun Peninsula, extending into the Black Sea west of Sinop, has striking forests, sand dunes, and lagoons.

En Route   Some fine old villages punctuate Route 755 as it heads inland from Amasra. Along this route, note the traditional Ottoman houses: square, half-timbered buildings with tile roofs and overhanging second stories. You'll see the first of these in **Bartin,** just south of Amasra.

Safranbolu

★ ❹   *97 km (60 mi) south of Amasra on Rte. 755.*

Tucked behind a modern town of the same name, old Safranbolu has preserved a slice of the past, with artisans in open storefronts plying their crafts and cars banned from the town center. The historic district holds many old Ottoman houses. Some buildings here are open to the public, including the **Kaymakam Evi** (Governor's House), which has been restored with furnishings of 200 years ago. The 17th-century *arasta* (market hall) once served the tanners' and cobblers' guilds.

Lodging

$–$$ 🏨 **Havuzlu Konak.** The hotel has been restored to resemble a typical affluent Safranbolu house in Ottoman times. Painstaking attention has been given to detail, from the embroidered floral motifs on the blinds to the *havuz* (pool) in the breakfast room from which it takes its name. The excellent restaurant serves the Safranbolu kebab of grilled lamb, tomato sauce, and yogurt on pita bread and topped with cheese. On the same grounds is the Küçük Konak, a seven-room version of the Havuzlu Konak with access to the same facilities but with no showers in the rooms. ⊠ *Haci Halil Mah. 18,* ☎ *372/725–2883,* ℻ *372/712–3824. Havuzlu Konak: 11 rooms with shower. Restaurant, outdoor café. MC, V.*

Kastamonu

★ ❺   *98 km (60 mi) from Safranbolu on Rte. 30.*

The medieval city of Kastamonu was once the stronghold of Alexius Comnene, the founder of the Comnene dynasty in Constantinople (1081), who recaptured it from the Seljuk Turks during the First Crusade. The **Comnene fortress** has survived, thanks to Tamerlane and his hordes, who swept through in the early 15th century and for some reason decided to rebuild the fortress rather than raze it. For an incredible view of the countryside, drive up to the castle past splendid 19th-century Ottoman mansions—run-down, but still occupied. The Seljuks are represented in Kastamonu by the 13th-century Atabey Mosque; the Isfeniyar Beys by the Ibn Neccar Mosque (1353); the Ottomans by the 16th-century Yakup Ağa mosque and seminary complex. The **Karanlık Bedestan,** a covered bazaar built in the 1470s, is still in use, bearing few signs of change through the intervening centuries. The **town museum** is housed in an attractive old building where Atatürk announced the abolition of the fez in 1926, though if you don't read Turkish, the exhibits in the museum may be incomprehensible to you.

OFF THE   **MAHMUT BEY CAMI** – This 14th-century mosque with exquisite wood
BEATEN PATH   carvings is the chief attraction of the village of Kasaba, 15 km (9 mi)
               north of Kastamonu on the road to Daday, west of Route 765.

En Route   An old stone bridge with five arches spans the Gökırmak River at
             Taşköprü (which means Stone Bridge), northeast of Kastamonu on Route
             30. Nearby, at Ev Kaya, is an interesting 6th-century BC rock tomb,
             with colonnades and a frieze. Just before the town of Boyabat, Route
             785 branches northeast, rolling through tobacco fields and over the
             wild forests of the Damaz Pass, to return you to the coast at Sinop.

Sinop

★ ❻ *192 km (119 mi) northeast of Kastamonu on Rtes. 30, 785, and 10.*

Known in ancient times as Sinope, Sinop is the oldest city on the Black
Sea Coast, reputedly founded by the Amazon queen Sinova. Legend
has it that Sinova attracted the interest of Zeus, who, to get on her good
side, offered to grant her one wish. Sinova requested everlasting vir-
ginity, thus foiling Zeus's amorous intentions. In the 7th century BC,
this region was colonized by an Aegean kingdom called Miletus, who
imported their Greek culture; ruins of a 2nd-century BC **Hellenistic temple** still stand near the Municipal Park in the center of town. The park
also marks the birthplace of the Cynic philosopher Diogenes (about
400–325 BC), who reportedly lived in a large earthenware tub and
preached a way of life that included the disregard of conventions, even
suggesting that people should feel free to make love in public like
dogs—*kyon* in Greek, hence "cynic."

The first **citadel** at Sinop is believed to have been built by the Hittites,
though the present layout dates from the Pontic King Mithridates IV,
who ordered its reconstruction in the 2nd century BC. The **mosque** bearing the name of Alaaddin Keykubat, the prominent Seljuk sultan, was
built in 1214; its splendid original *mihrab* (prayer niche) is displayed
in Istanbul's Museum of Islamic Art. The **Alaiye Medrese** seminary,
now a museum with some interesting tombs, was built in 1262 by the
Grand Vizier of Keykubat, Süleyman Pervane. A walk through Sinop
reveals many other small mosques, tombs, and fountains: the Saray and
Fetih Baba mosques, both built in 1339; the Çifte Hamam, built in 1332;
and a 7th-century Byzantine church, Balat Kilise, standing within the
grounds of a ruined palace. The church retains some frescoes, though
they are badly damaged; its fine icons are displayed now in the city
museum. On a hilltop at the edge of town, the 14th-century **Sayid Bilal
mausoleum** provides a good view of the town. Sinop is set on the neck
of a narrow peninsula with the sea on either side. The pleasant beaches
here are usually empty.

Lodging

$$ ☷ **Melia Kasım Hotel.** Though hardly memorable, the Melia is gener-
ally regarded as the best lodging in Sinop. ⊠ *Gazi Cad. 41,* ☎ *368/261–
4210,* ☏ *368/261–1625. 57 rooms with bath. No credit cards.*

$ ☷ **Karakum Motel.** Just outside town, the Karakum has a private
beach and bungalows with ramshackle charm. ⊠ *On the waterfront,*
☎ *368/261–4210,* ☏ *368/261–1625. 60 rooms with bath. Restau-
rant, bar. No credit cards.*

En Route   The thermal springs in **Bafra,** near the mouth of the Kızırmak River
             on the way to Samsun, supply a 13th-century *hamam* (Turkish bath).
             Bafra is a good place to buy tobacco and caviar.

Samsun

❼ *168 km (104 mi) from Sinop on Rte. 10.*

Developed as a port under the Ottomans, Samsun is still a booming commercial harbor. It was here that Atatürk landed on May 19, 1919, after World War I, slipping away from the Allies occupying Constantinople to launch his campaign for Turkish independence. May 19 is now a national holiday. The Atatürk Monument opposite the government house is the largest dedicated to the great leader outside of Ankara. The **villa** he occupied, in the city park, is open to the public as a museum. There you can see a summer suit, silverware, pajamas, and a shaving set that belonged to him. Next door are an archaeological museum (closed in the winter) and a small art gallery. ⊠ *Luna Park,* ☎ *362/431–6828.* 🎫 *40¢.* ☉ *Tues.–Sun. 8–noon and 1:30–5:30.*

Dining and Lodging

$–$$ ✕ **Cumhuriyet Restaurant.** The best restaurant in town outside the major hotels, the Cumhuriyet, which opened in 1934, serves the normal range of cold mezes and grilled meats and prides itself on its *kuzu tandir* (baked lamb). ⊠ *Saathane Meyd., next to bread bakery,* ☎ *362/431– 2165,* 🗏 *362/432–6896. MC, V.*

$ ✕ **Divanrama Restaurant.** On the second floor of a minimall in the center of downtown, the Divanrama has a good selection of fish, seafood, kebabs, and mezes. ⊠ *İstiklal Cad. 102,* ☎ *362/230–6219. MC, V.*

$ ✕ **Elit'e Restaurant.** The flavorful crust and tasty toppings on the special Turkish pide at this informal restaurant make the short drive toward Sinop from the center of Samsun worthwhile. ⊠ *Atatürk Bulvarı Körfez Mah., Kurupelit,* ☎ *362/457–6565. No credit cards.*

$$–$$$ ✕🏨 **Büyük Samsun.** For this undeveloped strip of coastline, this hotel
★ is about as good as things get. Some rooms have terraces overlooking the water, but make sure your toilet works before you commit to a room. The room rate varies according to location (the king-size suite is $150). The hotel's restaurant is the best in town. For lunch, try the *kebap 19 mayis,* a dish commemorating the day of Atatürk's arrival in Samsun. ⊠ *Sahil Cad.,* ☎ *362/435–8018,* 🗏 *362/431–0740. 114 rooms with bath. Restaurant, bar, pool, tennis court. MC, V.*

$ 🏨 **Hotel Yafeya.** Cheap, clean, and eminently acceptable, the Yafeya sits right on the main square. A rooftop terrace has a clear view of the sea. Reasonably priced suites have minibars and color TVs. ⊠ *Cumhuriyet Meyd.,* ☎ *362/435–1131,* 🗏 *362/435–1131. 96 rooms with shower. Restaurant, café. MC, V.*

AMASYA, ZILE, AND TOKAT

The terrain becomes more mountainous and less lush as one swings away from the coast toward the ancient Pontic capital of Amasya, the ruined Seljuk fortress at Tokat, and the rural village and fortress at Zile. The change is so great that you may forget just how near the Black Sea is. There aren't any beaches in this area, but it does contain one of the longest rivers in Turkey, the Yeşilırmak in Amasya.

Amasya

★ ❽ *131 km (81 mi) south of Samsun on Rte. 795.*

According to its most famous son, the geographer-historian Strabo (circa 63 BC–AD 19), Amasya was founded by the Amazon queen Amasis, but its epoch of glory was as the first capital of the kingdom of Pontus, which lasted from the decline of Alexander the Great's empire until the Romans took the town in 47 BC. The Seljuks moved in after 1071, followed by the Mongols in the 13th century and the Ottomans in the beginning of the 15th.

The historic center of Amasya is on the right (southern) bank of the Yeşilırmak (Green River). Old Ottoman houses line the riverside, with a break for a shady park with tea gardens. The equestrian statue of Atatürk in the central square is a good starting point for a walk. Westward along the tree-lined river (down Ziya Paşa Bulvari) is a row of overhanging houses and several old bridges. A banner on a house on the north bank marks the restored 19th-century **Hazeran Mansion,** which has a very small ethnology museum that is open Tuesday–Sunday 8:30–11:45 and 1:45–4:45. Admission is less than a dollar.

A 16th-century **bedestan** (covered bazaar) anchors the marketplace that runs for several blocks between Ziya Paşa Bulvari and Atatürk Caddesi. Behind the bazaar, away from the river, is the **Burmaı Minare Cami** (Mosque with the Twisted Minaret), built in 1242; its extravagant fluted minaret is an architectural oddity. The **Fethiye Cami,** a few blocks south of Burmaı Minare Cami, was first built as a Byzantine church in the 7th century and became a mosque in 1116.

The two-domed **Sultan Beyazıt Cami,** set on a shady terrace along the river, was built in 1486. The imposing mosque has a fine *mimber* (pulpit) and mihrab made of marble and blue tiles inscribed with quotations from the Koran. The mosque is only open during prayers, but if you're not planning on praying, you can't enter. ⊠ *Mustafa Kemal Paşa Cad.* 🖾 *Free.*

The collection of the **Amasya Museum** covers the nine civilizations that have ruled over the city. Wood carvings, astronomy instruments, old coins, and tombs make this a worthwhile stop; the Tomb of Sultan Mesut is on the museum grounds, alongside several Mongol mummies. ⊠ *Atatürk Cad., across from Sultan Beyazıt Cami,* 🕾 *358/218–4513.* 🖾 *75¢.* ☉ *Tues.–Sun. 8:15–11:45 and 1:45–5:15.*

The **Gök Medrese** (Blue Seminary), built in 1276, is now a museum containing among other things the mummies of its Seljuk founder, Seyfeddin Torumtay, and a few of the town's Mongol rulers. The Gök Medrese is only open during prayer time, but visitors who haven't come to pray are prohibited. Atatürk Caddesi near the Blue Seminary is lined with tranquil little *türbes* (tombs) containing the mortal remains of such dignitaries as Prince Sehzad, Halifet Gazi, Mehmet Paşa, and Sultan Mesut. ⊠ *Atatürk Cad.* 🖾 *Free.*

Unless you're prepared for a big climb, Amasya's **citadel** (The Castle of Amasya), high above the north bank of the Yeşilırmak, is only accessible by car (follow the small signs on the east side of the river). In the few bits of ruined tower and wall that remain upright, you can attempt to distinguish the different stones used by various builders, from the Greeks through the Romans to the Seljuks. The view from atop the citadel makes it the perfect spot for a picnic.

A short but steep path leads north from the Alçak and Hükümet bridges, up a cliff face and past the remains of the Pontic palace to the **Kral Kaya Mezarlaıri** (The Kings' Tombs). The well-preserved rock tombs of the first four Pontic kings are impressively floodlit at night. Fourteen in all, the earliest ones date from the late 4th century BC.

Dining and Lodging

$–$$ ✕ **Çakallar Aile Gazinosu.** You need a car to reach this restaurant, but
★ it's well worth the trip into the hills south of Amasya. While you eat
your fish dish or meat kebab, you can watch the sunset and take in a
panoramic view of the entire area. There's live music at night and outside seating in the summer. ✉ *Off Mustafa Kemal Cad.,* ☎ *358/218–
6289. MC, V.*

$ ✕ **Çiçek Lokantasi.** This cozy restaurant on a market street near the
square serves basic Turkish fare, including delectable kebabs and pide.
✉ *Kocacık Carşişi 4A,* ☎ *359/218–1337. No credit cards.*

$ ✕ **Öğretmen Evı.** This restaurant, on the north end of Hükümet
Köprüsü (Government Bridge), hangs over the river and has great
views. A "Teacher's Club," it caters to the locals; it's very cheap and
not at all touristy. The decor is unmemorable, but the traditional Turkish grilled meat dishes are not. ☎ *No phone. No credit cards.*

$–$$ ✕🏨 **Grand Amasya Hotel.** Though unexceptional, this is the best bet
in Amasya. It's well run, the restaurant is good, and the setting is nice.
Try to get a room with a terrace overlooking the river. The dining room
has a view of the Yeşilırmak. Sample the *menemen,* a Turkish dish with
eggs and potatoes. ✉ *Elmasiye Cad.,* ☎ *358/218–4054,* 📠 *358/218–
4056. 50 rooms with shower. MC, V.*

Zile

❾ *88 km (55 mi) from Amasya, south and southeast on Rte. 180 to Rte.
190 southwest from Turhal.*

From the fortress above Zile's **Uli Cami** mosque, built in 1296, you can
gaze over the scene of Julius Caesar's victory over the Pontic king Phar-
nakes II. This battle inspired Caesar's celebrated terse message to the
Roman Senate: *"Veni, vidi, vici"* ("I came, I saw, I conquered").

Tokat

❿ *115 km (71 mi) southeast of Amasya on Rte. 180.*

Tokat's Seljuk **hilltop fortress,** with 28 towers, is a crumbling ruin, but
still intact is **Garipler Cami,** a mosque built in 1074. **Gök Medrese** (Blue
Koran), a seminary built in 1275, is now a museum full of tiles and
Byzantine frescoes. ✉ *Gazi Osman Paşa Bul.,* ☎ *356/228–1509.* 🎫
$1. ☉ *8:30–12:30 and 1:30–5:30 (depends on mood of custodian).*

Tokat contains several mausoleums of Seljuk origin—those of El-
bukasim and Halef Gazi, Acikbas, Nurettin Sentimur, and Sumbul Bab—
and the Hatuniye school and mosque, built in 1485 by Beyazıt II in
honor of his mother. Another atmospheric Seljuk bridge spans the
Yeşilırmak River here.

En Route Route 850 winds northeast from Tokat back toward the coast. It re-
joins Route 10 at Ünye.

EAST TO TRABZON AND SUMELA

Ünye

⑪ *95 km (60 mi) east of Samsun on Rte. 10.*

The small port of Ünye, a popular weekend spot for Samsun's mon-
eyed classes, has splendid beaches and campgrounds around its
crescent-shape bay. In the Middle Ages this was the western border of
the Trebizond Empire, but the only notable architecture standing today

is an 18th-century town hall. Outside town are caves where Mediterranean seals breed.

Lodging

$$　☎ **Kumsal Hotel.** Five km (3 mi) outside Ünye on the way to Samsum, the Kumsal is clean and simple, with whitewashed walls, wooden shutters, and balconies overlooking a lush garden. Each room has a color TV, but there's no guarantee you'll find English programming. Spacious, affordable suites are well-suited to large families. ⊠ *Samsun Asfalti Üstü, Gölevi Köyü,* ☎ FAX *452/323–4490. 32 rooms with shower. Restaurant, bar, sauna, beach. MC, V.*

$　☎ **Belediye Çamlık.** Set in a pine forest, this little seaside motel has its own beach. Rooms are bare, with low wooden beds. Nine rooms have small kitchens, which aren't necessary since the hotel's restaurant serves good, inexpensive food. ⊠ *On Ünye's waterfront,* ☎ *452/323–1085. 13 rooms with bath. Restaurant, bar. No credit cards.*

Ordu

⑫　*75 km (47 mi) east of Ünye on Rte. 10.*

Outside the town of Ordu, a few ruins from the 5th-century BC Greek settlement of Kotyora survive on the beach at Bozzukale. Ordu itself is a port city dominated by a once resplendent 8th-century basilica that at press time (summer 1996) was being restored.

Lodging

$$　☎ **Hotel Balıktaşı.** For the relatively undeveloped eastern Black Sea Coast, the newish (1995) Balıktaşı is considered a luxury resort. Its pool overlooks the sea. ⊠ *Sahil Cad. 13/1, Güzelyalı Mah.,* ☎ *452/223–0611,* FAX *452/223–0615. 34 rooms with shower. Restaurant, bar, pool, sauna, beach, dance club. MC, V.*

Giresun

⑬　*45 km (28 mi) east of Ordu on Rte. 10.*

The Roman general Lucullus, who was something of a gourmand, reputedly introduced the cherry to Europe after first tasting one in Kerasous, the name by which Giresun was formerly known. Today the town spreads over a cape below a ruined Byzantine fortress, where there is now a pretty city park. Some ramparts still rise from the cliffs to guard the tomb of Seyyit Vakkas, who helped the Turks win Kerasous in battle in 1461. Jason and the Argonauts are reported to have stopped here and attributed the temple they found on the island (Buyuk Ada) facing the town to the Amazon god of war; a small teahouse stands here today, and you can take a swim in complete solitude.

The Şehir Müsezi, once an 18th century church, is now the small city museum. It displays Byzantine relics, old carpets, and jewelry. ⊠ *Eastern edge of town, 2 blocks from Rte. 10,* ☎ *454/212–1322.* 🖾 *75¢.* ☻ *Daily 8–5.*

En Route　Route 10 heading east from Giresun passes an enticing waterfall at Çağlayan, some ruined churches, and inviting beaches, before coming to **Tirebolu,** ancient Tripolis or Triple Town. The name refers to the three 14th-century Genoese fortresses in the area: Andos, near Espiye; St. John, atop Tirebolu itself; and Bedrama, 15 km (9 mi) inland on the Harşit River (with an exceptional panoramic view). Between the pleasant fishing ports of Görele, Vakfıkebir, and Akçaabat, the road turns inland, up into densely wooded hills and narrow vales, before entering cosmopolitan Trabzon.

Trabzon

⓮ *476 km (296 mi) east of Amasya on Rte. 100 E. to Rte. 885.*

In its glory days, Trabzon, the Trebizond of old, was the sort of place that epitomized the exotic East for European travelers. Early in the 14th century, a Venetian friar named Odoric described the city as "a haven for the Persians, Medes, and all the people on the farther side of the sea." Built of golden towers and glittering mosaics, probably with family money diverted from the royal till before the fall of Constantinople, Trebizond was the capital of the empire founded in 1204 by Alexius Comnene, grandson of Andronikos I, emperor of Byzantium. Alexius's successors continued to live well while playing off their powerful Muslim neighbors against one another. Genoese and Venetian colonies at Trebizond ensured extensive cultural interaction with the West; Marco Polo, among others, came to visit, and Trebizond's own Cardinal Bessarion returned the favor by pursuing a successful career at the Medici court. The glory came to an end when the Turkish sultan Mehmet the Conqueror swept through in 1461.

At first glance the city may well disappoint you, with its squalid port area and far too much concrete strewn about. But if you push on, up İskele Caddesi, you'll reach a pleasing central square atop the promontory, **Atatürk Alani** (also called Taksim, or Park, Meydanı), full of trees and tea gardens and surrounded by most of the city's hotels and restaurants.

Maraş Caddesi leads west out of Trabzon's central square into the maze of the **covered bazaar** (just past Cumhuriyet Caddesi), which includes a 16th-century bedestan used by local jewelers. The city's largest mosque, the Çarşi Cami (built in 1839), is joined to the market by an archway. Trabzon's oldest church, the **Küçük Ayvasil** (⊠ Iskander Paşa quarter, off Hükümet Cad.), also known as St. Anne's, was built in the 7th century and restored in the 9th century.

Trabzon's Comnene **citadel,** situated between two ravines, is still imposing. Its ramparts were restored after the Turkish conquest in 1461 (an effective job of saber rattling by Sultan Mehmet), although the remains of the Byzantine palace are insignificant. No army ever took Trabzon by force, though many tried. Within the citadel walls is the 10th-century Church of Panaghia Chrysokephalos (the Virgin of the Golden Head), which was the city's most important church for several centuries, until the Hagia Sophia was built. The Ottomans converted it into a mosque, the Ortahisar Cami, in the 16th century. ⊠ *Kale Cad.; from Hükümet Cad. (off Maraş Cad.), follow the Tabakhane Bridge over the gorge, turn left.*

A good view of Trabzon can be had from **Iç Kale Caddesi** south of the citadel. You'll also be able to make out three other Byzantine monuments, all south of the Atatürk Alani: the Yeni Cuma Cami (New Friday Mosque), built as the Church of St. Eugene in the early 13th century; the 13th-century Teokephastos Convent, on the other side of the hill; and the Kudrettin Cami, consecrated as the Church of St. Philip in the 14th century. Hagia Sophia is visible about 3 km (2 mi) to the west of Atatürk Alani.

★ Trabzon's best-known Byzantine monument, the 13th-century **Hagia Sophia** (Church of the Holy Wisdom), sits on a green hill overlooking the Black Sea. The ruined church, also known as Aya Sofya, has some of the finest Byzantine frescoes and mosaics in existence. It was converted into a mosque in Ottoman times and first opened to the public as a museum in 1963. The west porch houses the real masterpieces:

frescoes of Christ preaching in the temple, the Annunciation, and the wedding at Cana, executed in a style that shows strong Italian influence. As at Istanbul's Hagia Sophia, the artworks here were not destroyed by the Ottomans, only hidden under a hard layer of plaster. ⊠ *Kayakmeydan Cad., no phone.* ☎ *$1.* ☉ *June–Sept., Tues.–Sun. 8–6; Oct.–May, Tues.–Sun. 8–5.*

Atatürk Köşkü, Atatürk's summer villa (though he didn't actually spend much time here) is now a museum. The attractive white gingerbread house, set by a small forest, makes for a pleasant visit. ⊠ *Soğuksu Cad., 7 km (4 mi) southwest of Trabzon's central square, no phone.* ☎ *30¢.* ☉ *June–Sept., daily 8–7; Oct.–May, daily 9–5.*

Dining and Lodging

$$ ✕ **Süleyman Restaurant.** This upscale restaurant has four prix-fixe menus that include six to nine courses (if you count alcohol as a course) and a choice of à la carte dishes. A small indoor waterfall, a view of the Black Sea, musical performers in the evening, and good service make for a pleasant dining experience. ⊠ *100 Yil Parki Olimpik Yüzme Havuzu,* ☎ *462/325–0550,* ℻ *462/325–7085. MC, V.*

$ ✕ **Cosandere Restaurant.** On the banks of a stream beside the road from Maçka to Sumela, this restaurant is an ideal lunch spot for visitors to the Monastery of the Virgin (☞ Sumela, *below*). The specialties are *sutlac* (rice pudding) and *ayran* (buttermilk), but the köfte, which you grill on an individual barbecue at your table, are excellent as well. The restaurant is only open in summer. ⊠ *Mereyemana Yolu., no phone. No credit cards.*

$$ ✕▥ **Hotel Usta.** Renovated in 1993, the Usta, at press time, was being refurbished again, after which each room will have air-conditioning, heat, and a color TV. Long-range plans include a new building. At the moment, rooms are clean and simply furnished. The hotel can be a little hard to find, as the entrance is in an alley off İskele Caddesi, to the north of the main square. The restaurant (☎ 462/326–5704) is exceptional. The large, mirrored room lacks character, but the menu offers a substantial range of traditional Turkish fare. As at the hotel, the staff is courteous and attentive. ⊠ *Telgrafhane Sok. 1, İskele Cad.,* ☎ *462/326–5700,* ℻ *462/322–3793. 86 rooms with baths. Restaurant, bar. MC, V.*

$$ ▥ **Horon Hotel.** One block off Trabzon's main square, the Horon is clean, quiet, and has parking and valet services. At press time, its renovated restaurant was just about to open. ⊠ *Siramağazalar Cad. 125,* ☎ *462/321–1199,* ℻ *462/321–6628. 39 rooms with shower. Restaurant, bar, breakfast room. No credit cards.*

$–$$ ▥ **Hotel Özgur.** For years the best hotel in Trabzon, the Özgur has recently been renovated and has almost been restored to its former if simple glory. Its new restaurant serves pizza and burgers. In summer you can have tea in the garden or dine on the terrace, both in the back of the hotel. When booking, be aware that the hotel overlooks the main square; rooms at the front tend to be noisy. ⊠ *Atatürk Alanı 29,* ☎ *462/326–4703,* ℻ *462/321–3952. 50 rooms with shower. 2 restaurants. AE, MC, V.*

En Route Route E97, heading southwest from Trabzon inland toward Erzurum, follows a tunnel through the mountains. Somewhere around here in 401 BC, a ragtag army of Greek mercenaries wearily retreating from supporting a failed coup attempt against Artaxerxes, the king of Persia, first saw the Black Sea and knew they would get safely home. Their commander, a young Athenian officer named Xenophon, wrote the story of that march across Anatolia many years later in a famous book called the *Anabasis*

(The Ascent). Follow this highway 31 km (19 mi) from Trabzon and turn left at Maçka to get to Sumela. It's not the easiest place to reach—it's 23 km (14 mi) from Maçka, and the road isn't the best.

Sumela

⑮ *47 km (29 mi) south of Trabzon on Rte. 885 to Maçka, and then east on road to Altındere National Park.*

★ Sumela (Mereyemana in Turkish) is the site of the **Monastery of the Virgin.** The monks who founded the retreat in the 4th century carved their cells from sheer rock. Built to house a miraculous icon of the Virgin painted by St. Luke, this shrine was later rebuilt by Alexius III, who was crowned here in 1340—an event depicted in the frescoes of the main church in the grotto. Where chunks of the frescoes have fallen off—or been chipped away or scribbled over by over-enthusiastic souvenir hunters and graffiti artists—three layers of plaster from repaintings in the 14th and 18th centuries are clearly visible. Tolerant Ottoman sultans left the retreat alone, but after the Greeks were expelled from Turkey in 1922, the Turkish government permitted monks to transfer the Virgin icon to a new monastery in Greek Macedonia. The frescoes themselves are not as well preserved as those at Trabzon's Hagia Sophia, but the setting—a labyrinth of courtyards, corridors, and chapels—is incredible. At press time, workers were busy renovating the monastery and its surrounding rooms, but they weren't too optimistic about finishing anytime soon (grumbled one, "My great-grand-children will work here"). From the parking lot, pick up a well-worn trail for the rigorous 40-minute hike to the monastery, which clings to the cliff face over 820 feet above the valley floor and disappears completely when the clouds come down. ⊠ *Altındere National Park, no phone.* ⚏ *$1.* ☾ *Daily 8–7, in winter 9–5.*

OFF THE BEATEN PATH   **ZIGANA PASS** – From Sumela, you could continue on to Erzurum on Routes 885 and E97 (which are the same road in places), crossing (on Route 885) the hair-raising Zigana Pass, a stunning rift some 2,025 meters (6,645 feet) high, and descending to the low brushwood and yellow dust of the vast, arid Anatolian plateau.

En Route   Perhaps the most scenic portions of the coastal Black Sea drive are the 189 km (117 mi) northeast from Trabzon to Hopa. Densely wooded slopes sometimes tumble straight into the sea, but are more often broken by rice paddies and intensely green plantations where women in bright-striped aprons pick tea from early May to the end of October. Occasional tea factories exude black smoke, the only pollution on the coast.

Rize

Rize, the tea capital, sits above a small bay beneath the foothills of the Pontic mountains. For an untrammeled view, head to Zıraat Park, near the town's western entrance. Don't miss Rize's ruined Genoese castle (Rize Calesi), which sits high on a slope above the sea.

Lodging

$–$$ 🏨 **Hotel Keles.** The lodgings here are simple but acceptable, and the restaurant is good. ⊠ *Palandöken Cad. 2,* ☎ *464/217–4612,* 𝔽𝔸𝕏 *464/ 217–1895. 28 rooms with shower. No credit cards.*

OFF THE BEATEN PATH   **ÇAMLıHEMŞIN AND HOPA** – Beyond Rize, a 22-km (13-mi) jog inland from Ardesen will bring you to the village of Çamlıhemşin, a good center for mountain hiking and trout fishing. The bustling frontier town of

Hopa is journey's end for the Turkish Maritime Line boats as well as for cars; the remaining 22 km (13 mi) to the Georgian border are under military control.

THE BLACK SEA COAST A TO Z

Arriving and Departing

By Boat

Turkish Maritime Lines (✉ Rıhtım Cad. 1, Karaköy, Istanbul, ☎ 212/244–0207, reservations 212/249–9222 or ✉ Trabzon Liman Isletmesi, Trabzon, ☎ 462/321–2018 or 462/321–7096) operates two weekly ferries between Istanbul and the Black Sea ports of Giresun, Ordu, Samsun, Sinop, and Trabzon during summer. The trip from Istanbul to Trabzon takes a day and a half and costs from $10 for a Pullman seat to $25 for a bed and shower; cars cost $25. Sleeper cabins and car spaces sell out quickly in summer, so reserve in advance.

By Bus

You can get anywhere you want along the coast by bus. There is daily service from Istanbul (Esenler bus terminal ☎ 212/658–0505) to Samsun (bus terminal ☎ 362/238–1706), which takes about 12 hours and costs around $10. From Istanbul to Trabzon (bus terminal ☎ 462/325–2397), the daily service takes 20 hours and costs $12. There is also daily service to these cities from Ankara (bus terminal ☎ 312/310–4747).

By Car

The quickest way to the east from Istanbul is to take the E80 toll road (Ucretli Gecis) to Düzce and then cut up north along Route 655 to Akçako to join Route 10, which follows the coast the rest of the way east. The slower but more picturesque Route 20 passes through Şile to join up with Route 10 at Karasu. From Ankara, you can take the E89 north to Dörtdivan and then Route 750 to join Route 10 at Zonguldak; to explore only the eastern section of the coast, take E88 east through Kırıkkale, then head northeast along Route 190 toward Çorum to join Route 795 to Samsun, where you join Route 10.

By Plane

The airports at Istanbul (☞ Istanbul A to Z *in* Chapter 2) and Ankara (☞ Ankara and Central Anatolia A to Z *in* Chapter 6) are the jumping-off points for the western half of the coast. There are also daily flights from both airports to Trabzon via Turkish Airlines (☎ 212/663–6363 in Istanbul) or Istanbul Airlines (☎ 212/231–7526 in Istanbul). Fares are about $50–$60 one way.

Getting Around

By Boat

See Arriving and Departing, *above.*

By Bus

Bus service between towns runs frequently and is inexpensive. You can get schedules at the local tourist information office or directly from the bus station in each town: **Amasya** (☎ 358/218–1239), **Erzurum** (☎ 442/212–3969), **Kars** (☎ 474/223–9992), **Ordu** (☎ 452/223–0672), **Sinop** (☎ 368/261–5415), and **Trabzon** (☎ 462/325–2397).

By Car

The coast road from Istanbul, Route 10, winds along cliffs, takes an occasional hairpin turn, and can be rough in spots. It is, however, passable, and once you get past Sinop the road improves significantly.

RENTAL CARS

Avis has an office in Trabzon (⊠ Gazipasa Cad. 20/b, ☎ 462/322–3740). There are also several local companies around the main square in Trabzon (Atatürk Alani). As elsewhere in Turkey, local companies offer cheaper rates than international names, but not all companies include comprehensive insurance coverage in the price. Check the small print before agreeing on terms.

Contacts and Resources

Emergencies
Police (☎ 155). **Ambulance** (☎ 112).

Guided Tours
For a first-class customized tour of the Black Sea with a local guide, consider Tour Select, an Istanbul-based company that works jointly with sister company Megatrails in New York (in Istanbul, ☎ 212/232–4885, FAX 212/232–4889; in the U.S., ☎ 800/547–1211 or ☎ 212/888–9422, FAX 212/888–9819).

Visitor Information
Tourist offices: **Amasya** (⊠ Pirinci Cad., ☎ 358/218–7428, and Mustafa Kemal Bul. 27, Mehmetpasa Mah., ☎ 358/218–7427, FAX 358/218–3385); **Giresun** (⊠ H. Avni Öğütçü Sok. 11, ☎ 454/212–3190, FAX 454/216–0095); **Kars** (⊠ Ortakapı Mah., ☎ 474/223–2300, FAX 474/223–2724); **Ordu** (⊠ Hükümet Konağı, A Blok Kat: 1, ☎ 452/223–1607, FAX 452/223–2922); **Samsun** (⊠ Talimhane Cad. 6, 19 Mayis Mah., ☎ 362/431–1228, FAX 362/435–2887); and **Trabzon** (⊠ Atatürk Alani, Meydan Parkı Köşesi, ☎ FAX 462/321–4659).

8 The Far East

The far east of Turkey is a harsh but beautiful region, with lonesome plains, sun-scorched desert, and imposing black mountains—the kind of countryside for adventuring on an epic scale.

THE POPULATION OF TURKEY'S eastern provinces is primarily Kurdish. In recent years clashes between the Turkish armed forces and the PKK (Kurdistan Workers' Party), a Kurdish separatist group that wants to carve an independent state out of portions of Turkey, Iran, Syria, and Iraq, have restricted the movements of foreign visitors. At press time (summer 1996) the State Department of the United States continues to advise Americans not to travel in the area unless the journey is essential. Neither the Turkish army nor the PKK targets foreign travelers in the region (horrendously, the civilian death toll since the full-scale rebellion began in 1984 is estimated at 20,000, mostly innocent Kurds caught in the crossfire). Even so, because of the unpredictable nature of the conflict, be aware that a visit to the far east is not without risk.

Revised and updated by Scott McNeely

You can minimize that risk substantially by basing yourself in larger towns (there are direct flights from Istanbul and Ankara to Erzurum, Diyarbakır, Gaziantep, Kars, and Van); if you need to travel between them, do so only in daylight using a reputable bus company. It is possible to rent a car in Erzurum and Gaziantep, but the long distances and poor road conditions should make you think twice before tackling eastern Turkey in a private car. Terrorism is less of a consideration: Army roadblocks appear every few dozen miles (keep your passport handy), and Turkish soldiers will always give you an honest appraisal of the situation in their area. If a soldier warns you off a particular road, follow his instructions.

Up-to-date information about the situation in the eastern provinces can be obtained from the State Department hot line (in U.S. ☎ 202/647–5225) or from the American Consulate in Istanbul (☎ 212/251–3602, FAX 212/252–7851) and the American Embassy in Ankara (☎ 312/439–2740, FAX 312/440–9222).

Pleasures and Pastimes

Ancient Sites
The far east of Turkey has a staggering inventory of ancient sites, a few of which top many travelers' must-see lists despite the difficulties of travel in the region. Moving from the northeast to the southwest you can visit the remarkable Armenian kingdom of Ani; Mt. Ararat, where, according to Genesis, Noah's Ark came to rest after the Great Flood; the mighty, black basalt fortress at Diyarbakır; the birthplace of the patriarch Abraham in Şanlıurfa; and the awe-inspiring temple and sculptures atop Mt. Nimrod.

Dining and Lodging
Visitors to eastern Turkey don't come for the culinary experience or to stay in sumptuous lodgings. Restaurants serve standard Turkish cuisine, enlivened occasionally with such Kurdish specialties as *sac tava* (lamb and green peppers lightly roasted in sunflower oil) and lamb stew served with fresh flat bread. Kurdish sheep and goat cheeses are deliciously pungent, and you'll have no trouble finding excellent baklava and *pasta* (pastries). Be vigilant about what you eat, however, as standards of cleanliness are lower here than in the rest of Turkey. Diarrhea is a common complaint—drink only bottled water and eat plenty of fresh yogurt. As for accommodations, it's best to approach with humble expectations. Two hotels, though, deserve special attention: Diyarbakır's Otel Büyük Kervansaray and, a few kilometers below the summit of Mt. Nimrod, the Otel Kervansaray Nemrut. For charts that

explain meal and room rates at the establishments in this chapter, *see* Dining and Lodging Price Categories at the front of this book.

Shopping

Erzurum has an authentic Oriental bazaar, with particularly talented metalworkers; Şanlıurfa's is marvelously medieval. Van is noted for its weavings, especially its kilims and traditional Kurdish fabrics.

Exploring the Far East

A drive from Istanbul to Lake Van takes 25 grueling hours, and even if you fly directly to eastern Turkey, you still face long, hard outings from site to site within the region, with highways and facilities at best basic and often primitive. Whether you fly, drive, or arrive by bus, odds are that you will start your tour in the north at Erzurum (if you're coming from Ankara or the Black Sea Coast) or in the south at Diyarbakır (if you're coming from the Mediterranean); the region's two main airports are near these cities. Unless you rent a car in Erzurum or Gaziantep (☞ The Far East A to Z, *below*), the most efficient way to visit the main sights listed in this chapter is on a guided tour from Kars, Doğubayazıt, Kâhta, or Diyarbakır.

Great Itineraries

Eastern Turkey is an unwieldy region, and without some sort of strategy you will spend too much time on long-distance buses, fantasizing about a vacation from your vacation. To visit eastern Turkey's main sights, you'll need at least 10 days and plenty of patience. The following itineraries are for travelers with less time and a lower tolerance for crowded long-distance buses.

IF YOU HAVE 3 DAYS

Numbers in the text correspond to numbers in the margin and on the Lake Van and the East map.

Begin your visit in 🔛 **Erzurum** ①. On day one, visit the Seminary of the Twin Minarets and the Great Mosque, and perhaps make an afternoon trip to the Çoruh River Valley. On day two, travel to 🔛 **Kars** ② to view its old Georgian fort and to pick up the military permit that allows you entry to the ruins of the medieval Armenian town of **Ani** ③, which you will visit on day three.

IF YOU HAVE 7 DAYS

Spend day one in 🔛 **Erzurum** ①. On day two, drive or take a bus east to 🔛 **Doğubayazıt** ④, a sleepy agricultural town near the Iranian border. On day three visit Doğubayazıt's **İşak Paşa Saray,** followed by a drive around the base of **Mt. Ararat** ⑤. On day four head south to 🔛 **Van** ⑦ and visit its castle, set above smooth **Lake Van** ⑥. On day five visit the island of **Akdamar** ⑧, and continue west to 🔛 **Diyarbakır** ⑩. On the morning of day six visit Abraham's birthplace in **Şanlıurfa** ⑬, then head to the summit of 🔛 **Mt. Nimrod** ⑪ for one of the finest sunsets in Turkey. On day seven enjoy sunrise from Mt. Nimrod before heading to your next destination.

When to Tour the Far East

Travel in eastern Turkey involves a lot of "don'ts"—don't travel alone, don't travel at night, and don't travel in areas where PKK guerrillas are active (contact your embassy for information and become an avid reader of the English-language *Turkish Daily News*). If possible, don't visit eastern Turkey in the height of summer—average daytime temperatures for August are 36°C (97°F) in Erzurum, 38°C (100°F) in Van, and 39°C (102°F) in Diyarbakır.

Winter is harsh but beautiful in eastern Turkey, and tourism is focused on the ski resorts of Palandöken (near Erzurum), Tekman, and Sarıkamış (near Kars). Spring and fall are the most temperate seasons, with occasional rainfall and breezy evenings. At higher elevations—particularly in Erzurum and Kars—nighttime temperatures are blissfully cool in May, June, September, and October.

In the wake of the Gulf War the number of tourists in eastern Turkey dropped considerably; so, too, did the number of festivals and folk events in all but the smallest towns. In the last two years organized events have made a slow comeback: Van now hosts a music festival in mid-May, and there's a low-key music and food fair on Mt. Nimrod in mid-June. Local tourist offices should have current lists.

NORTHEASTERN TURKEY
Erzurum to Ani

One day is sufficient to see Erzurum's mosques and museum, and to rent a car or arrange bus transportation to Kars. The only reason for stopping in Kars is to obtain the mandatory permit for visiting the sprawling 10th-century ruins at Ani. Depending on the season, the northeast's sparsely populated, high-altitude plains are either snowbound or baking hot; only as you approach Ani do dusty flatlands give way to rugged hills carpeted with wildflowers. In spring and summer Kurdish farmers set up isolated tent villages in the hills near Ani, both to graze sheep and to tame the wild horses that roam here in the hundreds.

Erzurum

➊ *880 km (546 mi) east of Ankara on Rte. E88 to E80, 300 km (186 mi) southeast of Trabzon on Rte. E97.*

Erzurum occupies a strategic spot along the old trade routes to Russia, India, and Persia—a fact quickly recognized by the Byzantines, who made this their eastern bastion. The city fell to the Seljuks in AD 1071, after the battle of Manzikert, and they built most of the sights that remain today. Still a strategic spot (as you can see from the Turkish military barracks), Erzurum has developed into a sprawling, rather somber city, now the largest in eastern Anatolia, with factories and high-rise apartments that spread across an otherwise barren plateau at an elevation of 1,950 meters (6,696 feet). You can ski in the surrounding mountains as late as mid-March. The most interesting sights are along Cumhuriyet Caddesi in the center of Erzurum.

Sultan Alaaddin Keykubat II sponsored the **Çifte Minareli Medrese** (Seminary of the Twin Minarets), which was built in 1253 at the height of the Seljuk Empire. The seminary is renowned for its twin blue-tiled minarets and for the elaborate interlocking spirals carved on the main portal. Inside at the far end of an unkempt courtyard sits the Hatuniye Türbesi, a 12-sided chamber that once held the tomb of the sultan's daughter. ⊠ *Cumhuriyet Cad., east end of street opposite traffic circle, no phone.* ▣ *20¢.* ☉ *Daily 9–5:30.*

The **Ulu Cami** (Great Mosque) was built in 1179 with seven wide naves and a fine colonnaded courtyard. The exterior is plain, even severe. Inside are dozens of solemn columns and a small but dazzling pair of stained-glass windows. Visitors are not allowed at prayer times, and women are asked to cover their heads. ⊠ *Cumhuriyet Cad., 1 block west of Çifte Minareli Medrese, no phone.* ▣ *Donation requested.* ☉ *Daily 9–noon and 1–8.*

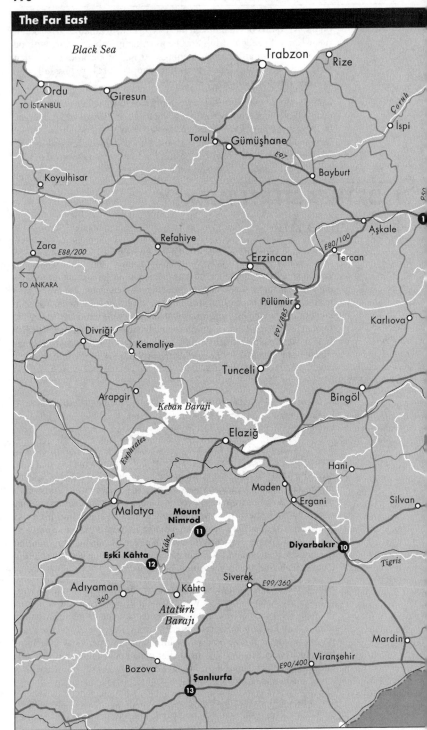

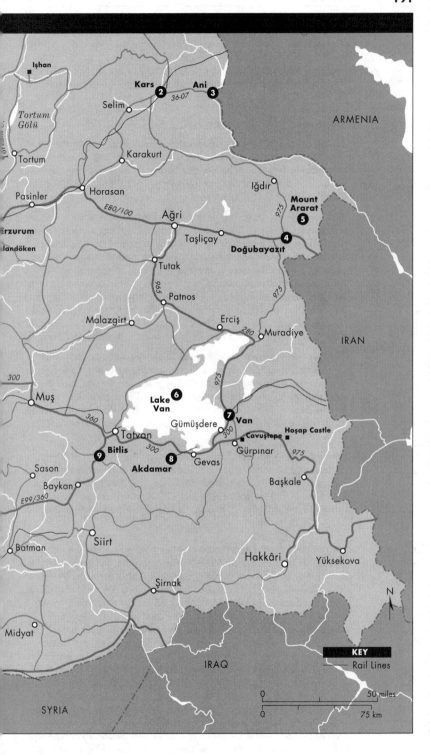

Işhan

Kars **2** 36-07 Ani **3**

Selim

ARMENIA

Tortum Gölü

Tortum

Karakurt

Iğdır

Mount Ararat **5**

Pasinler

Horasan

E80/100

Ağrı

Taşliçay

Doğubayazıt **4**

975

rzurum

landöken

Tutak

965

Patnos

Malazgirt

Erciş

280

Muradiye

IRAN

300

Muş

975

Lake Van **6**

360

Gümüşdere

Van **7**

Tatvan

Hoşap Castle

Çavuştepe

Bitlis **9**

300

8

Gevas

Gürpinar

975

Başkale

Akdamar

Sason

Baykan

E99/360

Siirt

Batman

Hakkâri

Yüksekova

N

Şirnak

Midyat

KEY
Rail Lines

0   50 miles
0   75 km

IRAQ

SYRIA

Erzurum's **citadel,** notable for its precisely hewn blocks, was started in about AD 400. Today the poorly kept ruins attract more soccer-playing kids than tourists, but do yield a sweeping view of Erzurum and beyond. Notice the few cannons scattered about, some Ottoman and some left by the Russians, who invaded Erzurum in 1882 and 1916. Bring a flashlight if you want to climb the citadel's rickety clock tower. ✉ *Tebriz Sok.; from Ulu Cami, cross Cumhuriyet Cad. and walk 3 blocks up small alley.* 💴 *40¢.* ☉ *Generally dawn–sunset, though actual hrs vary at whim of caretaker.*

The classical 16th-century **Lala Mustafa Paşa Cami,** built by the grand vizier of the same name, looks rather similar to the mosques designed by Sinan in Istanbul. The mosque faces the 17th-century Caferiye Cami. ✉ *Cumhuriyet Cad., at Menderes Cad., 2 blocks west of Ulu Cami.* ☉ *Daily 9:30–sunset.*

★ The **Yakutiye Medrese,** one of Erzurum's best sights, is a 14th-century seminary built by a Mongol emir. Mongol buildings are less refined than Seljuk ones, and many of Yakutiye's surviving embellishments—notably the stark portal, heavily carved with animal figures and floral patterns—were taken from contemporary Seljuk designs (the Mongols were usually more interested in conquering the next town than in building unique monuments). The ethnographic museum in the seminary's former prayer rooms displays Seljuk and Ottoman glasswork, jewelry, and armor. ✉ *Cumhuriyet Cad., 2 blocks west of Lala Mustafa Paşa Cami, no phone.* 💴 *25¢.* ☉ *Weekdays 8:30–noon and 1:30–5.*

The two-story **Rüsem Paşa Bazaar** is packed with brightly shining samovars, kilims and carpets, and Muslim prayer beads made from a lightweight, jet-black mineral called *oltutaş.* The bazaar itself is not especially photogenic, unless you're obsessed with plumbing fixtures and 14-karat jewelry. More appealing are the first-floor courtyard and tea garden. ✉ *Menderes Cad., 3 blocks north of Cumhuriyet Cad., no phone.* ☉ *Daily 9–7.*

At the **Erzurum Müzesi** (Erzurum Museum), Egyptian coins, Roman pottery, and Seljuk tilework are on display; the best pieces are the old Turkish kilims and carpets, home furnishings, and weapons. ✉ *Paşalar Cad.; from PTT office, walk west on Cumhuriyet Cad. and head south at traffic circle. No phone.* 💴 *75¢.* ☉ *Tues.–Sun. 9–noon and 1:30–5:30.*

OFF THE BEATEN PATH   **TORTUM AND ÇORUH RIVER VALLEYS** – North from Erzurum, the Tortum and Çoruh River valleys offer some interesting walks, but in summer bring plenty of water and avoid mid-afternoon sun scorchings. Tortum, 59 km (37 mi) north of Erzurum on Route 950, has a handful of restaurants, teahouses, and fruit stands. About 23 km (14 mi) beyond Tortum on Route 950, look on the left side of the road for the trailhead to Haho, where you can visit a well-preserved mosque originally built in the 10th century as a monastery by the Armenian prince David of Tayk (one of several by that name); allow two hours round-trip for the hike. Back on Route 950, it's another 5 km (3 mi) to the long and narrow Tortum Gölü (Lake Tortum). The highlight here is the 47-meter (154-foot) Tortum Şelalesi waterfall at the lake's northern end. Continue on Route 950 for 23 km (14 mi) and, on the right side of the road, pick up the hiking trail to the village of Ishan. Here you'll see the 10th-century Church of the Mother of God, built in the shape of a cross, with bas-reliefs carved on the exterior walls. The setting is spectacular, an oasis of tall green trees backed by barren peaks.

Dining and Lodging

Eating at the hotels in Erzurum is your best bet, though there are acceptable, inexpensive Turkish restaurants along the main street, Cumhuriyet Caddesi. The local specialties are kebabs served either with yogurt or *Iskender* (a large helping of thin tomato sauce).

$$ **✕ Güzelyurt.** Erzurum's finest restaurant is full of surprises: starched
★ white tablecloths, efficient service, and delicious Turkish food. The house specialty is *mantarli güveç* (mushrooms, lamb, and vegetables baked in a clay pot and topped with melted cheese). ⊠ *Cumhuriyet Cad. 12,* ☎ *442/218–1514. No credit cards.*

$ **✕ Salon Çağin.** This is an informal, friendly place to sample above-average Turkish cuisine. You'll be shown dishes and asked to point at whatever looks appealing. ⊠ *Cumhuriyet Cad. 20/C,* ☎ *442/218–9320. No credit cards.*

$ **✕🏠 Büyük Erzurum.** Although the furniture is somewhat worn and the walls bare, the three-star Büyük is friendly, and you'll find a good bit of English spoken. The top-floor restaurant is one of the best in Erzurum. The bus station is on the opposite side of town, but the hotel is an easy five-minute walk to Cumhuriyet Caddesi. ⊠ *Aliravi Cad. 5,* ☎ *442/218–6528,* 🖷 *442/212–2898. 50 rooms with bath. Restaurant. MC, V.*

$$$ **🏠 Palandöken Dedeman.** This popular ski lodge has a good restaurant and helpful staff, though it's only open from October to mid-May. Reservations are advised on winter weekends, when the hotel is inundated with wealthy students from Erzurum University and fugitive businessmen from Ankara. Ski equipment is available, and the hotel also provides airport transfers from Erzurum. ⊠ *Palandöken, 6 km (4 mi) south of Erzurum,* ☎ *442/316–2414,* 🖷 *442/316–3607. 115 rooms, most with bath. Restaurant, indoor pool. AE, MC, V.*

$$ **🏠 Dilaver.** Erzurum's plushest hotel is the three-star Dilaver, in the center of town and within walking distance of the main sights. The rooms are clean and modern, if somewhat lacking in character, and equipped with satellite TVs and direct-dial phones. ⊠ *Pelit Meyd., Asaği Mumcu Cad.,* ☎ *442/235–0068,* 🖷 *442/218–1148. 75 rooms with bath. Restaurant, 3 bars, air-conditioning, minibars. MC, V.*

$$ **🏠 Otel Oral.** Clean and quiet, this hotel's only drawback is its location on the outskirts of town. Still, the rooms (which average $60 per night) are comfortable, with TVs and refrigerators; the staff is helpful; and there's a good restaurant. ⊠ *Terminal Cad. 6,* ☎ *442/218–9740,* 🖷 *442/218–9749. 90 rooms with bath. MC, V.*

$ **🏠 Örnek Otel.** Absolutely inexpensive ($12 per night) and centrally located, this place is popular with Turkish business travelers and young couples. It's nothing special, and hot water is promised but rarely delivered. The rooms have antique phones and color TVs with fuzzy reception. Still, you could pass a night here in reasonable comfort. ⊠ *Kazim Karabekir Cad. 7,* ☎ *442/218–1203. 27 rooms, some with shower. No credit cards.*

Outdoor Activities and Sports

SKIING

The popular ski resort of **Palandöken** is only 6 km (4 mi) south of Erzurum, so expect crowds in peak season (December–March). The runs are good for beginning and intermediate skiers, but advanced skiers may find themselves dreaming of the Alps. The snow is usually deep and powdery. You'll pay $15–$20 per day for a lift ticket and rental equipment. In winter there are daily buses (weather permitting) from Erzurum's bus station. In summer most everything on the mountain shuts down. Traveling by car from Erzurum, take Route E80 east toward Ağrı and look for a right-hand turnoff marked TEKMAN. Follow this road until it eventually branches right.

Kars

② *211 km (131 mi) from Erzurum to Kars via Rte. E80 northeast through Pasinler, Horasan, and Karakurt, then north on Rte. 957.*

Kars looks like the frontier town it is: forbidding and grayish, set on a 1,750-meter (5,740-foot) plateau and forever at the mercy of the winds. Ever since the Seljuk sultan Alpaslan forced the last Armenian prince to abdicate in AD 1064, Kars has been besieged by invaders: the Akkoyun, the Mongol warriors of Tamerlane, and, three times in the 19th century, czarist armies from Russia. The Turks, under the leadership of Kazım Karabekir, retook the city in 1920, and Kars was formally ceded to Turkey after the war of independence in 1921. The Russian influence is still obvious in many buildings and in the rigid grid of streets that form the town's small, dusty center.

If you're traveling onward to Ani, you must obtain a permit at the tourist office in Kars—on the west side of town at the intersection of G.A.M.E. Caddesi and Faik Bey Caddesi, it's open daily 8–noon and 2–5:30—then take the free permit to police headquarters farther west on Faik Bey Caddesi to have it stamped. Finally, go to the Kars Museum (☞ *below*) on Cumhuriyet Caddesi and buy tickets to the site (the caretaker at Ani does not sell them). If you hire a guide, he will take care of the paperwork for you.

İç Kale (Kars Castle) is a 10th-century fort that overhangs Kars from a high, rocky vantage point. In 1386 Tamerlane swept violently through the region and razed Kars Castle. Most of the surviving fortifications were commissioned by Lala Mustafa Paşa in 1579. Today the castle houses an army barracks and is of little interest; only the panoramic views of Kars merit the 20-minute walk uphill. ⊠ *Kale Cad., no phone.* 🎟 *Free.* ⊙ *Daily 2 PM–sunset.*

The **Kümbet Cami** (Drum-Dome Mosque), at the foot of the hill by Kars River, is obviously not Turkish—originally the Armenian Church of the Twelve Apostles, it was built in the 10th century. You can still make out the Apostles on the exterior of the drum-shaped cupola. The mosque is often locked, in which case the only view is through a rusty gate. Just to the northwest is the Taşköprü, a bridge of Seljuk origin dating from the 1400s. ⊠ *Kale Cad., at foot of İç Kale, no phone.* 🎟 *Free.*

Kars Museum, near the train station on the eastern edge of town, is very difficult to find—take a taxi. Two floors of displays cover Kars's many rulers: Roman, Greek, Seljuk, and Ottoman, and there are pieces of Armenian churches and a Russian church bell. Buy tickets here for Ani, and take a minute to study the wall-size Ani site maps. ⊠ *Cumhuriyet Cad., on road to Ani,* ☎ *474/212–2387.* 🎟 *75¢.* ⊙ *Daily 8–5:30.*

NEED A BREAK? Kars has two excellent *hamamı* (Turkish baths). Both are on the Taşköprü stone bridge near the foot of Kars Castle, and both are open daily 7 AM–11 PM. A bath and massage at either cost $7. The 16th-century **Mazlumağa Hamamı** (☎ 474/212–2284) is for men only. The 18th-century **ılbeyoğlu/Muradiye Hamamı** (☎ 474/223–1765) is exclusively for women.

Dining and Lodging

Kars is one of the few towns in the east where young men and women meet openly for a cup of coffee or a meal. Even so, there aren't many good places to eat. You can have a passable meal at kebab salons along

Atatürk Caddesi and Kazım Paşa Caddesi, two parallel streets in the center of town. The local specialties are honey and Kaşar cheese, both displayed in copious quantities in nearly every shop window.

$ ✕🏨 Hotel Karabağ. Kars's most comfortable hotel is the centrally located, three-star Karabağ, catering to Russian and Turkish businessmen with direct-dial phones, room service, satellite TVs, and 24-hour hot water (a rarity in Kars). The adjoining restaurant serves above-average Turkish cuisine. ⊠ *Faik Bey Cad. 84, at Atatürk Cad.,* ☏ *474/212–2585,* 🖷 *474/223–3089. 50 rooms, most with bath or shower. Restaurant, bar, air-conditioning, room service. MC, V.*

$ 🏨 Hotel Temel. The popular budget choice ($12 per night) in Kars has fickle hot water, but everything is clean and the management helpful. Ask to see a few rooms before choosing, as some have small balconies. The sunny breakfast salon is an oasis of calm, but avoid the bleak smoke-filled restaurant. ⊠ *Kazım Paşa Cad. 4/A,* ☏ *474/223–1376. 28 rooms, some with bath. Restaurant. No credit cards.*

Ani

★ ❸ *42 km (26 mi) east of Kars on Rte. 36–07.*

Until the Mongol invasion of 1236, Ani (also called Ocaklı) was the chief town of a medieval Armenian kingdom, with 100,000 inhabitants and "a thousand and one churches," according to historical sources. Although it was occupied by the Mongols, Ani still had a large Armenian population well into the 14th century. In 1319 it was struck by a terrible earthquake, after which the townspeople began to leave. The latest inscription to be found in the city is dated 1348. Scarcely half a dozen churches remain today, and all are in shambles. Even so, the sprawling site is breathtaking, with hundreds of weather-beaten ruins set on a triangular promontory bounded on two sides by steep river gorges. Equally majestic is the surrounding countryside, a mix of severe mountains, tiny Kurdish settlements, and fields of wildflowers fading to the horizon.

The ruins at Ani straddle the Alaçay River, which forms a natural border with Armenia. It's a sensitive military area—machine-gun towers keep a close watch on it—and to visit the site you must obtain a permit in Kars (for instructions, ☞ Kars, *above*). The caretaker at Ani does not sell permits or tickets.

You enter **Ani** through the **Aslan Kapısı** (Lion's Gate), one of three principal portals in Ani's extensive city walls, which stretch for over 2,500 meters (8,200 feet). The 10-meter (32-foot) walls were raised in AD 972 by the Armenian king Ashot III, though the lion relief itself was added by the Seljuk sultan Menuçehr in 1064. A small trail makes a circle through Ani; following it clockwise the first major ruin you encounter is the **Keseli** (Church of the Redeemer), a huge quadrangular cathedral built in 1035. Its dome (1036) was struck by lightning in the 1950s and is now half-collapsed. There are three churches at Ani dedicated to St. Gregory, the Armenian prince who converted his people to Christianity. The best preserved is the **Nakışlı**, built by an Armenian nobleman, Tigran Honentz, in 1215. Nakışlı is the most impressive ruin in Ani, not the least because it stands at the foot of a small ravine with a view over the Arpaçay River. Inside, note the remarkable cycle of murals depicting the Virgin Mary and St. Gregory. The striking **Convent of the Three Virgins** stands on a rocky outcrop lower down the gorge.

Clinging to the heights overlooking the Arpaçay River, the **Menuçehr Cami** (1072) was originally an Armenian building, perhaps even a palace.

Climb up to the first citadel and continue on to the second at the far edge of town, where the two gorges converge. From here you have a good view of the many cave dwellings in the walls of the western gorge, which once housed the city's poor.

The best view of Ani's ruins is from the **İç Kale** (citadel), perched on a rocky plateau at the site's southeast end above a trail that cuts a steep path down to the river. Bring a flashlight for the climb inside the citadel's precarious tower and mind your footing. *No phone.* 🖂 *$1.* ⊙ *Daily 8:30–5.*

MT. ARARAT AND LAKE VAN

Fighting between PKK militants and the Turkish government discourages most travelers from trekking to the perpetually snowbound summit of Mt. Ararat. Instead, the region's few tourists (largely Turks and Iranians) console themselves with the İşak Paşa Saray, a striking mountain palace not far from sleepy Doğubayazıt.

After the rough and rugged scenery of Mt. Ararat, the arid plains around Lake Van are a disappointment unless you have your own transportation and are prepared to spend a few days touring off the beaten path. Otherwise, make a quick stop at the island of Akdamar, at Lake Van's southern end, and do your best to enjoy the dusty six-hour drive west to Diyarbakır.

Doğubayazıt and Mt. Ararat

286 km (177 mi) east of Erzurum on Rte. E80 to Doğubayazıt.

❹ The rough frontier town of **Doğubayazıt** (pronounced doe-YOU-bye-ah-zoot) is a good base for visiting Turkey's highest mountain, the majestic Mt. Ararat. You'll share the town with farm equipment, sheep, and Iranian tourists. The lack of carpet and kilim shops makes it easy to wander the main street, Çarşı Caddesi, unmolested.

★ Doğubayazıt's only sight, **İşak Paşa Saray,** is in the mountains to the southeast of town. The fortified palace was built in the late 17th century by local potentate Çolak Abdi Paşa and his son, İşak. The interior of the building is extremely ornate, a fantastic mixture of Georgian, Persian, and Ottoman styles. Gold-plated front doors were carted off by Russian troops in 1917.

Late afternoon is the best time to visit, when the sun casts a deep orange glow over the palace and the ruins of a 12th-century citadel carved into the opposite (and inaccessible) mountainside. There's a teahouse immediately above İşak Paşa Saray and a makeshift restaurant about 200 meters below the site. Otherwise, the only hints of civilization are a cluster of Kurdish mud-brick houses and the occasional Kurdish musician wandering from house to house in search of an audience. ⊠ *6 km (4 mi) southeast of town on road to Göller, no phone.* 🖂 *$1.* ⊙ *Mon.–Sat. 10–5.*

❺ An extinct volcano, snow-covered even in summer, **Mt. Ararat** (Ağri Daği in Turkish) soars 5,137 meters (16,850 feet), dominating an arid plateau. According to Genesis, after the Great Flood "the waters were dried up from off the earth; and Noah removed the covering of the ark, and looked, and behold, the face of the ground was dry." The survivors, as the story goes, had just landed on top of Mt. Ararat. Many other ancient sources—Chaldean, Babylonian, Chinese, Assyrian—also tell of an all-destroying flood and of one man who heroically escaped its consequences. Scientists generally agree that sometime during the 4th millennium BC, a veritable cataclysm may have occurred, accompanied by rains and floods. But did Noah's Ark really exist? Since medieval times, the locals here have sold Christian pilgrims old planks reputedly from the ark; the modern ark hunt dates from 1876, when an Englishman named James Bryce discovered on the peaks "amid blocks of lava, a piece of wood about 4 feet long and 5 inches wide, which had obviously been shaped by means of a tool." Fragments of ancient timber, embedded in the ice, have been brought back by various ark-hunting expeditions since then, but radiocarbon dating tests have proved inconclusive. Satellite photos showed a boat embedded in a glacier at 3,750 meters (12,500 feet), but on-the-spot examination of one of these "boats" proved it to be nothing more than a freak formation in the strata. Even so, expeditions by Christian fundamentalist groups constantly make new claims, and the mystery continues, as compelling in its way as that of Scotland's Loch Ness monster. Of interest to fans of the *X-Files* and *In Search Of . . .* will be the second Noah's Ark, "discovered" in the 1980s on a hillside 20 km (12 mi) southeast of Ararat. Most tours from Doğubayazıt (☞ Guided Tours *in* The Far East A to Z, *below*) visit the site, but don't get your hopes up. To the untrained eye, this Ark is nothing more than a pile of rocks, albeit with intriguing potential.

Because of ongoing PKK activity, mountain climbers must obtain permission from the Turkish authorities in Ankara, usually four months in advance. If you haven't made advance arrangements, in Doğubayazıt make inquiries at Trek Turizm in the Hotel İsfahan (☏ 472/312–4363) or Til-Tur Travel (☞ Guided Tours *in* The Far East A to Z, *below*). On the way up the mountain, you must brave spiders, snakes, and bears, as well as suspicious military patrols, snowstorms, and avalanches. The highly negotiable rate for the four- to six-day summit trek is $900–$1,200 per person.

Dining and Lodging

The hotels in Doğubayazıt have the best restaurants, but don't overlook the family-run kebab and *pide* (Turkish pizza) salons that line Çarşı Caddesi. One of the best is Tad Lokantası (✉ Çarşı Cad. 12, ☏ 472/311–2784), clean, friendly, and a good place to try brain soup and the local version of sac tava. They also serve a spaghetti-like dish with butter and garlic. The local dessert specialty is *aşure,* a nut-and-raisin pudding that's nicknamed "Noah's Pudding."

$ ✕⛱ **Hotel Grand Derya.** Doğubayazıt's most luxurious hotel was thor-
★ oughly refurbished a few years back, and all the fixtures—porcelain sinks, satellite TVs—are still shiny. The rooms themselves are comfortable if plainly decorated; the management clearly put more effort into renovating the lobby and public spaces. The hotel restaurant is one of the best in town. ✉ *Emniyet Cad., near PTT office,* ☏ *472/312–7531,* FAX *472/312–7833. 70 rooms with bath. Restaurant, bar. MC, V.*

$ ⛱ **Hotel İsfahan.** The somber lobby and bar here are decorated in traditional kilims, and a sightseeing room on the fifth floor has especially good views of Mt. Ararat. The hotel restaurant isn't bad, but the rooms are shabby and not worth the money. ✉ *Emniyet Cad. 26,* ☏ *472/312–4363,* FAX *472/312–7369. 73 rooms with shower. Restaurant, bar. No credit cards.*

$ ⛱ **Hotel Kenan.** Budget travelers appreciate the two-star comfort of Hotel Kenan, the reasonable prices ($10 per night, plus $4 for breakfast), and the cozy lobby and bar area. The rooms are less than fancy, and some are poorly ventilated; ask to see a few before choosing. ✉ *Emniyet Cad., off Çarşı Cad.,* ☏ *472/312–7869,* FAX *472/312–7871. 52 rooms, most with shower. Restaurant, bar. No credit cards.*

$ 🛏 **Sim-Er Motel.** The modern three-star Sim-Er, 5 km (3 mi) east of town, is clean, fairly attractive, and, as a result, popular with tour groups and truck drivers en route to Iran. It has magnificent views of Mt. Ararat, another plus. ⊠ *Off Rte. E80,* ☎ *472/312–1643. 130 rooms with shower. Restaurant. No credit cards.*

Lake Van and Environs

171 km (106 mi) from Doğubayazıt, west on Rte. E80 and south on Rte. E99/975, continuing past Muradiye to town of Van.

❻ The landscape at **Lake Van** (Van Gölü) is eerily barren and desolate, a result of winter flash floods and intense summertime heat—in August the average daytime temperature is 38°C (100°F). But it is Turkey's largest and most unusual lake, 3,738 sq km (1,443 sq mi) of brackish water surrounded by mighty volcanic cones, so travelers continue to come. Lake Van was formed when a volcano blew its top and blocked the course of a river, leaving the newly formed lake no natural outlet; as a result the water is highly alkaline, full of sulfides and mineral salts, much like the Dead Sea. Lake Van's only marine life is a small member of the carp family, the *darekh,* which has somehow adapted to the saline environment. Recreational water sports are nonexistent, and beaches along the rocky shores are few and far between. Swimming in the soft, soapy water is pleasant, but try not to swallow any—the taste is horrible. The towns of Adilcevaz and Ahlat, on Lake Van's north shore, are worth visiting only if you're in the area; most travelers head instead to Van and the nearby island of Akdamar, along the lake's southern shore.

❼ **Van** first appears in history 3,000 years ago, when it was the site of the Urartian capital of Tushpa, whose formidable fortress—built on a steep cliff rising from the lakeshore—dominated the countryside. (The Urartians first appeared in this region in the 12th century BC, and by the mid-8th century BC ruled an empire extending from the Black Sea to the Caspian Sea, only to be wiped out over the next 150 years by various rivals, primarily the Assyrians.) The old city, nestled below the southern cliff, was destroyed in battles with the Armenians and Russians during World War I. The melancholy jumble of foundations cannot be sorted out; only two vaguely restored mosques, one 13th-century, the other 16th-century, rise from the marshland. When it came time to rebuild the city after the war, the residents selected a higher, healthier spot, 5 km (3 mi) inland. Thus Van was robbed of a waterfront setting and, as a result, now looks like the tedious sun-scorched outpost it truly is. As the commercial center of southeastern Anatolia, Van has numerous banks, sleek European clothing shops, and a large university, but one afternoon is enough to cover the main sights.

Steps—considerably fewer than the 1,000 claimed in local tourist handouts—still ascend to **Van Castle** (Van Kalesi), the sprawling Urartian fortress on the outskirts of town. A path branches right to Urartian tombs in the sheer southern rock face; a cuneiform inscription here honors King Xerxes, whose Persian troops occupied the fortress early in the 5th century BC. The crumbling ramparts are still impressive, but as is true so often in these parts, it is the view from such a vantage point that makes the steep climb worthwhile. A taxi from the new town should cost no more than $4 one-way. Cheaper *dolmuşes* (shared taxis) depart regularly from Beş Yol, a large intersection two blocks west of the Büyük Urartu hotel.

The new city has little to recommend it besides a large new mosque and the small but well-arranged archaeological and ethnographical **Van Müzesi** (Van Museum), which displays many Urartian artifacts: rich, golden jewelry; belts and plates engraved with lions, bulls, and sphinxes;

and a carved relief of the god Teshup, for whom their capital was named. ⊠ *1 block east of Cumhuriyet Cad.,* ☎ *432/216–1139.* ☜ *50¢.* ◷ *Tues.–Sun. 9–noon and 1:30–6.*

OFF THE
BEATEN PATH

ÇAVUŞTEPE AND HOŞAP CASTLE – From Van, drive 35 km (22 mi) south on the Hakkari Road to Çavuştepe, where you can clamber around the stone foundations of a ruined 8th-century BC Urartian fortress-city, Sardurihinli. Nearby are temple ruins and a 6th-century BC sacrificial altar. Admission to the citadel is 50¢, though it's sometimes difficult to find the caretaker. Continue 15 km (9 mi) southeast on the same road to Hoşap Castle, a dramatic fortress looming over a river chasm. The 17th-century complex, which was used as a base to "protect" (i.e., ransack) caravans, included a palace, two mosques, three baths, and a dungeon. The great gate, with its carved lions and an inscription in the Farsi language of Persia, is quite a show of strength; a tunnel carved through bedrock leads inside from here. Bring a flashlight, as there are no lights within the castle, which is open daily 8–5. Admission is 75¢.

❽ On the tranquil, uninhabited islet of **Akdamar,** among wild olive trees, stand the scant remains of a monastery, including the truly splendid **Church of the Holy Cross.** Built in AD 921 by an Armenian king, Gagik Artzruni of Vaspurakan, it is very much a cousin to the Armenian churches at Ani in construction. Incredible high-relief carvings make this church a work of art. Nearly the entire story of the Bible is told here, from Adam and Eve to David and Goliath. Along the top is a frieze of running animals; another frieze shows a vineyard where laborers work the fields and women dance with bears; and, of course, King Gagik is depicted, offering his church to Christ. To reach Akdamar from Van, follow Route 300 to Gevaş. Entering Gevaş you will spot ferries waiting at the landing to collect the required number of passengers—between 10 and 15—for the 20-minute ride. Depending on how many people board the ferry, the cost is $3–$5 per person. If other tourists don't turn up, you must pay $25–$40 to charter the entire boat, depending on your ability to haggle. ⊠ *Rte. 300, 56 km (35 mi) west of Van, no phone.* ☜ *$1.25.* ◷ *Daily dawn–sunset.*

❾ **Bitlis,** west of Akdamar (and south of Tatvan), is a green oasis among towering mountains on a tributary of the Tigris. Its two principal landmarks are a sprawling castle built above the town by one of Alexander the Great's generals, and the odd 12th-century Ulu Cami (Grand Mosque)—apparently its sponsor ran out of money before its conical dome could be built. Bitlis is nearly halfway between Van and Diyarbakır, making it a convenient place to stop for lunch, but there's little reason to linger.

Dining and Lodging

Though Van is not a culinary oasis, for once you're not limited to hotel restaurants—local businessmen have created a demand for upscale eateries along Cumhuriyet Caddesi, Van's lively main street. The best is probably **Sultan Sofrası** (⊠ Cumhuriyet Cad., opposite PTT office, ☎ 432/216–7498), a modern spot that serves a delicious, massive plate of *közde piliç* (grilled chicken) along with the usual kebabs and soups. Also note the cluster of breakfast-only restaurants—serving fresh bread, honey, herb-scented cheese, and olives—behind and immediately north of the large tea garden on Cumhuriyet Caddesi.

$$ 🏨 **Büyük Urartu.** This well-run three-star hotel, one of the town's
★ best, is also educational, since the manager is a professor of archaeology. The decoration carries Urartian motifs. Guest rooms are small, though still pleasant; some face the noisy street, so ask to see a few be-

fore choosing. The attached restaurant is quite acceptable, though a bit overpriced. ⊠ *Hastane Cad. 60,* ☎ *432/212–0660,* 𝖥𝖠𝖷 *432/212– 1610. 87 rooms, 70 with shower. Restaurant, bar. MC, V.*

$ ▦ **Hotel Bayram.** The management here is overseeing a slow but thorough renovation. You'll be given a choice between a cheaper unrenovated room (as low as $12 per night) and a more expensive double with new furniture and bathroom fixtures. The Bayram will never be a luxury choice, but simply a clean and friendly spot right in the center of town. ⊠ *Cumhuriyet Cad. 1/A, entrance on Çakmak Cad.,* ☎ *432/216– 1136,* 𝖥𝖠𝖷 *432/216–5758. 32 rooms, most with shower. No credit cards.*

$ ▦ **Hotel Yakut.** This new three-star hotel is on the south side of town, on a busy side street filled with vegetable markets and carpet shops. The comfortable, spacious rooms ($30 per night) have satellite TVs and direct-dial phones. Business travelers will appreciate the fax and photocopy center. ⊠ *Kazım Karabekir Cad. 4, off Cumhuriyet Cad.,* ☎ *432/214–2832,* 𝖥𝖠𝖷 *432/214–2833. 64 rooms, most with shower. Restaurant, bar. MC, V.*

SOUTHEASTERN TURKEY

Diyarbakır, Mt. Nimrod, and Şanlıurfa

The photo is famous: a series of decapitated stone heads rising out of the sand, framed against a hypnotic blue sky. The image appears on postcards and tourist brochures throughout Turkey, seducing travelers by the hundreds to add Mt. Nimrod to their itineraries. It's an especially feasible detour if you're coming from Cappadocia, thanks to tour operators who operate overnight trips from Nevşehir and Göreme. Traveling by car, it makes sense to include the bazaar and ruins at Şanlıurfa, and perhaps the medieval citadel at Mardin. The region's largest city, Diyarbakır, has a few historic sights and is convenient if you're arriving from Van or Erzurum.

Diyarbakır

★ ❿ *357 km (221 mi) from Van on Rte. 300 to Rte. E99.*

Defended by a stretch of impregnable black basalt walls, three layers thick in places, Diyarbakır commands the rough, dusty plain 195 km (121 mi) west of Bitlis. With its great walls, one would think the stronghold of Diyarbakır could survive any siege; in fact, it seems to have fallen to about every petty raider who passed this way. One of the oldest cities anywhere, set in what is widely accepted as the "cradle of civilization" (the area between the Tigris and Euphrates rivers), Diyarbakır has seen a lot of raiders in its 5,000 years. The Hurrians were probably first, founding a city called Hurri-Mitanni. The Assyrians absorbed it, renaming it Amida in the process. Next came a century of Urartian domination, followed by the familiar succession of Medes, Persians, Macedonians, Romans, Sassanids, and Byzantines. In the 7th century several Arab Muslim groups battled with one another for possession of this strategic crossroads. They gave the city its present name, Diyarbakır, "City of the Bakır Tribes." Later came the Turkomans, the Ortokids, the eastern and western Seljuks, and the Mongolian hordes. Finally, Selim I took it for the Ottomans in 1515, the beginning of a long and relatively calm period.

Diyarbakır's Roman influence is evident in the layout of the old town: a rough rectangle with two main streets connecting the four gates, one at each compass point. Connecting the four primary gates are the **city walls,** reconstructed by Emperor Constantius in AD 349 and further restored by the Seljuks in 1088. On the whole, the walls remain in good shape along their entire length of 5½ km (3 mi). Of the original 72 towers, 67 still stand, decorated with myriad inscriptions in the language of every conqueror and with Seljuk reliefs of animals and men; you can explore their inner chambers and corridors. To make a circuit of the city walls on foot, start at the **Mardin Kapısı** gate on the south side near the Otel Büyük Kervansaray and take the wall-top path west toward the **Urfa Kapısı** gate, also called the Bab El Rumi. About halfway, you will come to the twin bastions, **Beden Burcu** and **Yedi Kardeş Burcu**, added to the fortifications in 1208. From here, you can see the old Ottoman bridge over the Tigris, called **Dicle Köprüsü.** Continue clockwise along the city wall and you'll eventually reach another gate, the **Dağ Kapısı**, which divides Diyarbakır's old and new towns. Farther east inside the ramparts are the sad remains of the Artakid palace, surrounded by a dry, octagonal pool known as the **Lion's Fountain.** Not long ago, there were two carved lions here; where the second one went is a mystery.

The ruins of the old town's **İç Kale** (Inner Fortress), a circular and heavily eroded section of the city walls, are notable for the 16th-century **Hazreti Süleymaniye Cami,** which is also known simply as the Citadel Mosque. The mosque has a tall, graceful minaret and is striped with black basalt and pale sandstone, a favorite design of this city's medieval architects. Its courtyard fountain is fed by an underground spring that has probably supplied cold, clear water to the city for all its 5,000 years. ⊠ *İzzet Paşa Cad., no phone.* ☉ *Daily dawn–sunset, except at prayer times.*

In the center of the old city stands the **Ulu Cami** (Great Mosque), very possibly the oldest mosque in Turkey. Though its present form dates from the 12th century, in an older form it served as a Byzantine basilica; its colonnades and columns are made from bits and pieces of earlier Greek buildings. Note its Arabic courtyard plan, which contrasts with the covered and domed mosques common in Turkey. ⊠ *Gazi Cad., opposite Yapi Kredi bank, no phone.* ☉ *Daily 10–sunset.*

Diyarbakır's **bazaar** encompasses the half-dozen streets surrounding Ulu Cami; most stalls are shrines to wrought metal, plumbing fixtures, and plastic shoes. Across the street from the mosque is the grand 16th-century Hasan Paşa Han, a photogenic caravansary now mostly used by carpet and souvenir dealers.

Zinciriye Medrese, a former seminary, now houses the local **Archaeological Museum,** where the exhibits cover 4,000 years of history. ⊠ *Gazi Cad.,* ☏ *412/221–2755.* 🎫 *50¢.* ☉ *Mon.–Sat. 8:30–noon and 1:30–5:30.*

The old town's most recognizable mosque is the **Kasım Padişah Cami** (1512), famous for its Dört Ayaklı Minare (Four-legged Minaret), which appears to be suspended in the air (the minaret balances upon four basalt columns, a marvel of medieval engineering). Legend has it that your wish will come true if you pass under the minaret seven times. ⊠ *Yenikapı Cad., no phone.* ☉ *Daily 10–sunset.*

Dining and Lodging

$ ✕ **Güneydoğu.** A newer and comparatively fancy dining spot, the Güneydoğu has decent Turkish entrées and air-conditioning, a blessing in the height of summer. ⊠ *İnönü Cad. 32/A,* ☏ *412/221–2597. No credit cards.*

$ ✕ **Hevser Beyaz Köşk Ocakbaşı.** This mouthful of a name is hard to ★ spot in the clash of competing restaurant signs along İnönü Caddesi; look for a red-and-orange entryway opposite the main PTT office, 150 meters (500 feet) west of Hotel Aslan. The airy courtyard garden sits in the shadow of the city wall, the perfect atmosphere for sampling a traditional Kurdish dish such as sac tava. ⊠ *İnönü Cad.,* ☎ *412/228–3950. No credit cards.*

$$ ✕⛆ **Demir Hotel.** The four-star Demir is one of Diyarbakır's better lux-
★ ury hotels. Facilities include a swimming pool, an excellent rooftop
restaurant, secure parking, and a terrace for music and dancing. ⊠ *İzzet Paşa Cad. 8,* ☎ *412/221–2315,* FAX *412/222–4300. 60 rooms with shower. 2 restaurants, 2 bars, indoor pool. V.*

$$ ⛆ **Otel Büyük Kervansaray.** There's something particularly apt about
★ the Turkish concept of turning old caravansaries into fancy four-star
hotels. This is an attractive newcomer, in a 16th-century building with
sandstone walls and traditional furnishings. The rooms are comfortable
enough, but what you're really paying for is the atmosphere—and the
swimming pool. ⊠ *Gazi Cad.,* ☎ *412/228–9606,* FAX *412/223–7731.
45 rooms with bath. Restaurant, bar, outdoor pool. MC, V.*

$$ ⛆ **Turistik.** If you're feeling nostalgic for a 1950s-style hotel, try the
Turistik. Guest rooms are larger than average and comfortable, and
the garden restaurant, around a fountain, is appealing. Front rooms
can be a bit noisy. ⊠ *Ziya Gökalp Cad. 7,* ☎ *412/224–7550,* FAX *412/
224–4274. 52 rooms with shower. Restaurant. MC, V.*

$ ⛆ **D. Büyük Otel.** If it weren't in the sun-baked east of Turkey, the D.
Büyük might be accused of having art deco tendencies. The rooms ($26
per night) are high on style, with sleek bathroom fixtures and color-
matched sheets and curtains—not to mention satellite TVs and direct-
dial phones. ⊠ *İnönü Cad. 4,* ☎ *412/228–1295,* FAX *412/221–2444.
23 rooms with shower. No credit cards.*

$ ⛆ **Hotel Aslan.** The Aslan, one of the better inexpensive ($20 per
night, plus $3 for breakfast) hotels in Diyarbakır, is on the border of
the old and new towns, a short walk west from the Dağ Kapısı gate.
All rooms have showers with 24-hour hot water. ⊠ *Kıbrıs Cad. 23,*
☎ *412/224–7096,* FAX *412/224–1179. 36 rooms with shower. Restau-
rant. No credit cards.*

Mt. Nimrod and Environs

*169 km (104 mi) from Diyarbakır west on Rtes. E99 and 360 past
Adıyaman to town of Kâhta; to reach mountain take Rte. 02–03 north.*

★ ⓫ **Mt. Nimrod** (Nemrut Daği) rises 2,150 meters (7,052 feet) above the
Anatolian plain, a ruddy outcrop of rock and stunted trees overlook-
ing a vast network of natural and manmade lakes, all part of Turkey's
controversial GAP (Southeast Anatolia Project). In 1984, in an effort
to harness the Tigris and Euphrates rivers, the Turkish government began
damming and flooding valleys at the foot of Mt. Nimrod, forcing
dozens of villages to relocate and causing a diplomatic stir from Dam-
ascus to Baghdad (neither Syria nor Iraq is pleased that water supplies
can now be turned off at a moment's notice). Practically speaking, GAP
has shortened travel times to Mt. Nimrod from Diyarbakır and
Şanlıurfa, with car ferries making frequent daily trips year-round.

Approaching from the west, minibuses run to the peak from both
Adıyaman and Kâhta ($40–$75 depending on the length of the tour);
if you drive to the summit yourself, the trip from Kâhta takes a good
two hours. Because of severe winter weather conditions, the trip should
be undertaken only between May and October—even then, when it is
baking down on the plain, there are strong winds and a stiff morning
chill at the summit. Tour guides recommend setting out at 2 AM to reach
the summit at sunrise. You can then return before the fierce midday

heat. The sunrise is lovely, but if you start later you'll avoid the sunrise tourist rush and the coldest part of the morning.

Cars must park 1 km (½ mi) below the sepulchral mound that tops the ocher-pink, cone-shape pinnacle of Mt. Nimrod. The hike up from here takes a good 20 minutes and can be tiring, given the altitude. When you finally reach the summit, though, you'll meet a stupendous spectacle. Temples stand on two terraces—one facing the rising sun, the other the setting sun—with a pyramid of small rocks, the **Tumulus of Antiochus,** between them. The man responsible for the fantastic project, King Antiochus I, is buried somewhere underneath (though they have tried, archaeologists have yet to find him—all attempts at excavation have caused cave-ins). From 64 to 32 BC, Antiochus was king of Commagene, a tiny Roman puppet state founded by his father, Mithridates the Great (it lasted until its annexation to Rome in AD 72). The kings of Commagene grandly claimed descent from Alexander the Great, and so young Antiochus reasoned that if Alexander was a god, he must be one, too. He set a veritable army of slaves to work building a suitable monument to himself. Enthroned on the two terraces are massive white statues of gods, Antiochus seated among them as an equal.

Originally 26 feet–30 feet high, the statues have been decapitated over the centuries by the forces of erosion and earthquakes; in 1926 a thunderstorm brought the last one—Tyche, goddess of fortune—crashing down. Their gigantic heads are nowadays set upright on the ground around the tumulus; note how they combine the Greek harmony of features with Oriental headgear and hairstyles. On the east terrace, left to right, they are: Apollo, Tyche, Zeus (at center, with his pointed cap and bushy whiskers), Antiochus, and Heracles. The west terrace is a mirror image of the east, with the addition of some fine relief carvings portraying Antiochus shaking hands with Apollo, Zeus, and Heracles, all with smiles and dignity. The inscriptions carved everywhere mostly describe the Commagenes and their religious practices; the message on the throne of Antiochus reads, "I, Antiochus, caused this monument to be erected in commemoration of my own glory and of that of the gods." Given the severe temperatures and strong winds at the summit, and the overall isolation of the site, one wonders why Antiochus didn't choose a more inviting location—a question best discussed over a steaming cup of tea at the wee visitor center or in the ramshackle tea shed on the summit itself. Bring your own food and water. ⊠ *Nemrut Daği,* ☎ *416/737–1231.* ☞ *$1.* ☉ *May–late Oct., daily sunrise–sunset.*

Along the road back from Mt. Nimrod to Kâhta, you pass other remarkable relics of Commagene in **Eski Kâhta** (Old Kâhta). Cross the Kâhta River on the Seljuk bridge to see, carved into the rock, a stunning relief of Antiochus I's father, Mithridates, being greeted by Heracles. Higher up on the rock face are copious inscriptions proclaiming the glory of the Commagene dynasty; on the top of this peak stand the foundations of an ancient acropolis with colored floor mosaics. Also in Eski Kâhta, Yeni Kale (New Castle) was built by the Mameluks over a smaller Commagene fortress. Recross the Kâhta via the Cendere Köprü, a single-span bridge with two tall columns on one end and one on the other, built by the Roman emperor Septimus Severus in the 3rd century AD.

Dining and Lodging

There are few decent restaurants in Adıyaman or Kâhta; you're better off stopping for lunch or dinner just below the summit at the Otel Kervansaray Nemrut.

$–$$ ✕🏨 **Otel Kervansaray Nemrut.** One of two places to stop on Mt. Nimrod itself, the caravansary is in a low stone building near a waterfall

8 km (5 mi) from Mt. Nimrod's summit. The location is stunning, and the rooms are clean and wonderfully quiet. The restaurant is one of the best for miles. ⊠ *Nemrut Daği, Karadut Köyü, 54 km (34 mi) from Kâhta,* ☎ *416/737–2190,* FAX *416/737–2085. 14 rooms with shower. Restaurant, pool, camping. Open year-round. MC, V.*

$ ✕🏨 **Bozdoğan.** This modern, relatively new hotel, the best place in Adıyaman, also has the town's best restaurant. ⊠ *Atatürk Bul., Adıyaman,* ☎ *416/216–2716,* FAX *416/216–3630. 54 rooms with shower. Restaurant. No credit cards.*

$ ✕🏨 **Hotel Euphrat.** This hotel on Mt. Nimrod was built in the 1960s, and its age shows. Many rooms haven't been occupied for years, so ask to see a few before choosing. The adjoining restaurant is Hotel Euphrat's only bright spot. ⊠ *Nemrut Daği, Karadut Köyü, 54 km (34 mi) from Kâhta,* ☎ *416/737–2175 (or 312/427–5831 in Ankara for reservations),* FAX *416/737–2179. 55 rooms, 43 with shower. Restaurant, outdoor pool, camping. No credit cards.*

$ 🏨 **Hotel Kommagene.** This is really a guest house ($15 per night, breakfast not included) with pretensions of being a hotel, but there are old kilims decorating the lobby and a shady terrace, and the restaurant is quite decent. ⊠ *Rte. 360, Kâhta,* ☎ *416/715–1092,* FAX *416/725–5548. 24 rooms with shower. Restaurant. No credit cards.*

$ 🏨 **Hotel Selçuk.** Generally considered one of the better places to stay in Kâhta, the Selçuk is often booked up by tour groups. Guest rooms are clean and comfortable, and the restaurant is on a shady terrace. ⊠ *Adıyaman Yolu, Kâhta,* ☎ *416/715–2369. 58 rooms with shower. Restaurant, outdoor pool. No credit cards.*

Şanlıurfa

★ ⓑ *143 km (89 mi) southeast from Kâhta on Rte. E99, or 180 km (112 mi) southwest from Diyarbakır on Rte. E99.*

Şanlıurfa (more commonly called Urfa), at the edge of the Syrian desert, is a sleepy frontier town most famous as the birthplace of the biblical patriarch Abraham. Half a dozen mosques crowd around the cave where Abraham reputedly was born, and a pool near the cave is filled with sacred carp.

It is possible to bypass Urfa on the way from Diyarbakır to Mt. Nimrod, either by taking a car ferry across Atatürk Reservoir or by simply staying on Route E99 as it turns west, toward Bozova, on the outskirts of Urfa. But it's worth spending a few hours roaming the town's colorful bazaar and poking around its vast fortress.

Urfa's old town, at the southern foot of Divan Caddesi, is a remarkable mix of Babylonian, Assyrian, Roman, Byzantine, and Ottoman architecture, albeit heavily eroded over the centuries. The most impressive monument is the **Urfa Kale** (Urfa Fortress), a motley collection of pillars, upturned stones, and broken columns at the top of a wide staircase. It's impossible to detect any one architectural intent here, probably because the fortress has been razed and rebuilt at least a dozen times since the 2nd century BC. ⊠ *Kale Cad., no phone.* 🎫 *50¢.* ☉ *Daily 9–6.*

Legend has it that Abraham was born in the **Hazreti Ibrahim Doğum,** a natural cave hidden behind the Hasan Paşa mosque. Men and women enter through separate doorways. Most people huddled inside this small, dark cavern have come to pray, not to snap photos. ⊠ *Göl Cad., no phone.* 🎫 *Free.* ☉ *Daily sunrise–sunset.*

Gölbaşı Park, locally famous for its carp-filled pools, is a shady oasis on hot days. A short walk east leads to Urfa's **bazaar,** where in summertime a knot of merchants, sweating profusely, waits patiently in the sun for the rare tour group. A few lucky families own stalls in the covered caravansary, where you'll find the best selection of dried fruits, gold jewelry, and miscellaneous plumbing fixtures.

OFF THE
BEATEN PATH

MARDIN – If you have your own transportation, Mardin, only 30 km (19 mi) from the Syrian border, is a worthwhile day trip from Şanlıurfa. Mardin is defended by a medieval sandstone citadel—one so impregnable that neither the Seljuks in the 12th century nor the Mongols in the 13th managed to capture it. At the tail end of the 14th century, Tamerlane did conquer the city, but when he returned in 1401 to crush the revolt of his own brother, Isa, the citadel resisted even Tamerlane. Most of the other outstanding buildings in Mardin are Islamic: the Lâtifiye Cami (1371); the Seljuk Ulu Cami, dating from the 11th century, restored in the 15th century, and disfigured in the 19th; and the Sultan İsa Medrese (1385), renowned for its exquisite stone carvings. Tour operators from Diyarbakır include Mardin on many itineraries, or you can drive yourself in about two hours. ✉ *From Şanlıurfa take Route E90 east for 161 km (100 mi), or from Diyarbakır take Route E97 southeast for 94 km (58 mi).*

THE FAR EAST A TO Z

Arriving and Departing

By Bus

Erzurum, the main hub of the regional transportation system, is about 15 hours from Ankara ($20), 20 hours from Istanbul ($26), and nine hours from Trabzon ($14). The region's other main hub, Diyarbakır, is about 13 hours from Ankara ($15), 18 hours from Istanbul ($24), and 10 hours from Erzurum ($14). A half-dozen bus companies serve the region.

By Car

From Trabzon, a twisty, mountainous road (E97 to Aşkale, then E80) covers the 322 km (193 mi) to Erzurum. The drive from Ankara is a whopping 882 km (530 mi) across much of Anatolia, first on Route E88, then on E80. From Adana, on the Mediterranean Coast, take E90 to Şanlıurfa then E99 to Diyarbakır, a total distance of 536 km (321 mi). Gas stations are plentiful, and roadside hotels and restaurants help break up the long, dusty, hot drives.

By Plane

Turkish Airlines and **Istanbul Airlines** (☞ Air Travel *in* the Gold Guide for phone numbers) both have daily scheduled flights from Istanbul and Ankara to Erzurum, Diyarbakır, and Van, and from Ankara to Gaziantep, Kars, Malatya, and Batman. The fares, set by region, are about $75 one-way no matter where you're flying. There are less frequent flights from Istanbul to Gaziantep and from Ankara to Elazığ, Erzincan, Sivas, and Şanlıurfa.

By Train

Not the best option, a train ride from Ankara to Erzurum (26 hours) and Van (38 hours or more) is brutally slow. Per-person fares are $16 (first class) to $60 (sleeper bunk).

Getting Around

By Bus

Within the eastern region, buses take a long time—Erzurum is 11 hours from Diyarbakır, eight hours from Van, four hours from Kars—

but you can get wherever you want to go without spending much money. There's an *otogar* (bus station) in each of the main towns.

By Car

With fewer services and more heavy trucks than on the Mediterranean or Aegean coast, these are not Turkey's best roads. To make matters worse, a series of dams under construction in the region can make existing highways impassable. Some sample distances: Erzurum to Kars, 212 km (131 mi); Erzurum to Van, 361 km (223 mi); Van to Diyarbakır, 408 km (252 mi).

Avis has two offices in eastern Turkey, in Erzurum (☎ 422/218–8715, FAX 422/233–2193) and in Gaziantep (☎ 342/336–1194, FAX 342/336–3058), near Şanlıurfa. Economy rates are $45–$55 per day with unlimited mileage; the drop-off fee is $100. **Vis Rent-a-Car** (☎ 422/234–4400), a small company in Erzurum opposite the Otel Oral, charges a bit more and requires you to return the vehicle to Erzurum.

Contacts and Resources

Emergencies

Police (☎ 155).

Guided Tours

Dagcılı Federasyonu (Turkish Mountaineering Club, B.T.G.M., ✉ Ulus Işhanı, A Block, Ulus, Ankara) is a good source of information about guided mountain-climbing tours, including treks to the summit of Mt. Ararat.

In Doğubayazıt, Mehmet Arik of **Til-Tur Travel** (✉ Belediye Cad. 30, ☎ 472/311–2643) arranges day trips to Mt. Ararat, the Iranian border, and Kurdish mountain villages for $10–$15 per person; look for the office marked METEOR on the road to İşak Paşa Saray. Mr. Arik is also an excellent guide for the three- to four-day Mt. Ararat summit trek, provided you make advance arrangements for the mountain permit.

Diyarbakır is rife with guides, many of whom are dishonest and looking to make a quick buck. One exception is Mehmet Nalbant (☎ 412/235–0642), a fluent English speaker who arranges overnight trips to Mt. Nimrod ($25–$40 per person). The three-day grand tour—Mardin, Şanlıurfa, and Mt. Nimrod—costs $85–$100 per person.

Visitor Information

Even before the current troubles, the number of tourists visiting eastern Turkey was relatively low. There will usually be someone in the tourist information offices below who knows at least a few words of English, but callers would be advised to have a Turkish speaker on hand to help with translation.

Adıyaman (✉ Atatürk Bul. 184, ☎ 416/216–1008, FAX 416/216–3840). **Ağri** (✉ Özel İdare Binası Kat 1, ☎ 472/215–3730, FAX 472/215–3918). **Bitlis** (✉ İl Halk Kütüphanesi Binası, ☎ 434/226–5304, FAX 434/226–5305). **Diyarbakır** (✉ Kultur Sanayi, ☎ 412/221–7840). **Erzurum** (✉ Cemal Gürsel Cad. 9/A, ☎ 442/218–5697, FAX 442/218–5443). **Kars** (✉ G.A.M.E. Cad., at Faik Bey Cad., ☎ 474/223–2300, FAX 474/223–8452). **Van** (✉ Cumhuriyet Cad. 19, ☎ 432/216–2018, FAX 432/216–3675).

9 Portraits

Turkey at a Glance: A Chronology

The Art of the Kilim

Books and Videos

TURKEY AT A GLANCE: A CHRONOLOGY

ca. 9000 BC   First agrarian settlements in the world are established in southern Turkey and northern Iraq.

6500–5650 BC   Catalhoyuk flourishes, the largest early agricultural community yet discovered and the oldest known site with religious buildings.

2371–16 BC   Reign of King Sargon of Akkad, whose empire reached from **Mesopotamia** to the southern parts of Anatolia (Asia Minor), the area that is now Turkey.

ca. 2200–1200 BC   Indo-European invaders include the **Hittites,** who establish an empire in Anatolia, pushing out the Mesopotamians.

1296 BC   Hittites defeat the Egyptian pharaoh **Ramses II,** at the battle of Kadesh, halting Egypt's northern advance and strengthening their hold over Anatolia.

ca. 1200 BC   New waves of invaders break up the Hittite empire.

1184 BC   The traditional date for the end of the legendary Trojan War, the accounts of which are believed to be based on a real conflict.

ca. 1000 BC   West coast of Asia Minor settled by Aeolians, Dorians, and Ionians from Greece.

ca. 657 BC   Foundation of **Byzantium** by Megarian colonists from Greece, led, according to legend, by Byzas, after whom the city was named.

559–29 BC   Reign of **Cyrus the Great,** the founder of the Persian empire, who subdues the Greek cities of Asia Minor, defeats the **Lydian** king, Croesus, reputedly the richest man in the world, and unifies Asia Minor under his rule.

334 BC   **Alexander the Great** conquers Asia Minor, ending Persian domination and extending his empire to the borders of India.

323 BC   Alexander the Great's sudden death creates a power vacuum and his vast empire disintegrates into a number of petty kingdoms.

190 BC   The Seleucid monarch **Antiochus III,** defeated by the Romans at the battle of Magnesia, cedes his territory west of the Taurus mountains to Rome.

133 BC   **Rome** consolidates its military and diplomatic gains in the region by creating the province of Asia Minor.

AD 284–305   Reign of the emperor **Diocletian,** who divides the Roman Empire into eastern and western administrative branches and shifts the focus of power eastward by establishing Nicomedia (İzmit) as a secondary, eastern capital.

325   The Ecumenical **Council of Nicaea** (İznik), the first attempt to establish an orthodox Christian doctrine.

330   The emperor Constantine establishes Christianity as the state religion and moves the capital of the Roman Empire from Rome to the town of Byzantium, which is greatly enlarged and renamed **Constantinople** ("City of Constantine").

527–63   Reign of **Justinian I.** The Byzantine empire reaches its military and cultural apogee. Hagia Sophia is rebuilt and rebuilt again.

674–78   Arab invaders sweep through the Byzantine Empire and lay siege to Constantinople before being repulsed.

1037   The **Seljuk Turks,** nomad tribes from central Asia recently converted to Islam, create their first state in the Middle East.

1071   The Byzantine Emperor Romanos IV is defeated by the Seljuk sultan Alp Arslan at the battle of Manzikert (Malazgirt), opening Anatolia to Turkish settlement.

1081–1118   Reign of emperor **Alexios I Commenus,** who successfully deals with the threats of Venetians and crusaders. His daughter Anna chronicles the history of the time in the *Alexiad.*

1204   Constantinople is sacked by the **Fourth Crusade,** the Byzantine emperor is expelled, and a Latin Empire of Constantinople is established.

1243   The Seljuk sultan is defeated by Genghis Khan's Golden Horde at Kosedag and the Seljuk empire disintegrates into petty states.

1261   The Byzantine emperor Michael Palaeologus is restored to a greatly weakened throne.

1300   Traditional date of the foundation of the **Ottoman Empire** at Bursa under **Osman I** (1258–1326). Over the next century Osman and his sons conquer much of Anatolia and southeastern Europe.

1402   The Mongol leader Tamerlane (Timur) defeats the Ottoman emperor Bayezit near Ankara, leading to a decade of civil war among his sons.

1453   Constantinople, the rump of the once mighty Byzantine Empire, falls to the Ottoman sultan Mehmet II.

1462   Mehmet II begins building a new palace at Topkapı.

1520–66   Reign of **Süleyman the Magnificent,** under whom the Ottoman Empire stretches from Iraq to Algeria. Ottoman culture reaches new heights, epitomized by the magnificent buildings of the architect Sinan.

1571   The defeat of the Ottoman fleet at **Lepanto** by an alliance of European states dents the legend of Turkish invulnerability.

1609   Work begins on the building of the Blue Mosque in Constantinople.

1683   The failure of the Ottoman siege of **Vienna** marks the high point of Turkish expansion into Europe and the beginning of a decline. Over the next century most of eastern Europe is detached from the empire.

1774   The Treaty of Kuchuk Kainarji (Küçük Kaynarca) brings the Ottoman Empire under the influence of Catherine the Great's Russia, and the Eastern Question is posed for the first time: Who will get the Ottoman lands when the empire falls?

1807   Sultan Selim II is overthrown by the Janissaries, the Ottoman praetorian guard, whose influence has grown to dominate the imperial court.

1826   The sultan Mahmut II (1808–1839) massacres the Janissaries in the Hippodrome and attempts to introduce reforms, including compulsory male education; but the empire continues to disintegrate under the forces of nationalism.

1853–55   The **Crimean War.** Britain and France support "the sick man of Europe" in a bid to prevent Russian expansion into the Mediterranean. Florence Nightingale nurses the sick and wounded at Scutari (Uskudar).

1876–1909   Reign of sultan Abdül Hamid II, who begins as a constitutionally minded liberal and ends as a despot.

1877–78 The Western powers come to the aid of the Ottomans after they are defeated in another **Russo-Turkish** war, but most of the empire's territory in Europe is lost.

1889 Birth of **Mustafa Kemal.**

1908 The "Young Turk revolution" compels Abdül Hamid to grant a new representative constitution.

1909 Abdül Hamid reneges on his reforms and is deposed by the Young Turks, who replace him with his brother, Mehmet V, the first constitutional sultan.

1911–13 The disastrous **Balkan Wars** discredit the liberal movement and a military government takes power under Enver Pasha.

1914–18 Enver Pasha's decision to enter World War I on the side of the Central Powers precipitates the final collapse of the Ottoman Empire. Despite repulsing an Allied landing at **Gallipoli,** the Turkish armed forces are resoundingly defeated, and the Ottomans are forced to accept humiliating peace terms, including the occupation of Constantinople.

1919–22 Greek forces invade Western Anatolia and are finally defeated by General Mustafa Kemal, the hero of the Turkish resistance at Gallipoli.

1922 The Mudanya Armistice recognizes the territorial integrity of Anatolia. Under the leadership of Mustafa Kemal, the sultanate is abolished and Mehmet VI, the last sultan, goes into exile.

1923 October 29: The **Turkish Republic** is proclaimed, with Ankara as its capital and Mustafa Kemal as its first president and leader of the sole political party, the Republican People's Party.

1924–34 Mustafa Kemal, soon to be renamed Atatürk ("Father of Turks"), introduces sweeping reforms, including the secularization of the legal system, the banning of the fez and veil, the enfranchisement of women, the introduction of a Latin alphabet and calendar, and the introduction of surnames.

1930 The name Istanbul is officially adopted.

1938 Atatürk dies.

1939–45 Turkey remains neutral throughout most of World War II, only declaring war on Germany in the final months in order to secure a seat at the new United Nations, of which the country becomes a founding member.

1950 Other parties are allowed to stand in the general elections and **Adnan Menderes** is elected prime minister as leader of the Justice Party. But the transition to multiparty democracy proves problematic as mounting civil unrest prompts three military coups over the next 30 years.

1974 Turkey invades **Cyprus** in the wake of a failed, Greek-sponsored military coup, resulting in the island's partition.

1980 The republic's third military coup brings Chief of Staff **Kenan Evren** to power. Turgut Ozal, a U.S.-educated engineer, takes control of the economy and introduces radical, Western-oriented, free market reforms.

1983 **Turgut Ozal** is elected prime minister in the first post-coup elections.

1987 Turkey applies for full membership in the European Union.

1993 **Tansu Çiller** is appointed as Turkey's first female prime minister, succeeding Süleyman Demirel, who replaces the late Turgut Ozal as president.

1994 **Kurdish Separatists** set off bombs in Istanbul and continue their struggle against government forces in the southeast. Local elections bring **pro-Islamic militants** to power in Istanbul, Ankara, and other cities in Anatolia.

1996 Turkey moves closer to **economic integration with the European Union.** The bloody struggle between the Turkish military and the separatist Kurdish nationalists continues. Tansu Çiller is forced out as prime minister in early 1996, but later in the year becomes part of a coalition controlled by the Islamic Welfare Party's Necmettin Erbakan.

THE ART OF THE KILIM

WHAT ARE KILIMS? The word *kilim* simply means a flat-woven rug, or a rug without a knotted pile. There are many variations used in different languages: *gelim* in Iran, *kelim* in Afghanistan, *palas* in the Caucasus, *bsath* in Syria and Lebanon, *chilim* in Romania and kilim in Turkey, Poland, Hungary, and Serbia. Flat weaving is found in some form all over the world, from the Great Plains of North America to Scandinavia and Indonesia. At times there is only a structural similarity in what is produced, but the disciplines imposed by the materials and techniques often result in strikingly similar designs and compositions.

Until recently the kilim has been considered the poor relation of the Oriental knotted carpet by collectors and traders alike. For generations this view has prevailed, and the majority of books on rugs dismiss the kilim in a few sentences as an inferior and simple tribal product. In the last two decades, however, there has been an explosion of interest in the decorative, utilitarian, and collectible qualities of these remarkable objects. Today, kilims captivate an ever-widening audience throughout the Western world. And Anatolia is leading the kilim-producing world in both the quality and quantity of the modern production.

Kilims have been an essential piece of decorative, practical, and portable furniture for the peoples of the Middle East and Asia for a very long time. Together with jewelry, clothing, tent furnishings, and animal trappings, kilims have helped to form the identity of a village or nomadic tribal group. They were made for use on the floors and walls of tents, houses, and mosques and as animal covers and bags. Most kilims were made for family and personal use, although some villages and towns became famous in the 17th and 18th centuries for their fine commercial production, and remain so today. Family wealth was stored up in kilims, knotted rugs, precious metals, and animals, and at times of famine or crisis any of these possessions could be bartered for grain or be exchanged into local currency for use in the nearest market town.

Kilims have always played a central role in the family as part of the dowry or bride price. Then, as now, marriage involved much more than the union of two people. The girl, betrothed at an early age, became an instrument of liaison between families, to the mutual commercial, financial, and political benefit of all parties concerned. The joint wealth of the two families was consolidated with rugs, jewelry, and other items; the dowry also consisted of animals and grazing, water, and irrigation rights. The young girl, learning alongside her mother and other members of her family, made her own dowry of kilims and textiles as a labor of love. Each piece embodies the inheritance of family traditions and tribal folklore. The position and status of a family were directly related to the quality and quantity of the bride's dowry, and this explains to some extent why the kilim has in the past had so much effort, craftsmanship, and creativity lavished upon it with no prospect of financial gain from the marketplace or bazaar.

In the late 19th and early 20th centuries, tribal groups began to lose their cohesion in the face of commercial and government pressures. Once tribes became sedentary and had to survive by trade and barter, they copied whichever designs were fashionable and salable. Marriages between tribes became more common, increasing the intermingling of often totally different cultures and confusing the heritage of traditional arts. These changes were often accompanied by a decline in craftsmanship, but the fusion of clans and tribes of fundamentally different origins has sometimes resulted in exquisite and unusual kilims, which have appeared on the market during the last few decades.

Workshop production of kilims in villages usually indicates a nomadic tribe that has settled, in ancient or modern times, continuing to weave for domestic, and latterly for commercial, reasons. Present-day Turkey has become the center for the village and workshop production of kilims for export and trade; orders are placed by fax, and many designs and colors are inspired by Western interior designers. Chemical dyes are used, and yet it is interesting to see the reemergence of the rich, glowing colors of natural dyes, matched with ancient and often long-forgotten motifs and symbols, to satisfy an ever-growing demand for more-traditional kilims.

The reasons for making kilims have changed greatly in recent years. Utility and religious and cultural significance have largely been replaced by profit and commerce. By looking at many different kilims, old and new, from many different areas, one can begin to appreciate those that are original and not mass produced. These are the genuine article—kilims that retain their true ethnic identity, woven without compromise and with a craftsmanship that reflects love and heritage in their making.

Until the 20th century many tribes were utterly self-sufficient in their weaving, a situation unknown in Europe since the Middle Ages. The source of the wool or animal hair, the streams to soak the fleeces, the plants and compounds for dyeing, and the timber to make the frame for the loom were all found within tribal boundaries, whether the tribes were nomadic or semi-nomadic. Kilims from different geographical, and hence tribal, areas show startling variations in color and texture, and this is in part due to the very specific localized sources of these basic raw materials.

Throughout central Asia the dominant source of yarn has always been the domesticated sheep, of which there are three types: fat-tailed, long-tailed, and fat-rumped. Fat-tailed sheep are found throughout Asia; their tails can develop to an enormous size—30 or 40 pounds. Long-tailed sheep are found on the southern borders of Afghanistan and fat-rumped sheep in Turkestan, a tribal area of central Asia. The quality of wool from all sheep depends entirely on climate and pasture, and the wool from the fat-tailed sheep is famous for its hard, coarse, and long staple, which gives a lustrous shine with excellent dye-taking qualities. Unlike flocks in the more developed world, where breeding has produced fleeces of uniform color, sheep are found throughout Asia that are brown, black, white, and a misty red, all in one flock, and sometimes all on one animal.

Camels, goats, and horses also provide a source for yarn. Goat hair is used for its strength and its attractive, high sheen. The warps of saddle and donkey bags, animal covers, and some of the kilims of central Asia are made of goat hair or of goat hair and sheep's wool combined. The sides of the kilims, the selvages, are often of goat hair. Camel hair is used for both the weft and warp in kilims, to rich and subtle effect, especially when it is left undyed. Horse hair from the mane and tail is often tied in tassels on bags, and, like goat hair, it gives added strength in binding and finishing a kilim.

WHITE COTTON HAS always been used by certain tribes and is becoming increasingly popular as a way of highlighting designs and patterns. Unlike white wool, cotton does not turn cream or ivory in color with age. Its structural qualities are also much valued. Since the turn of this century, cotton has tended to replace wool in the warps of Anatolian kilims. This is a good indication of how commercial zeal can influence traditional practice. Previously, there was no alternative to wool or local materials, and a weaver would never have parted with cash for cotton to weave into a kilim that she was not intending to sell for profit. Cotton-and-wool mixtures are found in 19th-century kilims, and the spinning of the materials together results in a fine yarn that is strong yet supple.

A distinctive feature of kilim weaving is that individual color sections are completed before the weaver moves on to other areas of the rug. This is in total contrast to knotted-pile carpets, where the weaver works straight across the carpet in horizontal lines of knots, using many different colors in close succession. The kilim weaver will work on one block of color, laying perhaps 20 wefts before beating them down with a comb and moving on to the adjacent color.

Traditional nomadic weavers were unable to carry large quantities of prepared wool with them and so would use whatever color and texture of wool came to hand each time the portable loom was set up. Because of this, the exact colors that the weaver had planned for the design could not always be found, and the kilim became an endlessly shifting colorscape.

Until the mid-19th century only colored dyes from animal, vegetable, and mineral sources were known, and there were thriving industries associated with the cropping and mining of the raw materials throughout Asia. In towns and villages, yarn would be taken to professional dyers, and naturally dyed yarn could be bought in the markets. All kilims made before the 1850s were, therefore, naturally dyed, a process that has continued until very recently. Nomadic or seminomadic peoples, making kilims for their own use, sometimes had access to natural dyestuffs—substances that grew wild amongst their grazing animals—and so the women would collect herbs, flowers, and roots for their own special color recipes. The migratory life only allowed for the carriage of small quantities of dyed wool, made up a batch at a time, and this is one explanation for the natural variations in color found in the older kilims.

A WHOLE SPECTRUM of natural colors can be obtained from the flowers, fruit, vegetables, and insects—even the earth—in kilim-producing areas. All natural dyes (with the exception of yellow) retain their colors extraordinarily well, but they do begin to fade naturally after about 50 years and will run if not well fixed. The positive aspect of this is that a kilim will mellow beautifully over the years if traditionally made with natural dyes.

In the late 19th century, weavers began experimenting with chemical dyes, achieving, at times, only limited success. However, with chemical dyes, weavers had a complete and relatively easy choice of colors, free from the limitations, and the natural aesthetic integrity, of the natural sources available to them in their homelands. Vivid oranges and yellows that had been so difficult to fix in the past were now readily available. The use of chemical dyes spread rapidly, spawning village industries and reaching even the least accessible and most self-sufficient weavers of all, the nomadic tribeswomen.

Kilims produced in the first flush of this new craze display a rather startling use of many different, not always harmonious colors, and until recently some chemical dyes, such as aniline and acid-base dyes, corroded the wool, faded quickly, and would not withstand washing with detergents. But chemical dyes do not always result in clashing color effects, or poor durability. In the last 40 years chrome-mordanted colors have been developed that are indistinguishable, when used well, from natural dyes. Ironically, it is in these same 40 years that the natural-dye lobby among consumers and collectors in the West has met with some success. Classes of instruction in the art of natural dyeing and a price premium for kilims with vegetable dyes have ensured a contemporary revival in traditional techniques among the kilim producers of Anatolia.

There is no representation of the Deity in Islam, either in the form of the written word or through the depiction of people (man being made in God's image). In Islamic art some figurative forms, human and animal, are permitted, but in many cases it is considered disrespectful to walk over them, thus precluding their use in knotted rugs and kilims. For the tribal weavers, however, connections with their natural environment, with their animals, and with their family groups are very strong and deeply rooted and will override religious taboo. So, although recognizable objects are depicted in their rugs, they will never be seen to form part of a complete, pseudorealistic picture.

Two factors other than religion influence the designs that a weaver will choose for her kilim. One is the discipline of the weaving techniques themselves, which produce mostly abstract patterns; the other is the natural environment in which the weaver lives and from which she will adapt motifs to represent lakes, rivers, flowers, petals, trees, and leaves, or domestic and wild animals. She will incorporate images from her own household, such as a kettle, teapot, ewer, comb, beater, or lamp, as well as, more recently, objects of Western influence, including cars and bikes and even helicopters and automatic rifles.

Perhaps the most familiar motif used on kilims is the Tree of Life, which, to the weaver, could represent equally well the presence of water in desert lands, or the family, with the trunk as the father and the branches as the children. Another symbolic motif is the talismanic evil eye, or *nazarlik,* used to deflect evil and to balance the adverse effects on the kilim of other motifs, such as the spider or scorpion.

On many modern kilims, made in the last 40 years or so, ancient motifs have been misrepresented or given a new twist because the weaver has not been aware of the origins of the design she is using. Modern weavers often work from "cartoons" or pictures of old rugs, re-creating them for an enthusiastic Western market. Original motifs will be modified in this process to suit a preordained shape or weaving technique, and so the evolution of the ancient design continues under modern conditions.

Yet the roots of tribal traditions are deep within the mind of the weaver. An English textile-designer friend traveled to Anatolia recently with a design for a kilim that was totally divorced from traditional uses of color as dictated by the weaving methods. His major difficulty was finding a weaver who could understand this alien composition. Why were certain colors appearing where they were, and why were certain shapes, unrelated to traditional methods, being used? Here was a pattern that departed from the inbuilt and centuries-old methods. The weavers may be able to absorb small design changes within a basically traditional format, but it would be impossible for them to change their whole style of expression, even temporarily. Pattern for them makes no sense unless it is an integral part of the whole woven composition.

Until recently there were, generally speaking, three clear-cut categories from which to choose when buying a kilim: There were antique flat-weaves made over 100 years ago, before the influences of export trade began to be felt; there were old kilims, made in this century, some of whose compositions clearly display the blending of different tribal and regional traditions; and there were modern, largely commercially produced kilims, woven in village workshops, often to orders from retailers in the West and often much removed from their local, traditional techniques and patterning.

A fourth category, however, has developed—the new facsimiles being produced in Anatolia. These are completely traditional in style and form and are made largely as a response to the increasing Western demand for authentic, quality weavings. Many have been specially commissioned by Western dealers, and most are made for export. Various grades are available, determined by the quality of the weaving—from coarse to very fine—and by the complexity of patterning in the overall composition. Most of these kilims are chemically dyed, and those that do make use of vegetable and natural dyes enjoy a considerable premium in price.

The safest purchase in terms of financial investment is, without doubt, an antique kilim. But it is dangerous to assume that a kilim is rare, or excellently designed and constructed, simply because it is old; there have always been good weavers and bad weavers. Anyone interested in buying an antique kilim should take time to examine as many old and antique rugs as possible and should talk to a knowledgeable, trustworthy dealer to get a clear idea of which rugs are considered important and collectible.

Collectibility is not determined by the vagaries of fashion. A rug is collectible if it is rare or unusual and if it is very well woven; these are unchanging qualities, and one may assume that such a rug will increase in value as an investment. Antique kilims are invariably the most expensive to buy, both in the West and in their country of origin; ironically, there is often a much better choice in Europe and North America, in terms of price and kilim type, than there is in Anatolia or central Asia.

VERY FINE ANTIQUE kilims are obviously too expensive for many people, but large numbers of old, traditional weavings can be found to suit most budgets. Old kilims are not yet considered a financial investment in themselves and should really be valued for their decorative and practical qualities on a personal level. Until about 40 years ago, few kilims were produced for commercial gain, and so traditional kilim shapes and compositions were made, and weaving techniques practiced, as they had been for generations. Antique kilims are now very difficult to find in their countries of origin, and the same will soon be true of traditional old kilims. Their increasing rarity will doubtless be reflected in their rising values.

Of the modern production, it is safe to assume that the finest facsimiles of antique weaving and dyeing techniques will become the investments of the future, and the highest-quality naturally dyed Anatolian replicas will definitely improve and mellow with age and use.

In Anatolia, kilims can be recognized by their tribe and area of origin to within a group of villages or even a single village. Many distinctive kilims of the 19th century can be attributed to the area around Bergama and Balikesir, in western Anatolia, now one of the last strongholds of the Yoruk peoples. Most of the antique Balikesir kilims are patterned with an interlocking grid of blue on a red ground, with dazzling results. More recent Balikesir kilims are varied in design, often decorated with medallions of different sizes on a plain ground, with simple side and end borders or skirts.

IT IS UNUSUAL to find kilims from Anatolia with any area left undecorated, and those from the Manastir region are therefore easy to recognize. The kilims have very strong and simple compositions, usually on a tomato-red or black ground with a plain central field decorated with very few designs. The *mihrab*, the ceremonial mosque archway, is represented in Manastir kilims by a distinct, floating line rather than by a pattern.

The village of Mut lies south of the Taurus mountains, another region of the seminomadic Yoruk pastoralists. The kilims from this area are often found with dark warps of goat hair or brown wool. Brightly colored medallions are set against a red ground, usually a pair of designs in a mirror image.

Aydin is a town near the Aegean Coast and is a productive source of kilims, often woven in two halves and joined together. As with most western Anatolian kilims, the Aydin examples are brightly colored with small patterns.

The town of Konya lies at the south and center of a most prolific weaving area, that of west-central Anatolia, once known as Karaman. Konya kilims are made wholly of wool and are often large, woven in two or three pieces, with a predominantly white or cream background color into which is woven a strong central series of oval medallions.

The kilims of the central area of Anatolia around Kayserı are very loosely woven, and the older examples have a silky and flat texture. Modern Kayserı kilims are generally red and black, fading to pinks and grays.

Maylatya is in Kurdish country and gives its name to the numerous kilims that are produced in the area by both Kurds and Turkic peoples. Woven in two pieces with warps of white wool, the kilims are usually long, relatively narrow, and difficult to make. Commonly, three central medallions are split by the central joint, at times most irregularly, and the white sections of the composition are given brilliance by the use of white cotton yarn. Some of the longest Anatolian kilims are found in the Malatya area. Known as band kilims, they can exceed 15 feet in length; and each of the two sections is often, and most unusually for Anatolia, a complete composition in itself. They are sometimes cut and sold as runners. Predominant colors are red and blue with striking white bands.

Woven by Kurds, most Sivas kilims, and indeed most of the kilims made anywhere east of here, are prayer mats in muted colors with a strong single and central mihrab motif. All are made in one piece, and the mihrab is bordered by three narrow bands full of floral designs.

Prayer rugs from around Bayburt and Erzurum are woven in predominantly yellow or ocher colors with tiered central mihrabs surrounded by stylized floral designs, especially carnations. Many of the kilims have their year of weaving woven into the design. Just east of this area is the village of Bardiz, where most of the Karabagh or modern Bessarabian kilims are made. The Kurdish weavers are excellent copyists and have been producing these large floral-pattern kilims since the 1920s, using European tapestry designs such as those from Aubusson and Savonnerie in France. Curiously, these were themselves derived from the original Ottoman floral kilims of the 17th century— a full circle of design ideas.

The remote and mountainous district of eastern Anatolia around Van has maintained many clans of seminomadic Kurds, largely undisturbed for thousands of years. The kilims are, unusually, square and are generally in two pieces; many examples bear a resemblance to the kilims of northwest Persia and the Caucasus, made by other Kurdish groups. Kilims from Van are well made with good-quality wool and will last for many years.

The kilims from the Kars area, close by the Russian border, are typical of most Kurdish work—either long narrow strips or small prayer rugs. Thick, dark wool warps give a ribbed effect, and, in general, colors are browns, pinks, and oranges.

The area of European Turkey known as Thrace is thought to be the region of origin for many distinctive kilims. The typical composition is simple, often the Tree of Life in its many forms, surrounded by a floral border with animal and leaf motifs. Those from around the town of Sarkoy are of the finest quality.

When seeking out kilims, do not assume that those bought in Turkey will be cheaper than those for sale in the West. A rug bought in an Istanbul bazaar may often be just as expensive as in London or New York, if not more so. And do beware of the hidden costs and regulations governing a sale for personal export. These include shipping, packing, and handling charges, as well as export and import tax. All these expenses add up and can mean that the overall cost is considerably more than you at first calculate. But for the memories and stories associated with the purchase of a kilim in a bazaar—the haggling, the playacting, and the gallons of sweet tea consumed before the deal is struck—there is no substitute.

— By Alastair Hull and Nicholas Barnard

Alastair Hull is a collector, expert, and dealer in kilims. Nicholas Barnard is a writer and organizer of original tribal-art exhibits.

BOOKS AND VIDEOS

Homer's *Iliad* is still the most evocative reading on the Trojan War and the key players of Turkish antiquity. The keenest insight into the ancient ruins you will encounter on your trip comes from George Bean, author of *Aegean Turkey, Turkey Beyond the Meander, Lycian Turkey,* and *Turkey's Southern Shore.* John Julius Norwich's three-volume *Byzantium* chronicles the rise and fall of one of history's great empires.

Mary Lee Settle provides a vision of Turkey that is both panoramic and personal in *Turkish Reflections.* The book marks Settle's return to the country that was the setting for her novel *Blood Tie,* a 1978 National Book Award winner. Dame Freya Stark, one of the most remarkable travelers of our century, chronicles her visits to Turkey in *The Journey's Echo* and *Alexander's Path.* Only a piece of Mark Twain's *Innocents Abroad* is about Turkey, but it offers a witty glimpse of the country as it used to be. Hans Christian Andersen also wrote a memorable travelogue, *A Poet's Bazaar: A Journey to Greece, Turkey and Up the Danube.* Agatha Christie's *Murder on the Orient Express* provides the proper atmosphere for a trip to Istanbul, the terminus of the noted train. The *Letters and Works of Lady Mary Wortley Montagu* is a significant and entertaining book that delightfully documents life in 19th-century Ottoman Turkey—including the much-quoted passages about the harem—through the eyes of Lady Montagu, the wife of a consul.

For an introduction to Turkish literature, track down a copy of *Anatolian Tales* or *Memed, My Hawk,* by Yaşar Kemal, one of the country's most famous modern novelists. Orhan Pamuk's *White Castle,* published in the United States and Great Britain, is for those who want to sample a contemporary writer with great talent and technical expertise.

Western movies tend to play up Turkey's exotic aspects. Director Joseph L. Mankiewicz's *Five Fingers* (1952), an Ankara-based spy thriller based on the book *Operation Cicero* by C.L. Moyzisch, is noteworthy both for its action and clever dialogue ("Counter espionage is the highest form of gossip"). Peter Ustinov won an Academy Award for best supporting actor for his performance in the Jules Dassin–directed museum-heist film *Topkapi* (1964), which also stars Melina Mercouri and Maximillian Schell. Alan Parker directed the film version of *Midnight Express* (1978), about Billy Hayes's days in a Turkish prison following a drug conviction. The film's relentlessly horrific depiction of Hayes's experiences (some of which do not occur in his memoir) made the Turkish government exceedingly gun-shy about allowing Western moviemakers into the country. When *Midnight Express* was finally shown on Turkish TV in the mid-1990s, newscasters interviewed people in the street who wept over the country's portrayal on-screen and the influence they feared the film may have had on perceptions of Turkey in the West. Peter Weir's *Gallipoli* (1981) follows the exploits of two Australian soldiers preparing for and fighting in the historic battles in the Dardanelles during World War I. Critics generally praise the film, though some have noted a lack of sensitivity to the Turks.

TURKISH VOCABULARY

Words and Phrases

	English	Turkish	Pronunciation
Basics			
	Yes/no	Evet/hayir	**eh**-vet/**haw**-yer
	Please	Lütfen	**lewt**-fen
	Thank you	Tesekkür ederim	tay-shake-**cure** eh-day-**reem**
	You're welcome	Rica ederim	ree-**jaw** eh-ay-**reem**
		Bir sey değil	beer shay **day**-eel
	Sorry	Özür dilerim	oh-**zewr** deel-air-eem
	Sorry	Pardon	**pahr**-doan
	Good morning	Günaydin	goo-eye-**den**
	Good day	Iyi günler	ee-yee gewn-**lair**
	Good evening	Iyi akşamlar	ee-yee awk-shom-**lahr**
	Goodbye	Allahaismarladik	**allah**-aw-ees-mar-law-deck
		Güle güle	**gew**-leh-**gew**-leh
	Mr. (Sir)	Bay, or Bey	buy, bay
	Mrs. Miss	Hanım	ha-nem
	Pleased to meet you	Tanıştığımıza memnun oldum	tawnesh-tumu-**zah** **mam**-noon ohl-doom
	How are you?	Nasıl sınız?	**gnaw**-sull-suh-nuz

Numbers

	one	bir	beer
	two	iki	ee-**kee**
	three	üc	ooch
	four	dört	doort
	five	beş	besh
	six	altı	awl-tuh
	seven	yedi	yed-dy
	eight	sekiz	sek-**kez**
	nine	dokuz	doh-**kooz**
	ten	on	own
	eleven	onbir	**own**-beer
	twelve	oniki	**own**-ee-kee
	thirteen	onüç	**own**-**ooch**
	fourteen	ondört	**own**-**doort**
	fifteen	onbeş	**own**-besh
	sixteen	onaltı	**own**-awl-tuh
	seventeen	onyedi	**own**-yed-dy
	eighteen	onsekiz	own-sek-**kez**
	nineteen	ondokuz	**own**-doh-**kooz**
	twenty	yirmi	yeer-mee

twenty-one	yirmibir	**yeer**-mee-beer
thirty	otuz	oh-**tooz**
forty	kırk	kirk
fifty	elli	el-leeh
sixty	altmış	**ought**-mush
seventy	yetmiş	**yet**-mish
eighty	seksen	sex-an
ninety	doksan	dohk-**san**
one hundred	yüz	yewz
one thousand	biṇ	bin

Colors

black	siyah	**see**-yah
blue	mavi	**mah**-vee
brown	kahverengi	**kah**-vay-**ren**-gee
green	yeşil	yay-sheel
orange	portakal rengi	pohr-tah-kawl ren-gee
red	kırmızı	ker-muz-eh
white	beyaz	**bay**oz
yellow	sarı	sah-**reh**

Days of the Week

Sunday	Pazar	Poz-**ahr**
Monday	Pazartesi	Poz-**ahr**-tes-sy
Tuesday	Sali	Saul-luh
Wednesday	Çarşamba	Char-shom-**bah**
Thursday	Perşembe	Pair-shem-**beh**
Friday	Cuma	**Joom**-ah
Saturday	Cumartesi	Joom-**ahr**-tes-sy

Months

January	Ocak	Oh-**jock**
February	Şubat	Shoo-**bought**
March	Mart	mart
April	Nisan	Nee-**sahn**
May	Mayıs	My-us
June	Haziran	Hah-zee-**rahn**
July	Temmuz	**Tem**-mooz
August	Ağustos	Ah-oos-tohs
September	Eylül	Ay-**lewl**
October	Ekim	Eh-**keem**
November	Kasım	Kaw-sem
December	Aralık	Ah-raw-**luk**

Useful Phrases

Do you speak English?	Ingilizce biliyormusunuz?	in-**gee-leez**-jay bee-lee-**your**-moo-soo-noose
I don't speak Turkish	Turkçe bilmiyorum	**tewrk**-chah **beel**-mee-your-oom
I don't understand	Anlamıyorum	On-**lah**-muh-your-oom
I understand	Anlıyorum	on-**lew**-your-oom

I don't know	Bilmiyorum	**beel**-meeh-your-oom
I'm American/	Amerikalıyım	ahm-ay-**ree**-kah-lew-yum
I'm British	Ingilizim	**een**-gee-leez-um
What's your name?	Isminiz nedir?	ees-mee-niz nay-der
My name is . . .	Benim adım . . .	bay-**neem** ah-dumb
What time is it?	Saat kaç?	sought **kawch**
How?	Nasıl?	**naw**-sill
When?	Ne zaman?	**Nay** zoh-mawn
Yesterday	Dün	dewn
Today	Bugün	**Boo**-gown
Tomorrow	Yarın	**Yaw**-run
This morning/ afternoon	Bu sabah/ ögleden sonra	**boo** saw-bah/ **ow-lay**-den sewn-rah
Tonight	Bu gece	**boo** ge-jeh
What?	Efendim?/Ne?	**eh**-fen-deem/neh
What is it?	Nedir?	**neh**-deer
Why?	Neden/Niçin?	**neh**-den/**nee**-chin
Who?	Kim?	kim
Where is . . .	Nerede . . .	**nay**-ray-deh
. . . the train station?	. . . tren istasyonu?	tee-**rehn** ees-**taws**-yone-oo
. . . the subway station?	. . . metro durağı?	metro doo-**raw**-ugh
. . . the bus stop?	. . . otobüs durağı?	oh-tow-**bewse** doo-**raw**-ugh
. . . the terminal? (airport)	. . . hava alanı?	haw-**vah ah**-lawn-eh
. . . the post office?	. . . postane?	post-**ahn**-eh
. . . the bank?	. . . banka?	**bahn**-kah
. . . the hotel?	. . . oteli?	oh-**tel-ly**
. . . the museum?	. . . müzesi?	mews-zay-**see**
. . . the hospital?	. . . hastane?	hoss-**taw**-neh
. . . the elevator?	. . . asansör?	aw-sahn-**seur**
. . . the telephone?	. . . telefon?	teh-leh-**fon**
Where are the restrooms?	Tuvalet nerede?	too-vah-**let** nay-ray-deh
Here/there	Burası/Orası	**boo**-rah-seh/ **oh**-rah-seh
Left/right	sağ/sol	saw/soul
Is it near/ far?	Yakın mı?/ Uzak mı?	Yaw-**kin** muh/ Ooz-**ahk**-muh
I'd like . . .	istiyorum . . .	**ess**-tee-your-room
. . . a room	. . . bir oda	beer oh-**dah**
. . . the key	. . . anahtarı	**on**-ah-tahr-eh

. . . a newspaper	. . . bir gazete	beer **gauze**-eh-teh
. . . a stamp	. . . pul	pool
I'd like to buy . . .	almak istiyorum . . .	ahl-**mock** ees-tee-your-room
. . . cigarettes	. . . sigara	see-**gahr**-rah
. . . matches	. . . kibrit	**keeb**-rit
. . . city map	. . . şehir planı	shay-**hear plah**-nuh
. . . road map	. . . karayolları haritası	**kah**-rah-yow-lahr-**uh** hah-ree-tah-**suh**
. . . magazine	. . . dergi	dair-gee
. . . envelopes	. . . zarf	zahrf
. . . writing paper	. . . mektup kağıdı	**make**-toop **kah**-uh-duh
. . . postcard	. . . kartpostal	cart-poh-stall
How much is it?	Fiyatı ne kadar?	fee-yacht-eh **neh** kah-dar
It's expensive/cheap	pahalı/ucuz	pah-hah-**luh**/oo-**jooz**
A little/a lot	Az/çok	ahz/choke
More/less	daha çok/daha az	da-ha choke/da-ha oz
Enough/too (much)	Yeter/çok fazla	**yay**-tehr/**choke** fahz-lah
I am ill/sick	Hastayım	**hahs**-tah-yum
Call a doctor	Doktor çağırın	dohk-tore **chah**-uh-run
Help!	İmdat!	eem-**dot**
Stop!	Durun!	Doo-**roon**

Dining Out

A bottle of . . .	bir şişe . . .	**beer** she-shay
A cup of . . .	bir fincan . . .	beer **fin**-john
A glass of . . .	bir bardak . . .	beer **bar**-dock
Ashtray	kül tablası	kewl tahb-lah-**suh**
Bill/check	hesap	heh-**sop**
Bread	ekmek	ekmek
Breakfast	kahvaltı	**kah**-vaul-tuh
Butter	tereyağ	tay-**reh**-yah-uh
Cocktail/aperitif	kokteyl, içki	cocktail, **each**-key
Dinner	aksam yemeği	**ahk**-shom yem-ay-eeh
Fixed-price menu	fiks menü	fix menu
Fork	çatal	**cha**-tahl
I am a vegetarian/ I don't eat meat	vejeteryenim/ et yemem	vegeterian-**em**/ et yeh-**mem**
I cannot eat . . .	yiyemem . . .	**yee**-yay-mem
I'd like to order . . .	ısmarlamak isterim . . .	us-mahr-lah-**muck** ee-stair-em

I'd like . . .	isterim . . .	ee-stair-**em** . . .
I'm hungry/ thirsty	acıktım/ susadım	ah-**juck**-tum/ soo-saw-**dum**
Is service/the tip included?	Servis fiyata dahil mi?	service **fee**-yah-tah dah-hee-**mee**
It's good/bad	güzel/güzel değil	gew-**zell**/gew-**zell day**-eel
It's hot/cold	sıcak/soğuk	suh-**jock**/soh-**uk**
Knife	bıçak	buh-**chock**
Lunch	öğle yemeği	**ew**-leh **yem**-ey-ee
Menu	menü	meh-**new**-yew
Napkin	Peçete	**peh**-che-teh
Pepper	Karabiber	kah-**rah**-bee-bear
Plate	tabak	tah-**bock**
Please give me . . .	Lutfen bana verirmisiniz . . .	**loot**-fen bah-nah vair-**eer**-mee-see-niz
Salt	tuz	tooz

INDEX

NOTES

NOTES

NOTES

Fodor's Travel Publications

Available at bookstores everywhere, or call 1–800–533–6478, 24 hours a

Gold Guides
U.S.

Alaska

Arizona

Boston

California

Cape Cod, Martha's
Vineyard, Nantucket

The Carolinas & the
Georgia Coast

Chicago

Colorado

Florida

Hawai'i

Las Vegas,
Reno, Tahoe

Los Angeles

Maine, Vermont,
New Hampshire

Maui & Lāna'i

Miami & the Keys

New England

New Orleans

New York City

Pacific North Coast

Philadelphia &
the Pennsylvania
Dutch Country

The Rockies

San Diego

San Francisco

Santa Fe, Taos,
Albuquerque

Seattle & Vancou

The South

U.S. & British
Virgin Islands

USA

Virginia & Mary

Washington, D.C

Foreign

Australia

Austria

The Bahamas

Belize & Guatemala

Bermuda

Canada

Cancún, Cozumel,
Yucatán Peninsula

Caribbean

China

Costa Rica

Cuba

The Czech Republic
& Slovakia

Eastern &
Central Europe

Europe

Florence, Tuscany
& Umbria

France

Germany

Great Britain

Greece

Hong Kong

India

Ireland

Israel

Italy

Japan

London

Madrid & Barcelona

Mexico

Montréal &
Québec City

Moscow, St.
Petersburg, Kiev

The Netherlands,
Belgium &
Luxembourg

New Zealand

Norway

Nova Scotia, New
Brunswick, Prince
Edward Island

Paris

Portugal

Provence &
the Riviera

Scandinavia

Scotland

Singapore

South Africa

South America

Southeast Asia

Spain

Sweden

Switzerland

Thailand

Tokyo

Toronto

Turkey

Vienna & the Dɛ

Fodor's Special-Interest Guides

Alaska Ports of Call

Caribbean Ports
of Call

The Complete Guide
to America's
National Parks

Disney Like a Pro

Family Adventures

Fodor's Gay Guide
to the USA

Halliday's New
England Food
Explorer

Halliday's New
Orleans Food
Explorer

Healthy Escapes

Kodak Guide to
Shooting Great Travel
Pictures

Net Travel

Nights to Imagine

Rock & Roll
Traveler USA

Sunday in New York

Sunday in
San Francisco

Walt Disney World for
Adults

Walt Disney World,
Universal Studios
and Orlando

Wendy Perrin's S

Every

Smart Traveler Sl
Know

Where Should W
Take the Kids?
California

Where Should W
Take the Kids?
Northeast

Worldwide Cruis
and Ports of Call

Special Series

Affordables
Caribbean
Europe
Florida
France
Germany
Great Britain
Italy
London
Paris

Bed & Breakfasts and Country Inns
America
California
The Mid-Atlantic
New England
The Pacific Northwest
The South
The Southwest
The Upper Great Lakes

Berkeley Guides
California
Central America
Eastern Europe
Europe
France
Germany & Austria
Great Britain & Ireland
Italy
London
Mexico
New York City
Pacific Northwest & Alaska
Paris
San Francisco

Compass American Guides
Alaska
Arizona
Canada
Chicago
Colorado
Hawaii
Hollywood
Idaho

Maine
Manhattan
Montana
New Mexico
New Orleans
Oregon
San Francisco
Santa Fe
South Carolina
South Dakota
Southwest
Texas
Utah
Virginia
Washington
Wine Country
Wisconsin
Wyoming

Citypacks
Atlanta
Hong Kong
London
New York City
Paris
Rome
San Francisco
Washington, D.C.

Fodor's Español
California
Caribe Occidental
Caribe Oriental
Gran Bretaña
Londres
Mexico
Nueva York
Paris

Exploring Guides
Australia
Boston & New England
Britain
California
Caribbean
China
Egypt
Florence & Tuscany
Florida

Germany
Ireland
Israel
Italy
Japan
London
Mexico
Moscow & St. Petersburg
New York City
Paris
Prague
Provence
Rome
San Francisco
Scotland
Singapore & Malaysia
Spain
Thailand
Turkey
Venice

Fodor's Flashmaps
Boston
New York
San Francisco
Washington, D.C.

Pocket Guides
Acapulco
Atlanta
Barbados
Budapest
Jamaica
London
Munich
New York City
Paris
Prague
Puerto Rico
Rome
San Francisco
Washington, D.C.

Mobil Travel Guides
America's Best Hotels & Restaurants
California & the West
Frequent Traveler's Guide to Major Cities

Mid-Atlantic
Northeast
Northwest & Great Plains
Southeast
Southwest & South Central

Rivages Guides
Bed and Breakfas
Character and Cl
in France
Hotels and Coun
Inns of Characte
Charm in France
Hotels and Coun
Inns of Characte
Charm in Italy
Hotels and Coun
Inns of Characte
Charm in Paris
Hotels and Coun
Inns of Characte
Charm in Portug:
Hotels and Coun
Inns of Characte
Charm in Spain

Short Escapes
Britain
France
Near New York (
New England

Fodor's Sports
Golf Digest's Bes
Places to Play
Skiing USA
USA Today
The Complete Fo
Sport Stadium G

Fodor's Vacation Planners
Great American
Learning Vacatio
Great American
Sports & Advent
Vacations
Great American
Vacations
Great American
Vacations for
Travelers with
Disabilities
National Parks a:
Seashores of the :
National Parks o

WHEREVER YOU TRAVEL, *H*ELP IS NEVER FAR AWAY.

From planning your trip to providing travel assistance along the way, American Express® Travel Service Offices are always there to help.

Turkey

Pamfilya Tourism Inc. (R)
Keykubat Caddesi
Zeybek Apt. 63/A
Alanya
242/513 24 66

Turk Ekspres (R)
Cinnah Caddesi 9/4 Cankaya
Ankara
41/467 334

Pamfilya Tourism Inc. (R)
Isiklar Caddesi 57/B
Antalya
242/243 15 00

Turk Ekspres (R)
Cumhuriyet Caddesi
Hilton International, Hotel Lobby
Istanbul
212/241 02 48

Pamfilya Tourism Inc. (R)
Ataturk Caddesi
No. 270/1, Alsancak
Izmir
232/463 65 93

Pamfilya Tourism Inc. (R)
Hastabe Caddesi, Sohretler Sitesi
Sokak 21/B
Kemer
242/814 19 81

Pamfilya Tourism Inc. (R)
Kenan Everen Bulvari
Sirin Yer Mahallesi
Marmaris
252/412 55 37

Pamfilya Tourism Inc. (R)
Cami Sok Koyu
Haliil Yesil Ipek Dukkanlari
Side
242/753 13 45

Travel

http://www.americanexpress.com/travel